LONDON
RESTAURANTS

THE MINI ROUGH GUIDE

There are more than one hundred Rough
Guide travel, phrasebook, and music titles,
covering destinations from Amsterdam to
Zimbabwe, languages from Czech to Thai,
and musics from World to Opera and Jazz

Forthcoming titles include

Dominican Republic • Laos
Jerusalem • Melbourne

Rough Guides on the Internet

www.roughguides.com

Rough Guide Credits

Text editor/Series editor: Mark Ellingham
Typesetting: Helen Ostick
Design: Henry Iles
Cartography: Nichola Goodliffe
Photography: Giles Stokoe
Proofreading: Elaine Pollard

Publishing Information

This first edition published February 1999 by
Rough Guides Ltd, 62–70 Shorts Gardens, London WC2H 9AB.
Reprinted in May 1999.

Distributed by the Penguin Group:

Penguin Books Ltd, 27 Wrights Lane, London W8 5TZ
Penguin Books USA Inc., 375 Hudson Street, New York 10014, USA
Penguin Books Australia Ltd, 487 Maroondah Highway,
PO Box 257, Ringwood, Victoria 3134, Australia
Penguin Books Canada Ltd, 10 Alcorn Avenue,
Toronto, Ontario, Canada M4V 1E4
Penguin Books (NZ) Ltd, 182–190 Wairau Road,
Auckland 10, New Zealand

Typeset in Bembo and Helvetica to an original design by Henry Iles.
Printed in Spain by Graphy Cems.

Mapping is based upon the Ordnance Survey maps with the
premission of the Controller of Her Majesty's Stationery Office,
© copyright.

© Charles Campion 496pp, includes index
A catalogue record for this book is available from the British Library.
ISBN 1-85828-470-8

The publishers and authors have done their best to
ensure the accuracy and currency of all the information
in *The Rough Guide to London Restaurants*, however, they
can accept no responsibility for any loss, injury or
inconvenience sustained as a result of information or
advice contained in the guide.

LONDON
RESTAURANTS

THE MINI ROUGH GUIDE

written and edited by
Charles Campion

additional research and reviews
**George Theo, Margaret Clancy,
Sarah Dallas, Susan Grimshaw,
John Edwards, John Davis,
Sam Cook** and **Ann-Marie Shaw**

About Rough Guides

Rough Guides have always set out to do something different. Our first book, published in 1982, was written by Mark Ellingham. Just out of university, travelling in Greece, he took along the popular guides of the day but found they were all lacking in some way. They were either strong on ruins and museums but went on for pages without mentioning a beach or taverna, or so conscious of the need to save money that they lost sight of Greece's cultural and historical significance. Also, none of the books told him anything about Greece's contemporary life – its politics, its culture, its people and how they lived.

So with no job in prospect, Mark decided to write his own guidebook, one which aimed to provide practical information that was second to none, detailing the best beaches and the hottest clubs and restaurants, alongside interesting accounts of sights both famous and obscure, and up-to-the-minute information on contemporary culture. It was a guide that encouraged independent travellers to find the best of Greece, and was an immediate success, getting shortlisted for the Thomas Cook travel guide award, and encour-aging Mark and a few friends to expand the series.

The Rough Guide list grew rapidly and the letters flooded in, indicating a much broader readership than anticipated, but one which uniformly appreciated the Rough Guide mix of practical detail and humour, irreverence and enthusiasm. Things haven't changed. The same writers who began the series are still the caretakers of the Rough Guide mission today: to provide the most reliable, up-to-date and entertaining information to independent-minded travellers of all ages, on all budgets.

Rough Guides now publish more than 100 titles, written and researched by a dedicated team based in Britain, Europe, the USA and Australia. We have also created a unique series of phrasebooks, along with an acclaimed series of music guides, and a best-selling pocket guide to the Internet. We also publish comprehensive travel information on our Web site: **www.roughguides.com**

About the Author

Charles Campion is an award-winning food writer and restaurant reviewer. He writes the "Off The Beaten Track" column for *ES*, the *London Evening Standard* magazine, which won him the Glenfiddich "Restaurant Writer of the Year" award, and contributes to radio and TV food programmes, as well as a variety of magazines including *Bon Appetit* in the US. His most recent book publication was *The Livebait Cookbook* with chef Theodore Kyriakou.

Before becoming a food writer, Charles worked in a succession of London ad agencies and had a spell as chef-proprietor of a hotel and restaurant in darkest Derbyshire.

Help Us Update

We've tried to ensure that this first edition of *The Rough Guide to London Restaurants* is as up to date and accurate as possible. However, London's restaurant scene is in constant flux: chefs change jobs; restaurants are bought and sold; menus change. There will probably be a few references in this guide that are out of date even as this book is printed – and standards, of course, go up and down. If you feel there are places we've underrated or over-praised, or others we've unjustly omitted, please let us know: comments or corrections are much appreciated, and we'll send a copy of the next edition (or any other Rough Guide if you prefer) for the best letters. Please address letters to Charles Campion at:

Rough Guides, 62–70 Shorts Gardens, London WC2H 9AB or Rough Guides, 375 Hudson St, 9th floor, New York, NY 10014.

Or send email to: mail@roughguides.co.uk

CONTENTS

CENTRAL LONDON

THE CITY & EAST LONDON

NORTH LONDON

CONTENTS

INTRODUCTION

Anyone who has lived or worked in London knows that, while it may seem like one big metropolis to the outsider, it is really a series of villages. If you live in Clapham, you know about Clapham and Battersea, and maybe Brixton or Chelsea, while Highgate or Shepherd's Bush are far-off lands. And vice versa. Yet almost every restaurant guide is divided up by cuisine, which assumes that this is your first criterion when choosing a place to eat. It shouldn't be. If you're meeting friends in Camden your best options might be Greek or Spanish; in Brick Lane or Southall they might be Indian. But you want to know about that oddball great restaurant, too: whether it's a star like Chez Bruce in Wandsworth or a brilliant restaurant-pub like The Anglesea Arms in Hammersmith.

This Rough Guide – published for the first time in 1999 (and that really does mean 1999 and not Autumn 1998!) – divides London into five sections (Central; City & East; North; South; West) and then breaks these down into the neighbourhoods, with restaurants arranged alphabetically in each section. Keep it handy and it will tell you where to eat well anywhere from Soho to Southall.

The first thing to say about the 320 restaurants selected and reviewed in this book is that they can all be recommended – none have been added simply to make up the numbers. There are some very cheap places and there are some potentially pretty expensive places, but they all represent good value. The only rule is that it must be possible to eat a meal for £35 **a head or less**. In some of the haute cuisine establishments that may mean keeping to the set lunch, while in some of the bargain eateries £35 might cover a blow-out for four. This guide contains restaurants for every possible occasion from quick lunches to celebratory dinners. It also covers many different kinds of food – forty-six separate cuisines – if you use Indian as a catch-all term (as we do) to cover everything from South Indian vegetarian restaurants to Pakistani grillhouses.

Prices and Credit Cards

Price is one of the most difficult areas for any restaurant guide to master. Every review in this book has at the top of the page a **spread of two prices** (eg. £12 –£40). The first figure relates to "What you could get away with": this is the minimum amount per person you are likely to spend on a meal here (assuming you are not a non-tipping, non-drinking skinflint). The second relates to what it would cost "If you don't hold back". Wild diners with a taste for fine wines will leave even our top estimates far behind, but they are there as a guide. For most people, the cost of eating at a restaurant will lie somewhere within the spread.

For a more detailed picture, each review sets out the prices of various dishes. At some time in the guide's life these specific prices (and indeed the overall price spreads) will become out of date, but they were all accurate when the book left for the printer. And even in the giddy world of restaurants, when prices rise or prices fall, everyone tends to move together. If this book shows one restaurant as being twice as expensive as another, that relationship is likely to remain.

The reviews also keep faith with original menu spellings of dishes wherever possible – so you'll find satays, satehs, and satés – all of which will probably taste much the same. Hieroglyphics have been kept to a minimum, so opening hours and days are spelled out, as are the credit cards accepted. Where reviews specify "all major credit cards accepted", that means at least Amex, Diners, Mastercard and Visa. Acceptance of Visa and Mastercard usually means Switch and Delta, too; we've specified the odd exception but if you're relying on one card it's always best to check when you book.

Getting off the fence . . .

Every restaurant reviewed in this book is whole-heartedly recommended . . . but it would be a very strange person who did not have favourites, so here are mine:

Best British/Modern British

1. Chez Bruce Wandsworth: p.332
2. Richard Corrigan at the Lindsay House Soho: p.162
3. St John Clerkenwell: p.226
4. Redmond's Sheen: p.376
5. The Anglesea Arms Hammersmith: p.400
6. Ransome's Dock Battersea: p.318
7. The Fifth Floor Knightsbridge: p.89

Best Chinese

1. Fung Shing Chinatown: p.37
2. Mr Kong Chinatown: p.40
3. Mao Tai Fulham: p.392
4. Mandarin Queensway: p.143
5. China City Chinatown: p.36

Best French

1. The Mirabelle Mayfair: p.111
2. Gordon Ramsay Chelsea: p.385
3. Novelli EC1 Clerkenwell: p.224
4. Paris London Café Holloway: p.270
5. 755 Fulham: p.395
6. Monsieur Max Hampton: p.454
7. Chinon Shepherd's Bush: p.438

Best Indian

1. Café Spice Namaste, Prescott Street City: p.212
2. Mirch Masala Norbury: p.367
3. Sarkhel's Southfields: p.336
4. The Brilliant Southall: p.445
5. Ma Goa Putney: p.427
6. Veeraswamy Piccadilly: p.134
7. Rasa Stoke Newington: p.297
8. Kastoori Tooting: p.363
9. Chor Bizarre Mayfair: p.108
10. Tabaq Balham: p.337

Best Italian

1. Zafferano Knightsbridge: p.93
2. Assagi Notting Hill: p.409
3. Del Buongustaio Putney: p.425
4. Tentazioni Tower Bridge: p.358
5. Vasco & Piero's Pavillion Soho: p.169

Best Thai/Southeast Asian

1. Singapore Garden Swiss Cottage: p.285
2. O's Thai Café Crouch End: p.263
3. Little Saigon Waterloo: p.192
4. The Piecrust Stratford: p.236
5. The Churchill Arms Notting Hill: p.412

Best Vegetarian

1. Rasa Stoke Newington: p.297
2. Kastoori Tooting: p.364
3. The Gate Hammersmith: p.403
4. Chutney's Euston: p.63
5. Sakoni's Wembley: p.304

Best Budget Meal

1. Café España Soho: p.148
2. The Piecrust Stratford: p.236
3. Mirch Masala Norbury: p.367

Best Extravagance

Best Bargain Extravagance

Charles Campion,
London.
January 1999

CENTRAL

Bloomsbury
& Fitzrovia

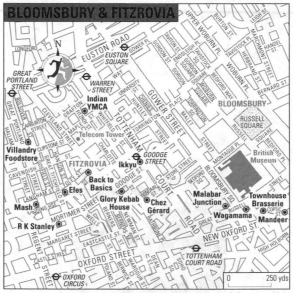

BLOOMSBURY & FITZROVIA

© Crown copyright

0   250 yds

Back to Basics

21a Foley St, W1 ☎ 0171 436 2181	⊖ Goodge Street
Mon–Fri noon–3pm & 6–10pm	All major credit cards

Back to Basics is a jolly, green-painted restaurant with canopies flaring out from the windows, and tables spilling outside when the weather is up to it. What you get here is a range of reliable fish dishes, prepared with care and occasionally with real panache, and served by friendly, attentive staff. Checked paper tablecloths, tables crammed together and the radio humming away in the background make this a good restaurant choice for a casual meal with friends.

The menu changes daily, according to what's good at the market, though the starters don't vary much – there's usually a choice of four hot appetizers and four cold ones. Portions are generous, so bear this in mind when ordering the likes of wild mushrooms with cream and sherry on grilled bread (£4.75), which comes with two thick slices of toast. Another tasty starter is Stilton and walnuts baked in puff pastry with grilled pears (£4.25), and the kitchen also does a fine homemade gravadlax with mustard dill sauce (£6.75), which is almost a meal in itself. Or you could skip starters and just play around with the bread (£2.45 for half a loaf), which arrives with three kinds of butter – anchovy, red pepper and garlic. You'll see the main course fish dishes – 'Today's Catch'– scrawled on a big blackboard. You might go for whole baby lobster salad, with red pepper mayonnaise (£13.50); if you do, get ready for the waitress to come over and tuck a plastic bib firmly into your collar. Fillet of red emperor bream, with rocket, aubergine, avocado and hoummous (£11.95) comes with ingredients piled high, while fillet of smoked haddock (£9.75) is served with a poached egg and spinach salad. There are non-fish dishes too. You can get a Scotch rib-eye steak with fresh horseradish and mustard (£10.95) or chicken breast with red wine, bacon, shallots and mushrooms (£8.50). Desserts are reliable and good; fail-safe options include bananas baked in foil with rum (£3.50), or bread and butter pudding with whisky sauce (£3.95).

This restaurant re-affirms your faith in the extra care taken by "owner drivers" – chef proprietor Stefan Pflaumer, who set up the restaurant some years ago, still runs the kitchens himself, and it shows.

£20–£45

Chez Gérard

8 Charlotte Street, W1 ☎ 0171 636 4975   ⊖ Goodge Street

Mon–Fri noon–3pm & 6.30–11.30pm, Sat 6–10.30pm   All major credit cards

Chez Gérard was set up to recreate the myth of a certain type of French restaurant. In such places the steak is good and the frites are fabulous. There is salad Niçoise, fish soup, snails and crème brulée. The bread is crusty and the service Gallic and off-hand. There's decent red wine. Twenty years ago such things held the appeal of being novel on this side of the Channel, today London's recent restaurant explosion makes it all seem rather tame. But you can never choose anything more satisfying than exactly what you want, and when the inner prompting shouts for steak frites you would be silly not to turn to Chez Gérard, because that's what they do best. It's not cheap, the service can be brusque, but you'll get a good steak cooked precisely as you wish and great frites – and in summer you might eat al fresco at one of the pavement tables.

Start with some oysters – rock oysters (£6.20 for 6; £9.30 for 9; or £12.40 for 12). Or chicken liver paté with toasted brioche (£4.50); or a dozen snails in garlic butter (£5.30), for a real belt of nostalgia. Steaks come in all shapes and sizes, Châteaubrind and Côte de boeuf are both for two people (£29.50 and £23.50 respectively). Everything off the grill comes with pommes frites and Béarnaise sauce. There's fillet steak (£15.10) or entrecôte (£11.90). This is also one of the few places in London where you can get onglet (£9.50), a French cut that is particularly tasty. There is also space on the grill for salmon, tuna, and chicken, and on the menu for a couple of vegetarian options. But don't kid yourself, you're here for the steak frites. Salad, side orders of vegetables, desserts (£3.95) – including tarte Tatin, and crème brulée – pass as if in a blur, though a decent selection of regional French cheeses (£3.95) are nicely in tune with the Gallic ambience. So too are the house wines (£9.50) which are so good that you can almost disregard the wine list.

The Charlotte Street Chez Gérard now stands at the head of a chain of brasserie branches. Loyalists would suggest that this, the original, remains a cut above its clones, though in truth they all look vaguely alike and deliver much the same standard. So when only steak frites will do . . .

Efes

80 Great Titchfield St, W1 ☎ 0171 636 1953	⊖ Oxford Circus / Great Portland St
Daily noon–11.30pm, Sun noon–11.30pm	All major credit cards

Efes has some of the finest kitsch seventies decor in London – walking through its doors is like entering a time warp – all stained glass chandeliers, banquettes and dark carpets. It is also a Tardis of a restaurant, the premises stretching right the way from Great Titchfield street through to Foley Street on the other side. The restaurant has been here, run by two brothers who have been responsible for the cooking as well as the front of house, for over 20 years now and in many ways time has stood still. Judging by the look of the waiters, so have they. A grumpier bunch would be hard to find.

That said, it's well worth enduring the surliness for the food here. You'll find a good range of meze – all the favourites – tarama (£3.25) a fetching shade of pink, a meltingly good imam bayildi (£3.25) and hummuz (£3.25) as well as some more unusual dishes. Try the special meze (£3.95 per person) for a range of their own choice, and enjoy the presentation – it matches the decor of the restaurant. A vast range of kebabs follow, from the classic sis kofte (£5.80) and doner kebab (£6.20) to the seftali kofte (£6.50), a herby lamb kebab that's wrapped in lamb fat before cooking to keep it moist – which tastes a good deal better than its description. If none of these take your fancy, there is a selection of steaks (£10.50), but that would really be missing the point. Or if decision-making is too taxing there are four set menus (£15.50–£16.50 per person, minimum 2), to include meze, kebab, salad, fresh fruit, baklava and Turkish coffee.

Efes is one of those places that every media and radio personality remembers with fondness. That's because it's less than five minutes walk from the BBC, and surrounded by media companies. Efes is an institution and one that should not be missed. If you don't have time for the whole experience but fancy a quick kebab, there is a take-away part of the shop front. Efes kebabs beat all the gnarled offerings from kebab shops in the Tottenham Court Road hands down.

Glory Kebab House

57 Goodge St, W1 ☎ 0171 636 9093   ⊖ Goodge Street

Mon–Sat noon–3pm & 5.30–11pm, Sun noon–3pm & 6–9.30pm   All major credit cards

The Glory Kebab House has been on this site, on the corner of Goodge Street, since 1939 – and, to be frank, it looks that way. This is a place that owes nothing to 1990s restaurant design or style; in fact, everything about it, from the dated frontage to the shiny black banquettes and chairs, seems locked into a time warp. It is run, as it always has been, by the Savva family and offers a haven of old-fashioned gentility – if there were a museum for Greek Cypriot restaurants this would be the star exhibit. It may be unfashionable but the food is very sound when compared with the flashier places, and much more keenly priced.

Start with old favourites. Taramosalata (£1.75) is creamy. Houmous (£1.75) is coarsely ground and tasty. Kalamari (£3.75) – strips of slowly stewed squid, pink and in a muddy-looking sauce – wins no points for presentation but is meltingly tender. Halloumi cheese (£2.50) is salty and rubbery just the way it ought to be. All are adorned with wedges of tomato. Main course choices are grills or stews, and come with either a combination of rice and a lettuce and tomato salad, or those strangely yielding roast potatoes. The sheftalia – skewer-grilled, minced lamb – is good (£6.15), as are the loukanika – spiced sausages (£6.25). Kleftiko (£6.25) is the real thing, a thick lamb shank cooked to the point where you can grab the protruding bone, twist and pull, and see it come away from the tender meat clean as a whistle. Lamb with aubergines (£6.25) is a pleasure. A Greek salad (£3.25) combines the tang of feta with lettuce and the ubiquitous tomato. To accompany it, explore the Cypriot wine list – like the food, these represent outstanding value with a dozen bottles that will please without breaking the bank.

On Cyprus – and at the Glory – the stout-hearted can sample a dish called trahana (£1.75). This is a soup made by mixing crushed wheat and yoghurt into a paste, drying it, and then reconstituting it. You end up with something like a sour, thin porridge. As with all truly horrid delicacies trahana is supposed to be good for you, and a single bowlful is reputed to cure the flu.

Ikkyu

67a Tottenham Court Road, W1 ☎ 0171 636 9280	⊖ Goodge Street
Mon–Fri & Sun noon–3pm & 6–10.30pm, closed Sat	All major credit cards

Ikkyu is busy, basic and full of people eating sound Japanese food at sensible prices – all in all a good match for any popular neighbourhood restaurant in Tokyo. What's more it is hard to find, which adds to the authenticity. Down the steps and through the twine fly screen and you've made it. The first shock is how very busy the place is – you are not the first person to discover what must be about the best-value Japanese food in London.

Nigiri sushi is good here and is priced by the piece – tuna (£2), yellow tail (£2.10), salmon (£1.70), mackerel (£1.40), or cuttlefish (£1.70). Or there's sashimi – running all the way from mackerel (£4.50) to an "assortment" (£13.50), or even sea urchin (£13.00). Alternatively, start with soba – cold brown noodles (£3.60), delicious. Then allow yourself a selection of yakitori – either a portion of "assorted" (£5), or mix and match from tongue, heart, liver, gizzard or chicken skin all at £1 a stick. You will need a good many skewers of the grilled chicken skin as it is implausibly delicious. Moving on to the main dishes, an order of fried leeks with pork (£7.20) brings a bunch of long onion-flavoured greens which may well be chives, although not so pungent, strewn with morsels of grilled pork. Whatever the green element is it is certainly not leeks. Or there's grilled aubergine (£3.40). Or rolled five vegetables with shrimp (£7.70) which is like a Swiss roll made with egg and vegetable and a core of prawn.

Ikkyu's menu rewards a bit of experiment as it has a good many delicious secrets, though the Japanese-favoured drink, shouchu and soda (£3.50), is perhaps not among them – shouchu is a clear spirit which tastes like clear spirit and the addition of soda does little to make it palatable. Asahi and Kirin beers (both £2.70) are a much better choice. Another doubtful order would be fermented soya beans topped with a raw egg (£3.10), which in Japan is thought to be the perfect way to start the day. It's available here, if you're curious, but something that combines such a challenging texture with such a strange taste is unlikely to woo you away from cornflakes.

£3–£6

Indian Student Hostel (YMCA) Canteen

41 Fitzroy Square, W1 ☎ 0171 387 0411	⊖ Warren Street
Mon–Fri 12.30–1.45pm, 7–8pm; Sat/Sun 7–8pm	Cash only

Sooner or later everyone who patrols this end of Fitzrovia pauses in front of the Indian Y.M.C.A. and looks in at the serried ranks of happy diners, only to notice that a good many of them appear to be neither Indian nor young men. This is the moment that sorts out the adventurers from the passers-by. The bold ones press the doorbell, and wait for the door to unlock, then, ignoring the signs limiting use of the facilities to students, ask if the canteen is open to the public. Apparently it is (on some unfathomable informal basis), and you're in, amid a lunchtime production line that makes Mezzo look slapdash.

The canteen's entire menu is portioned up into pretty little bowls and you go and collect what you want then you pay and carry your tray and cutlery to one of the long tables. It feels like a grown up and rather benevolent school dining hall. Your fellow diners may indeed be Indian students, but they are just as likely to be advertising folk from Charlotte Street, or office wallahs from Whitfield Street. A genuine bargain breaks down many barriers. For starters, have a plate of "bhajia" with pickle (£1) – vegetables fried in a spicy gram flour, the pickle fresh, green and hot – and a pile of poppadums, hardly a luxury item here at 20p each. Then pick up a plate piled with "special rice" (£1.20), which is pilau rice with vegetables, a well-flavoured base for the excellent curries. Mutton curry (£2.20) is rich, with lumps of tender meat; or there's chicken curry (£2), or fish curry (£2). Save room on your tray for dhal (£1), and a parata (50p).

The Canteen also has a range of puddings, all at 50p. These include the usual range of Indian delicacies but it takes some resolve not to opt for the nostalgic school dinner option – a bowl of delicious tinned peaches in their own syrup. Drinks, too, are strictly school fare: tap water or soft drinks in cans.

Malabar Junction

107 Great Russell Street, WC1 ☎ 0171 580 5230   ⊖ Tottenham Court Road

Daily noon–3pm & 6–11.30pm   All major credit cards

The cuisine at Malabar Junction is that of Kerala – the home province of the proprietor – and it is served up from two entirely separate kitchens and brigades of chefs, vegetarian and non-vegetarian, kept completely separate to comply with religious requirements. However busy it may be down in the kitchens, though, inside the restaurant all is calm. This is a top quality Indian restaurant, fully licensed, with a spacious dining room with comfortable chairs and a conservatory roof, none of which elegance is hinted at by the rather unprepossessing frontage at the Tottenham Court Road end of Great Russell Street.

Kerala is the spice capital of India, and all the Malabar dishes tend to be spicy and nutty – curry leaves, cinnamon, coconut, chilli, and cashew nuts prevail. There is also a good deal of fish. To start with try the spinach vadia (£3), these small chickpea doughnuts made with spinach and ginger are deep fried and served crunchy with two dipping sauces, yoghurt and tamarind. Or there's uppuma (£3.30), a kind of Eastern polenta – semolina fried in ghee with onions, spices and cashew nuts. The poori masala (£2.50) takes the form of two balloon-shaped, puffed breads with a potato cake that's not a million miles from bubble and squeak. For a main course, try some fish or seafood: the fish moilee (£7.50) runs the gamut of cinnamon , cloves, cardamom, green chillies, garlic, coconut and curry leaves, while the Cochin prawn curry (£7.90) is more tomatoey with huge prawns. Chicken Malabar (£5.50) applies much the same Keralan spice palate to chicken. From the array of vegetable dishes try avial (£3.50), a combination of all sorts of vegetables but with a host of woody and aromatic spices, and a plate of green bananas (£3.90), tangy and delicious.

You'll also find all the traditional southern Indian vegetarian favourites listed on the menu here – rava dosa (semolina pancake), uthappam (crisp lentil pancake), and iddly (rice and lentil cakes). As it seems to offer the best of both worlds, this may well be the perfect restaurant for any mix of vegetarians and fish (or meat) eaters.

The Mandeer

8 Bloomsbury Way, WC1 ☎ 0171 242 6202   ⊖ Holborn/Tottenham Court Road

Mon–Sat noon–3pm & 5–10pm   All major credit cards (evenings only)

This is the second address for the Mandeer restaurant but don't get the impression that Ramesh and Usha Patel are flighty – it is their first move in forty years. The Mandeer Ayurvedic Vegetarian restaurant is something of an institution. From its old premises just of the Tottenham Court Road smiling staff dished up very cheap, very good, very worthy Gujarati food, to everyone from penniless students to the highly religious. Nowadays the new Mandeer stands next to the centre for Tibetan studies in Bloomsbury Way, and it is full of much the same clientele as before. The food is just as good, too, and just as good value as it ever was. The most expensive dish on the menu is a thali at £14.50 and this brings you an absolute feast of Gujarati and Maharashtrian cooking: a well-balanced meal on a tray, featuring pilau rice, two purum puri, kadhi, dry potato, bindhi, aubergines, beans, two kachori, raita and papadom. There's a beer and organic wine list for the weak of spirit, but no smoking – as you'd expect of a 'medicinal' restaurant.

You can easily eat for a lot less – but there is much to tempt. Crisp, plump samosas, (£2.50) are served with date and tamarind chutney. Batata vada (£2.50) are mini hand grenades of spicy mashed potato, deep fried. Kachori (£3.75) are a revelation – deep-fried pastries filled with split mung beans, redolent of cinnamon and cloves. Breads are wholemeal and delicious – puris (two for £1.20), chapattis with ghee (two for £1.40) and parathas (£1.25). Bhindi (£5.50), from the Gujarati section of the menu, is a rich, dry curry of okra. The "beans of the day" (£4.25) may be anything from chickpeas to aduki beans. Panir mattar (£5.25) is cubes of Indian cheese with peas in a much reduced garlic and onion sauce. There are good concentrated flavours here, no wading through anonymous and wishy-washy sauces. Desserts are Indian and very sweet in the main, although the shrikand (£2.50) – a strained yoghurt with saffron, and cardamom – is pleasantly tangy.

Turn up at lunchtime and part of the dining room becomes a self-service buffet – good food, very low prices, cash only. There's a display board with the dishes on it: masala dosa with soup (£4.50); samosas (60p); batata vada (60p). As you would expect, it's busy.

Mash London

19–21 Great Portland St, W1 ☎ 0171 637 5555   ⊖ Oxford Circus

Mon–Fri 8am–4pm & 6pm–1am, Sat 11am–1am,

Sun 11am–10.30pm   All major credit cards

Mash is certainly modern – and it will probably go on looking modern for the next twenty years. At the back of a low and busy bar there stands a brewery, for like its antecedent in Manchester, Mash London combines a brewery with bar, cafe, and restaurant. It is open for breakfast, sells take-away packed lunches, and is always busy. Sometimes a restaurant has an indefinable something that guarantees it success: Mash London has been full since the day it opened and if you like the buzz (and the crowds of other people who like the buzz) you will be happy here. There are moments when the food is very good and it seldom slips much below okay. There is a wood-fired oven, and a wood-fired grill.

Starters are reasonably priced from £5.50 and range from brochette of wood-grilled onion bread, buffalo mozzarella, anchovy and chilli, to salad of raw fennel, red onion and honey-cured salmon, or twice cooked belly pork with a chunky green salsa – they are good at rich and earthy dishes here. A slightly more extravagant and delicious speciality is warm potato and octopus with fresh peas and mint (£6.90). To follow, there are pizzas, pasta, salads, fish from the wood-fire grill, mains and sides. Pizzas are more Californian than Italian, with toppings such as crispy duck, hoi sin, cucumber and Asian greens pizza (£9); pastas, like-wise, with such as wood-roasted pumpkin raviolo with wilted roquet, pecorino and roasted seed dressing (£7.50). And then there's wood-grilled baby artichoke salad with runner beans and shallots (£8.50); various fish served in a number of ways – with confit fennel, tapenade sauce and char-grilled courgette (£12.50); or how about wood-roasted suckling pig with charred leeks, apples, baby spinach and a cinnamon cider dressing (£12.50)? If these dishes sing out to you, you'll be very happy here as they are soundly cooked and well-presented.

The four beers made on the premises are probably an acquired taste – though anyone drinking enough of the fruit beer to acquire a taste for it deserves some sort of commendation for fortitude. There's a decent wine list, if you don't get along with the beer.

BLOOMSBURY & FITZROVIA ① MODERN EUROPEAN

CENTRAL

R.K. Stanley

6 Little Portland St, W1 ☎ 0171 462 0099   ⊖ Oxford Circus

Mon–Sat noon–11.30pm   All major credit cards

BLOOMSBURY & FITZROVIA ⑲ MODERN BRITISH

Beer and sausages: at first glance a prescription for German restaurant hell . . . a bierkeller with over-cheerful waitresses and over-large portions. Think again. R.K. Stanley's is a highly successful celebration of two of Britain's culinary strengths, presented in a stylish, modern take on an up-market American diner; the service is swift and friendly, and good value pricing belies its location – just to the North of Oxford Street. The food is well-cooked and tasty, and the inspiration for the sausages comes from all over the globe.

The centrepiece of the menu is a selection of different sausages, all of which are freshly made on the premises (and all of which are offered at £6 from 6–7pm). Bratwurst (£7.25) comes with choucroute, grilled bacon, caramelised pears, and champ mash. Game sausage (£7.25) comes with wine scented cabbage, mustard mash, glazed parsnips and pancetta. The vegetarian Glamorgan sausage (£7.25) comes with chunky tomato chutney, green vegetables, potato salad and crisp leeks. Thai sausage (£6.95) is made with pork, and comes with noodles, choi sum and spicy vegetables. Simple Stanley (£6.95) is a delight – a home-made pork sausage with onion gravy, spinach and champ mash. The chicken sausage (£7.25) comes with couscous, and salad. And the Caribbean style jerk sausage (£7.25) is hotter and served with plantain, chilli peppers and sweet potato mash. The starters range from a splendid plate of house savouries (£5.95) to diver-caught scallops with black pudding and mushy peas (£8). There is also a succession of alternative main courses – meat loaf (£8.95), roast plaice (£9.95) – and reliable puddings at under £5.

You should drink ale, lager, stout or porter here. There are dozens of interesting bottled ales on offer, ranging from Shepherd Neame's Spitfire – smooth and soft (£3.75) – to Fraoch Heather ale, which is brewed with the hand picked flowering shoots of the heather (£4.20). Or try Stanley's Stout from the keg (£2.70 a pint). The bottle prices might seem a bit high but you get some fine brews – and experimenting with rare beers, as ever, is a lot cheaper than trying fine wines.

CENTRAL

Townhouse Brasserie

24 Coptic St, WC1 ☎ 0171 636 2731   ⊖ Holborn/Tottenham Court Road

Mon–Fri noon–11.30pm; Sat 4–11.30pm; Sun noon–8pm   All major credit cards

Townhouse Brasserie is a bright modern restaurant with an eclectic French–Caribbean menu, and owners doing the cooking and service. Front of house Joanna Lewars and her Chinese–Jamaican husband Lloyd, who cooks, claim that running a restaurant is their dream come true and they look like they mean it. Their enthusiasm shines though in a friendly attention to detail and an eclectic menu. No wonder the Townhouse has a loyal clientele who treat the place like home.

A feature of the Townhouse menu is its 'light meals' section – on offer at both lunch and dinner – though traditional starter and main course sections also put in an appearance. The menu changes every couple of months and in winter concentrates on game which is the Lewars's great love. Light meals include seafood crêpe with white fish, Scottish salmon and fresh herb cream (£6.30), and char-grilled marinated quail with tempura style vegetables (£5.95). All are good and substantial enough to satisfy most appetites. 'Full' main courses on offer include a pan-fried Kingfish, Caribbean style with shallots & chilli aïoli (£9.50); char-grilled breast of duck with a pesto jus (£12.95), steamed whole sea bass with fennel and a cherry tomato dressing (£15.95). The Kingfish, a Jamaican speciality, is delightfully spicy; the duck is perfectly cooked; and the steamed sea bass is tender and good. Starters include fresh Mediterranean fish soup with fresh basil (£4.10), crispy nests of spicy prawns with spring onion and fresh ginger (£5.45), and warm goats' cheese with roast shallots and a tomato confit (£5.30).

Desserts are classic and home-made as well. Banoffee pie (£4.10) is as sticky as it should be; tart Tatin with crème fraîche (£3.75) is classically done and caramel rich; and there's a white and dark chocolate tart with double chocolate sauce (£4.10) to please chocoholics. The wine list is compiled to complement the food and there is a good selection of rich reds for the gamey side of the menu. Townhouse offers set lunches and dinners of £9.95/£12.45 for two/three courses, and also a good value Sunday brunch. A secret Georgian sitting room on the first floor caters for large dinner parties and functions.

Villandry Foodstore

170 Great Portland Street, W1 ☎ 0171 631 3131	⊖ Great Portland Street
Daily 8.30–11am, 12.30–3pm, 7–10pm	Amex, Mastercard, Visa

Both foodstore and restaurant, Villandry began in more fashionable but cramped surroundings in Marylebone High Street. Its success brought the need for larger premises and, thus installed in Great Portland Street, a handsome foodstore gives onto a modern, rather stark, dining room. Passing displays of asparagus priced at £9.50 a kilo may induce nerves among diners – and this is decidedly not a cheap restaurant – while the menu header reads like a warning, rather than a welcome: "Please allow time as all food is made to order. Please do not smoke. Thank you for coming." Nevertheless, if you're serious about your food, and you have time to wait for careful preparation, Villandry won't disappoint.

The Villandry menu changes daily, so you won't necessarily find all – or indeed any – of the dishes mentioned here. But you should experience the same care in quality, fresh ingredients – as you'd expect at the back of a quality, fresh foodstore – and critically exact cooking. On our visit, leek and potato soup with chives (£4.50) balanced earthy flavours evenly; the charcuterie (£8.00) was temptingly arranged; the asparagus and red onion salad with balsamic dressing and parmesan (£7.00) was fine, if a little weighted to the rocket (perhaps understandably given the shop price). The main courses were hugely impressive. Roast cod with pea mash and anchovy butter (£12.00) was spot on, the fish perfectly timed to the point where it becomes flaky and firm without losing moisture. The corn-fed chicken, sweet potato, cippoline onions, mushrooms and red wine sauce (£2.00) was suitably robust with morels enriching the gravy. Desserts include moist chocolate cake (£5.00), and as you'd expect from the array in the shop, there's an extensive and expensive cheeseboard (£8.00), served with terrific walnut and sourdough breads.

Wine prices, like the food, are distinctly West End though there are house selections from £11.50. Waters are (irritatingly) described by region: Badoit – Loire (£3.50), San Pellegrino – Italian Alps (£2.50). Service flows like glue, but the menu has already warned you that this might be the case. However, standards are high and the balancing of flavours suggests that the kitchen brigade know what they're doing and are not afraid to buck the fashionable trends.

Wagamama

4 Streatham Street, W1 ☎ 0171 323 9223   ⊖ Tottenham Court Rd

Mon–Sat noon–11pm, Sun 12.30–10.30pm   All major credit cards

Wagamama has been trendy – and packed – right from its opening, and its popularity shows no signs of falling off. Which is fair enough: this is as good a canteen as you'll find, serving simple, and generally rather good Japanese food at very reasonable prices. What it's not is a place for a relaxed or intimate meal. The basement interior is cavernous and mini-malist, while diners are seated side-by-side on long benches. At regular eating times, you'll find yourself in a queue lining the stairway (there are no reservations), and even mid-afternoon you'll encounter a sprinkling of customers slurping noodles. When you reach the front of the queue, you're seated and your order is punched into a hand held computer, then the code numbers for your dishes are written on the low-tech placemat in front of you – a legacy of the day when the radio ordering system failed. There's beer and wine available as well as free green tea.

Dishes arrive when they're cooked, so a party of four will be served at four different times. This system doesn't favour sharing – what you order is yours. Generally that means ordering a main dish – noodles in soup, fried noodles, or sauce based noodles – or a rice dish. Plus a side dish (which in other establishments would be listed as starters). The mains include a splendid chilli beef ramen (£7), slivers of sirloin steak in a vat of soup with vegetables and noodles (it's good etiquette to slurp these); yasai katsu curry (£5), boiled rice with a light curry sauce and discs of deep fried vegetables; and ebi katsu (£4.50), very tasty deep-fried king prawns with cilli and garlic sauce. A couple of interesting sides are gyoza (£3.40) – chicken dumplings, fried and delicious, and yaki soba (£4.50) – rich, pan-fried noodles. If this all sounds confusing, that's because it is: to enjoy Wagamama you'll need to go with the flow.

It's not often that a restaurant sees fit to offer a glossary which includes its own name. The menu here is a lengthy document, just the thing for a rainy afternoon at a seaside hotel but a little confusing in situ. Wagamama is described as "Willfulness or selfishness: selfishness in terms of looking after oneself, looking after oneself in terms of positive eating and positive living." The success of this formula has resulted in two more Wagama-ma's – at 10a Lexington St (Soho) and 101a Wigmore St (behind Selfridges) – with another due to open in Camden in Spring 1999.

Chinatown

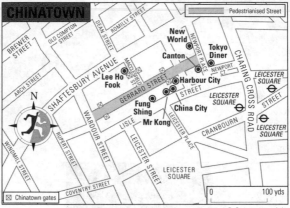

CHINATOWN

Pedestrianised Street

Leicester Square

Chinatown gates

0   100 yds

© Crown copyright

CENTRAL

Canton Restaurant

11 Newport Place, WC2 ☎ 0171 437 6220	⊖ Leicester Square
Daily noon–midnight (Fri & Sat until 1am)	All major credit cards

The Canton's charm is that it bridges the gap between the elite Chinese restaurants and the cheap and cheerful barbecue houses; thus while there is a steamed seabass on the menu there is still duck rice being prepared at a block in the window. The food is fresh and generally well-cooked although presentation can be rough and ready. The service is surprisingly friendly for Chinatown although the cramped tables make this more of a pitstop than a palace. Netherthless, the Canton is invariably busy and attracts a varied crowd ranging from tourists to waiters coming off shift at other Soho restaurants.

Smart Chinese starters like the gluey, sweet and sour, Capital spare ribs (£7.50) or the steamed fresh scallops (£1.80 each) are both good, but so are some of the bargain ones like hot and sour soup (£1.80) or the pancake rolls (four for £2.50). Take your pick. Then study the list of main dishes, which is unfeasibly long. In the bargain zone you'll find a plate of rice with cold pork and duck (£3.90) and fresh-tasting Singapore noodles (£3.90). Pricier and more ambitious but very good indeed are the squid in chilli and black bean sauce (£8) and the steamed fresh seabass (£15). Some items have a foot in both camps, especially the hot pot dishes. The stewed eel with roast pork (£9) is particularly tasty – not so cheap as the other dishes, but coming as it does in a stainless steel pot that holds a portion large enough to feed a family of four, it is terrific value and strongly recommended.

As recently as ten years ago the Canton was primarily a perch for night owls, and would stay open until the dawn. In those days they used to sell out bowls of congee – the sloppy and bland rice porridge that's served for breakfast in China. When trying to apply the brakes to a serious drinking session, fatty, garlicky foods that need a lot of chewing just won't do; congee on the other hand could have been tailor-made for the job. Since Chinatown became more respectable and the early-closing regime came into force at the Canton, congee has been dropped from the menu due to lack of demand.

CHINATOWN ⓣ CHINESE

China City

White Bear Yard, 25a Lisle Street, WC2 ☎ 0171 734 3388   ⊖ Leicester Square

Mon–Sat noon–midnight   All major credit cards except Diners

White Bear Yard lies off Lisle Street to the north. There's a large gate and an archway; go through the arch, cross the courtyard, and you'll come to a large glass-fronted Chinese restaurant which seats 500 diners on three floors. Go early and you will see the restaurant change from cavernously empty to bustling and packed. The service is "Chinatown-brusque" but a combination of good flavours, large portions, and sensible pricing keeps the clientele coming back for more. The menu stipulates a "minimum charge of £10 per person" but do not be put off – this is not an expensive restaurant and you have to go some to spend a lot more.

Both home-style dishes and less familiar exotic dishes are good here – this is a place in which to spread your wings and try something new. Naturally the menu includes sweet and sour pork, platters of mixed appetisers, crispy ducks with attendant pancakes, but why not start instead by trying the mixed seafood with fish straw soup (£3.50), rather like that old workhorse "crab meat and sweetcorn soup" but altogether more delicate. Whatever fish straw may be, (and you cannot tell from the evidence in the bowl) it is certainly delicious. Then sample some chicken – steamed with ginger and spring onion sauce (£8.50) it produces astonishingly rich flavours and satisfying chunks of meat. Alternatively, look in the section on hot pot dishes. Mixed seafood with bean curd in hot pot (£7), is a casserole containing fresh scallops, huge prawns, crisp mange tout and bean curd, all in a terrific sauce. The simpler dishes are good too; try fried ho fun with beef, dry (£4.50) – wide noodles with tender beef and a rich brown sauce, very comforting. And just to see something green on the table and so appease your conscience, order choi sum in oyster sauce (£4.50).

"Seasonal price" are two words to strike fear into the heart of even the most experienced diner. At China City you'll find them alongside all the lobster dishes. These include deep-fried lobster with garlic and chilli, and baked lobster with cheese and garlic. You'll get a straightforward answer on price – and it may just prove surprisingly accessible.

CENTRAL

Fung Shing

15 Lisle St, WC2 ☎ 0171 437 1539   ⊖ Leicester Square

Daily noon–11.30pm   All major credit cards

The Fung Shing was one of the first restaurants in Chinatown to take cooking seriously. Twenty or so years ago, when it was still a dowdy little place with a mural on the back wall, the kitchens were run by the man acknowledged to be Chinatown's number one fish cook – chef Wu. And when he died in 1996 his sous chef took over. The restaurant itself has changed beyond all recognition and now stretches all the way from Lisle Street to Gerrard Street, ever bigger and ever brassier. The menu is littered with interesting dishes. There's an array of particularly fine fish dishes. The portions are large. And while the prices creep ever upwards, they still offer really good value.

By Chinese restaurant standards the menu is not a huge one, topping out at around 160 dishes. To start with, ignore the crispy duck with pancakes (half for £10.50) – good but too predictable – and the lobster with noodles (£18 a lb. with noodles £2 extra) – too expensive. Turn to the steamed scallops with garlic and soya sauce (£2.40 each); nowhere does them better. Or the spare ribs – with chilli and garlic (£7.50) or barbecued (£7.50). Or the prosaically named mixed meat with lettuce (£8.50), a wonderful savoury mince with lettuce leaf wraps. Or you could happily order mains solely from the chef's specials: stewed belly pork with yam in hot pot (£9.50), crispy spicy eel (£10.95), cold spice and herb boiled chicken with jelly fish (half £14) – suspend your doubts it's amazingly delicious. The other dishes are good too – the perfect Singapore noodle (£6), crispy stuffed baby squids with chilli and garlic (£8.95), braised aubergine with black bean sauce (£7). The food here has that earthy, robust quality which you only encounter when the chef is absolutely confident of his flavours and textures – whatever the cuisine.

The Fung Shing is a class act, but what makes it doubly successful is the unusually (for Chinatown) gracious and patient service. This is a place where you can both ask questions and take advice with confidence.

£6–£20

Harbour City

46 Gerrard Street, W1 ☎ 0171 439 0171   ⊖ Leicester Square

Mon–Sat noon–11.30pm, Sun 11am–11pm   All major credit cards

Dim sum were invented in the Tang dynasty, and are best defined as small snacks eaten informally, and traditionally only served in the morning and afternoon. The Harbour City excels at dim sum, and this is the place to visit whether you are a novice or an expert. Do not expect a lot in the way of service, nor much help with the menu. But you will get a tasty, cheap and filling meal.

Call in any time between noon and 5pm and a pot of refreshing Chinese tea (20p) arrives with a pair of menus. Discard the main one and study the dim sum list. The dumplings – a dim sum mainstay – usually come three or four pieces to a portion, so it makes sense if everyone in the party starts by choosing three different ones (you can always re-order anything particularly delicious, as no dish takes more than ten minutes to arrive). In the steamed dumplings section try har kau (prawn dumpling £2), sui mai (meat dumpling £1.60), and fun kuo (a mixture of prawn and meat £1.60). These are all classics and come in bamboo steamers. Also good is the char sui pau (barbecued pork in a bun, like a steamed doughnut with a savoury middle £1.60), or try glutinous rice with meat wrapped in lotus leaf (£2.40), very sticky and rich – don't eat the leaf! Moving on to fried dumplings, there's wan ton with sweet and sour sauce (£1.60), spring rolls (prawn-filled and very delicious, £1.80), and paper-wrapped prawns £1.80 – prawns in paper thin pastry (£1.60). The "exotic dim sum" list also yields some treasures, among them scallop dumplings (£2), deep-fried crispy squid (£1.60), and deep-fried dumpling with chives and minced prawns (£1.60). This is one place where it is easier to overeat than spend a fortune.

Do not believe anyone who tells you that they enjoy chicken claws in "shy maiden" wine sauce (£1.60), this is a dish of chickens' feet served cold and scaly, and tastes about as nasty as it sounds. Do, however, try one small adventure: char sui cheung fun (£2.20), a translucent, jelly-like batter rolled around barbecued pork. This is really rather good.

Lee Ho Fook

4 Macclesfield Street, W1 ☎ 0171 734 0782   ⊖ Leicester Square

Daily 11.30am–11pm   Cash only

Despite glowing reports in many guidebooks, a good many people set out to eat at the Macclesfield Street Lee Ho Fook but never actually find it. This is a genuine Chinese barbecue house – small, Spartan, cheap and the food is good of its kind – but it is not so helpful as to have a sign, at least one in English characters. Thus, many potential non-Chinese diners find themselves ending up at the larger, grander, more tourist-friendly Lee Ho Fook around the corner in Gerrard Street. These then are the directions: Macclesfield Street runs from Shaftesbury Avenue in the North to Gerrard Street in the South; on the West side there is a back street called Dansey Place, and on the corner with a red and gold sign in Chinese characters and a host of ducks hanging in the window is Lee Ho Fook. Inside there's a chef chopping things at a block in the window, four or five waiters and seats for 22. Sit down and you get tea, chop sticks and a big bottle of chilli sauce placed in front of you. Tables are shared and eating is a brisk, no-nonsense business.

The main focus of the short menu is plated meals. You get a mound of rice with a splash of soy sauce "gravy" over it, and a portion of chopped barbecued meat balanced on top. Choose from lean pork loin (£4.10); crisp, fatty belly pork (£4); suckling pig (£6.50); soya chicken (£4.10); or duck (£4.10). You can mix and match – half pork half duck – order a "combination" mixed roast pork, soya chicken, and duck with rice (£5.50); or you can order the meats by portion without rice – duck (£5.50); suckling pig (£7). There's also a thriving take-away trade – a whole duck costs £18, a half £9.

Because of the specialised nature of this place the "other" menu items are all too easily overlooked. Try adding a plate of crisp vegetables in oyster sauce (£3.80) to your order. And before going for the barbecue, perhaps choose a bowl of wontun soup (£2.20) or the even more substantial wontun noodle soup (£2.80).

Mr Kong

21 Lisle St, WC2 ☎ 0171 437 7341	⊖ Leicester Square
Daily noon–3am	Amex, Mastercard, Visa

You have to wonder whether the eponymous Mr Kong flirted with the idea of calling his restaurant King Kong. Despite its marathon open hours at all regular mealtimes it's full of satisfied customers who would support such an accolade. Going with a party of six or more is most helpful when dining at Mr Kong, that way you can order, taste, and argue over a raft of dishes. You can share. If there's something you really don't like you can exile it to the other end of the table, if there's something wonderful you can call up a second portion. It's a strategy which means that you can never be caught out.

There are three menus here – the main menu (5 pages and 160 dishes or so); the "Chef's Specials" (70 more) and the "Today's Chef's Specials" (10 more). The main menu is rather safety first, but sliced pork, salted egg and vegetable soup (minimum of two £2.10 each) is something of a house speciality and very good and rich, the salted egg tasting pleasantly cheesy. Then try deep-fried crispy Mongolian lamb (£6.50) from "Today's": this is very crisp breast of lamb which comes with a lettuce leaf wrap – avoid the accompanying hoi sin sauce which is very sickly. Also from "Today's" there is braised shin of beef with fresh lotus root in hot pot (£6.50). Then turn to the "Chef's Specials" for sautéed dragon whistlers with dried scallops (£11), made with fresh pea shoots. Back to the main menu for a good, spicy Singapore noodle (£4.20), an interesting prawn dish in a spicy tomatoey sauce – Kon Chin king prawn (£7.50) – and some Chinese broccoli in oyster sauce – dark green, crunchy and delicious (£4.60). Portion sizes are generous and even when dishes contain exotic ingredients prices are reasonable. Just ignore the decor which falls somewhere between ordinary and grubby.

On the "Chef's Specials" you'll find steamed fresh razor clam with garlic "seasonal price"; when they are available that's about £2.50. They're tender, well-flavoured and worth every penny. Order a couple per person by way of an extravagance.

New World

1 Gerrard Place, W1 ☎ 0171 734 0396   ⊖ Leicester Square

Daily 11am–midnight   All major credit cards

When the 1990s saw the arrival of the mega-restaurants – giant 200 and 300 seater emporiums – the proprietors of this long-established Chinese restaurant were right to feel aggrieved, and ask what all the fuss was about. The New World seats between 400 and 600 depending on how many functions are going on at any one time. This is probably the largest single restaurant in Europe and it can comfortably swallow up a couple of huge Chinese wedding parties as well as getting on with the daily business of feeding thousands of people. When you arrive you will have to wait in a sort of holding pen just inside the door until the intercom screeches with static and you are sent off to your table. The system is properly inscrutable. The menu is leather-bound and nearly twenty pages long. It features everything you have ever heard of and quite a lot you haven't. You don't need it – go for the dim sum which are served every day from 11am until 6pm.

The dim sum come round on trolleys. Catch the eye of a waiter or waitress with a bow tie to order drinks and then you're at the mercy of the trolley pushers. Broadly speaking the trolleys are "themed", so you will get one that has a lot of barbecued meat; another that has ho fun – the broad noodles; another with steamed dumplings; another with soups; another with cheung fun – the long slippery rolls of pastry with different meats inside. A good mix would be to take siu mai (£1.50) and har kau (£1.50) from the "steamers" trolley. Then char sui cheung fun (£2.35), a long roll with pork. Then some deep fried won ton (£1.50) – little crispy parcels with sweet sauce. Perhaps something exotic like woo kwok (£1.50) – deep fried taro dumplings stuffed with pork and yam. And something filling like char sui pow (£1.50) – steamed doughnuts filled with pork – or nor mai gai (£2.35) – a lotus leaf parcel of glutinous rice and meats.

If you arrive after 6pm, you're on your own: there are literally hundreds of dishes on the main menus. However, Chinese functions apart, New World is really best as an in-and-out dim sum joint. It's about eating – and not, as the sticky carpet immediately declares, design and fripperies.

Tokyo Diner

2 Newport Place, WC2 ☎ 0171 287 8777   ⊖ Leicester Square

Daily noon–midnight   All major credit cards

Tokyo Diner offers conclusive proof that you needn't take out a second mortgage to enjoy Japanese food in London. Stacked up on three floors of a block that clings to Chinatown's silk skirts, this is a friendly eatery that shuns elaboration in favour of fast food, Tokyo-style. The place was actually set up by an Nipponophile Englishman, but the kitchen staff are all Japanese, and its far eastern credentials bear scrutiny. The decor, crisp and minimalist, leaves the food to do the talking, which it does fluently if the number of Japanese that walk through the doors are any indication. If you don't know your teppanyaki from your kamikaze, or your sushi from your sumo, you'll be glad of the explanatory notes on the menu. When your food arrives, pick a set of chopsticks, snap them apart – the menu recommends that you rub them together to rid them of splinters – and get stuck in.

Top seller is the soba noodle soup (£4.90), thin brown buckwheat noodles in a soya broth, which is pleasant, filling and very popular with the drop-by lunchtime trade. Don't be afraid of slurping it – as the menu note explains, slurping is okay. Or try the set lunch in a bento box: this comprises rice, noodles, sashimi and your choice of teriyaki, all for around £10. The bento will dispel the misconception that Japanese food is just for picking at, once and for all, though watch out for the little green mound of wasabi which will blow your head off if you're not careful (it should be mixed with soy sauce in a saucer). If you don't have appetite enough for a full-on bento box, skip the curry section (as the menu admits it's a bit like school food) and head straight for the sushi and sashimi. They too come in "sets" and if you like sushi try the nigiri set (£7.50) – very good value.

For washing it all down, the Japanese beer, Asahi (£1.99), is good – or there's complimentary Japanese tea. For a special treat try the rich, sweet plum wine (£2.99 for 125ml) which is surprisingly more-ish and quite delicious.

Covent Garden & Holborn

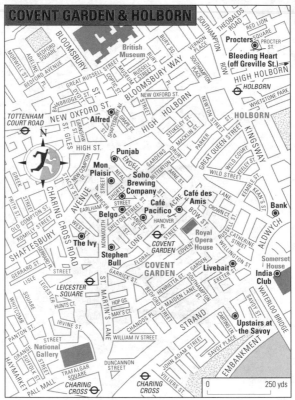

COVENT GARDEN & HOLBORN

Procters
Bleeding Heart
(off Greville St.)
British Museum
Alfred
Punjab
Mon Plaisir
Soho Brewing Company
Café des Amis
Café Pacifico
Belgo
The Ivy
Stephen Bull
COVENT GARDEN
Royal Opera House
Livebait
Bank
Somerset House
India Club
Upstairs at the Savoy
LEICESTER SQUARE
National Gallery
CHARING CROSS

© Crown copyright

0   250 yds

Alfred

245 Shaftesbury Ave, WC2 ☎ 0171 240 2566   ⊖ Tottenham Court Road

Mon–Fri noon–3.30pm & 6–11pm, Sat 6–11.30pm   All major credit cards

Many restaurants claim to be British but Alfred actually delivers, and in some surprising ways. While the menu is based upon unpretentious but inventive British cooking, the supporting cast of drinks completes the experience. There are 20 British beers on the menu, three of them on draught, and you are encouraged to drink beer rather than wine with your meal. A pleasant change. British wines feature too, seven in number including a champagne style and a dessert wine, all available by the glass. Even more unusual are the British eaux de vie and cider brandies on the list. If that doesn't tempt you, try one of the 28 whiskies including some rare single malts.

Continuing in Caledonian vein, the menu offers starters like haggis and neeps (£5.50) and whisky-cured salmon and cress salad (£6.00). Or try the potted chicken liver mousse, toast, pickles and chutney (£5.50); served like potted shrimps with a butter crust, it is rich and moreish. Main courses of fishcake, spinach and tomato (£8.95) or crispy belly pork, choucroute cabbage, chutney and mash (£9.95) do not disappoint either. The fishcake comes with crispy fried leek strips and a sauce well flavoured with tarragon. Crispy belly pork is all that the dish should be, meat that melts and crispy skin. Puddings include novel combinations like gingerbread and lavender custard (£4.50), with the home-made, highly-scented custard a very good taste amplifier for the gingerbread. Other welcome standards include roast guinea fowl, cabbage, bacon and pearl onions (£12.95), and calves liver with bubble and squeak (£10.95). Good simple ingredients are well cooked and very well presented. There is also an excellent value set menu, available at both lunch and dinner, which features many of the main menu dishes, at £12.95 for two courses and £15.90 for three courses.

Design at Alfred is minimalist Formica retro chic, and works well in its light and open corner situation. But the genuine bakelite ashtray, salt and pepper pot sets are cult items and deserve a place in the V & A. Ask if you can buy a set, but don't try to steal them as the staff watch over them like hawks.

Bank

1 Kingsway (corner of Aldwych), WC2 ☎ 0171 379 9797	⊖ Covent Garden
Mon–Fri 7–10.30am, noon–3pm, 5.30pm–11.30pm,	
Sat & Sun 11.30am–3.30pm, 5.30pm–11.30pm (Sun 10.30pm)	All major credit cards

A good many foodists believe that this restaurant is the closest London comes to re-creating the all day buzz and unfussy cuisine of the big Parisian brasseries. Bank opens for breakfast (Continental, Full English, or Caviar), lays on brunch at the weekend, does a good value pre-theatre (5.30–7pm) and lunch prix fixe (both are £13.90 for two courses, £17.50 for three) . . . has a lively bar packed with revellers . . . and then there's the other matter of lunch and dinner for several hundred. Whatever time of day, the food is impressive, especially considering the large numbers of people fed, and if you like the lively life you will have a great time here. If you're leaving after 10pm, incidentally, and want a taxi home, go for the cabs arranged by the doorman; black cabs are rare as hen's teeth around here after the Drury Lane theatres empty.

The menu changes seasonally, so dishes may come and go. Start with something simple – simple to get wrong that is – a Caesar salad (£6.50); or a hearty ham hock and lentil salad with a poached egg (£7.95); or push the boat out with a well-made terrine of foie gras (£12.50). Or go for shellfish. Bank is owned by one of London's leading catering fishmongers so crustacea such as cold lobster in shell (half £13.95, whole £26.50) or dressed crab and avocado pepper dressing (£12.50) should be reliable. The fish dishes are equally good, from the ambitious – seabream, caramelised endive, orange and cardamom sauce, (£15.95) – to the traditional – Bank fish and chips, featuring halibut, mushy peas and tartare sauce (£16.95). Meat dishes are well prepared brasserie fare such as grilled calves liver and bacon with celeriac mash (£14.95), roast rack of lamb herb crust and roast spring vegetables (£15.95). Puddings include a wonderful passionfruit creme caramel (£5.10), and a classic lemon tart (£5.90).

When Bank first opened many diners felt uneasy about the ceiling decoration – a modernist extravaganza of suspended armoured glass – and the tables around the edge were always the first to fill up. Thankfully, and as the insurance company predicted, the ceiling is safe and no-one seems to worry any more.

Belgo Centraal

50 Earlham St, WC2 ☎ 0171 813 2233	⊖ Covent Garden

Mon–Thurs noon–11.30pm, Fri/Sat noon–midnight, Sun noon–10.30pm

Restaurant closed but beerhall open 3–5.30pm	All major credit cards

The Belgians invented mussels, frîtes and mayonnaise – and Belgo has done all it can to help the Belgian national dish take over London. This – the Belgo group's flagship restaurant – is a massive metal-minimalist cavern accessed by riding down in a scissor powered lift. Turn left at the bottom and you enter the restaurant for booked places, turn right and you get seated in the beerhall where diners share tables. With 95 different beers, some at alcoholic strengths of 8-9%, it's difficult not to be sociable. But that's not to decry the quality of the food.

Belgo offers the best mussels in town and no mistake. A kilo of classic moules marinière served with frîtes and mayonnaise (£10.95) is fresh and clearly cooked then and there. Other varieties of moules on offer include Blonde/bacon, with Leffe beer and bacon (£10.95); Congo, with coconut cream and lemongrass (£10.95); and Provencale, with tomato, herbs and garlic (£10.95). But there are many alternatives for the non-mussel eater. Try carbonnade Flamande (£8.95) – beef braised in Geuze beer with apples and plums and served with frîtes; or waterzooi à la Gantoise (£9.75) – Belgian chicken and vegetable julienne in a light sauce. There are also five different asparagus dishes, three rôtisserie chicken dishes and whole Canadian lobsters for £16.95 served in three different ways. Desserts, as you might expect, are strong on Belgian chocolate. They include, amongst many others, a white chocolate creme brulée (£3.95), and traditional Belgian waffles with ice cream, cream and chocolate sauce (£3.95). Belgo delights in special offers too. There's a £5 lunch every day of the week which buys you wild boar sausages with Belgian mash and a beer, or half a kilo of mussels and salad. On Monday lunchtime anything on the menu is just £5.55. And there's a Belgo loyalty card that gets you a free £5 lunch for every four meals eaten at Belgo.

It's brilliant value, a great atmosphere and the food is very good. But the beer list at Belgo is awesome, making it a must-visit for that alone.

Bleeding Heart

Bleeding Heart Yard, off Greville St, EC1 0171 242 2056	⊖ Farringdon
Mon–Fri noon–3pm & 6–10.30pm	All major credit cards

Bleeding Heart Yard is a quiet little backstreet on the edge of Farringdon, close to both Holborn and Clerkenwell. Its eponymous restaurant-wine bar is targeted at City and law firm regulars but should appeal to practically everyone. The restaurant is downstairs in the basement and leather chairs, French waiters in black-tie and candles on every table create a sense of occasion. Bleeding Heart Yard is also a place for those who enjoy their wine just as much – if not more – than their food. Its cloth-bound, book-sized wine list has won the restaurant a Wine Spectator award and if you're an enthusiast it could easily take you all evening to read through. But don't be intimidated: although the Petrus '76 clocks in at £425 a bottle, a bottle of very good house Burgundy will set you back only £14.95.

Take your time when choosing from the tempting list of starters, which specializes in fish. The bisque de homard et ses croutons (£4.95) is a really outstanding lobster bisque with croutons; creamy and tangy. Or you might go for gateau de crabe et son choux aux epices (£6.95), a beautifully prepared fresh crab, served out of its shell and accompanied by sweet and sour sauce. Equally splendid are the coquilles St Jacques aux algues croquantes, sauce saki citronée (£8.50), a generous heap of grilled scallops served with crunchy seaweed and a delicious lemon saki sauce. For mains, you can't go wrong with the classics. Contre-filet de boeuf d'Ecosse (£14.50) is a fine slab of Scottish Beef, served with Béarnaise sauce and a picturesque little stack of pommes frites. Carré d'Agneau rôti aux petits pois et á la menthe (£13.95) is roasted rack of lamb with a very tasty purée made from peas and potatoes. The restaurant has its own pastry chef, which means you must leave room for pudding. All desserts are priced at £4.95. Tarte fine of apples on frangipani pastry with vanilla ice-cream is a work of art.

There's a macabre story behind the name of the restaurant; read about it on the back of the menu – perhaps after you have eaten?

Café des Amis

11–14 Hanover Place, off Long Acre, WC2 0171 379 3444   ⊖ Covent Garden

Mon–Sat 11.30am–11.30pm   All major credit cards

This is the re-incarnation of an old-established restaurant, just around the corner from the (as yet unreincarnated) Opera House. Where once it was Gallic shabby it is now all bleached, blonde wood. All is modern, all is clean and bright. The reincarnated menu sits uneasily with its French section headings – "Les plats", "Les poissons" – as it ranges across the globe, through Thai fishcakes, Chinese noodles, polenta fritters, and tuna carpaccio. The old clientele, many of whom used to have half a meal before the opera, and a dessert in the interval, are in shock. However, from a food point of view, there's only good to report. In the hands of a predominantly French team, the old bistro menu has been taken out and shaken into the 1990s. Service is efficient and friendly, while the set menus – two courses £9.95, three courses £12.50, served between 11.30am and 5pm – are a real bargain.

You might start with a dish like duck liver parfait (£5.75); it is served in a wedge and very smooth – modernity is imposed by a kumquat and seed mustard relish. Or there's a Continental fish soup (£4.50), the twist here being that it is a clear soup served up with croutons made from focaccio, and a saffron aïoli. The main courses run the gamut from roast rump of lamb with peach chutney and sage potatoes (£14.25) to leek and pork sausages, creamed feves and red onion rings (£8.95), and the omnipresent Thai fishcakes, with pak choi, tempura calamari, and cilantro mixed pepper salsa (£9.25) – large fishcakes, if a touch under seasoned. The set lunch features starters like cream of mushroom soup with tarragon dumplings or salad Niçoise, and mains like roasted hake with Belgian endive and red pepper butter or perhaps a cassoulet. The French dishes have been gently eased into line – salade Niçoise includes hard boiled quail's eggs and a slice of grilled tuna. The cassoulet is low on beans and sludge and high on chunks of sausage and meat. If you can suspend any purist tendencies, you will enjoy this. The cooking is well-judged, the presentation on the plate is good, and the prices are reasonable.

The winebar/bar under the restaurant is as dark and cavernous, as the restaurant above is light and bright . . . and so it should be!

Café Pacifico

5 Langley St, WC2 ☎ 0171 379 7728	⊖ Covent Garden
Mon–Sat noon–midnight, Sun noon–11pm	Amex, Mastercard, Visa

The salsa is hot at Café Pacifico – both types. As you are seated, a complimentary bowl of searing salsa dip with corn chips is put on your table. As you eat, hot salsa music gets your fingers tapping. The atmosphere is relaxed and you're soon in the mood for a cold Tecate (£2.60) or Negro Modelo (£2.80) beer. There are nine Mexican beers, a good selection of wines and dozens of cocktails. Parties can enjoy a pitcher of Margaritas to serve eight people for £27.45. But Pacifico's tequila list is the highlight. There are over sixty varieties, ranging from £2.50 to £18 a shot, and including very old and rare brands.

The menu is a lively mixture of old style Californian Mexican and new Mexican, so whilst favourites like fajitas, flautas and tacos dominate, there are also some interesting and unusual dishes. Portions are generous and spicy and many main courses come with refried beans and rice. Try Nachos rancheros (£6.50) for starters and enjoy a huge plate of corn chips with beans, cheese, sauce, guacamole, onions, sour cream and olives. It's excellent for sharing. Taquitos (£4.50) are good too, being baby, filled fried tacos that are very tasty, as are smoked chicken quesadillas (£4.75) which are flour tortillas with chicken, red peppers and avocado salsa. Main courses include degustacion del Pacifico (£9.50), which gives you a taste of almost everything. A burrito especial (£8.95) gives you a flour tortilla filled with cheese and refried beans covered with ranchera sauce and a choice of roast beef, chicken or ground beef. Refried beans at Café Pacifico are smooth and comforting and just the thing to balance the spicy heat. Roast beef is slow-cooked and falling apart tender. From 5pm you can select from a range of more modern Mexican dishes on the menu. These include ideas like cordero sabanero (£10.95) – breaded lamb ribs with habanero jelly and yogurt salsa.

Café Pacifico has been a place to party since 1978 and claims to be London's oldest Mexican restaurant. And, yes, they do have a bottle of Mescal with a worm in it.

India Club

143 Strand, WC2 ☎ 0171 836 0650　　　　　　⊖ Charing Cross

Mon–Sat noon–2.30pm & 6–10pm　　　　　　Cash only

When the India Club opened in 1950, the linoleum flooring was probably quite chic; today it has a faded period charm. Situated up two flights of stairs, sandwiched between floors of the grandly named Strand Continental Hotel (one of London's cheapest hotels), the Club is an institution, generally full, and mostly with regulars, as you can tell by the stares of appraisal given to newcomers. The regulars eat here because they have fallen in love with a strangely old-fashioned combination of runny curry and low, low prices. They don't mind paying a £2 a year membership fee for the right to buy cold bottles of Cobra beer from the hotel reception downstairs – they quite understand the inflexibility of English licensing arrangements. These stalwart customers can be split into two categories, suave Indians from the nearby High Commission and a miscellany of folk from the BBC World Service, hanging on precariously to their old Central London base, down the road in Bush House.

The food at the India Club pre-dates any London consciousness of the differential spicing of Bengal, Kerala, Rajisthan or Goa. It is Anglo-Indian, essentially, and well-cooked of its kind. Mughlay chicken (£4.80) is a wing and a drumstick in a rich brown, oniony gravy, garnished with two half hard-boiled eggs. Scampi curry is runny and brown with fearless prawns swimming through it (£5.80). Masala dosai is a well made crispy pancake with a pleasantly sharp-tasting potato filling (£2.90). Dhal is yellow and . . . runny (£2.90). Mango chutney is a revelation, thick parings of mango, each three inches long, chewy and delicious (40p). Breads are good – paratha (£1.50), puris (two for £1.30). Rice is white and comes in clumps (£1.80).

You should heed the kindly warning of your waiter about the "chillie bhajais" (£2.50), a dish as simple as it is thought-provoking. Long, thin, extra-hot green chillies are given a thick coating of gram flour batter and then deep fried until crisp. These are served with a side dish of coconut chutney which has a few more chopped chillies sprinkled through it. Eating this actually hurts. Console yourself by remembering that, however bad, a chilli burn only lasts for ten minutes.

The Ivy

1 West St, WC2 ☎ 0171 836 4751

Tube Leicester Square

Daily noon–3pm (Sun 3.30pm) & 5.30pm–midnight

All major credit cards

The Ivy is a beautiful old Regency-style restaurant – built in 1928 by Mario Gallati, who later founded Le Caprice. It has been a theatreland and society favourite throughout the century – Noel Cowerd was a noted regular – and never more so than today. The staff, so it is said, notice recessionary times only because they have to turn fewer people away. And that's no joke: The Ivy is booked solid, for lunch and dinner, right through the week. Its clientele include a lot of face-familiar actors and media folk, and to get a booking it helps to proffer a name of at least B-list celebrity. That said, there are tables to be had here if you book far enough ahead – or try at very short notice; or if you ask after a table in the bar area (nice enough, so long as your legs aren't over-long); or if you go for the weekend lunch, which is three courses for a bargain £15.50 plus £1.50 service charge.

And once you're in? Well, first off, whether you're famous or not, the staff are charming and unhurrying. Second, the food is pretty good. The menu is essentially a brasserie list of comfort food – nice dishes that combine simplicity with familiarity and which are invariably well-cooked. You could spend a lot here without restraint, surprisingly little if you limit yourself to a single course and pud. You might start with deep fried Cornish sprats (£5.75); or the famous risotto nero (£7.50), black with squid ink; or the eggs Benedict (£5.75). Then there's kedgeree (£9.25) and meatloaf (£9.75), and well-made versions of classic staples: calf's liver and bacon (£15.75); shepherd's pie (£9.75); salmon fishcakes (£10.75). Even the vegetable section is enlivened with homely delights like bubble and squeak (£2.50) and medium cut chips (£3). For dessert you might turn to Bakewell tart (£5.50) or sticky toffee pudding (£6), or perhaps finish with a savoury such as Welsh rarebit (£4) or angels on horseback (£4.50) – prunes wrapped in bacon.

The Ivy's present incarnation is the result of a 1990 makeover which meticulously restored the wood panelling and leaded stained-glass. It also involved a roll-call of British artists. Look around and you may notice works by, among others, Howard Hodgkin, Peter Blake, Tom Phillips and Patrick Caulfield.

Livebait

21 Wellington St, WC2 ☎ 0171 836 7161	⊖ Covent Garden.
Mon–Sat noon–3pm & 5.30–11.30pm	All major credit cards

This large bustling restaurant is an offshoot of the original Livebait in the Cut behind Waterloo station. You'll find the same black and white tiling, the same rather cramped diner booths, and much the same kind of menu. Since the early days – when all was unbridled eccentricity – things have calmed down a bit and some of the wilder combinations of ingredients have been tamed. But the emphasis is still on fish so fresh you expect to see it flapping on the slab, and superb crustacea. The breads are still a feature and service is friendly. The hand of big business – Livebait was bought from its creators by a large London restaurant group – is apparent, but the Livebait ethos is so irrepressible that this remains the most innovative fish restaurant in town.

As an amuse gueule you get a few fresh prawns to munch at along with the amazing Technicolor breads – which may include anything from red bread made with beetroot to yellow bread made with tagine. If you continue with seafood, you've any number of treats to choose from – vast crevettes with mayonnaise (£2.60 each), cock crabs (£7.60 each), hen crabs (£7.35 each), winkles, cockles, clams, oysters – maybe it is best to go for it, and have the two tier shellfish platter (£21.50), and if someone else is paying add a supplementary half lobster (pushing the price up to £39.50). The cooked starters are large and complex – anywhere else they could easily pass muster as main courses. They might include such constructions as oyster fritter with guacamole and Cajun potato fondant (£7.10); or pan-fried squid with white bean purée and red chilli jam (£6.40); or gratinée of Scottish king scallops on the half shell with Oriental leek and coral fricasée (£8.20). If you're not hugely hungry, you'd do well to order one for starter and another for your main course. Which is not to knock the mains, which are equally original, with such offerings as baked cutlet of hake, new potatoes and red onions in chilli oil (£14.85) or bluefin tuna, stuffed red pepper with polenta spinach and cheese (£16.90).

Livebait's food is exciting and the wine list is carefully chosen. But the beer list is also a delight. Bottles such as Marston's Pedigree or Young's Special complement the dishes superbly.

£17–£40

Mon Plaisir

21 Monmouth St, WC2 ☎ 0171 836 7243	⊖ Covent Garden
Mon–Fri noon–2.15pm & 5.50–11.15pm, Sat 5.50–11.15pm	All major credit cards

A table at Mon Plaisir can often comprise three generations. Loyal diners have been enjoying traditional French cooking here since the 1940s. The menu boasts: "Mon Plaisir is London's oldest French Restaurant and has for over fifty years been family owned …" The current manager is Phillipe Lhermitte, son of the family who inherited the premises in 1972 from the previous Viala family, themselves owners since 1943. The ambience and standards haven't changed and dishes have remained on the menu for decades. All the staff do a good French-accented English and the many cosy rooms give it a club-like atmosphere. Cooking is classical.

Starters include favourites like gratinée a l'oignon (£4.95), a rich onion soup that is meatily good; cassolette d'escargots a l'ail (£5.90), garlickly buttery and delicious; and salade d'endives au Roquefort, vinaigre aux noix (£5.50), a light crisp chicory salad with a dressing that turns simple leaves into a meal. Main courses feature dishes like thon facon Niçoise (£13.50); gigot d'agneau roti, legumes de Provence (£14.50); poulet roti Chasseur (£9.20); or entrecote grille, allumettes (£13.95). Vegetable accompaniments are the likes of gratin Dauphinoise (£2.50), epinards à la creme (£2.00) and haricots verts (£2.50). If you are still going for the puddings, there are reassuring standbys such as creme brulée, truffe au chocolat and tarte maison du jour (all at £5.50). All are as good as you would expect from a long-established, family-run restaurant. Dishes are cooked as if someone cares and it shows in the taste. Menus change (somewhat) as the seasons dictate and there is a prix fixe pre-theatre menu at £11.95 for two courses and £14.95 for three. There is also a very good value prix fixe lunch at £14.95. Wines are French and there is an excellent selection of better, well-selected clarets and burgundies.

Mon Plaisir is almost a museum piece of cooking in the traditional French style. When it closed for a while after a kitchen fire in 1998 it had an answerphone message: "Don't worry, we are not changing anything." It is very likeable.

Procters

30 Procter Street, WC1 ☎ 0171 242 6691   ⊖ Holborn

Mon–Fri 7.30–11pm   All major credit cards

Procters is something of an oasis, fenced off from Bloomsbury by a four lane highway, and surrounded by the dry and lawyerish offices around Red Lion Square. It describes itself as a wine-bar, though it's probably more restaurant, these days. Either way, the cooking here is consistently good: if Procters was the other side of Kingsway, in Covent Garden, or even just down the road in Clerkenwell, it would be jam-packed, and prices would doubtless be significantly higher. As it is, you're likely to find space amid a staunch band of regulars. It's a splendid place for an unpretentious lunch, or a good "wine bar" dinner.

The menu is seasonally driven and commendably simple so you will encounter starters like gravadlax of trout on a spiced potato cake with lemon sour cream (£5.75) – home-made and well-judged. Or a layered terrine of goats' cheese, herbed potato and pancetta (£5.75). Main courses divide into two camps – grilled Cumberland sausages with mashed potato and onion gravy (£10.50); and salmon and haddock fishcakes (£10.50) are simple, good and ever-present, with any threat to drop them causing rebellion amongst the regulars. While the rest of the mains are interesting dishes based on rounding up the usual suspects – seabass, rump of lamb, corn-fed chicken. The chargrilled calf's liver, smoked bacon and button mushrooms with parmentier potatoes and an Armagnac jus (£13.25) is precisely cooked and a good strong blend of flavours. The vegetarian options can also be attractive -.such as the salad of grilled butternut, baby corn, watercress and pine nuts with a sundried tomato pesto (£11.50).

It's probably to do with Procters split personality, but they take their wine very seriously here. The prices aren't wild but the choice is. There are often obscure and delicious wines to be had at low prices and there's a small box on the menu listing the current tip. Thus summer menus might list a rosé from Penedes like Mas Comtal Merlot D.O. Penedes 1996 at £12.95 a bottle or £3.60 for a large 175ml glass. Surprisingly fruity, and surprisingly cheap.

Punjab

80/82 Neal St, WC2 ☎ 0171 836 9787   ⊖ Leicester Square

Daily noon–3pm & 6–11.30pm   Amex, Mastercard, Visa

In 1951 Gurbachan Singh Maan took the decision to move his fledgling Indian restaurant from the City to new premises in Neal Street in Covent Garden, his plan being to take advantage of the trade from the nearby Indian High Commission. It was a strategy that has worked handsomely. Today his grandson Sital Singh Maan runs what is one of London's oldest curry houses, though one which has always been at the forefront of new developments – in 1962 the Maan family brought over one of the first tandoor ovens to be seen in Britain, and in 1989 they added the then-exotic chicken jalfrezi to their repertoire. Despite these forays into fashionable dishes, the cuisine at the Punjab has always been firmly rooted where it belongs . . . in the Punjab. This is a Sikh restaurant, as you'll realise straightaway from the imposing, turbanned waiters.

Punjabi cuisine offers some interesting, non-standard Indian dishes, so start by ordering from among the less familiar items on the menu. Kadu and puri (£2.10), for instance, a sweet and sharp mash of curried pumpkin served on a puri; or aloo tikka (£1.95), which are described as potato cutlets but arrive as small deep-fried discs on a sea of tangy sauce; or chicken chat (£2.60) – diced chicken in rich sauce. To follow, try the acharri gosht (£7.50) or the acharri murgha (£7.80) – the first is made with lamb and the second with chicken. This is a dish the Maan family are very proud of, the meat is "pickled" in traditional Punjabi spices and as a result both meat and sauce have an agreeable edge of sharpness. Chicken karahi (£7.10) is good, too – rich and thick, while from the vegetable dishes, channa aloo (£3.70) combines the nutty crunch of chickpeas with the comfort of potatoes. For refreshment turn to Kaylani lager (£3.50), a beer from Bangalore which comes in gratifyingly large bottles.

On the menu you'll also find benaam macchi tarkari (£7.50) and underneath the description "nameless fish curry, speciality of chef". This curry may be nameless but it is certainly not flavourless, with solid lumps of boneless white fish in a rich and tasty gravy.

Soho Brewing Company

41 Earlham Street, WC2 ☎ 0171 240 0606   ⊖ Covent Garden

Meals served noon–3pm & 6–11pm   All major credit cards except Diners

At first glance this is just another Covent Garden cellar, with a blonde wood floor and huge stainless steel bar. But appropriately enough (as the building was once the site of a thriving brewery), it is now a micro-brewery, Covent Garden's first. As well as the nest of squat copper tanks and purposeful pipes snaking their way to and fro across the ceiling, there's a stylish dining area, leading off an open kitchen. The food here is both modern and British and shows a careful choice of fresh ingredients. It is not a place for flights of culinary fancy but if you want some excellent beer (their own or imports), and entirely suitable food to accompany it, well, this is your place. Be warned, however, that in the evening the bar area is as packed as any other in Covent Garden.

A three-course, no-choice set menu is on offer at a bargain £7.95 (lunch) or £11.95 (dinner), both prices including a house beer but not service (10%). You might get chicken liver parfait; pan-fried escalope of cod; and walnut, chocolate and banana bread. Ordering from the menu, expect to see starters like a wild mushroom risotto with parmesan and chives (£5.50); caramelised apples, black and white pudding with bitter leaves (£5.50); gravadlax, cucumber mustard and dill (£5.50); linguini, roasted tomatoes and rocket (£5); and a Caesar salad (£5). Dishes from Italy, England, Scandinavia, and America: a perfect definition of Modern British cuisine. Main courses follow the same kind of pattern featuring the likes of baked cod, olive fennel and parsley salad (£10); loin of pork with mixed leaves, black beans, ginger and soy (£9); or grilled swordfish with couscous mint and coriander pesto (£10.50). The puddings are all at £4 – tarte Tatin, cheesecake, bread and butter pudding made with pannettone, and organic ice creams. The best choice of all (and a definite bargain) is the plate of cheeses from the nearby Neal's Yard Dairy (also £4). An opportunity to enjoy Montgomery's cheddar or Cashel blue at this price should not be missed.

The brewmaster here makes a very good wheat beer, also a New York inspired red beer, at getting on for £3 a pint, they could never be described as cheap but they are eminently quaffable.

Stephen Bull

12 Upper St Martin's Lane, WC2 ☎ 0171 379 7811   ⊖ Leicester Square.

Mon–Fri noon–2.30pm & 5.45–11.30pm Sat 5.45–11.30pm   All major credit cards

The decor at Stephen Bull is modern and the food is too. It's very much designer architecture in terms of an interior, but without being austere, and it's a good place to enjoy that much hyped style of cooking called Modern British. Dishes are genuinely innovative, created to introduce new combinations of flavours and textures, and surprising descriptions on the menu deliver satisfying results on the plate.

The starter section offers mixes like crab salad with gazpacho and tomato sorbet (£8.00); warm rabbit with black pudding and mustard (£7.00); and warm smoked eel, apple and cracked pepper chutney, pork crackling (£7.25). The rabbit is served as a sliced sausage of firm meat, the eel as slim fillets. Both are unconventional and exceptional. Main courses do not disappoint either. They might feature the likes of saddle of lamb wrapped in Suffolk bacon, penny bun and potato gratin (£14.50), or fricassée of chicken and veal sweetbreads, port and truffle oil (£14.00), or boned red mullet and sardines, sweet peppers, tapenade and roast bread (£14.00). Eating boned red mullet is such a delight and the lamb is served just pink with its penny bun garnish – or cepes as most people know them. Puddings include equally experimental departures. There's strawberry champagne consommé and vanilla parfait; warm prune and armagnac tart; orange confit and mascarpone ice-cream; banana, pecan and date pudding; or vanilla ice cream with butterscotch sauce for anyone with an ultra-sweet tooth. All are very good and all are priced at £5.50. The pudding menu also suggests five well chosen dessert wines to accompany them.

The wine list overall is thoughtfully laid out, in two sections: there's a Quick List for easy selection and a main long list divided not by the usual regions but by taste and texture. It is particularly useful if you are interested in trying new wine regions. Another innovation is Stephen Bull's pre-theatre menu that runs from 5.45 pm to 7.00 pm and from 10.30 pm to 11.30 pm. This features a good range of dishes and you can select a starter and dessert for £10 the pair – which really is a snip for cooking of this quality.

Upstairs at the Savoy

Savoy Hotel, 1 Savoy Hill, WC2 ☎ 0171 836 4343   ⊖ Charing Cross

Mon–Sat noon–midnight   All major credit cards

Walk in through the main doors of the Savoy Hotel in the Strand, pausing only to notice that traffic in the Savoy courtyard drives on the right, turn sharply left up the stairs, left again before you get to the American Bar and continue on as if you're a regular guest. Upstairs at the Savoy appears to be a secret in that it's hard to find, but once there you'll find impeccable service and the kind of cooking that justifies the Savoy's pricing. The front of house will greet you with genuine charm and bilingual waitresses seem to outnumber the customers. Come between 8pm and 10pm and you can have it all for under £20 with a set menu of £17.50/£22.50 for two/three courses, including an after-dinner coffee in the American Bar.

The Upstairs restaurant shares the famed Grill Room kitchen so expect cooking of a quite elaborate nature, if lighter than you might expect from a hotel like this. Starters offer variations on traditional themes like avocado and prawns with orange salad (£7.75), beef carpaccio with caviar of aubergine and foccacia toast (£7.50), and crunchy Caesar salad with butterfly sardines (£8.00). This latter was exceptional and easily enough for two. Main courses include standards like fried fish cake with fennel compote and grain mustard sauce (£12.95); smoked haddock kedgeree with soft poached egg and spinach (£12.95); and roast loin of lamb with pistachio and mint crust, Thai croquettes and roasted fennel sauce (£14.25). All well cooked and as accomplished as you would expect of the venue and at the price. The lamb is served very rare, so ask if you prefer it on the cooked side of pink. The Thai croquettes could be patented. Puddings are ornate. Coconut creme brulée with sesame seed tuile (£5.00) could do with having the coconut in the creme rather than on it, but poachèd summer fruits with fromage blanc sorbet (£5.50) is worth its spoon for the sorbet alone.

There's an excellent offering of tisanes and perfumed teas as well. Marco Polo is scented with fruits and flowers from China and Tibet, and Casablanca is Moroccan green tea with mint and bergamot. Afterwards, the front of house bids you a fond good night and you stroll through the Savoy like an honoured guest.

Euston &
King's Cross

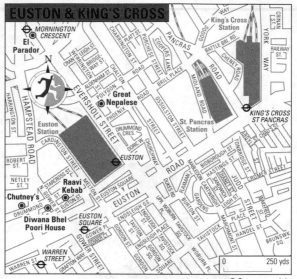

EUSTON & KING'S CROSS

MORNINGTON CRESCENT
El Parador
Great Nepalese
Euston Station
Raavi Kebab
Chutney's
Diwana Bhel Poori House
King's Cross Station
St. Pancras Station
KING'S CROSS ST PANCRAS
EUSTON
EUSTON SQUARE
WARREN STREET

0   250 yds

© Crown copyright

Chutney's

124 Drummond St, NW1 ☎ 0171 388 0604	⊖ Euston Square/Warren St
Mon–Sat noon–2.45 & 6–11.30pm, Sun noon–10.30pm	All major credit cards

Chutney's is quite a bargain. It does a buffet lunch for just £4.94, on offer every lunchtime from Monday to Saturday, and all day Sunday. This would be normal enough if the food were ropey or routine but Chutney's kitchen turns out well-flavoured, rich, varied, very tasty, vegetarian food. And therein lies the key: potatoes cost a great deal less than meat. Still, at Chutney's the chefs are skilled enough to leave even a carnivore red in tooth and claw pleasantly full of potatoes before they have a chance to pine for their meat ration. Service is attentive and while there are only 30 seats upstairs, downstairs there are another 100 so you will usually get a seat – though Sundays can be busy.

You would have to be foolish not to take advantage of the lunchtime offer, but if dining there's no shortage of dishes to tempt you, and an almost equally good bargain lies in wait in the form of Chutney's deluxe thali – a three-course meal priced at £6.95. If you're ordering from the menu, meals here tend to blur the distinction between starters and main course. From the section headed "Western India's Farsan" try ragara pattice (£2.50) which will bring a dish of chick peas in a fresh-tasting curry sauce and topped by two fried potato cakes. Or opt for the Chutney's special puri (£2.20). You get five of these amazing mouthfuls: little ball-shaped puris filled with potatoes and topped with sev. Open wide and pop the whole thing in; as you bite down it is soft, crunchy, rich, sweet, sour, sharp, creamy, and delicious – all at the same time. You must also try the rava onion dosa (£3.60) – a vast flat sheet that's not quite a pancake, crispy/caramelised on the outside and gooey with potato and onions on the inside where it has been folded. It comes with a knockout coconut chutney and a dish of sambhal. The Chutney's curries are very tasty, too, even simple things like mushroom bhajee (£2.30) and peas and potatoes (£2.60).

The breads here are essential. Good orders are the flaky, multi-layered plain paratha (£1.70), or a couple of small puris (£1.10), which are deep-fried chapattis.

Diwana Bhel-Poori House

121 Drummond St, NW1 ☎ 0171 387 5556   ⊖ Euston

Daily noon–11.30pm   All major credit cards

All varnished pine and shag-pile carpets, the Diwana Bhel-Poori House puts you in mind of a late-70s Wimpy bar. Only the Indian woodcarvings dotted around the walls give the game away – that and the heady scent of freshly blended spices. It's a busy place, with tables filling up and emptying at a fair crack, though the atmosphere is convivial and casual rather than rushed. There's no licence, so you can bring your own beer or wine (corkage is free – a charitable touch) though a full water jug is supplied on each table. This, the low prices (the costliest dish will set you back just £6.20), a chatty menu listing "tasty snacks", and fast, friendly service combine to create a deceptively simple stage for some fine Indian vegetarian cooking.

Starters are copious, ladled out in no-nonsense stainless steel bowls. The dahi bhalle chat (£2.30) is a cool, yoghurty blend of chick peas, crushed pooris and bulgar wheat, sprinkled with "very special spices". The dahi poori (£2.30) is a fragrant concoction of pooris, potatoes, onions, sweet and sour sauces and chilli chutney, again smothered in yoghurt and laced with spices. Stars of the main menu are the dosas, particularly the flamboyant paper dosa (£4.30), a giant fan of a pancake with coconut chutney, potatoes and dal nestling beneath its folds. Also superb is the house speciality, thali annapurna (£6), a feast of dal, rice, vegetables, pickles, side dishes, mini bhajees and your choice of pooris or chapatis – divine but unfinishable, especially if you make the mistake of ordering the monstrously proportioned side dishes as well.

Whatever feast you put together, do leave room for dessert, as there's a heavenly kulfi malai (£1.70) to dig into – a creamy pyramid of frozen milk flavoured with kevda, nuts and herbs. A rich but less sweet-toothed option is the shrikhand (£1.60), a western Indian dish with cheese, spices and herbs counteracting the sugar. Alternatively, try the Kashmiri falooda (£2.20) – cold milk with china grass and rose syrup, topped with ice cream and nuts. Though strictly speaking a drink, this is surely pudding enough for anyone.

El Parador

245 Eversholt St, NW1 ☎ 0171 387 2789   ⊖ Euston

Mon–Thurs 11am–3pm & 6–11pm, Fri noon–3pm & 6–11.30pm,

Sat 6–11.30pm, Sun 7–10.30pm   All major credit cards

El Parador is a small, no-frills Spanish restaurant and tapas bar – slightly stranded in the quiet little enclave around Mornington Crescent, between King's Cross and Camden. It serves very tasty tapas at very reasonable prices and has a friendly, laid-back atmosphere, even on busy friday and Saturday nights. It's a good place to spend a summer evening, with a lovely garden out the back, though this is no secret and the sought after tables here should be booked in advance.

As ever with tapas, the fun part of eating here is choosing several dishes from the wide selection on offer, and then sharing and swapping with your companions. The plates are small, so allow yourself at least two or three tapas a head – more for a really filling meal – and go for at least one of the fish or seafood dishes, which are treats. Merluza del Parador (£4.20) is a slab of melt-in-the-mouth hake baked with parsley and lemon; gambas salteadas (£4.20) is a portion of nice fat tiger prawns, pan-fried with parsley and hot paprika; mejillones (£3.60) are green-lipped mussels, grilled with coriander and olive oil. Carnivores shouldn't miss out on the jamon Serrano (£4.50), delicious Spanish cured ham, or the morcilla del Parador (£3.70), a savoury Spanish sausage served with new potatoes and peppers. Also good is cordera a la plancha (£4.20), grilled lamb with rosemary and olive oil. The ten vegetarian tapas include legumbres asadas (£3.80), a squishy mound of roasted peppers, aubergines, tomatoes, red onions and garlic; alcachofas del Parador (£3.40), artichoke hearts with garlic, red onion and basil; and calabaza salteado (£3.30), roast butternut squash with tomato, sage and onions. Desserts keep up the pace. Marquesa de chocolate (£3) is a luscious, creamy home-made chocolate mousse; flan de naranja (£2.80) is really good orange creme caramel.

Try a glass of the dryish Manzanilla (£2) to start or accompany your meal. It's a perfect foil for tapas. Or delve into El Parador's strong extensive selection of Spanish wines. Enjoyable choices include Muga crianza '97 (£14.50), a smooth white Rioja, and the Guelbenzu crianza '95 (£14), a rich and fruity red.

Great Nepalese

48 Eversholt St, NW1 ☎ 0171 388 6737	⊖ Euston / Euston Square
Mon–Sat noon–2.45pm & 6–11.30pm,	
Sun noon–2.30pm & 6–11.15pm	Mastercard, Visa

This bit of London behind Euston Station is distinctly seedy and the shops that are neighbours to the Great Nepalese offer strange products for probably quite strange people. Inside the restaurant, however, everything is re-assuringly normal, if a little old and faded, like the giant wall photo showing the Queen and Prince Phillip standing with the five living Gurkha holders of the Victoria Cross. This is a place that manages to combine friendly and homely service with authentic Nepalese food and just in case your nerve falters the menu also has a buffer zone littered with standard curry house favourites like chicken tikka masala and lamb rogan josh – the latter helpfully subtitled "a very popular lamb curry".

Don't order the lamb curry unless feeling profoundly un-adventurous. It may be a very nice popular lamb curry but the authentic Great Nepalese dishes are nicer still. Start with masco-bara, a large flying-saucer-shaped doughnut. It is made from black lentils, but without their black skins, so the result is a nutty-tasting, fluffy white mass with a crisp outside. It comes with a bowl of curry gravy for dipping (£3.25 plain or £3.65 with a hidden core of shredded lamb). Or try haku choyala (£3.50) diced mutton with garlic, lemon juice and ginger, spicy and agreeably sharp. For mains, the staff direct you to the dumba curry (£4.50), a traditional Nepalese style curry, reliant on the same rich gravy as the masco bhara, or the chicken ra piaj (£4.60), with onions and spices. Both are well recommended. Another very typical Nepalese dish is the butuwa chicken (£4.60). It combines ginger and spices with garlic and green herbs and is delicious. If you like dal, you shouldn't miss the kalo dal (£2.80), nutty and dark with black lentils.

A single note of caution. Beware the Coronation rum from Kathmandu. This firewater was first distilled in 1975 for the coronation of his majesty King Birendra Bir Bikram Shah Deva, and it comes in a bottle shaped like a glass kukri. You probably have to be a Gurkha to appreciate its finer points.

Raavi Kebab Halal Tandoori

125 Drummond St, NW1 ☎ 0171 388 1780   ⊖ Euston Square

Daily 12.30pm–10.30pm   All major credit cards

This small restaurant has been a fixture for over twenty five years, during which time Drummond Street has become one of the main curry centres of London. Competition here is more than just fierce, it is ludicrous, as well-established vegetarian restaurants compete to offer the cheapest "eat-as-much-as-you-can" lunch buffet. It is lucky that vegetables are such bargain ingredients. But the Raavi is not just about bargain prices – or vegetables. It specialises in halal meat dishes, especially grills, and on the menu claims to offer "probably the best grilled and cooked items in London". And indeed, when you fancy tucking into an item, this is a great place to come.

The grills here are good but hot – hot enough for the wildest chilli head. Seekh kebab (£2), juicy and well-flavoured, is straight from the charcoal grill in the doorway – and hot. Chicken tikka (£2.10), is hot. Mutton tikka (£2.20), is hot. And with the kebabs comes a khaki-coloured dipping sauce that is sharp with lemon juice, strongly flavoured with fresh coriander, and as you'd expect, hot with fresh chillies. Lamb quorma (£4.25) is not so fierce, a rich sauce with fresh ginger and garlic topped with a sprinkle of shaved almonds. Chicken daal (£3.25) is chunks of chicken on the bone, thoroughly delicious, bobbing on a sea of savoury yellow split-pea daal. Nan breads (90p) are light and crispy.

One curiousity on the menu is haleem (£3.90). This is a dish with origins that are shrouded in mystery. Some say that it was invented in the Middle East, and that is certainly where it is most popular today; other devotees track it back to Mogul kitchens. The recipe is arduous. Take some meat and cook it, add four kinds of daal, a good deal of cracked wheat, and two kinds of rice, plus spices. Cook for up to seven hours then add some garam masala. The result is a gluey slick of smooth and spicey glop from which signs of the meat have all but disappeared. And how does it taste? You'd be hard pushed to be more enthusiastic than, "not bad".

Islington

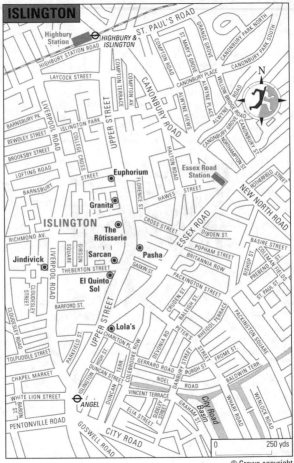

ISLINGTON

© Crown copyright

CENTRAL

El Quinto Sol

27 Upper St, N1 ☎ 0171 226 5300   ⊖ Angel

Mon–Thurs noon–10.30pm, Fri & Sat noon–midnight,

Sun noon-10.30pm   All major credit cards except Diners

There are dozens of restaurants, bars and cafés on Islington's Upper Street so the casual diner can stroll along to pick and choose. El Quinto Sol is at the beginning of the street and many pass it by in the expectation of more exotic or enticing fare further on. This is a shame as El Quinto Sol gives good value and features some interesting dishes – mostly Mexican but with Mediterranean pastas for Tex-Mex defectors. There are few better choices around here if you're in the mood for a spicy, well-flavoured and budget-priced meal.

For starters try Texan torpedoes (£3.95) – jalapeno peppers stuffed with cheese and served with sour cream. Or go for the Nachos, either plain with cheese and tomato salsa (£2.95), or with barbecued duck, mango salsa and cheese (£3.95), or with deep-fried calamari with a spicy dill and anchovy mayo (£3.95). Main courses include Mexican standards like fajitas, with a choice of vegetarian (£8.25), chicken (£8.95), beef (£9.25) or jumbo prawn (£10.50). All are sizzling, fresh and tasty. There's also Mexican-style barbecued salmon with sweet potato hash and red pepper chutney (£8.95); sizzling soft shell crabs (£11.95); and jambalaya of chorizo, prawns, chicken and catfish with south western rice (£8.95). Barbecued ribs with smoky sauce and shoestring fries (£7.95) are chewy and good, and Caesar salad with chicken and red chilli croutons (£6.55) works rather well, the chilli adding an unusual but welcome bite to an old favourite. Side orders include extra tortillas (a well spent 85p) and barbecue beans (ditto at just 95p). There's a rather good Mexican style dessert, too: fresh fruit chimichanga with caramel and chocolate sauce (£2.95). Drinks include Corona (£2.60), Sol (£2.55) and Dos Equis (£2.65) beers for a complete Mexican dinner, or there are wines (from £8.90 to a top whack £15.95).

The pavement outside El Quinto Sol is wide and perfect for the tables and chairs set outside there. With umbrella heaters intrepid diners can still enjoy an al fresco meal well into autumn and winter.

ISLINGTON ⑪ MODERN BRITISH

Euphorium

203 Upper St, N1 ☎ 0171 704 6909   ⊖ Highbury & Islington/Angel

Restaurant: Mon–Fri 12.30–2.30pm & 6–10.30pm, Sat 6–10.30pm, Sun noon–3.30pm

Bar open for light meals 9.30am–10.30pm daily   Amex, Mastercard, Visa

This Islington restaurant – which serves up Modern European food amid smart, minimalist decor – has been winning the praise of locals since it opened. The dining room is in a conservatory at the back, and despite being on the small side, manages to deliver a nice feeling of space, with large windows looking onto a courtyard and soft spotlights creating a mellow, comfortable atmosphere. Before eating, you might have a drink at the bar (which serves a good range of snacks throughout the day), where the modern glass front is perfect for taking in Upper Street's increasingly fashionable bustle. A big plus at Euphorium is the friendly, laid-back staff, who genuinely seem to enjoy themselves.

The bread is delicious – fresh from the ovens of the Euphorium bakery next door. The menu is short but varied and changes with the seasons. Starters might include stuffed grilled sardines with sundried tomato (£6.50), or aubergine and courgette cannelloni (£5.50), which uses courgettes in place of the pasta. The samosas of black bean, fresh crab and chilli (£7) are also good. If it's the right season, try the Irish rock oysters with horseradish cream (£7.00). For mains, you get a choice of around eight dishes, all bearing an eclectic European stamp. Grilled lamb's liver, chorizo, roast tomato and shallot dressing (£12.50) is a typical offering, while a chicken dish might come with a tasty combination of red wine sauce, roast shallots and shaved truffles (£15). Fish tends to be more simply handled; for example, a whole grilled seabass accompanied by braised baby fennel and peppered potatoes (£17.50), or roast cod with chilli sweetcorn macaroni and sorrel (£13). There's usually an imaginative veggie option, too, such as cauliflower fritters, broad bean curry and tahini dressing (£10.50). Leave room for pudding, as this is one of Euphorium's strengths. Parfait of whiskey and praline with almond biscuits, or figs in red wine and vanilla syrup with mascarpone and honey puffs (both £5.00) should induce an agreeable euphoria.

Beer-drinkers beware: the menu lists only one beer, and it's called 'Beer'. Have a look at the brief but well-chosen wine list instead.

CENTRAL

Granita

127 Upper St, N1 ☎ 0171 226 3222	⊖ Angel
Wed–Sat 12.30–2.30pm & 6.30–10.30pm, Tues 6.30–10.30pm,	
Sun 12.30–2.30pm & 6.30–10pm	Mastercard, Visa

Architecturally minimalist and modern, Granita is stark when empty at 7.30pm, but comes to life from 9pm with Islingtonites who look upon it as their local. Run by Vicky Leffman, front of house, and Ahmed Kharshoum in the kitchen, it offers some interesting modern ideas with influences from the Mediterranean and beyond. The menu is short, with around six starters and five main courses and changes weekly as, according to Vicky, Granita's clientele visit often and seek variety.

A typical starter at Granita is a pressed Mediterranean sandwich: aubergine, red pepper, courgettes, olives, bufala mozzarella, basil, rocket (£5.95) delivered exactly that – a concentrated sandwich of Mediterranean flavours. Or you might find wok-wilted spinach, scallops, crab, soy, red pepper, noodles (£7.50) – equally intensely flavoured, the pepper and soy carefully not dominant. For the main course, lamb shank braised in red wine, mash, roasted carrots (£11.75) was almost large enough to share and well executed, with the rich sauce and vegetables making for good unadorned tastes. Other main courses can include dishes like calves liver chargrilled, bulgar, lentils, chickpea salad, preserved lemon, yoghurt, sweet onion (£11.50), which demonstrate Granita's varied influences. Puddings feature a subtly flavoured ginger mascarpone cheesecake with chocolate crust (£4.75), and rhubarb ice cream, strawberry compote, or orange shortbread (£4.75). There is an excellent selection of sweet wines, too, including Elysium black muscat (£3.95) from the USA, which is almost sherry-like in its density, and a Tokaji Aszu 5 puttonus – the sweetest of the Tokaji's (£4.50). There are no side orders on the menu so whatever you order comes as complete as the descriptions promise. The wine list is equally cosmopolitan, with more choices from the new world than the old.

Tony Blair was a famed Granita habitué, prior to his ascension, and Granita is still a favourite with the social intelligentsia of north London and with visitors to the Almeida Theatre a few minutes' walk away. Set lunches of two (£11.95) and three (£13.95) courses are good value. All in all, worth a journey – and essential to book.

ISLINGTON ⑰ PACIFIC FUSION

Jindivick

201 Liverpool Rd, N1 ☎ 0171 607 7710   ⊖ Angel Islington

Mon 6–10.45pm, Tues–Fri noon–3pm & 6–10.45pm, Sat 10.30am–3.15pm

& 6–10.45pm, Sun 10.30am–3.15pm   All major credit cards except Amex

Jindivick is enigmatic and enthusiastically trendy – even for Islington. Just when you think you have got it sensibly pigeon-holed (Modern British cooking; eclectic Australian – Jindivick means "to burst asunder" in an aboriginal language; Pacific-rim-fusion) it seems to wriggle free. The menu changes daily, the food is always fresh and usually well-balanced, with the occasionally freaky dish. The service is engagingly laid back and the designer has done a good job of transforming what looks like an old pub into a comfortable, Islington-styled restaurant. It's a justly popular place and needs a bit of advance booking, especially for the Sunday brunch.

The menu changes daily. As a starter the "Jindivick Antipasti Platter" (£6.95) offers six bite-sized portions on a large oval plate, basically a bruschetta but more complex than usual with fine roast peppers, savoury chick peas and artichoke hearts. Jindivick's Caesar salad with shaved Parmesan (£4.95 or £6.95) is a good one with fine anchovies, and the chilled green vegetable, spring onion and yoghurt soup (£4.50) is fresh and clean tasting. For main courses some unusual fish get featured, perhaps grilled Emperor bream with asparagus and Vierge sauce (£13.95); or roasted pink snapper with saffron, olive and prawn butter and spinach (£13.95). Only slightly less exotic, the treacle roasted duck breast (£12.95) is served with shallots and pak choi and accompanied by tagliatelle apricots and rosemary. Pot roasted rabbit (£12.50), which comes with creamed herb and smoked bacon polenta and a red wine, mild aniseed and herb sauce, seems almost plain by comparison. When dessert time comes around, there are creations like mango and passionfruit semi-freddo with mango sorbet (£4.95), or fresh fig and plum puff pastry pizza with vanilla ice cream (£4.95).

Jindivick has won prizes for the brunch menu offered at the weekends, and rightly so with its excellent offerings of "The Full Monty" (£7.50) or, for the more adventurous, smoked kangaroo omelette (£7.95) or cajun spiced sardines (£6.95).

CENTRAL

Lola's

Upstairs in the Mall, 359 Upper St, N1 ☎ 0171 359 1932	⊖ Angel
Mon–Fri noon–2.30pm & 6.30–11pm, Sat noon–3pm & 6.30pm–11pm	
Sun noon–3pm & 7–10pm	All major credit cards

Lola's occupies the top floor of The Mall antique market in Islington, and as the shops are closed in the evenings it is slightly harder to find than the average restaurant. But follow the signs, climb the stairs and you will be in the realm of Carol George, Morfudd Richards and Juliet Peston, respectively the owners and chef. Lola's is very much a personal restaurant and the attention to detail and quality shows. It's a delightful building too, and the dining room has been arranged to make the most of the sky lights and features in daylight. In the evenings it's candles and cool piano, and very romantic.

The menu is hand-written daily, depending on what's in season and at the market, but on the starters menu you can expect dishes like sweet potato soup, tapenade toast (£4.75); spaghetti marrow gratin (£5.25); roast figs, goat's cheese, crisp Parma ham (£6.75); potato, onion, red pepper and fontina pizza (£5.25). Main courses include lemon risotto, rocket and parmesan salad (£9.75); roast halibut and panzanella style cous cous, harissa (£14.50); lamb chump, ratatouille, and pesto mash (£12.75); fillet steak, chips and Caesar salad (£12.75). If all this sounds enticing, it lives up to the promise. Steak, chips and Caesar salad is a good acid test of freshness and good cooking and Lola's comes up trumps on all fronts. Puddings similarly combine the highest quality of ingredients with simplicity. Try Greek yoghurt ice cream, fruit and honey (£5.25); chocolate truffle cake and ginger sauce (£5.50); or just for a glass of excellent vin santo with some cantuccini biscuits (£5.25). There is an interesting and very varied list of Old and New World wines with some fine wines at very affordable prices; it has obviously been compiled with care to complement the cooking at Lola's and makes it easy for you to accompany good food with well chosen wines.

Opened in 1996, Lola's has swiftly acquired a dedicated following, and the staff seem to greet half the customers as old friends. This is a good sign, but one that indicates you must book.

ISLINGTON ⑪ TURKISH

Pasha

301 Upper St, N1 ☎ 0171 226 1454   ⊖ Angel

Mon–Fri noon–3pm & 6–11.30pm,

Sat & Sun noon–midnight   All major credit cards (not Switch)

If you picture Turkish food as heavy and slick with oil, think again. Pasha is dedicated to producing fresh and light authentic Turkish food that's more suited to modern tastes. Cooking is done with virgin olive oil, fresh herbs, strained yoghurts and fresh ingredients prepared daily. It doesn't look like a traditional Turkish restaurant either, being open and modern looking with only the odd brass pot for decoration. It has clearly adapted well to its Upper Street location – so well in fact that the wine list helpfully offers spritzer as an item at £2.25.

For anyone new to Turkish cooking the menu is a delight. Dishes are clearly described so that you get a good idea of what dishes contain and try them on a no risk basis. Staff are helpful and will encourage you to eat in Turkish style with lots of small "meze" dishes. There are set menus of £9.95 for 12 meze and a Pasha Feast at £15.95 which gives diners ten meze plus main courses, dessert and coffee. These are for a minimum of two people. Starters include midye tava (£3.45), fried mussels Mediterranean style with walnut sauce; aranavut ciger (£3.95), lambs liver served with finely chopped onions and parsley; or fasulye piyas (£2.95), white beans with olive oil. Main courses are a more familiar selection of kebabs and dishes, but again there is a better than usual choice. Try kilic baligi (£9.95), fillet of swordfish marinated in lime, bayleaf and herbs and served with rice; or istim kebab (£8.95), roasted aubergine filled with cubes of lamb, green peppers and tomatoes with rice; or yogurtlu iskender (£7.95), a trio of shish, kofte and chicken on pitta bread soaked in fresh tomato sauce with fresh herbs and topped with yoghurt. Whilst the menu is mainly meat there are seven vegetarian and five fish selections on offer. Puddings include the usual Turkish stickies, but once again are light and freshly made.

Wines are priced fairly, there is Efes beer from Turkey (£2.25), and also that powerful spirit raki (£2.75) for a tongue-numbing blast of the real Middle East.

CENTRAL

£15–£30

The Rôtisserie

34 Upper St, N1 ☎ 0171 226 0122   ⊖ Angel

Mon & Tues 6–11pm, Wed–Fri noon–3pm & 5–11pm,

Sat noon–11pm, Sun noon–9.30pm   All major credit cards

The Rôtisserie is buzzing, cheerful, brightly-painted and unpretentious, with a commitment to quality underlying both food and service. Its South African owner makes regular trips to Scotland to lean on the farm gate and make small talk about Aberdeen Angus steers (who if they did but know it, will soon be visiting his grill), and his menu claim "Famous for our steaks" seems well earned. The kitchen also frets about the quality of their chips, which is no bad thing as the classic combination of a well-grilled steak with decent frites and some Béarnaise sauce is one of life's little luxuries. The restaurant's succcess has led to a couple of offshoots, offering much the same menu, at 56 Uxbridge Road, Shepherds Bush, W12 (☎0181 743 3028) and 316 Uxbridge Rd, Hatch End, Middx (☎0181 421 3778). There are presumably plans afoot for the rest of London's Uxbridge Roads.

The Rôtisserie starters are sensibly simple: a good Caesar salad (£3.95); tiger prawns peri peri (£4.50); char-grilled vegetable salad with pesto (£3.95). Having brushed aside these preliminaries, on to the steaks: Scottish Aberdeen Angus – 9oz rump (£10.95); 12oz sirloin (£13.95); 8oz fillet (£13.95). Carefully chosen, carefully hung, carefully cooked. All of them (and all other main courses) come with a good-sized bowl of French fries. If you don't want steak, try one of the other rotisserie items, such as the French, corn-fed chicken leg and thigh (£5.95); breast and wing (£6.95); or half a chicken (£9.95); or the wonderful spit roasted Barbary duck – half a duck with fruit chutney (£10.95). The rest of the menu covers the bases for non-meat eaters. There's a "grilled fish of the day" (£9.95), or vegetable brochettes with spiced rice (£7.95). Puddings are sound and range from apple and cinnamon cake with hot caramel (£3.50) to home-made ice cream (£3). But it will take able trencherman to get as far as dessert.

The South African influence is a constant lurking presence behind all the fabulous grilled meat so look out for the "monkey gland" sauce – rich and dark, and to a secret family recipe rumoured to include both Coca Cola and Mrs Ball's Chutney.

£10–£25

Sarcan

4 Theberton St, N1 ☎ 0171 226 5489   ⊖ Angel

Daily 11.30am–11.30pm   All major credit cards

Brash, basic and very busy, Sarcan drops a welcome pebble of reality into the maelstrom of trendy Islington. The food is Turkish, and sound enough. The service combines bustle with charm and the prices are low – perhaps all the competition round here helps keep them that way. Inside the decor is predictable, with a sort of Turkish-tourist-board feel to it, and a couple of tables perched outside on the pavement when the weather is up to it. Be warned that it can get very full and pretty rowdy on a Saturday night.

The menu is something of a magnum opus, the score is as follows: cold hors d'oeuvres 17; hot hors d'oeuvres 11; salads 3; main courses 17; specials 7; vegetarian mains 10; seafood dishes 4; and finally 3 different set menus. One starter achieves "must have" status, both on grounds of variety and value – the mixed meze (£4.50); this is a triumph, a large round plate divided up into sectors like the spokes of a wheel, and filled with a huge range of dips. Expect hummus, kisir (a kind of tabbouleh with wheat, mint and parsley), zetinyagli mercimek (a stunning green lentil salad), enginar (artichoke hearts), pilaki (kidney beans), ispanak tere ture (spinach and yoghurt), and many more! All served with rather good, round, flat and substantial Turkish bread – pide not pitta. From the hot starters go for hellim (grilled halloumi cheese) or borek (deep-fried cheese in filo parcels). If you haven't succumbed to the temptation to eat only starters, go for grilled meat, plainly cooked and served with both rice and salad. Beyti (£5.95) is made with round flat fillets of grilled lamb – surprisingly tender; or there's shish kofte (£4.95); or sucuk izgara (£4.95) spicy sausages. On the vegetarian menu you'll find melemen (£4.95) which is a Turkish style omelette – rather like a Spanish tortilla without the potato. And there is also fish and chips to tempt – actually swordfish and chips, kilic baligi (£7.45).

You cannot really eat at a Turkish restaurant without trying some offal: Albanian liver (£2.75) is chopped, fried liver, and despite its name a Turkish favourite. Uykuluk (£4.95) are sweetbreads and very tasty too.

Kensington

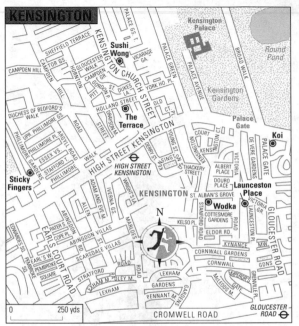

KENSINGTON

Kensington Palace

Round Pond

Sushi Wong

Kensington Gardens

Palace Gate

Koi

The Terrace

HIGH STREET KENSINGTON

HIGH STREET KENSINGTON

KENSINGTON

Launceston Place

Sticky Fingers

Wodka

N

0 — 250 yds

CROMWELL ROAD

GLOUCESTER ROAD

© Crown copyright

CENTRAL

80

Koi

1 Palace Gate, W8 ☎ 0171 581 8778   ⊖ High St Kensington

Mon–Sat noon–3pm & 6–11pm`,

Sun noon–3pm & 6–10.30pm   All major credit cards except Diners

The menu outside Koi explains that the word was first used about 2000 years ago to celebrate the birth of Confucius's son. King Shoko of Ro presented the philosopher with a fabulous Japanese fish known as Koi because it was so highly prized. High aspirations which neatly set the scene for this stylish and expensive Japanese restaurant. Or, perhaps more accurately, trio of restaurants, for Koi has three different areas: a teppanyaki area for 22, a sit-at sushi bar for 12, and tables on a raised dais with recesses for your legs. All are calming minimalist creations, and the food is as good as you'll find in any London Japanese restaurant – utterly fresh and beautifully presented. The only disappointment is that there's no Koi sushi!

You visit Koi (and pay its prices) essentially for the sushi. Nigiri sushi costs from £2.00 for salmon to £4.00 for Uni, and there are 17 varieties on the list. Rolled sushi (maki) costs from £3.00 for salmon to £11.50 for futomaki. Sashimi is £15.50 for tuna or salmon or £22.00 for assorted sashimi. The chef's special selection of sushi is £26.00 and worth it, though you can perhaps have more fun by sitting at the bar, watching and ordering as you go. The teppanyaki menu also offers 9 pieces of scallop for £13.50 or 150 grams of fish from £15.50 for salmon to £19.50 for turbot. Although dedicated to fish there are meat dishes, too. Fillet steak is £22.00 and 100 grams of foie gras is £18.00. The grill menu includes chicken yakitori (£5.50), eel (£13.50) and prawns with teriyaki sauce (£12.50). There is also a deep-fried section with assorted tempura (£12.50), minced prawns (£8.00), and beancurd fried and then served in broth (£6.50). Desserts are not a strong point in Japanese restaurants but there are red bean, green tea and chestnut ice creams (all at £2.80) which are refreshing and interesting. A large sake is £6.50 and there is a selection of Japanese beers.

Koi also does a selection of set dinners and the teppanyaki table is ideal for a party – preferably on expenses.

Launceston Place

1a Launceston Place, W8 ☎ 0171 937 6912	⊖ High Street Kensington
Mon–Fri 12.30–2.30pm & 7–11.30pm, Sat 7–11.30pm,	
Sun 12.30–3pm	All major credit cards except Diners

Launceston Place is a sister restaurant to trendy Kensington Place in Notting Hill Gate (p.413) but it's as different as they come. Launceston is comfortable and steady where Kensington is bustling and modish; its service is precise, the clientele is generally older, and the dining area is divided up into a series of inter-connecting rooms which gives everyone the illusion that they alone matter. The food is good: straightforward flavours, well-matched textures and a blend of old and new ideas. The menu changes regularly and the set lunch offers something of a bargain: choose from three starters, two mains, then three puddings and cheese (£14.50 for two courses and £17.50 for three). So for £17.50 you could be tucking into steamed razor clams with ginger, garlic and white wine cream, followed by roast duck breast with Summer fruits, and then plum cake with clotted cream – that's the kind of lunch you need a leisured lifestyle to truly appreciate. But if you can afford one of the houses round here, such a lifestyle probably comes as standard.

Starters combine old favourites with some unexpected twists so you might find tempura of oysters (£7.50) served with a spiced mango and cucumber relish. Or an oak-roasted wood pigeon (£7.50) may be teamed with ratatouille and garlic mayonnaise. Then there's seared foie gras (£9), with sweetcorn relish. The main courses are in a similar vein, with occasional flickers of heartiness – poached corn-fed chicken breast with artichokes and white beans and a tomato and tarragon broth (£14.50); or veal sweetbreads with oyster mushrooms (£17) – a simple dish but a terrific marriage of tastes and textures. Or there may be roast sea bass with crab mousse and citrus dressing (£16.50). Or peppered medallions of venison with damsons (£16). As befits such a grown up restaurant, there's all manner of game in season.

The window seats are great for watching the rich and famous sidle by, but it's a two way thing and they tend to stare back confidently. So no pastime for the faint-hearted.

£8–£25

Sticky Fingers

1a Phillimore Gardens, W8 ☎ 0171 938 5338   ⊖ High Street Kensington

Mon–Sat noon–11.30pm, Sun noon–11pm   All major credit cards

It should be enough to strike fear into the heart of any sophisticated diner, "a hamburger restaurant which is the pride and joy of a wrinkly rocker." But take heart. The food at Bill Wyman's Sticky Fingers is very good indeed. If there are times when you feel like a burger, the whole burger and nothing but the burger, or when your kids demand the same, then visit Sticky Fingers and you'll be well satisfied. Go in any other mood and the foreground music, the rock memorabilia, and the waves of children may prove oppressive.

Sticky Fingers make an effort to tempt adults and kids alike with their starters – barbecue chicken wings (£4.25); deep fried potato skins with sour cream and chives (£3.25) or cheese and bacon (£3.75); half a rack of spare ribs (£4.95); guacamole with corn chips (£3.95). And to follow they also offer pasta dishes, or specials like a char-grilled English lamb steak (£8.95) or herb crusted salmon fillet (£10.95). There are New York style sandwiches – house club (£7.95) is a multi-layered delight chicken, crisp bacon, tomato and so forth. There are even salads: Caesar (£6.95), or bang-bang chicken (£7.95). But this is all high class, International-hotel food and you are here for the real stuff: the burgers. The burgers here weigh in at 6oz. They are cooked to order, and somebody listens to what you say – medium turns out medium, and rare is suitably rare. They come in a good soft sesame seed bun. There's a choice of cheese – blue, Swiss and American. There's a choice of dressing on the side salad: herb, balsamic, blue cheese, Thousand Island, honey mustard and mayonnaise. Pick from a char-grilled burger (£7.25); bar-b-q burger (£7.75); cheeseburger (£7.75); cheese and bacon burger (£8.25); and the sticky stack (£10.95) – double burger with cheese, crisp bacon and fried onions.

For the studiously eccentric or BSE-wary, Sticky Fingers also purvey a decent enough lamb burger (£7.75), or an Oriental pork burger (£7.75), though if you're not eating beef then there's not a lot of point in being here at all.

KENSINGTON ⑪ JAPANESE

Sushi Wong

37–38 Kensington Church St, W8 ☎ 0171 937 5007   ⊖ High Street Kensington

Mon–Sat noon–2.30pm & 6–10.30pm, Sun 6–10pm   All major credit cards

Sushi Wong is the kind of name you either love or hate, but whichever side of the argument you take you'll concede that it is certainly slick – just like this deceptively-sized restaurant. On the ground floor there's a modernist Japanese restaurant-cum-sushi-bar seating about 25 people. Downstairs there's room for a further 60, including a teppanyaki table. Looking in from the street it's hard not to admire the bright yellow and blue colour scheme, and the tables each topped with ground glass which in turn is backed by a blue neon tube. In the face of all this brightness and modernity, the service is so low key that it almost seems timid, but is confident and efficient for all that.

Sushi is good here. Ordering the nigiri sushi "A" deluxe set (£18) brings a round lacquer tray with 6 pieces of salmon or tuna roll flanked by 10 pieces of sushi various – the chef's selection. The fish is fresh, the wasabi strong, the gari delicious and the sushi well-made. A good array at a good price. The menu emphasises roll sushi, ranging from "mixed roll" (£8) which delivers eighteen pieces made up of salmon, tuna and cucumber, to "Kensington roll" (£3.80), crispy salmon and asparagus subtitled "let's make it famous", and the winningly named "cheese roll" (£4.20) which brings together cheese, avocado and smoked salmon. There are also cooked rice dishes, among them tori teriyaki don (£6), which is chicken teriyaki on rice, and unagi don (£5.80) delicious grilled eel on rice. And then there are twelve noodle dishes including yaki soba (£6) and Sushi Wong ramen (£6.90) – egg noodles with chicken, prawns, egg and vegetables in miso broth.

The set lunch menus are appealing value. They offer a choice of starters – rolled sushi, chef's salad or agedashi tofu – then you pick between tonkatsu (£10.50) – deep-fried pork loin with rice and miso soup – or sushi set (£11.80) – five pieces of nigiri sushi and 6 pieces of cucumber roll plus miso soup. Or for the hungry and eager to try all, there's Sushi Wong bento (£14.80) which is a combination of sushi, chicken teriyaki, tempura and fruit with rice and miso soup.

CENTRAL

The Terrace

33C Holland St, W8 ☎ 0171 937 3224   ⊖ High Street Kensington

Mon–Sat noon–2.30pm & 7–10.30pm, Sun 12.30–3pm   All major credit cards

The Terrace is a small, modern restaurant hidden amongst the residential streets north of Kensington High Street. Its dining room is small, but as the name proclaims there is a terrace fronting onto the street where a handful of tables await diners with the nerve to brave the British weather. The food is simple and seasonal modern British. Presentation is unfussy and the standard of cooking is generally high; elsewhere you would probably expect the prices to be a tad lower but here – in Kensington on the way to Holland Park – they represent quite decent value.

The menu changes regularly. Starters like smoked haddock and red onion tartlet (£6.50) are well executed, while ordering the sautéed foie gras (£9.50) brings a huge portion of liver bedded on a warm salad with grilled new potatoes and bacon, an impressive bargain of a dish but not to be trifled with. Or there's char grilled scallops (£7.50), served with a wild leaf salad and an orange and thyme beurre blanc. The Terrace salad (£5) could be anything from a competently made Caesar to a combination of grilled spiced aubergines, plum tomatoes and goat's cheese. Soups veer towards the exotic, such as watercress and lime soup with creme fraiche (£4.50). At first glance the main courses are standard fare – cod, tuna, chicken, lamb – but they're all made from fresh ingredients which deliver good strong flavours. Grilled pork chop with date and apple chutney and grilled asparagus (£11.50) is particularly good, as is the braised lamb shank with mint mash and roasted baby carrots (£13). Or there's char grilled tuna (£12.50), accompanied by bashed Jersey potatoes and French beans with quail's eggs and a cherry tomato salsa, and a fine wild mushroom risotto (£10.50) which comes with a splash of truffle oil and plenty of Parmesan. The dessert section ranges from chocolate fudge pot (£4.50) to apricot and lemon grass creme brulée (£4.50).

Regulars are easily spotted, they're the ones tucking into the excellent value (and constantly changing) set lunches – £12.50 for two courses, £14.50 for three.

£14–£35

Wódka

12 St Albans Grove, W8 ☎ 0171 937 6513	⊖ High Street Kensington
Mon–Fri 12.30–2.45pm & 7–11pm, Sat & Sun 7–11pm	All major credit cards

Wódka is a restaurant which lies in wait for you. It's calm, and bare; the food is better than you expect, well-cooked, and thoughtfully seasoned. There is a daily lunch menu which represents extremely good value at £9.90 for two courses and £12.50 for three, a large proportion of the dishes being refugees from the evening à la carte. Where, you wonder, is the streak of madness that helped the Polish cavalry take on German tank regiments with sabres drawn? On shelves behind the bar, that's where. In the extensive collection of moody and esoteric vodkas which are for sale both by the shot and by the carafe.

The soups are good, for starters: zur (£3.90) is a sour rye and sausage soup, parsnip soup (£4.50), rich and creamy. Blinis are also the business: they come with smoked salmon (£6.90), aubergine mousse (£4.90), foie gras (£8.90) or 40 grams of oscietra caviar (£19): a lunchtime selection will get you all except the caviar. Also good is the kaszanka (£5.25) – grilled black pudding with one salad of fresh green leaves and another made from lentils, onions and white beans. For main course the fish cakes (£9.90) with leeks and a dill sauce are firm favourites with the regulars (many of whom are from nearby Penguin Books). When available, the roast partridge comes with a splendid mash of root vegetables and the mashed potato is also worthy of special praise. Puddings tend to be of the over sweet, under-imaginative gateaux variety, but the vodka will ensure that you won't be worrying about that.

Consider the vodka list with due attention. There's Zubrówka (made with bison grass); Okhotnichya, (for hunters); Jarzebiak, (that's rowan berries); Cytrynówka, (lemon); Sliwowica, (plum); Sliwówka (plum, but hot and sweet); Czarna Porezecka, (blackcurrant); Ananas (pineapple); Krupnik (honey, and served hot); Roza (rose petals); Goldwasser (made with flakes of gold and aniseed); Soplica (which is a mystery) and a host more. They cost from £2.25 to £2.75 a shot, and from £33.90 to £37.90 per 50cl carafe. Remember this simple test: pick any three of the above names and say them quickly. If anyone shows signs of understanding you need another shot.

Knightsbridge & Belgravia

KNIGHTSBRIDGE & BELGRAVIA

HYDE PARK CORNER

Pizza on the Park

KNIGHTSBRIDGE

KNIGHTSBRIDGE

The Fifth Floor (Harvey Nichols)

SCOVILLE ST.

DUPLEX RW.

WILLIAM ST.

WILLIAM M.

WILTON PLACE

WILTON ROW

GROSVENOR CRESCENT

OLD BARRACK YD.

TREVOR SQ.

TREVOR PLACE

RAPHAEL ST.

LANCELOT PL.

TREVOR SQUARE

HARRIET ST.

HARRIET ST. WALK

SQUARE

LOWNDES

KINNERTON STREET

CRESCENT

BELGRAVE MW. N.

BELGRAVE SQUARE

MONTPELIER MEWS

KNIGHTSBRIDGE

N

HANS CRESCENT

BASIL ST.

SLOANE

Zafferano

MOTCOMB ST.

Motcomb's

WEST HALKIN ST.

LOWNDES ST.

BELGRAVE M. W.

BROMPTON

HANS ROAD

BROMPTON PL.

BEAUFORT GS.

PAVILION

COTTAGE WALK

CADDOGAN

BELGRAVIA

CHESHAM PLACE

LOWNDES PLACE

BEAUCHAMP PL.

O Fado

OVINGTON SQUARE

WALTON PL.

PONT ST.

STREET

HANS ST.

PONT

STREET

CADOGAN STREET

CHESHAM PLACE

CHESHAM STREET

LYALL MEWS

LYALL STREET

EATON MEWS NORTH

WALTON

LENNOX GDN. MWS.

OVINGTON ST.

LENNOX GARDENS

CLABON MEWS

CADOGAN SQUARE

CADOGAN LANE

CADOGAN PLACE

EATON PLACE

EATON MEWS WEST

EATON SQ.

HASKER ST.

MILNER ST.

0   250 yds

© Crown copyright

The Fifth Floor

5th Floor, Harvey Nichols, Knightsbridge, SW1 ☎ 0171 235 5250　⊖ Knightsbridge

Mon–Fri noon–3pm & 6.30–11.30pm,

Sat noon–3.30 & 6.30–11.30pm, Sun noon–3.30pm　　All major credit cards

Harvey Nichols is almost a synonym for upmarket fashion: the place where Ab Fabbers come to shop. Its Knightsbridge store has many floors, a couple of restaurants, a rather notorious bar (B- and sometimes A-celebrity shoppers in need of a gasper), a café, a conveyor belt sushi bar, and a very smart food hall and wine department. The Fifth Floor restaurant is the smartest of the lot and so you would rightly infer that it is not cheap. What you get for your money, however, is very accomplished cooking, attentive but not overbearing service, fine wines and good times. The dining room is a large one and is separated from the lively bar by nothing more formidable than a velvet rope. The menu is long and interesting and as well as the à la carte there is a three-course prix fixe lunch menu which offers half a dozen choices for each course at a surprisingly accessible price – £23.50.

The main menu is broadly seasonal, and it is left to the daily specials to introduce game, mushrooms, spring vegetables, and new season's this and that. The cooking is satisfying and the flavours are pronounced – there is nothing wishy-washy here. Amongst the starters you'll find Henry's black bean soup (£6.50) – tasty, rich and satisfying. Another star dish is the hot buttered crab with a potato pancake and a verjuice sauce (£11.50), the crisp clean tang of un-ripened grape juice perfectly balancing the richness of the crab. Or there's the laconically named shrimp Caesar (£9.25) – take a Caesar salad with a good mustardy dressing and pour a panful of small brown shrimps cooked in butter over the top. Main courses range from roast fillet of brill, olive oil mash, cepes a la Grecque (£16.50) to grilled spiced breast of duck, pickled cherry salsa, Lyonnaise potatoes (£13.50); or roast halibut steak with clams, bacon and laverbread. Puddings are suitably greed inspiring.

As you would expect from a restaurant that is fifty feet from its own smart wine department, there's a pretty smoky wine list. And for after dinner, 28 different Cognacs ranging from Hennessy VS (£6 a measure) to the very grown-up Richard Hennessy (£110 a measure).

Motcomb's

26 Motcomb St, SW1 ☎ 0171 235 6382	⊖ Knightsbridge
Mon– Fri noon–3pm & 7–11pm, Sat 7–11pm, Sun noon–3pm	All major cedit cards

The walls at Motcomb's groan under the weight of its owner's collection of artwork. It's an eclectic mix and, depending upon your table, you could find yourself staring at a native woman, an elephant, a nostalgic advert for champagne or Keith Richard holding a kitten. Eye-level mirror panelling, warm yellow walls and subtle lighting make this an intimate and relaxing place to be – belying the fact that it's popular with business-people and also something of a favourite with horse racing folk. The service is a sensitive blend of steady and experienced, which suits the clientele just fine.

Seafood and game (in their due seasons) are the things to order. Kick off with a serious plateful of warm scallops and bacon (£8.50), or the crab soup with brandy (£5.50), which is served ad lib at table from a big tureen. There is also a very sound smoked salmon and trout terrine with brown toast (£6.50). For main courses, the Dover sole shows how very good a simple dish can be (price varies, but expect to pay around £15-20); it is plainly cooked in virgin olive oil – they are "very conscious of your cholesterol" at Motcomb's. The grilled lobster (around £20) is also pleasingly simple, and comes with a set of cutlery that wouldn't look out of place beside a dentist's chair. Very popular, though neither game nor seafood, is the roast crispy duck with sweet and sour sauce (£12). Puddings vary from visit to visit – your waiter will be able to put you wise to the current options. If you're lucky, these will include the rich bread and butter pudding.

There's an exhaustive wine list specialising in fine white burgundies and respectable clarets. Since this is not a bad place to choose for a simple celebration, the house champagne appeals at a wholly reasonable £26.50. But if you were really pushing the boat out, there's a 1983 Graves at £240. Those on a tighter budget will be pleased to learn that prices start from £10.50. And the three-course set lunch is something of a bargain at £12.95.

O Fado

45/50 Beauchamp Place, SW3 ☎ 0171 589 3002   ⊖ Knightsbridge

Mon–Sat noon–3pm & 6.30–12.45pm, Sun noon–3pm   All credit cards except Diners

O Fado, is owned, staffed and largely frequented by Portuguese, though the waiters also need to speak Japanese, or at least refer to the food glossary on the wall when taking orders from the regulars who come here for the seafood. Pretty in pink and bedecked with hand-painted azulejos, it is quite a romantic restaurant, seductively lit with a few nooks and crannies that are bagged quickly – so book ahead.

The menu and wine list are exhaustive. Favourite dishes among Japanese diners include octopus salad (£6.50), and arroz de marisco (£25 for two), the Portuguese take on paella. But those wanting to get in the mood for their summer holiday should try the crisp and salty grilled sardines (£3.50) or caldo verde soup (£2.60), followed by a spicy piri piri chicken and fries (£7.90) that should send French chefs scuttling for their cooking manuals. Finish off with pastels de nata (95p each): custard tarts Portuguese style. More sophisticated options are the shellfish crepe with brandy sauce (£4.60), or mussels with a twist – served in olive oil and coriander together with the usual wine and garlic (£5.50). Popular with Portuguese families for Saturday lunch is cozido a Portuguesa, a bean and sausage stew (£9.50). Give them a day's notice and bring five friends. Bacalhau a cataplana (£9.80) is a dish of salt cod and clams, pressure cooked in a rich tomato sauce, and surprisingly delicious. Look out for daily specials such as suckling pig (£15.00) but ask the price as they can prove expensive. If you still have room after the sumo wrestler portions try the arroz doce (£2.80), rice pudding, it's wonderful. The tarta da laranja (£2.80), moist, eggy orange cake, pudim flan (£3.20), cream caramel, and molotof (£3.20) – not a bomb but an egg white soufflé – are all good as well. To accompany your meal, try the Borba VQPRD 1996: delicious and a snip at £11.90.

This place is called O Fado for a reason, as mid-evening the house singer begins the haunting, lyrical strains of Fado ballads, with guitar accompaniment, and diners listen appreciatively if they know what's good for them. It's all a lot quieter at lunchtime.

KNIGHTSBRIDGE & BELGRAVIA ⑰ PIZZA

Pizza on the Park

11 Knightsbridge, SW1 ☎ 0171 235 5273	⊖ Hyde Park Corner
Mon–Sat 8.15am–midnight, Sat 9.30am–midnight,	
Sun 9.30am–11.30pm	All major credit cards

For Pizza on the Park read Pizza on The Road – busy Knightsbridge lies between Hyde Park and the forecourt tables that front this popular restaurant. Happily, things improve greatly inside, where palms, woodwork, white tiles and spotlights conjure the elegant ethos of Pizza Express, the chain to which this place once belonged.

Fans of Pizza Express will find the evening menu reassuringly familiar. Aficionados will make straight for the dough ball starter – £1.75 worth of deliciously crusty, warm bread dipped in garlic butter. You can be sure your pizza toppings will be fresh, as they're laid out for your inspection in big glass bowls along the back of the dining room, adding a cheery splash of colour to the affair. This is one place where they're not afraid to go heavy on the anchovies, capers and olives. If those ingredients take your fancy then opt for the Napolitana (£5.95), the Neptune, the Capricciosa or the Four Seasons (all £6.50). For those in need of a touch more fire, the American Hot (£6.55) is a classic, laden with pepperoni and green pepper. When choosing the Quattro Formaggi (£6.10), it's worth remembering that this a seriously cheese-laden affair dauntingly rich. Of the handful of pasta offerings, the cannelloni (£6.30) is rich, creamy and an excellent alternative to pizza. Puddings are generous; the apple pie (£2.65), which actually tastes home-made, is a real winner.

But that's where similarities to Pizza Express end. Pizza on the Park also offers a choice of all day breakfasts from 8.15am: a Continental (£4.00) with a pastry, orange and a hot drink, and a somewhat out of place English breakfast (£4.95) of eggs, tomato, mushroom, toast and coffee. Alternatively, should you saunter in around 3.15pm, you can partake of a three-course afternoon tea (£6.95) or various snacks. Visit on a Sunday and you can listen to a live jazz band as well. If you can't wait that long, the downstairs restaurant has a jazz band every night, but you will have to pay a music charge for the privilege.

CENTRAL

Zafferano

15 Lowndes St, SW1 ☎ 0171 235 5800	⊖ Knightsbridge
Mon–Sat noon–2.30pm & 7–11pm	All major credit cards

This is a very exciting place to eat. The decor is a touch bleak, service is quick and slick, but the food . . . the food is amazing. This is what Italian food is like when it is trying very hard – not too precious, rooted firmly in tradition, wonderful natural combinations of tastes and textures. Unsurprisingly, everyone who is anyone has noticed this restaurant, so booking ahead has become a necessity. It is worth the wait. Zafferano sticks to good value fixed price menus: two or three courses at lunch (£17.50 and £20.50) and two, three or four courses at dinner (£26.50, £32.50, and £36.50). This is your opportunity to recognise Italian instincts, enjoy a pasta course – and go for the four!

The menu changes each season and is "tinkered" with every month or so. There is also a list of four or five daily seasonal specials and these almost invariably include some fish dishes. The lunch-time menu is a shortened version of the dinner menu and the few dishes which attract a supplement tend to be fish and crustacea, which seems fair enough. The kind of antipasti you can expect are lingua di manzo in salsa verde (thinly sliced ox tongue with a gherkin and herb sauce); insalata di spada al Verde (swordfish and yellow bean salad with olive oil and herbs); and mozzarella di bufala (buffalo mozzarella with baked aubergine). On to the pastas and risotti – ravioli di boraggine (borage parcels with herbs and olive oil), tagliolini alle zucchini e bottarga (hand-made egg pasta with courgette and dried tuna roe), risotto all ortiche (nettle risotto). Or there's sometimes a splendid and simple saffron risotto. Then the mains – anatra arrosto con farro al balsamico (roast duck with pearl spelt and balsamic vinegar); coda di rospo salsa di noci, apperi e barbe di frate (baked monkfish with a walnut and caper sauce). These dishes are always well-balanced and always well cooked.

For pudding shun the cheesecake; the hot chocolate tart; the lemon and marscapone tart . . . they are all delicious, but not quite so delicious as the tiramisú!

Marylebone

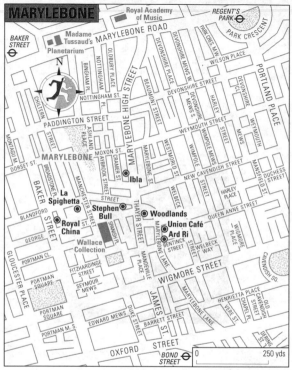

MARYLEBONE

Royal Academy of Music

REGENT'S PARK

PARK CRESCENT

BAKER STREET

Madame Tussaud's
Planetarium

MARYLEBONE ROAD

PARK CRES. M.W.

WILSON PLACE

DEVONSHIRE PLACE

DEVONSHIRE STREET

PORTLAND PLACE

BINGHAM PL.

NOTTINGHAM PLACE

OLDBURY PLACE

BEAUMONT STREET

DEVONSHIRE MEWS W.

DEVONSHIRE MEWS S.

HARLEY STREET

WEYMOUTH MEWS

WEYMOUTH STREET

NOTTINGHAM ST.

PADDINGTON STREET

MARYLEBONE HIGH STREET

WIMPOLE MEWS

CHILTERN STREET

ASHLAND PLACE

MOXON ST.

MARYLEBONE

DORSET ST.

MONTAGU ST.

BROADSTONE PL.

BAKER STREET

BLANDFORD

GEORGE

GLOUCESTER PLACE

PORTMAN CL.

PORTMAN SQUARE

PORTMAN SQUARE

PORTMAN M.S.

MANCHESTER STREET

AYBROOK STREET

CRAMER ST.

Ibla

La Spighetta

Stephen Bull

Royal China

Wallace Collection

ST.

THAYER STREET

SPANISH PL.

FITZHARDINGE STREET

SEYMOUR MEWS

MANDEVILLE PLACE

EDWARD MEWS

DUKE STREET

JAMES STREET

BARRETT ST.

OXFORD STREET

BOND STREET

NEW CAVENDISH STREET

WIMPOLE STREET

WELBECK STREET

MARYLEBONE LANE

Woodlands

Union Café

Ard Ri

BENTINCK STREET

WELBECK WAY

WIGMORE STREET

MARYLEBONE LANE

HENRIETTA PLACE

VERE ST.

QUEEN ANNE STREET

HARLEY PLACE

MANSFIELD ST.

DUCHESS STREET

WIGMORE PLACE

CAVENDISH SQ.

CAVENDISH ST.

OLD CAVENDISH STREET

CHAPEL PL.

DEERING ST.

0   250 yds

© Crown copyright

96

CENTRAL

Ard Ri Dining Room

At The O'Conor Don, 88 Marylebone Lane, W1 ☎ 0171 935 9311   ⊖ Bond Street

Mon–Fri noon–2.30pm & 6–10.30pm, Sat 6–10.30pm   Amex, Mastercard, Visa

The Ard Ri dining room is to be found over the O'Conor Don – and that is where you should begin your investigations. The pub is large, crowded and jolly and serves one of London's finest pints of draught Guinness. When you have taken enough fuel on board, make your way up the stairs. The decor in the dining room is comfortable/homely and unpretentious. There's a fireplace – with a real fire in season – and tables and chairs assembled from various junkshops that probably called themselves antique dealers. The food is simple and good. Service is friendly.

The main menu changes monthly to reflect the seasons and although it is not set out that way, there tends to be a balance between modern Irish dishes on the one hand and traditional Irish fare on the other. Thus as starters you might choose hot buttered Irish oysters (£7.50), or soufflé of fresh crab with a crab sauce (£6.95). Lamb fillet, black pudding, lamb's lettuce and herb dressing (£5.25) has a foot in both camps. For main courses traditional Irish lamb stew (£12.95) is counterpoint to seared tuna loin, avocado and bacon, new baby potatoes and lime dressing (£13.95). Or there's roast saddle of rabbit, glazed root vegetables, Colcannon and shallot jus (£13.45), or sauté of veal cutlet, pickled white cabbage, Irish boxty, sauce of cepes (£14.95) a multi-faceted multinational if ever there was one. The side orders provide rich pickings: sautéed field mushrooms, champ, Colcannon (all at £2), and carrot mash (£1.50). Puddings are backed by a good all-Irish cheeseboard which is well worth sampling.

There's a set menu – £16.50 for two courses, £19 for three, both including coffee – which represents excellent value, as you get to choose more or less anything from the main menu. You could end up with a meal of smoked haddock with potato cake and mustard sauce; beef in Guinness casserole with carrot mash; and treacle tart with clotted cream.

Ibla

89 Marylebone High St, W1 ☎ 0171 224 3799	⊖ Baker St/Great Portland St
Mon–Sat noon–2.30pm & 7–10.15pm	Amex, Mastercard, Visa

At first glance Ibla looks most unpromising – perhaps because it has retained the odd shade of green that somehow suited the previous occupant, the upmarket delicatessen-restaurant Villandry (now transplanted to Great Portland Street – see Fitzrovia, p.30). But persevere – it will be worth it. Along with well laid dining tables at the front, there is a nod to the shop-like premises with a small attempt to sell smart packets of pasta and the like. If possible, ask for a table in the back room, a pretty yet functional square space painted beetroot red, and settle down for some excellent Italian fare.

The menu – uncompromisingly Italian – changes weekly and works on a set price basis, of £13–£16 for the short lunch menu and a rather longer one at £18.50–£21.50 for dinner. Starter offerings are to the order of tartare of crab with pesto dressing, or calamari and fennel salad, or warm salad of monkfish in sweet bread to start. Main courses might include roast calves' liver with pancetta, or stuffed aubergine with taleggio, while the pastas, all home-made, can be taken as either first or main course. The less Italian sounding dishes, such as salmon with herb crust, are in general less interesting, but the chef really knows his stuff and all will be zingily fresh, well seasoned and perfectly presented. Puddings are equally thoughtful, but suffer from being at the end of a filling Italian meal ... you'll be lucky if you have any room for them.

The picky might take issue with the all Italian wine list, which will be confusing to anyone but a connoisseur, and the service, which has more attitude than you might enjoy – ask for an espresso with milk separately and you may well find yourself told that this is not correct. But on the positive side, the staff are perfectionist, and they will only take as many customers as the kitchen can cope with. A kitchen that's not overstressed is a kitchen that is at its best – which means that you can be sure your meal will be just as it should be. And you should be able to put up with a few quirks for food like this.

La Spighetta

43 Blandford St, W1 ☎ 0171 486 7340	⊖ Bond Street/Baker Street
Mon–Fri noon–2.15pm & 6.30–10.30pm, Sat 6.30–11pm,	Amex, Mastercard, Visa

Walk past La Spighetta and you could be forgiven for thinking that this is the least popular small pizza and pasta joint in London. You will see five or six tables, generally deserted, and you'll be lucky if there is a member of staff within sight. But venture inside and down the stairs and you will discover a large basement restaurant buzzing with activity. At lunchtime there is the Marylebone office crowd (advertising, Marks & Spencer staff), at dinner it's more local (young professionals); either way, this is a place where people are happy to spend their own money. The decor is more practical than elegant, with bare table tops, terracotta and cream walls, and banquette seating, while the kitchens are open plan, with a magnificent pizza oven dominating the room. But it's the food – well-cooked and well-priced – that you're here for.

Even if you had planned to drop in for just a bowl of pasta, it's worth considering Spighetta's first courses. Legumi marinati alla griglia (£6.50) is light, fresh and simple; mozzarella di bufala, pomodoro e salsi di olive (£7.00) reminds you what mozzarella really can taste like. Most starters come in two sizes which make them perfect to share between two people. A short choice of pastas and a full list of pizzas follow, alongside daily special meat and fish main courses. But the pastas and pizzas are so good that you'd be advised to stick to them. A linguine alle vongole e peperoncino (£8.00) is dressed with fine olive oil and actually tastes of clams, and the pizza Napoli (£6.50) really tastes of tomato, anchovies and capers. Puddings are classic Italian and consistently good. If you have room, try the panna cotta al frutti di bosco (£4.00).

La Spighetta is the sort of restaurant which everyone would like as their local pizza and pasta joint: simple food at sensible prices, a good buzz most times of night, but no real need to book. If it has a fault, it's that the service is a bit rushed and slightly forgetful. But at this price and with cooking of this standard, that's hardly a gripe.

CENTRAL

MARYLEBONE ⑪ CHINESE/DIM SUM

Royal China

40 Baker St, W1 ☎ 0171 487 4688   ⊖ Baker Street/Bond Street

Mon–Sat noon–11pm, Sun 11am–10pm

Dim sum served daily until 5pm   All major credit cards except Diners

Like its elder sibling – at 13 Queensway, W2 (☎0171 221 2535) – this branch of the Royal China is a black and gold palace. The effect is a kind of "cigarette-packet-chic" and smacks of the 70s. But don't let that put you off. The food is not as expensive as the decor would have you believe, the service is efficient and brisk rather than that special kind of rude and brisk you may encounter in Chinatown, and the food is really good. One knowledgeable chef-critic describes the Royal China's sticky rice wrapped in a lotus leaf as the "best ever".

You could eat well from the Royal China's full menu but it is the dim sum here that are most enticing. Like everything else in the Royal China the small booklet that comprises the dim sum menu is bound in gold. It goes from "Today's Chef Special", through dim sum, to lunch time noodle and rice dishes. The most famous dim sum here is the roast pork puff (£1.80) – this is unusual in that it is made from puff pastry, very light and with a sweetish filling of char sui. From the "specials" try the lobster dumpling (£3.50) and Thai style fish cake (£2.30), both of which are good. Also worth noting are prawn and chive dumpling (£2.20); pork and radish dumpling (£1.80); and seafood dumpling (£2.20) – a selection of three. The glutinous rice in lotus leaves (£3) really is the best ever – rich and not too "gamey", two parcels come in each steamer. The Royal China cheung fun (£2.70) is another sampler providing one of each filling – prawn, pork and beef. They take their cheung fun seriously here, with a total of eight variants including mushrooms and dry shrimp (£3). The fried rice dishes and the noodle dishes are well priced (£5–£7).

This may well be the place to take the plunge and try chicken's feet. Spicy chicken feet (£1.80) come thickly coated in a rich and spicy goo and to be frank this sauce is so strongly flavoured that if it weren't for the obvious foot shapes you could be eating almost anything.

CENTRAL

Stephen Bull

5–7 Blandford St, W1 ☎ 0171 486 9696	⊖ Baker St/Bond St
Mon–Fri 12.15–2.15pm & 6.30–10.45pm, Sat 6.30–10.45pm	All major credit cards

MARYLEBONE ⑪ MODERN BRITISH

Stephen Bull understands his customers and their little foibles only too well. While a good many of London's hotspot restaurants chase an ever-younger client base by searching four corners of the globe for the next great food fad, the customers at his Marylebone restaurant are of an older generation. They want something more foodie than faddie and could equally be found at the tables of any smart restaurant in provincial France. Mind you, so could Mr Bull's staff who are decked out in crisp white shirts and ankle-length black aprons. The cooking here is serious stuff, and the menu changes just often enough to reflect the seasons.

Start simple. Mixed dressed leaves, herbs, salted almonds and French beans (£6.50) is a pleasing combination of textures and not over-oily. Sautéed scallops, linguine, parsley, chilli, and olive oil (£8.50) may sound like a recipe but is skilfully made to allow the delicate briny flavours to hold their own with the chilli. Fish soup with rouille, gruyere and croutons (£5.50) is faithful to the time-honoured formula used by generations of provencales – and the same accolade applied to the duck and foie-gras rilettes with toasted brioche and chutneys (£8). In season, main dishes may include a roast partridge, braised Savoy cabbage, roast parsnip, foie gras and Madeira (£15); or a well-judged pan-fried plaice with aubergine and potato rösti, girolles, shitake and confit garlic (£15). Of the rest, osso bucco and calf's tongue, potato gnocchi, braised celery and oregano (£10) and noisette of lamb, sweetbreads, pea purée caramelised shallots and mint jus (£15) are suitably robust and vegetarians are catered for with dishes like papardelle, wild mushrooms, Parmesan, cream and truffle oil (£10), and spicy vegetable quesadilla, black bean salsa and Manchego cheese.

Desserts (£6) include some hearty, rich offerings: a block of double chocolate fudge cake with pineapple, or steamed maple pecan pudding with butterscotch sauce and vanilla ice cream. If that all sounds a spoon too far, wimps can always pick the iced praline parfait with poached pears. Or there are well-chosen farmhouse cheeses served with great home-made oatcakes (£6.50).

CENTRAL

MARYLEBONE ⊕ MODERN BRITISH

Union Café & Restaurant

96 Marylebone Lane, W1 ☎ 0171 486 4860   ⊖ Bond St

Mon–Fri 9.30–11.30am, 12.30–2pm & 6.30–10.30pm,

Sat 11am–10.30pm   Mastercard, Visa

The Union Café is a light, airy restaurant tucked into a quiet corner off the South end of Marylebone High Street. The decor is modern and simple (no-nonsense wooden tables, large windows, a stainless steel kitchen on show at the back), and the food – modern European – is both tasty and imaginative. During the day, this is a bright, sunny place for breakfast or lunch, while in the evenings, spotlights give the place a warm glow.

The daily menu is handwritten on an A4 sheet and has a good balance between adventurous dishes and more traditional ones. Portions aren't huge, so if you're hungry, go for a full three courses. Depending on your mood, you might start with something interesting like panzanella with anchovies (£6.25), which is a salty and well-flavoured bread salad, or goat's cheese with beetroot, fennel, chive and rocket salad, where the ingredients are piled prettily on top of each other. Or there's the more traditional Scottish oak-smoked salmon with horseradish and watercress (£7.50), which can also be taken as a main course (£12.50). There are usually a couple of soups to choose from – hot and sour, grilled chicken soup (£4.50) has a great tang. Main dishes are feisty and colourful. Though there are generally only four or five to choose from, veggies and carnivores are equally well catered for, and there are always a couple of fish dishes. Deep-fried brill in beer batter (£12.75) comes on a bed of spinach; roast chump of lamb with herb roasted butternut squash and sugar snap peas (£13) is hearty and satisfying. Vegetarians might go for chargrilled aubergine, tomato, mozzarella, oregano and black olive pizza (£9), which is definitely a cut above even a good pizza house offering. Desserts are indulgent and include the likes of strawberry mascarpone and marsala cream cake (£4.50) and bitter chocolate ice cream (£4) – both delicious.

Think of the Union Café for breakfast. Kick-start your day with tropical fresh fruit salad (£4.50) or Pink grapefruit juice (£2.50), or go for the full Monty with waffles with banana, maple syrup and cream (£5).

CENTRAL

Woodlands

77 Marylebone Lane, W1 ☎ 0171 486 3862	⊖ Bond St
Daily noon–2.30pm & 6–10.30pm	All major credit cards

The Marylebone Lane branch of this South Indian vegetarian restaurant group has been trading for some years, ignored by many locals simply because of the vegetarian tag – but adored by all those who have been through the doors. The interior is rather classier than most local Indian restaurants, with simply decorated white and artist-painted walls, adorned with a few Indian artefacts, and a huge skylight rendering electric light unnecessary during the day. Large tables are built for comfort rather than practicality, giving diners plenty of room for their food, but making it very awkward to get in and out without disturbing the table next door. There are more Asian faces in this restaurant than English, and even on a Monday lunchtime the room is filled with chatter and laughter.

The food is as dramatic looking as it is good to eat. Kick off with a masala dosa (£4.25), a great cone of pancake looking like nothing so much as a nun's wimple, with a well-spiced potato and onion filling, served with an excellent coconut chutney and sambar. Or try the tomato and onion uthappam (£3.50), an Indian version of a pizza made with lentils. Follow it with a thali – the mini thali (£9.95) has all that you are likely to want on it including pappadom and desert; the Delhi royal thali (£10.95) offers even more. The breads are well made, especially the chappati (£1.95 for 2) and the lachadar paratha (£2.35 for 2), and if you can possibly manage it, leave room for pudding. The jaggary dosa (£2.75) is sweet-toothed heaven and the gajjar halwa (£2.75) better than most.

Service is very helpful and if you don't really know your way around South Indian food this as good a place as any to start. If you ask for guidance they won't let you order too much or eat things in the wrong order. It is also an ideal place to take someone who has dietary difficulties as ingredients used here are generally obvious and if you have doubts about the suitability of a dish for a wheat, nut or even dairy allergy, the staff will generally know the answer.

Mayfair &
Bond Street

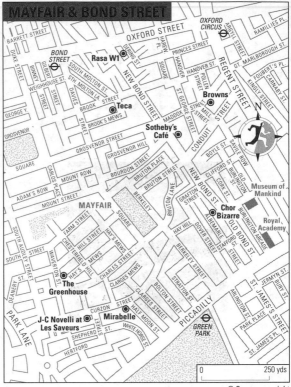

MAYFAIR & BOND STREET

OXFORD STREET

OXFORD CIRCUS

BARRETT STREET

DUKE STREET

BOND STREET

Rasa W1

GILBERT ST

BINNEY STREET

SOUTH MOLTON ST

STH. MOLTON LA.

DAVIES STREET

WEIGHHOUSE STREET

GEORGE Y.

GROSVENOR

GROSVENOR SQUARE

CARLOS PLACE

MOUNT ROW

ADAM'S ROW

MOUNT STREET

MAYFAIR

CHESTERFIELD HILL

HILL STREET

HAY'S MEWS

FARM STREET

SOUTH AUDLEY STREET

WAVERTON ST

CHARLES STREET

CLARGES MEWS

The Greenhouse

DEANERY ST

PARK LANE

J-C Novelli at Les Saveurs

CURZON STREET

Mirabelle

SHEPHERD ST

HALF MOON ST

WHITE HORSE ST

HERTFORD ST

BROOK STREET

Teca

BROOK'S MEWS

Sotheby's Café

GROSVENOR STREET

GROSVENOR HILL

BOURDON STREET

BERKELEY SQUARE

HAY HILL

Chor Bizarre

BRUTON STREET

BRUTON LANE

GRAFTON STREET

ALBEMARLE STREET

DOVER STREET

STRATTON ST

BERKELEY STREET

BOLTON STREET

CLARGES STREET

GREEN PARK

DUKE STREET

LANCASHIRE CT

NEW BOND STREET

HANOVER SQUARE

PRINCES STREET

HANOVER ST

Browns

HANOVER STREET

POLLEN STREET

ST GEORGE STREET

MADDOX STREET

MILL STREET

CONDUIT STREET

REGENT STREET

BOYLE ST

SAVILE ROW

CLIFFORD ST

CORK ST.

NEW BOND ST.

OLD BOND ST.

BURLINGTON GARDENS

Museum of Mankind

Royal Academy

Burlington Arcade

STAFFORD ST

OLD BOND ST.

PICCADILLY

ARGYLL STREET

RAMILLIES PL.

GT MARLBOROUGH ST.

LOUBERT'S PL.

CARNABY ST

KINGLY STREET

N

JERMYN ST.

ST. JAMES'S STREET

BURY ST.

PARK PLACE

ARLINGTON ST

ST. JAMES'S ST.

| 0 | 250 yds |

© Crown copyright

CENTRAL

106

Browns

47 Maddox St, W1 ☎ 0171 495 4565	⊖ Oxford Circus/ Bond St
Mon–Sat noon–11pm	All major credit cards

There are so many Oxford graduates in London, nostalgic for their student days when proud parents would take them for a reliable and unchallenging lunch at Browns, that it's no wonder various branches have sprung up across the capital. As you walk into this one, you'll see what is at first glance a long thin room, but in fact the restaurant is deceptively large; ask to sit at the back if you want to observe the hustle and bustle, but don't actually want to be part of it. Even in this rather awkwardly shaped premises, Browns has been able to create their familiar, unmistakably English feel which with judicious use of old glass, wood, and mirrors manages to be light and casual at the same time. Daily specials are chalked up on blackboards.

The menu at Browns has exactly the sort of dishes you would expect: a collection of old favourites with here and there a smattering of comfort food. And it does that very well. You can choose to kick off with anything from half a dozen oysters (£6.75) or moules marinières (£5.45) to a duck liver parfait (£4.95), and not be disappointed by any of them. There is a small range of pastas (around £8.50), hot sandwiches (around £8.00) and salads (£8.50–£12.00), which are served as main course sizes. Plus there's a decent selection of simple main courses – something unusual in London these days. The char-grilled chicken breast with fresh tarragon butter (£9.65) couldn't be simpler, the traditional salmon fishcakes with lemon mayonnaise (£8.95) are slightly stodgy but nice. If you want the pure Browns experience and you're hungry enough, try the steak, mushroom and Guinness pie (£8.95), a dish on which the restaurant has always staked its reputation.

There's no need to book at Brown's but you may have to wait for five or ten minutes for a table at lunchtime. In the meantime, have a drink at the bar and look at the rest of the clientele. The borderline between bar and restaurant is very blurred here and at least half the clientele have only dropped by for a classy drink after work.

£20–£40

Chor Bizarre

16 Albemarle St, W1 ☎ 0171 629 9802   ⊖ Green Park

Mon–Sat noon–3pm & 6–11.30pm, Sun 6–10.30pm   All major credit cards

Chor Bizarre is something of a novelty in London as one of a handful of Indian restaurants that has a "head office" in India. Indeed the London Chor Bizarre is a copy of the one in the Broadway Hotel in Delhi. Its name is an elaborate pun (Chor Bazaar translates as thieves market) and, like the Delhi branch, the London restaurant is furnished with an amazing clutter of Indian antiques and bric-a-brac. Every table, and each set of chairs, is different and you may find yourself dining within the frame of an antique four poster bed. The food is similarly eccentric, but very well prepared and strikingly authentic. It does, however, carry the kind of price tag you'd expect of Mayfair.

Start with simple things such as pakoras (£4) – vegetable fritters; or samosas (£4), which are fresh, full of potato and peas, and served with fine accompanying chutneys. Kebabs are taken seriously here, too: gilawat ke kebab (£9) is a Lucknow speciality – made with lamb. Gazab ka tikka (£9.50), a best seller in Delhi, is a kind of chicken tikka deluxe. Then for your main course, choose dishes like baghare baingan (£8) which is a Hyderabadi dish combining aubergine, peanuts and tamarind. Or one of the dum pukht dishes where the food is cooked slowly in a sealed pot – the chooza dum pukht (£11) is made with chicken. Breads are also impressive, including an excellent naan (£2), pudina paratha (£2.50) – a mint paratha, and stuffed kulcha (£2.75) – choose from cheese, potato or mince.

There is an extensive selection of imposing set menus, which are a good way to tour the menu without watching your wallet implode. South Indian Tiffin (£21) features chicken Chettinad, Kerala prawn, porial, and sambal, served with rice and Malabari parathas on a banana leaf. Kashmiri tarami (£22) is a copper platter with goshtaba, mirchi korma, rajmah, al Yakhni, tamatar chaaman andnadru haaq on rice, prededed by a starter of dry cooked lamb ribs. Or there is the Royal Repast (£31) – two starters, one item from the tandoor, two non-vegetarian main courses, three vegetarian mains, two breads, rice, two desserts and coffee! Vegetarians can have a veggie version.

The Greenhouse

27a Hay's Mews, W1 ☎ 0171 499 3331	⊖ Green Park
Mon–Fri noon–2.30pm & 6.30–11pm, Sat 6.30–11pm,	
Sun noon–3pm & 6–10pm	All major credit cards

Make your way down an alleyway, just around the corner of the cabbies' favourite Mayfair petrol stop, and you find yourself walking under a long canopy into the reception of The Greenhouse. For somewhere located on the ground floor of a rather nasty Mayfair apartment block, this is a remarkably attractive restaurant. The room has a light, spacious feel and the gardening theme is brought home with topiary bushes, flowerpots and picture windows. It's all classic, country English – stable and a little staid, but undeniably well done.

The Greenhouse offers a good value lunch at £16.50 for two courses, £21.50 for three, which might be watercress soup followed by salmon or chicken, and desserts from the menu. Ordering from the carte brings more ambitious starters like home-cured spiced herring with potato, bacon and spring onion (£5.50), which provides an elegant sufficiency and tastes very good; and jellied bacon and parsley with watercress and mustard (£5.50), which is a lot better than it sounds. There is also an acknowledgement of more fashionable cooking with honey glazed quail with cucumber and mushrooms (£8.00), and what is now almost de rigueur on smart menus, risotto – here it is made with truffles, girolles, peas and mint (£9.50). Main courses score highly with a meltingly-good herb roasted chicken with asparagus (£15.00), or roast cod, creamed cabbage, leeks and broad beans (£15.50). And then there are more classical dishes, featured on the daily changing lunch specials (£19.50 for two courses). Mussels with garlic and parsley deep fried cod and chips is a regular on a Friday, while Tuesdays promises Lancashire cheese and onion tart followed by boiled ham, creamed spinach and butter beans. Whatever the day, if you can, save room for the signature dessert, bread and butter pudding (£4.90).

The Greenhouse proprietors are Mr and Mrs Levin and suitably enough they offer as house wine Le Vin de Levin – very drinkable and excellent value at £12.

Jean-Christophe Novelli at Les Saveurs

37a Curzon St, W1 ☎ 0171 491 8919	⊖ Green Park
Tues–Fri noon–3pm & 7–10.30pm, Sat 7–10.30pm	All major credit cards

Jean-Christophe Novelli is one of those chefs who has worked his way up to owning a small chain of restaurants. This is his flagship. The prices tend towards Mayfair but the irreverent and innovative cuisine do not. On an underlying strata of French classicism, Jean-Christophe Novelli piles up flavour after flavour and texture after texture. It doesn't always work but it is always exciting. The restaurant offers a fixed price menu – two courses £25 and three courses £29.50 – but on top of that there are extra charges for vegetables, and the menu is dotted with supplements where dishes contain luxury ingredients or expensive fish. So be aware that this is a special treat with a bill to match.

The menu changes every four months and trying to second guess what the next menu will bring is as difficult a task as second guessing Jean-Christophe Novelli's imagination. Starters are complex here . . . no, that's not really accurate, every dish is complex. How about tartare of crab and home-cured trout with cucumber croque quail's egg and caviar? Or cervela of cured salmon and foie gras with a fine herb fromage blanc? Or New Forest wild mushrooms wrapped in a thin pancake steamed and served with a light vintage port sauce? Fish dishes are equally elaborate – mille feuille of Dover sole and aubergine, confit tomatoes with tomato and anchovy sauce – strong tastes. The meat dishes will include the obligatory pig's trotter and feature a host of strong and earthy combinations – such as a lasagne of beef daube and shitaki mushrooms with leek purée and foie gras emulsion, or rabbit paupiette, confit leg and cutlet on a bed of fresh pea risotto with a fine herb velouté. Puddings are stupendous, with or without the trademark sugar twirls: fig tarte fine with pistachio ice cream; Amaretto creme brulée in a white chocolate cup; they taste as good as they sound.

To really push the boat out, the special "menu dégustation" makes a good deal of sense – four courses for £45. Such menus represent the chef's idea of his most impressive dishes, and who should know better?

Mirabelle

56 Curzon Street, W1 ☎ 0171 499 4636   ⊖ Green Park

Mon–Fri noon–2.30pm & 6–11.45pm, Sat & Sun 6–10.30pm   Amex, Mastercard, Visa

Everyone hoping to open their own restaurant should go and have lunch at the Mirabelle. It's not just the touch of Marco Pierre White (London's own culinary Rasputin), the whole operation is superlative. Forgive them the mind-numbingly arrogant and extensive wine list – it climaxes in an 1847 vintage Chateau d'Yquem at £30,000 – and concentrate on the food, which is quite reasonably priced for such haute cuisine. The ingredients are carefully chosen. The presentation on the plate is stunning. The surroundings are elegant, and the service attentive. There's a very elegant bar, too, which really does invite a pause for a drink before and maybe after a meal. Go on, splash out – it really is worth it.

Start with a great classic – omelette "Arnold Bennett" (£8.50) – no wonder Arnold liked these omelettes – rich and buttery with smoked haddock, light and delicious. Or there's Bayonne ham with celeriac remoulade (£9.50). Or a truffled parsley soup with a poached egg (£6.50). Step up a level for some triumphant foie gras "en terrine" dishes: gelée de Sauternes, toasted brioche (£16.95) or "parfait en gelée" with toasted Poilane bread (£8.95). Believe it or not these two are actually bargains. For a fishy main course, how about sea bream with citrus fruits, olive oil, coriander (£13.50)? Or the classical option: grilled lemon sole – pomme pont neuf, beurre Maître d'hôtel (£14.50). In the meat section there's pork chop with mirabelles, apple sauce, jus marjolaine (£12.50) – this is served off the bone and with some notable mashed potato. Or there's liver and bacon (£13.50); an entrecôte with fresh snails (£14.95); and that blast-from-the-past, veal escalope Holstein (£14.50). Puddings (all at £7.50) are deftly handled. The star is a hot caramel soufflé amandine.

Go for the set lunch, don't let the wine list sneak up on you (there's a decent enough Montes Sauvignon Blanc for £16), and you could be enjoying a combination of dishes such as salad frisée Lyonnaise, then pajarski of wild salmon with sorrel, then lemon tart, and finally coffee. Three courses £17.95, two courses £14.95. It's a steal.

Rasa W1

6 Dering Street W1 ☎ 0171 629 1346   ⊖ Bond Street

Mon–Sat 12.30–2pm & 6–10.30pm, Sun 6–10.30pm   All major credit cards

Rasa W1 is a multiple contradiction, a Keralan restaurant that is pricy, elegant, fashionable, upmarket, and still strictly vegetarian. They also claim that it is the only non-smoking Indian restaurant in Britain. Service is friendly and Rasa seems completely at ease with itself. It's under a year old but there's none of the newness of many new restaurants. The menu is littered with unfamiliar and homely dishes and they are all worth investigation. Lean heavily on the helpful advice available.

Start with the pre-meal snacks (£4) and you will never be satisfied by a few curling pappadoms again, as five different variations on the pappadom theme are accompanied by seven fresh chutneys. Acchappam is a fascinating three dimensional honeycomb affair, the chena upperi are root vegetable crisps. The chutneys are stunning – there's a garlic pickle of genuine virulence and what is described by Das the proprietor as "Mum's special" – a terrific concoction made from sharp green mangoes. Don't miss these. Highlights on the starters menu are banana boli (£4.25) – deep fried plantain fritters; Mysore bonda (£4.25) – potato, ginger and curry leaf cakes; and cashew nut pakoda (£4.50) – a kind of peanut brittle made with cashews. With the main courses (which are served the traditional way on banana leaves in the evenings), try as many of the different rices as possible: tamarind (£3.50); lemon (£3.25); and thakkali choru (£3.75), which is rice cooked in milk and tomato juice – very delicate. The curries are fascinating and unusual. Kadachakka stew (£6.25) is made with breadfruit; bagar baingan (£5.75) is rich with aubergines; moru kachiathu (£5.75) is an unusual combination of sweet mangoes and green bananas. Also look out for the mottakrose thoran (£5.25) which is a dish of fried potatoes and cabbage – Indian bubble and squeak.

Going for the set menu often seems like a cop out but this is one place where you'd be foolish not to consider it. The Kerala feast costs a not insubstantial £22.50 a head but brings waves of dishes, each one seemingly better than the last. There are also likely to be a few off-menu delights – Mum's specials – and they really are special.

Sotheby's Café

34-35 New Bond St, W1 ☎ 0171 408 5077   ⊖ Bond Street

Mon-Fri 9.30–11.30, noon–3pm, 3–4.45pm (tea)   All major credit cards

If you like the idea of eating in an art collection attached to a famous auction house, and rubbing shoulders with international art dealers and collectors, you will enjoy Sotheby's Café. It is quintessentially English and boasts a quiet atmosphere even though sited on one side of the main hall of Sotheby's. It is also that rare thing in London restaurants nowadays – somewhere you can get a proper English afternoon tea.

The lunch menu is short and changes daily with seasonal variations. Warm asparagus with citrus butter (£5.95) is prepared with very fresh vegetables and a good tang of lemon in the butter. Vichyssoise (£4.50) is smooth creamy and subtle. Grilled cod with warm salad of cannellini beans, leeks, radicchio, citrus dressing (£12.95) is good – accompaniments which do not overpower the very fresh and just-cooked cod. Lobster club sandwich (£10.95) is an interesting idea. Large chunks of fresh lobster in a fresh mayonnaise served in a club sandwich making for an ideal light lunch. There are puddings like strawberry ice cream, fresh strawberries and lemon biscuits (£4.50) and pear and almond tart with clotted cream (£4.50). They are also good and the pear tart tastes as if it is freshly made that morning. There is also a large range of teas, herbal teas and other infusions. Wines are chosen by Serena Sutcliffe, who runs the wine auction department, and the café is managed by Sally Heyes who greets customers with a delightful English charm and grace making you feel quite at home.

The afternoon tea menus offer Welsh rarebit (£4.25), Dumfries smoked salmon with brown bread (£6.50) and chicken club sandwich (£6.50). There are complete afternoon tea menus at £4.50 and £8.50, the latter including cucumber and ham and egg sandwiches and home-made cakes. Breakfast extends to Scottish smoked salmon and scrambled eggs with toast (£7.25), but sadly no bacon and eggs. Whatever time of day, visitors who come just for the food are made very welcome – you don't have to feel that you need to go home with a paperweight or an old master. However, in keeping with the reverential atmosphere, a notice whispers "please, no smoking or mobile phones".

MAYFAIR & BOND STREET ⊕ ITALIAN

Teca

54 Brooks Mews, W1 ☎ 0171 495 4774   ⊖ Bond Street

Restaurant: Mon–Sat noon–2.30pm & 7.30–10.30pm

Bar: Mon–Sat noon–midnight   All major credit cards

There was a time when Brooks Mews was deserted save for all the patient chauffeurs waiting with their gleaming limos round the back of Claridges. Not any more. Teca has a splendid corner site at the Avery Row end and when the weather co-operates tables and chairs at this quality (and quality-priced) restaurant spill out onto the street. Within, the restaurant has clean lines and an elegance to match the clientele – ladies who lunch, clearly delighted to find somewhere that is both stylish and comfortable, and so close to the lairs of the Bond Street couturiers. The cuisine here is modern Italian, if there is such a thing, and the chefs take a lead from chefs like Cavallini at the Halkin and Marchesi in Italy.

The menu is market driven and changes regularly. The list is short but the dishes on it are well balanced, well cooked and well presented, which more than makes up for brevity. When they are in season you should look out for starters like insalata di quaglia con pecorino (£8.50), a perfectly roast quail, tender and juicy, halved and placed upon broad beans and pecorino cheese. Or carpaccio di salmone con avocado (£7.50) – familiar ingredients in a new guise. From "paste e risi" choose ravioli di melanzane e taleggio (£8) – rich aubergine and Taleggio cheese; the orecchiette alle cime di rape e triglie (£8) – orecchiette with broccoli and red mullet; or there's crema di piselli con marscapone e cipolotti (£6.50) – a traditional combination, pea soup with marscapone and spring onions. Main courses tend to be light and pretty. Even the coscia di conigilo farcita alle olive con spinaci saltati (£12.50) – a rabbit leg stuffed with olives and served with sautéed spinach which looks the part as well as tasting delicious. Or there may be medaglioni di coda di rospo alla griglia con carciofi e patata (£16.50) – grilled monkfish medallions with artichokes and potatoes, peasant fare for sophisticated peasants!

Teca means treasure chest, and in this instance refers to the glass-fronted wine store where all sorts of fine Italian wines lie in wait for people with wallet enough to enjoy them.

CENTRAL

Paddington &
Edgware Rd

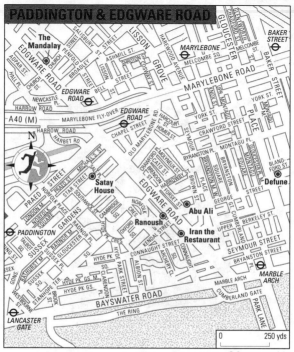

PADDINGTON & EDGWARE ROAD

The Mandalay

Satay House

Ranoush

Abu Ali

Iran the Restaurant

Defune

MARYLEBONE

BAKER STREET

PADDINGTON

LANCASTER GATE

MARBLE ARCH

MARYLEBONE ROAD

A40 (M) MARYLEBONE FLY-OVER

BAYSWATER ROAD

THE RING

CUMBERLAND GATE

PARK LANE

0 — 250 yds

© Crown copyright

Abu Ali

136-138 George St, W1 ☎ 0171 724 6338   ⊖ Marble Arch

Daily 9am–midnight   Cheque or cash only

You can only suppose that in the Lebanon going out to eat is man's work. That certainly seems to be the case around the Oxford Street end of the Edgware Road, where you'll find Abu Ali's bustling café. This is an authentic place: a Lebanese equivalent to a northern working man's club, a bit Spartan in appearance, with honest, terrific value food, and pavement tables outside, where men gather to smoke a pipe or two and discuss the world. Although you are unlikely to find many Lebanese women here, women diners get a dignified welcome. There's nothing intimdating about the place or its clientele.

You will want a selection of starters. Tabbouleh (£2) is bright green with lots of fresh parsley, lemon juice, oil, and only a little cracked wheat – it even tastes healthy. Hommos (£2) is rich and spicy, garnished with a few whole chick peas and Cayenne pepper. Warak inab (£2.50), are stuffed vine leaves served hot or cold, thin and pleasantly sour. Kabis (£1.50) is a plate of tangy salt and sour pickles – cucumber, chillies, and red cabbage. For main dishes there's kafta billaban (£5.50) – minced lamb kebabs served hot under a layer of sharp yoghurt and with a sprinkling of pine kernels; or there's kibbeh bissiniyeh (£5) which is a strange dish, a ball of mince and pine kernels is coated with a layer of mince and cracked wheat, then it is baked until crispy in the oven. The plain grilled meats are also good: try the boned-out poussin – farrouge moussahab (£6). To drink, there is mint tea (£2) – a Lipton's teabag and a bunch of fresh mint in every pot – or soft drinks.

Inside and outside Abu Ali's the air is full of the sweet scent of bubble pipes. They cost £5 a go, and you can have either apple or strawberry. The long strands of black tobacco are mixed into a squelchy mess with chopped fruit and then covered with a piece of foil, on top of which is placed a chunk of blazing charcoal – you are on your way to clouds of sweet-smelling smoke. Some of the cognoscenti take this procedure a step further and replace the water through which the smoke bubbles with ice and Appletise.

Defune

61 Blandford St, W1 ☎ 0171 935 8311	⊖ Marble Arch
Mon–Sat noon–2.30pm & 6–10.30pm	All major credit cards

For a restaurant renowned for serving some of London's top sushi, Defune is a remarkably unpretentious place – the elderly bar stools, Formica counter and Japanese rock music in the background give no clues. The bill does. Sit at the mid-point of the counter and watch the two sushi chefs pirouette from fish to fish. This is great theatre, as they present the sushi portions to the diners with a synchronised exclamation – "Hai!" Don't make the mistake of putting your beer on the top ledge of the counter as the sushi is served straight onto it. Pour a little soya sauce from the elegant china flagon into the saucer in front of you; and add as much of the super-fiery wasabi as you like, then take your wooden chopsticks, dip the piece of sushi in the sauce and eat it. There are usually two pieces per portion. In between sushi varieties clean the palate with a morsel of the gari or pickled ginger which is also plonked on the counter; it is unreservedly delicious.

Start by asking to see the "sushi menu", which is a "look-and-point" series of pictures with prices, then off you go. Sake – salmon (£4.80) – is rich and smooth, if you like smoked salmon you'll like this. Maguro – tuna (£5) – is meaty in texture. Ebi – cooked shrimp (£4.80) – are rather bland, but amaebi – raw sweet shrimp (£7.20) – are delicious. Anago – eel (£7.20) – rather surprisingly comes hot off the grill and with a special sauce. Suzuki – sea bass (£4.80) – is fresh tasting. Maki toro is a roll sushi, fine scrapings of tuna meat from next to the skin served up with pickles (£4.80). Hotate – fresh scallops (£6.20) – are splendidly sweet.

Some of the sushi are a touch more testing. Uni – sea urchin either from Iceland or Chile, allegedly with a subtle difference in taste (£8.20) – is one of the most extraordinary textures you'll ever encounter. Mirugai – giant clam, beaten to death on the counter in front of you (£6.20) – combines an agreeable texture with a less agreeable taste.

Iran the Restaurant

59 Edgware Rd W2 ☎ 0171 723 1344   ⊖ Marble Arch

Daily noon–midnight   All major credit cards except Diners

In comparison with the very basic cafes and very glitzy eateries that are its neighbours, Iran the Restaurant reeks of sophistication. The interior is not over-gaudy; the staff are helpful; and the food is simple, tasty and freshly cooked. It's very difficult to put you finger on just what makes one restaurant hospitable and another merely acceptable, but at "Iran the Restaurant" they manage to put you completely at your ease however unfamiliar the cuisine may be. You do pay for this consideration – the portions are not huge, prices are West End, and there is a 15% service charge added – but all-in-all it is worth it.

The first thing to do is marvel at the bread chef. In pride of place there is a special oven dedicated to making Iranian bread (£2), which is about the size of a tea towel, thin and chewy, and with crisp edges. It is full of perforations courtesy of a tool that looks like a cross between hedgehog and rolling pin. The oven is so hot that it cooks in about 35 seconds. It is very, very good. Accompany it with some torshi litteh (£3.95) – mixed pickles. Plus halim bademjon (£3.95) – aubergines with dried yoghurt, fried onions and mint. And tapulla salad (£3.95) – a parsley-rich tabboulleh. Borani is also tempting (£3.95) – spinach with fried onion and yoghurt. Go on to something from the grill. The lamb here is very well cooked and not greasy: kebab barg (£10.95), fillet with grilled tomato, and kebab koobideh (£9.95), minced lamb kebabs, stand out. Then there is a section of koresht dishes. At least one of you should order the koresht fesenjon (£11.95), a chicken dish with a delicious sauce made from walnuts pumpkin and pomegranate sauce. Vegetarians, or anyone who wants to accompany their grilled meats, can order a portion of this sauce on its own (£7.95).

If the wine list here were a car, it would be a Ferrari. It goes from Beaujolais Villages, Domain Soitel, (£13.75) to Chateau Margaux 1981 (£444.50) in the space of just eight bottles.

£5–£15

The Mandalay

444 Edgware Rd W2 ☎ 0171 258 3696	⊖ Edgware Road
Mon–Sat noon–2.30pm & 6–10.30pm	All major credit cards

In the Edgware Road Desert – North of the Harrow Road but South of anything else – Gary and Dwight Ally, Scandinavian-educated Burmese brothers, have set up shop in what must be an ex-greasy spoon. The resulting restaurant is rather bizarre, with just 28 seats, the old sandwich counter filled with strange and exotic ingredients, greetings and decoration in both Burmese and Norwegian, Gary in the kitchen and a smiley, talkative Dwight as front of house.

Gary and Dwight have perhaps correctly concluded that their native language is unmasterable by the English, so the menu is written in English with a Burmese translation – an enormous help when ordering. But the food itself is pure un-expurgated Burmese and all freshly-cooked. The local cuisine is a melange of different local influences, with a little bit of Thai and Malaysian and a lot of Indian, and a few things that are distinctly their own. To start there are pappadoms (2 for £1.20) or a great bowlful of prawn crackers (£1.90) which arrive freshly fried and sizzling hot (and served on domestic kitchen paper to soak up the oil). First courses range from spring rolls (from £1.70 for 2), and samosas (£1.70 for 4), to salads like raw papaya and cucumber (£3.50) or fermented tea leaf (£3.50) which is a great deal better than it sounds. There are soups, noodle soups and all manner of fritters as well. Main courses are mainly curries, rice and noodle dishes, with plenty of ginger, garlic, coriander and coconut, and using fish, chicken and vegetables as the main ingredients. The cooking is good, flavours hit the mark, portions are huge, and only one dish costs over £6.00. Vegetable dishes are somewhat more successful than the prawn ones, but at this price it's only to be expected.

Even with its eccentric setting, tiny room and no-smoking restrictions, Mandalay has built up a loyal following over the years. The tables are tiny and the acoustics are good so be careful what you talk about – you are as likely to sit next to a dustman as an ex-pat Burmese diamond dealer.

Ranoush Juice Bar

43 Edgware Rd W2 ☎ 0171 723 5929   ⊖ Marble Arch

Daily 9am–3am   Cheque and cash only

Ranoush is a Lebanese bar-style restaurant on busy Edgware Road, with counter service and room for just a few tables. The decor, which is all black marble and stainless steel, is smart and whatever time of the day you pop in there'll always be people queuing up for the superb array of vegetables and shawarma – the heir apparent to a doner kebab. After midnight the place buzzes, as clubbers and late-night revellers pile in to re-charge their batteries. Towards the back, a juice bar serves up an impressive selection of freshly-squeezed fruit juices. This is the place to come for a superior take-away; to sit down to a great-value meze; or to finish off a wilder night with some rehydration and a timely belt of vitamins and minerals – as supplied by a long cool fruit juice..

Once inside, pay for your food at the till and take your receipt to the food counter. Ranoush's popular mixed meze (£9) is a generous plate piled high with six different portions of goodies. You can take your pick from wonderfully fresh offerings, which usually include mousakaa bizeit (fried aubergine cooked with tomato sauce, onions and chick peas), batata harra (cubes of potatoes fried with garlic and coriander), sambousek (pastry filled with mince meat and pine kernels), pickles, Lebanese salad, hommos and falafel. Round it off with a helping of lamb or chicken – both moist and piping hot. If you haven't got the appetite for such a feast, you might go for a straightforward chicken shawarma (£3.50), which comes with just the right amount of relish and tomatoes – absolutely delicious. Then there are the sweet pastries – a whole counter devoted to baklawa and the like. Especially good are the lady fingers, small cubes of almond pastry (4 for £1).

Ranoush isn't licensed, but you're unlikely to hanker after booze once you've tasted their juices. The freshly-squeezed banana, mango, melon, and pineapple varieties (£1.50) are all good, but the king of the range is the Ranoush fruit cocktail (£1.75). This is a creamy, refreshing blend of all of the above, and will send you singing into the night.

Satay House

13 Sale Place, W2 ☎ 0171 723 6763   ⊖ Paddington

Tues–Sun noon–3pm & 6–11pm   All major credit cards

Why is it that starters always seem to have the edge on main courses? This depressingly accurate rule of thumb can be explained in part by the fact that you get to the starters first – when your appetite is still a contender. The Satay House breaks this rule. Here the starters are pretty pedestrian and the satay, for which the establishment was named, particularly ordinary. But do not be downcast for the main courses are spectacularly good. Simply adjust your expectations and ordering policy to suit. This is also one of the few Malaysian restaurants in London that is actually Malaysian run (most are owned by Chinese restaurateurs cashing in on something new), and in consequence the Satay House attracts a knowledgeable Malaysian clientele. Service is friendly and the light, bright dining room is more often full than empty.

Order the satay (£4.30 for six sticks) only if you must – the sauce is chunky but underseasoned. It's much better to make a start elsewhere on the menu, perhaps with a murtabak (£4.70) off the breads list; this is an eggy Malaysian bread wrapped around minced meat and served like a small plump pillow, with bright orange, sweet pickled onions – it is very delicious indeed and the onions have an almost addictive quality. Continue with nasi lemak (£6.00), rice cooked in coconut milk topped with crisp whole peanuts, still in their little red jackets, and slivers of deep-fried anchovy, or one of the excellent noodle dishes – either mee, mee hoon, or kway teow goreng (£4.70) – with meat, prawns, egg and vegetables. Among the main dishes, standouts include the rendang daging (£5.30) – beef cooked for days and served almost dry but spectacularly tender – and the ayam goreng beriada (£4.70) – chicken pieces on the bone covered in chilli paste and fried. Try some specials, too: an order of sambal belacan (£2.50) produces fiercely salty and fishy chillies, fish paste and cucumber. Cinalok (£2.50) brings you four giant prawns in a fiery sauce from Malacca.

The Malaysian customers all drink odd fluorescent-coloured drinks made from sugar cane, or soya beans, or lichees, or guava, or else dark brown tea with condensed milk and ice. Happy exploring.

Piccadilly & St James's

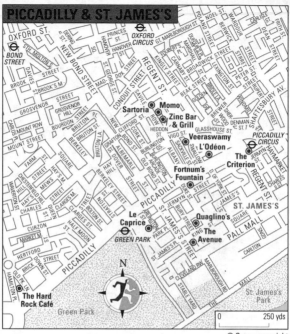

PICCADILLY & ST. JAMES'S

The Avenue

7/9 St James's Street, W1 ☎ 0171 321 2111   ⊖ Green Park

Mon–Thurs noon–3pm & 5.45pm–midnight, Fri & Sat noon–3pm

& 5.45pm–12.30am, Sun noon–3pm & 5.45–10pm   All major credit cards

Avenue was one of the first banker-led restaurants in London – the owner Chris Bodker got a bunch of City chums to join him in setting up the kind of restaurant where he and they would choose to eat. The result is a stark yet stylish barn of a place, with white walls and pale cherry wood chairs, and an enormous video wall of moving images around the bar seating area. Entrance is through a glass door, part of a great glass plate fronting the restaurant, and greeting is by designer-clad actor-actress-looking hosts. Inside it's very noisy but with a real upbeat atmosphere. There is not much subtlety about this place – wear your choicest clobber to feel most at home and do not be afraid to gawp.

Cooking is well executed and the menu is a fashionable mix of English and Italian. First courses are generally salads and pastas – a baby gem salad with poached egg and parmesan (£5.75) is simple but fine; or a courgette and asparagus tagliatelle (£5.75/9.75), offered in two sizes to give more choice to the surprisingly meanly-served vegetarians. Main courses are generally more substantial and err towards nursery food: Avenue fish fingers (£11.75), smoked haddock fishcake with Welsh rarebit (£12.95), and calf's liver with gnocchi and Parma ham (£14.95) – a posh version of liver and bacon with mash. For those watching their waists, try the rare seared tuna with red onion salad (£15.95). Puddings – mixed berries with marshmallow (£5.50), treacle tart with lemon mascarpone (£6.50) – are generally unchallenging, and for those with a sweet tooth.

Avenue is huge, and as such you are likely to be able to get a table even when it's fully booked. Somebody is bound to cancel at the last minute. Alternatively go at lunchtime when there's a good set menu at £17.50/19.50 for two/three courses; it is also available as a pre- or post-theatre menu (5.45–7.30pm & after 10.15) at £14.50/£16.50. But whenever you go, have a drink at the bar before or after a meal. It's a fun place.

The Criterion

224 Piccadilly, W1 ☎ 0171 930 0488   ⊖ Piccadilly Circus

Mon–Sat noon–2.30pm & 6–11.30pm,

Sun noon–3pm & 6–10.30pm   All major credit cards except Diners

To go through the revolving doors behind Eros and into the Criterion Brasserie is to be instantly seduced. The room of this, one of the most accessible of Marco Pierre White's restaurants, is one of the most beautiful in London with its high vaulted gold mosaic'd ceiling, delicate golden petal lamps, wooden floors, and lighting at just the right level to flatter both the room and the diners. It was built, inspired by Byzantine church interiors, in the 1880s, hosted dinner dances in the 1920s, and – astonishingly – was lined with formica from 1960 until restoration in 1984. These days it must look as good as any since its dinner dance heyday. A translucent curtain divides the restaurant from the bar area, adding a soft focus effect, and beautiful front of house staff await you. Providing you've booked and you are on time, they will be perfectly charming.

Once within, there is no getting away from the Marco Pierre White influence – the Anglo French cooking is of the pure White school and a stylised portrait of the master stares at you from the menu. The menu changes every couple of months but you'll always find the classics. Start with the velvety soft veloute of asparagus (£3.95) – a dish that in other hands might be plain asparagus soup – or the clean-cut terrine of veal and bacon, sauce gribiche (£8.95). Follow with caramelised skate wing with roast winkles and capers (£13.95), which is hard to beat, or the signature smoked haddock "kedgeree" (£11.95). Meat main courses are every bit as good. The Criterion's veal Holstein (£14.95) is as good as the dish gets, and the spiced pot roast pork with young vegetables (£12.75) is excellent. Try to leave room for pudding (£6.75), which ranges from a Granny Smith creme brulée and a Roux style lemon tart to a simple English summer pudding.

Great classical cooking at non-suicidal prices is what this restaurant is about. The only problem is that to keep the prices at these levels they seem a little too keen to manage more than one sitting a night and you tend to get hustled through your dinner. For the best service, therefore, go at lunchtime when there's a bargain priced set menu (£14.95) and you can keep your table all afternoon.

Fortnum's Fountain

181 Piccadilly, W1 ☎ 0171 973 4140	⊖ Piccadilly Circus/Green Park
Mon–Sat 8.30am–8pm	All major credit cards

The main entrance to Fortnum's Fountain Restaurant is at the back of the store on Jermyn Street. This makes it a draw for those working and shopping in the surrounding area, though the core clientele of this rather traditional English restaurant are well-to-do retired folk who use Fortnum and Mason to shop, or wish that they still could. The Fountain reflects their taste and is utterly dependable, delivering just what you expected – and ineed hoped for – in its well prepared, very English, breakfasts, lunches, teas and early dinners. The ingredients, as you'd expect of London's smartest and most old-fashioned delicatessen, are top class. And the Fountain itself is a very pretty room, with classical murals all around.

The Fountain is deservedly famous for its selection of Fortnum's teas and coffees accompanied by cream teas and ice cream sundaes and on any given afternoon you will see small children being treated to their idea of heaven by elderly relatives. But the restaurant serves a very decent breakfast all day from 9am – the full English (£10.95) is rather better than in many hotels, and the Lock Fyne kippers (£6.50) a bit of a find, while a more formal lunch and dinner menu is available from 11.30am to 3pm and 6pm to 8pm. The best things to order are those where the Fortnum ingredients stand up as specialities on their own. Montgomery Cheddar and Colston Basset Stilton (£9.95) served with home–made pickles is quite unbeatable. Fortnum & Mason London-smoked salmon is another real treat, as is a trio of sliced cold pies (£10.95). If you want something more substantial, there is also a classic range of old fashioned grills – from scotch fillet steak (£15.95) to Dover Sole (£16.50). The occasional nod to modernity – a Caribbean crumble (£10.95) or salmon and scallop in filo pastry (£10.95) – is perhaps best avoided.

The restaurant is always busy, and though they turn tables you will not be hurried. The down-side is that there is no booking. That is great for shoppers but if you are on a schedule avoid peak lunchtime.

The Hard Rock Café

150 Old Park Lane, W1 ☎ 0171 629 0388   ⊖ Hyde Park Corner

Daily 11.30am–12.30 am (Sat 1am)   All major credit cards

The Hard Rock Café is a genuine celebration of rock'n'roll which makes its location, in the trad Hyde Park hotel-land strip, all the more strange. Perhaps it was chance, or clever marketing, as the bulk of the cafe's customers are tourists? Whatever the reason, this is the original Hard Rock Café, here since the 70s, as well as being the original theme restaurant (and as such a hard act to follow). The queue to get in is as legendary – there is no booking and you will find a queue almost all day long, every day of the year – and it kind of adds to the occasion. Once in, there is a great atmosphere, created by full-on rock music, dim lighting, and walls dripping with rock memorabilia. The Hard Rock food is not bad either, predominantly Tex-Mex and burgers.

They like their paperwork here: as well as three separate menus – including a life-sized guitar-shaped one; a seasonal special menu and a bar menu (which also lists the merchandise available – should you be in any doubt) – there is a memorabilia catalogue, modestly named the Hall of Fame, which shows the floor plan of this rock'n'roll museum. The dishes on offer enjoy an appropriately rock-oriented vocabulary. B.B. wings (boneless bodacious wings – £5.25) are graded classic rock (medium) or heavy metal (hot). The burgers here (£7.25) knock spots off those at the High Street burger restaurants and cover the spectrum from natural veggie burger (£7.25) to "pig sandwich" (£7.35). Among the Tex-Mex dishes, the grilled fajitas (£11.90) are pretty good. Choose from chicken, beef or vegetarian; all come with bits and pieces for parcelling up with sour cream and guacamole. Puddings are self-indulgent, with an eco-friendly ethos reflected in Brazil nuts and the like. The hot fudge brownie (£4.25) elevates goo to an art form.

Check out the Elvis stairs at the back (they're actually the lower floor fire escape) where there's even a copy of this junk-food lover's last will and testament. Why are there no Internet reports of the King being sighted here? It's just the sort of place he would like.

Le Caprice

Arlington House, Arlington St, SW1 ☎ 0171 629 223	⊖ Green Park
Daily noon–3pm (Sun 3.30pm) & 5.30pm–midnight	All major credit cards

No socialite in London worth their salt is not a regular at this deeply chic little restaurant behind the Ritz – everyone from royalty downwards uses it for the occasional quiet lunch or dinner. That's not because they'll be hounded by well-wishers or because photographers will be waiting outside. They won't. This restaurant is discreet enough to make an oyster seem a blabbermouth. It's not even particularly plush or comfortable, with black and white tiled floor, big black bar, and cane seats. What keeps Le Caprice full day-in-day-out is its personal service, its very good, properly-prepared food . . . and a bill that holds no surprises.

The much-copied menu is enticing from first moment. Plum tomato and basil galette (£6.75) is simplicity itself, but with decent ingredients that taste of what they should. Broad bean houmous with Lebanese bread (£6.25) is a bright green garlicky heaven; dressed Cornish crab with landcress (£13.50) is so fresh and clean it makes you wonder why other restaurants can't produce it. In season there's usually game, such as a grouse salad with elderberries (£12.50) – perfectly hung breast of grouse with tender salad leaves. Or as an equally gutsy option there may be grilled veal chop with truffled Savoy cabbage and ceps (£19.50). If you can cope with pudding, try the Bakewell tart with plum jam and Jersey cream (£6.00) to see just what classic English puds are about.

Expense aside, the only trouble with Le Caprice is the struggle to get a table. It is so permanently booked up that they only really accept reservations from people they know, or people who book well in advance. If you are able to plan well enough ahead, you should go just for the experience, otherwise you'll have to befriend a regular. But this has its advantages, too. The fly-by-night fashion people won't be found here and it's almost too chic and grown up to find hip designer-wear. All you need to look the part is a Continental tan, a little jewellery, Italian clothes, and a few old-fashioned laughter lines.

PICCADILLY & ST JAMES'S ⑪ MODERN FRENCH

L'Odéon

65 Regent Street, W1 ☎ 0171 287 1400	⊖ Piccadilly Circus
Mon–Sat noon–2.45pm & 5.45–11pm, Sun noon–4pm	All major credit cards

The view from the bar at L'Odéon, or from any of the numerous window tables, is a good one. You are not high above some park or other, nor watching the Thames roll by, but you look down on the splendid curve of Regent Street, and the bustle of people rushing about their business. What could be more relaxing than to see others hurrying about when you don't have to? The bar here, with its piano, professionally mixed cocktails and reasonably priced champagne, has become a favourite meeting place for both early and late evening drinks and can get crowded. The restaurant is sub-divided into chunks of seating so that although it totals several hundred covers you never seem to be "lost in space". The room itself is stylish, and the service West End slick.

The kitchen here is run by a protegé of French superstar-chef Pierre Gagnaire, and represents the newer, braver face of contemporary French cooking. Good quality British ingredients are given a shake and a twist, resulting in an ever-changing, ever-evolving menu that combines novel inspirations – starters like poached egg on sardine velouté – with old favourites like a main course of grilled entrecôte Béarnaise sauce, pommes paille (£19.95). Other main courses may be dishes like fricasée of Dover Sole fillets with sage and onion compote and a cream sauce (£19.25); or roast farmhouse chicken with parmesan served with basmati rice (£14.50); or pan-fried seabass with peppery butter sauces (£16). The puddings catch the eye, too, with the likes of poached apple in saffron with dried fig ice cream (£4.50); or baba a la Parisien (£5).

The set lunch is well worth investigating with a choice from two starters, mains and puds: two courses £16.50, three courses £19 (including cover charge). That could be lightly spiced fish soup with coriander – grilled onglet with Dauphinoise potatoes – panna cotta with peaches. Or free-range egg poached with ratatouille – Torbay sole, beurre noisette with capers – chocolate tart with vanilla ice cream. Each Sunday there's also a serious brunch menu.

CENTRAL

Momo

25 Heddon Street, W1 ☎ 0171 434 4040   ⊖ Piccadilly/Oxford Circus

Mon–Fri 12.30–2.15pm & 7–11.15pm, Sat 6.30–midnight, Sun 6–9.30pm.

Sat & Sun brunch 11am–4pm   All major credit cards

Momo is an attractive and very trendy Moroccan restaurant, tucked away (a neighbour to the Zinc Bar & Grill) in a backwater off Regent Street. For dinner, you usually have to book at least a week in advance, and to opt for an early or late sitting. If you go for the late shift, be prepared for a noisy, night-club ambience, especially on Fridays and Saturdays. The design of the place is clever, with bold geometric kasbah-style architecture, decked out with plush cushions and lots of candles. Downstairs there's an even more splendid-looking Moorish bar, annoyingly reserved for members-only – a shame, as Momo is the kind of place you could happily carry on the evening, especially if you're booked in for the earlier (7–9pm) of its two dining slots.

Whenever you arrive, get into the mood with a Momo special (£6.00), a blend of vodka, lemon juice and sparkling water, topped with a pile of chopped mint. While you're downing that, you can check out the starters. Briouat de poulet safrone (£5.75) are mouth-watering little parcels of paper-thin pastry filled with chicken and saffron, while salade Zaalouk (£5.75) is a soft mound of grilled aubergine, soaked in garlic, olive oil and coriander. Or you might try sardines farcies á la chermoula (£5.75), sardines stuffed with parsley, garlic, cumin and lemon. For main course, there are seven tagines to choose from – North-African-style stews served in a large clay pot. Try the duck (£12.50) – not something you'd find in Morocco, but delicious all the same. Alternatively, opt for couscous – brochette de volaille (£12.00) combines the staple with marinated chicken and a pot of vegetables. Or treat yourself to the Fes speciality of pastilla (£11.00), a super-sweet pigeon pie in millefeuille pastry. Desserts (all around £5.00) include a milk pastilla, the pastry floating in a bowl of sweet milk flavoured with cinnamon and orange blossom water; plain and good oranges in cinnamon; or couscous saffae – a sort of pudding with raisins, almonds and cinnamon.

Finally, don't miss a trip to the toilets downstairs. Your journey there will be enlivened by candles on the stairs and maybe a bongo player. And the men's urinal is an installation of some beauty.

PICCADILLY & ST JAMES'S ⊕ MODERN BRITISH

Quaglino's

16 Bury St, SW1 ☎ 0171 930 6767   ⊖ Green Park

Daily noon–3pm, Mon–Thurs 5.30pm–midnight,

Fri & Sat 5.30pm–1am, Sun 5.30–11pm   All major credit cards

In 1929 Giovanni Quaglino opened a restaurant in Bury Street which became an instant success. He was a daring innovator – and is reputed to have been the first person to serve a hot dishes as hors d'oeuvres. The thing his new restaurant had above all else was glamour. When Sir Terence Conran re-designed and re-opened Quaglino's over sixty years later his vision was essentially the same. Love it or loathe it, Quaglino's is glamorous, and when it first opened it attracted a glamorous and sophisticated crowd. Inevitably, with such a huge restaurant, that early exclusivity is a fading memory (and all the better for it), but Quag's still has what it takes: the elegant reception, the sweeping staircase into the bar which overlooks the main restaurant, and then another one down to restaurant level. However shy you are, you'll still get buzz from making an entrance here.

The menu is simple, classy and brasserie style with very little to scare off the less experienced diner. Given the size of the restaurant it is best to go for the simpler dishes that need less finishing and exactitude – with this number of people to feed, the head chef is not going to have a chance to get to every plate. The fabulous display of seafood at the far end of the restaurant makes it tempting to stick to the plateau de fruits de mer (£27.50 per person) which is as good as you would hope, or lobster mayonnaise (£29.00). Fish and chips (£12.50) is served with home-made chips and tartare sauce and is excellent, while entrecôte Béarnaise (£16.00) is a treat when served, as it is here, properly cooked. Puddings are straightforward and fine, too.

Quaglino's staff can be brusque but marshalling large numbers of glamour seekers is a testing enough job to make anyone a little tetchy, and you can always avoid this altogether by staying in the bar, which offers highlights from the menu – including all the seafood. Furthermore Quaglino's is open very late, which makes it perfect for a genuine "after-theatre" dinner.

CENTRAL

Sartoria

20 Saville Row, W1 ☎ 0171 534 7000	⊖ Piccadilly Circus/Oxford Circus
Mon–Sat noon–3pm & 6.30–11pm, Sun noon–3pm	Amex, Mastercard, Visa

The pressure on finding restaurant sites in the West End was bound to put the squeeze on other kinds of real estate – hence Sartoria, a modern building on the corner of Saville Row which has been prized by Sir Terence Conran from the grip of the tailoring fraternity. It is a handsome space – long and stylish – and makes a few low-key design references to tailoring (beyond the name). There's a glass wall to the wine store and part of the restaurant is set back, up a step, and can be used as a salle privé; the walls here have glass cases full of half finished suits complete with pins and chalk marks. The food at this self-styled bar-ristorante is upscale Italian and the pricing is more Saville Row than off-the-peg.

The menu breaks things down into many sections – antipasti, zuppa, pasta, risotto all make an appearance before it finds its way to pesce and carne. There seems to be one impenetrable item in every menu section – perhaps put there to encourage you to question the waiter; it takes a pretty sure grasp of Italian to know that dragoncella means tarragon. Suddenly, deep-fried artichokes and lamb sweetbreads with dragoncella (£7.50) becomes comprehensible, and delicious. Insalata of artichokes, boiled salted lemons and almonds (£6.95) is delicious and fresh-tasting. While amongst the pasta dishes there's mandilla di saea (£7.25) which is even mysterious when translated: these "silk handkerchiefs" are thin sheets of pasta coated with a fresh green sauce. The risotto is precisely cooked, particularly a risotto with rabbit, borlotti beans and rosemary (£11.50). Scallops with asparagus, anchovies and rosemary (£17.95) is a splendid combination of tastes and textures. On the dessert menu there's another star turn – green tomato tart with zabaglione (£6), a strange but very delicious combination.

Before getting to grips with the wine list here you'd better make sure your tailor equips you with deep pockets. "Super Tuscans" are well represented, as well as all manner of other noble Italian bottles whose prices inspire a sharp intake of breath. For the more cautious, house wine runs at £14 a bottle – and it's not at all bad.

£18–£35

Veeraswamy

Victory House, 101 Regent Street, W1 ☎ 0171 734 1401	⊖ Piccadilly Circus
Mon–Sat noon–2.30pm & 5.30–11.30pm,	
Sun 12.30–3pm & 6–10pm	All major credit cards

Veeraswamy is Britain's oldest-surviving Indian Restaurant, founded in 1927 by Edward Palmer following a successful catering operation at the British Empire Exhibition. Its next owner was Sir William Steward who pulled in the rich and famous throughout the post war boom – their numbres included the King of Denmark whose penchant for a glass of Carlsberg with his curry is said to have first established the link between Indian food and beer. The latest owner is Namita Panjabi (who also owns Chutney Mary – p.383), and she has swept Veeraswamy into the modern era. The old and faded colonial decor has gone, and so have the old and faded dishes. In their place there's an elegant, modern restaurant painted in the vibrant colours of today's India, and an all-new menu of bold, modern, authentically Indian, dishes of all kinds – from street food to regional specialities. It's a bit of a shock to find an Indian restaurant like this – but a pleasant one. You do, however, need to adjust your pattern of ordering. Main dishes come as a plate, with rice and sometimes vegetables. They're not designed for sharing – and you definitely need one each.

Street food makes great starters: pani puri (£4), rich with tamarind; ragda pattice (£4) – spiced potato cakes with chick pea curry. Or there's machli ki tikki (£4.75) – fish cakes; or fresh oysters exquisitely stir-fried with Keralan spices (£7.50). The main dish curries are well spiced and with a depth of flavour. Plum dopiaza (£11.50) is a lamb curry with chillies, caramelised onions and plums; or try Karwari red fish curry with poppy seeds and red chillies; or for milder palates there's malai murgh, an amazing white chicken curry with almonds, cinnamon and green chillies (£11). The biryanis are a revelation, too: particularly good is the Andhra green biryani (£11.50) – lamb and rice cooked slowly in a sealed pot with lots of green herbs and nuts. Vegetarian dishes are also grandstand affairs and include such as guchhi biryani (£13.50) – morels stuffed with panir cheese and then slowly cooked with rice..

Like its sister restaurant Chutney Mary, Veeraswamy does an excellent Sunday lunch – £11 for one course, £12.50 for two, £13.95 for three.

The Zinc Bar and Grill

21 Heddon Street, W1 ☎ 0171 255 8899 ⊖ Piccadilly Circus/Oxford Circus

Mon–Wed noon–11 pm, Thur–Sat noon–midnight   All major credit cards

Fronted by decorated glass panels and a crustacea bar, The Zinc Bar and Grill is a classic Conran gastro-space. Ashtrays are £4.50 each and Zinc boasts the longest zinc bar in London and more drinks on the menu than food choices. It's in a more or less traffic-free cul-de sac and so can boast an attractive, Parisian-styled outside terrace that is only closed in winter. All of which makes it doubly attractive to a lively crowd of young after-work Soho drinkers

The menu offers French brasserie food adapted for an English palate. Start with ham and parsley terrine (£4.50) though, and you will enjoy jambon persillée as good as any from across the Channel. Goat's cheese and aubergine tart (£4.75) brings you soft textured puree-like creamy flavours. Calves' liver and bacon (£9.25) is served either pink or well done – you can't have it medium – but even when ordered well done it was tender. Lamb shank, parsnip, mash and lentils (£9.50) is generous and cooked to fall off the bone. Pommes frites (£1.95) are fine, and mushy peas (£2.50) authentically bitty. Zinc green salad (£2.50) comes seasoned with finely shredded salad onion and chive. Lemon tart (£4.00) is smooth and sweet rather than sharp, and rhubarb bread and butter pudding (£4.50) comes with a proper custard made with eggs. There's a massive choice of wines and other drinks, from Pink Zinc (£6.50) – a mixture of raspberry liqueur and champagne – to citron pressé (£1.95). House wines from £2.75 a glass up are excellent. There are also simple but good menus for lunch and dinner at £8.95 for two courses and £11.50 for three – on offer if you order from noon to 7.30pm Monday to Friday – and a special Saturday lunch menu at £10 for two courses and £12.50 for three (served from noon to 6pm). These make Zinc better value.

Zinc changes by the hour. Arrive at 7pm and you will find a casual jazzy tempo after work drinking place, but within an hour it's a fast tempo lively eatery. Either way, go there in a groups to enjoy a lively buzz and the piled dishes of crustacea. It's ideal for parties. It's not a place for quiet or a romantic dinner à deux.

Queensway &
Westbourne Grove

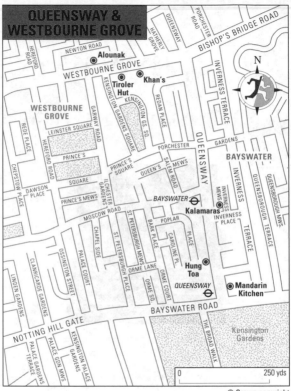

QUEENSWAY & WESTBOURNE GROVE

NEWTON ROAD
Alounak
WESTBOURNE GROVE
Tiroler Hut
Khan's
HATHERLY GROVE
QUEENSWAY
PORCHESTER ROAD
BISHOP'S BRIDGE ROAD
INVERNESS TERRACE

N

HEREFORD ROAD
WESTBOURNE GROVE
GARWAY ROAD
LEINSTER SQUARE
KENSINGTON GARDENS SQUARE
KENSINGTON GDS. SQ.
REDAN PLACE
PORCHESTER GARDENS
BAYSWATER

REDE PLACE
PRINCE'S
HEREFORD ROAD
PRINCE'S SQUARE
SALEM ROAD
QUEEN'S MEWS
QUEENSWAY
INVERNESS
QUEENSBOROUGH TERRACE
QUEENSBOROUGH MWS.

CHEPSTOW PLACE
DAWSON PLACE
SQUARE
ILCHESTER GARDENS
PRINCE'S MEWS
MOSCOW ROAD
POPLAR
BAYSWATER
Kalamaras
INVERNESS MEWS
INVERNESS PLACE

CLANRICARDE GARDENS
LINDEN GARDENS
OSSINGTON STREET
PALACE COURT
CHAPEL SIDE
ST PETERSBURGH MEWS
ST PETERSBURGH PLACE
BARK PLACE
CAROLINE PL.
ORME LANE
ORME COURT
ORME SQ.
Hung Toa
QUEENSWAY
Mandarin Kitchen

NOTTING HILL GATE
PALACE GARDENS TERRACE
PALACE GARDENS
KENSINGTON PALACE GARDENS
KENSINGTON PALACE MWS
BAYSWATER ROAD
THE BROAD WALK
Kensington Gardens

0   250 yds

© Crown copyright

138

Alounak

44 Westbourne Grove, W2 ☎ 0171 229 0416	⊖ Bayswater/Queensway
Daily noon–midnight	All major credit cards

Westbourne Grove has always had a raffish cosmopolitan air to it, which makes it the perfect home for this the second branch of Alounak to be set up – actually the third if you count its early years in a Portakabin opposite Olympia station. Don't be put off by the dated sign outside: this place turns out really good, really cheap Iranian food. The welcoming smell of clay oven-baked flat bread hits you in the face the moment you walk through the front door, creating a sense of the Middle East that's enhanced further by the gentle gurgling of an Italianate fountain, and the strains of Arabic music that underpin your conversation.

The sizeable contingent of Middle Eastern locals dining here testifies to the authenticity of the food on offer. As an opening move, you can do no better than order the mixed starter (£8), a fine sampler of all the usual dips and hors d'oeuvres, served with splendid freshly-baked flat bread. And then follow the regulars with some grilled meat, which is expertly cooked. Joojeh kebab (£6.70) is melt-in-the-mouth baby chicken, packed with flavour. The chicken fillet (£6.90) may be from an older bird, but it's no less tender for it. As you would expect from a Middle Eastern restaurant, lamb dishes feature heavily. A good way to try two-in-one is to order the chelo kebab koobideh (£8.50), marinated lamb fillet coupled with minced (lamb) kebab, which is deliciously rich and oniony. In the bamieh polo (£5.90), okra and diced lamb in tomato sauce, the ladies fingers are more like babies' fingers: the smallest, chubbiest okra known to mankind. Worth looking out for are the daily specials: if you can engineer your visit on a Tuesday, the special is zereshk polo (£5.90), a stunning chicken dish served on saffron steamed rice mixed with sweet and sour forest berries.

Round things off with a pot of Iranian black tea (£3), sufficient for six, and served in ornate glass beakers. Infused with refreshing spices, it does a great job of cleaning the palate, leaving you set for a finale of select Persian sweets. Beware of unpronounceably named yoghurt drinks.

£4–£20

Hung Toa

51 Queensway, W2 ☎ 0171 727 5753	⊖ Bayswater / Queensway
Daily 11am–11pm	Cash only

It is easy to find the Hung Toa: just look out for the much larger New Kam Tong restaurant, and two doors away you'll see this small and Spartan establishment. The Hung Toa is actually part of the same group as the Kam Tong, as is the Thai restaurant over the road (which is where all those singularly appetising ducks hanging up in the windows of the three establishments are roasted). The reason to choose the Hung Toa above its neighbours is if you fancy a one plate (or one bowl) meal. Despite a long and traditional menu, featuring mainly Cantonese and Szechuan dishes, its strengths lie in its barbecued meat with rice, noodle dishes, and noodle soups. All attract the hungry and are keenly priced.

The very first thing on the menu is good – Hot and Sour Soup (£1.60). Uncannily enough this is both hot (fresh red chillies in profusion) and sour. There are also a dozen different noodle soups – priced at between £3.60 and £4. Then there are twenty dishes that go from duck rice (£3.70) to shrimps and egg with rice (£4.70). Plus about thirty noodle, fried noodle, and ho fun dishes at prices ranging from £2.40 to £5.50. The fried ho fun with beef (£3.70) is a superb rich dish, well-flavoured brisket cooked until melting on top of a mountain of ho fun. And the barbecued meats displayed in the window are very good, too – rich, red-painted char sui, soya duckling, crispy pork and duck – all shuttled across from the kitchens over the road.

Towards the front of the menu, and hailing from Canton, you'll find a succession of congee dishes. Congee is one of those foods people try and then remark "interesting" without meaning it. Plunge in at the deep end, try "Thousand years egg with sliced pork congee" (£3.70). This is a thick, whitish, runny porridge made with rice; stunningly bland and under-seasoned, but tasting faintly of ginger. As well as containing pork there's the "thousand year" egg, the white of which is a translucent chestnut brown and the yolk a fetching green, but inscrutably tasting just like an ordinary hard boiled egg.

Kalamaras

60 Inverness Mews, W2 ☎ 0171 727 9122   ⊖ Bayswater/Queensway

Daily 5.30–11pm   All major credit cards

For a great many years there were two Kalamaras restaurants in Inverness Mews – "Mega" and "Micro" – both flying the flag for Greek (rather than Greek Cypriot) food. The remaining Kalamaras occupies the "Micro" site. Arm yourself with a bottle of good wine, or some beers before visiting, as it is that rare thing amongst London restaurants – unlicensed. And they don't charge corkage either. There is an abundance of late night supermarkets and the Marks and Spencer in Whiteley's is close at hand, so you should have no trouble. Suitably laden, make your way into the mews where you'll find a genuine looking Greek taverna dedicated to mainland Greek cooking.

Start with agginares me koukia (£4.50) – a stew of fresh artichoke hearts, broad beans and dill; or varkoula (£7.50) – baked courgettes with salmon; or octapodi (£5.50) – grilled octopus with oregano and parsley. There is also avgolemono (£2.60) – a traditional Greek lemon chicken and rice soup. Other "mezedes" include melitzanes me scordalia (£4.60); fried aubergine with garlic, scordalia (£2.60) – a not-for-the-faint-hearted garlic dip; spanakotyropites (£3.50) – crisp filo parcels with spinach and onions; and yoghourtosalata (£2.60) – home made yogurt with olive oil, garlic lemon and fresh mint. You could do worse than eat Attic style and just order mezedes until you are stuffed. But if you still have room, main course offerings are good and tasty being more stew and baked than the grill and kebab variety. Moskharaki stifado (£7.90) is chunks of veal lightly stewed with tomatoes and herbs; gourounopoulo fournou (£7.10) is thin steaks of pork casseroled with lemon juice; and soutzoukakia Smyrneika (£7.50) is small fingers of minced meat cooked in the oven in a herby sauce. There is also freska psaria – fresh fish such as red mullet, grey mullet, sea bass and others as available in the market and priced from £9.50 to £12.50.

Puddings (all at £2.10) include favourites like baklava – the one with honey and nuts; kaitifi – the shredded wheat one; and the Kalamaras speciality of bouyatsa – layers of filo pastry with a vanilla custard cream, served hot. Or you could opt for plain, good Greek yogurt and honey.

Khan's

13–15 Westbourne Grove, W2 ☎ 0171 727 5420	⊖ Bayswater
Daily noon–3pm & 6pm–midnight	All major credit cards

If you're after a solid, inexpensive and familiar Indian meal, Khan's is the business. This restaurant in busy Westbourne Grove is a long-standing favourite with students and budget-wary locals, who know that the curries here may be the staples of a thousand menus across Britain, but they're fresh, well-cooked, and generously portioned. Just don't turn up for a quiet evening out. Tables turn over in a blink of an eye, service is perfunctory (this isn't a place to dally over the menu), and it's really noisy. Try to get a table in the vast, echoey ground-floor, where blue murals stretch up to high ceilings – it feels a bit like dining in an enormous swimming pool. The basement is stuffier and less atmospheric. Wherever you sit, be prepared to be hurried on your way by the waiters – unless you keep ordering regular supplies of Cobra beer.

There are some tasty breads on offer. Try the nan-e-mughziat (£1.60), a coconut-flavoured nan with nuts and sultanas, or the keema nan, which comes stuffed with minced meat (£1.45), or the paneer kulcha (£1.45), bulging with cottage cheese and mashed potatoes. You might also kick off with half a tandoori chicken (£2.75), which is moist and well cooked, or there's a creditable chicken tikka (£3.80). For main dishes, all those curry house favourites are listed here – meat madras or vindalu (£3.10); prawn biryani (£5.25); chicken chilli masala (£3.20); king prawn curry (£6.20) – and it all tastes unusually fresh. Especially good is the butter chicken (£4.70), while for lovers of chicken tikka masala – the murgh tikka masala (£3.70) will appeal. There's a typical array of vegetable dishes, too: mutter paneer (£2.60) bhindi (£2.70); sag aloo (£2.60); vegetable kofta (£2.60), and vegetable curry (£2.60). Desserts include kulfi (£2.15), chocolate bombe (£1.60) and various ice creams – or you could try the lemon or orange delight (£1.70). A pint of lager will set you back £1.90, and there's a small selection of wines; a bottle of Chardonnay costs £8.50, or you can get a glass of house white or red for £1.60.

Cast your eye around the tall, tiled ground floor and front windows and you'll find enough architectural clues to confirm that this was once a Cardomah coffee bar.

Mandarin Kitchen

14-16 Queensway, W2 ☎ 0171 727 9012	⊖ Queensway
Daily noon–11.30pm	All major credit cards

London has its fair share of French fish restaurants, and there are famous English fish restaurants, so why does it seem so odd to come across a Chinese fish restaurant? Part of the mystique of the Mandarin Kitchen, which you'll find at the Kensington Gardens end of Queensway, is the persistent rumour that they sell more lobsters than any other restaurant in Britain. (When taxed with this myth, the management will confirm that they regularly have 100 lobster days!). This is a large restaurant, busy with waiters deftly wheeling four-foot-diameter table tops around like giant hoops as they set up communal tables for large parties of Chinese who all seem to be eating . . . lobster. What's more, as the menu observes, "we only serve the finest Scottish wild lobsters, simply because they are probably the best in the world".

Whatever you fancy for the main course, start with as many of the steamed scallops on the shell with garlic soya sauce (£1.80 each) as you can afford. They're magnificent. Then decide between lobster, crab, or fish. If you go for the lobster, try ordering it baked with green pepper and onion in black bean sauce (it is priced at about £15 per lb depending on the season), and be sure that you order the optional extra soft noodle (£1.20) to make a meal of it. The crab is tempting, too. Live crabs are shipped up here from the South coast, and a handsome portion of shells, lots of legs and four claws baked with ginger and spring onion is a pretty reasonable £12. Fish dishes require more thought – and an eye to the per lb prices. The menu lists "the fish we normally serve" as sea bass, Dover sole, live eels, live carp, monkfish, Chinese pomfret and yellow croaker. Sea bass comes steamed whole at £17–19 per lb depending on season. The roast eel fillets with garlic and chili (£7.90) are notable, and strongly flavoured. The monkfish (£9.90) is meaty and delicious.

After seafood "the-never-ending-menu" wanders off amongst old favourites, plus a number of veal chop dishes under "chef's specials" – such as roasted veal chop with Mandarin sauce (£9.90) – so a seafood allergy is no excuse for you to miss the Mandarin.

£15–£25

The Tiroler Hut

27 Westbourne Grove, W2 ☎ 0171 727 3981   ⊖ Queensway

Mon–Sat 6.30pm–12.15am, Sun 6.30–11.15pm   All major credit cards except Diners

The Tiroler Hut is one of the Grove's longest-serving restaurants, here since 1967, promoting the virtues of rustic Austrian cooking and culture. Don't be put off by the "tourists only" signals sent out by the sandwich board proclaiming "live-music, yodelling and cow bells", and venture down the stairs. This is a family restaurant run by Josef Friedman and his wife, it's not expensive and the cooking is authentic. Furthermore, Josef so obviously delights in playing the accordion, cow bells and whatever that you'd have to be in a very sour mood to deny him the pleasure.

The chef here is Peter Eckbauer, and he has had charge of the kitchens for nearly 25 years. His cooking is straighforward Austrian home fare and none the worse for that. Start with his gulash soup (£3.50), dark, pungent, and full of chunks of meat and potatoes, or try the Tiroler speck, (£4.50) German air-cured ham – dry very smoky and certainly the equal of its more famous Italian and Spanish counterparts. For a main course brave the consonants of gebratene schweinshax'n bratkartoffeln und rotkraut (£8.70), a formidably-sized roast pig's knuckle, with sauté potatoes and red cabbage. Knuckle also appears in the regional speciality eisbein (£8.70), this time boiled and served with sauté potatoes and sauerkraut. Another very Austrian dish is the bauer-schmauss (£11.50), a soggy cricket-ball-sized dumpling with sauerkraut and a host of grilled meats, served with a glass of schnapps alongside. The sauerkraut is very good here, peppery and not too redolent of vine-gar. The menu also runs to schnitzels, fish, bratwurst, noodles, and Hungarian goulash. Sample a bottle of Erdinger weiss beer (£3), or the malty, dark brown Erdinger Dunkel (£3). If you suspect that the rigours of the cow bell performance may stimulate an intense need for refresh-ment, a two-litre stein of beer (£10.80) is indicated.

Austrians have a thing about liver dumplings. One Tirolean village – seeking a coveted place in the Guinness Book of records – made a dumpling containing a tonne of liver, so large it had to be lifted into the soup by crane. Small wonder then, that Josef is inordinately proud of his leberknödel suppe (£3.20).

Soho

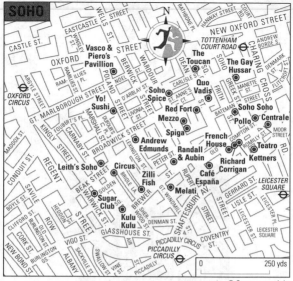

© Crown copyright

Andrew Edmunds

46 Lexington St, W1 ☎ 0171 437 5708	⊖ Oxford Circus/Piccadilly Circus

Daily 12.30–3pm (Sat/Sun from 1pm) & 6–11pm (Sun 10.30pm)   All major credit cards

For a man who obtained a restaurant by default, Andrew Edmunds has done well. Starting as a wine bar 12 years ago, this romantic and intimate little place is popular with 20- and 30-somethings who are drawn like moths by the candle light. Everything is well thought out, yet informal. There are fresh flowers on every table, and a pepper mill that doesn't disappear after your first grind. Edmunds owns the next-door print shop, and his pictures hang here teasing diners about the dangers of drinking too much. The good, modern European cuisine and friendly service lead you to expect a much larger bill. There are daily specials and eclectic weekly menus, consistently good and imaginative, as is the wine list: try a bottle of the 1996 Corbieres (£9) and you won't be disappointed. The only criticism is that tables are so close together you may end up sharing your neighbour's after-dinner cigarette while you tuck into your starter.

Starters are excellent and offer many vegetarian choices. The menu changes daily but you can expect the likes of roast leek Nicoise (£4.50), tender and sweet; or a lovely, clean-tasting broad bean, tabouleh and feta salad (£4.25). For main courses, fish is a good choice here – always precisely cooked, never overdone. Wild sea bass with rocket, coriander and fennel salad (£10) can be the most expensive thing on the menu but it is money well spent, delivering a good-sized portion of fish perched on top of a mound of fresh salad. But head chef Rebecca St John Cooper also caters for heartier appetites. You might find a dish like rabbit in creamy black-eyed peas and spinach (£8.50) – rich and substantial; and you'll wish the dinner ladies at your school had served his meatloaf with mash and porcini mushroom sauce (£8). For pudding, the chocolate mousse cake and tiramisu (both £3.25) are reassuringly velvety and rich. Round the whole thing off with a smooth cup of coffee and you'll want to become a regular.

Andrew Edmunds' restaurant is a very laid back affair and the favoured haunt of local literary types. You won't qualify as a regular until you know the name of the restaurant dog.

Café España

63 Old Compton St, W1 ☎ 0171 494 1271   ⊖ Tottenham Court Road

Daily noon–midnight   Mastercard, Visa

Situated as it is at the heart of Soho's pink strip (at the Wardour Street end of Old Compton Street), and nestled amongst hard core shops and video stores, Café España is a remarkably balanced restaurant. From the outside it looks rather like a traditional and tourist-focussed trattoria. But once through the door, tripping over the dessert trolley, you'll be greeted by a friendly maitre d' and led up the stairs to join a hubbub of hungry Soho folk with a nose for a bargain.

The menu gives a nod to the trattoria with a short list of pastas, but it is Spanish cooking you should be going for here – and if you are anything less than seriously hungry, it's best to make that tapas. Mejillones a la marinera (£3.95) delivers enough mussels for a small main course; a portion of tortilla (£4.00) is the size of a saucer and is likely to be cooked especially for you; while ordering the jamon Serrano (£5.25) brings a huge portion – and at a price you'd be hard to match wholesale. If you are after something more substantial there's plenty of choice, mostly simple grills. Try chuletas de cordero a la brasa (£8.95) – lamb chops; higado de ternera (£7.95) – calf's liver and bacon; or rodaballo a la plancha (£11.50) – grilled turbot. Or there are the traditional paellas – Valenciana and marinera (£19.50 to feed two people) – though these are slightly less exciting. Service is swift if a little harassed. To keep food prices at this level needs a turn-around of custom, but the waiters are nonetheless friendly and polite. And given the number of people in the place, you can be sure that whatever you are eating is freshly prepared – the volume of ingredients they must get through will be huge.

To enjoy Café España to the maximum, go with friends, so you can have a decent selection of tapas. But don't try to recreate an Iberian holiday with a surfeit of sangria – the stuff served here is a dark and dangerous West End concoction that is really quite horrid.

Centrale

16 Moor Street, W1 ☎ 0171 437 5513　　⊖ Leicester Square / Tottenham Court Road

Mon–Sat noon–9.45pm　　　　　　　　　　　　　　　　　　Cash only

In a grid of streets full of bottom-dollar belly-fillers, Centrale stands out, with an idiosyncratic charm beloved by its clued-in regulars. Don't be misled by its down-at-heel exterior – there's something special about sweeping through the plain glass door and sliding into one of its cracked black vinyl banquettes, forced into cosy, chatty proximity with strangers across a narrow red Formica table. Maybe it's the tininess of the place, maybe it's the omnipresent crush of students, maybe it's just that the cappuccino comes in smoked-glass cups, but it feels effortlessly friendly – and strangely glamorous. Odd when this is basically a place to line your stomach with cheap pasta before going on to a pub or club.

Centrale's menu is artless – orange juice (80p) appears as a starter – and the portions are substantial. Appetisers include home-made minestrone (£1.50), salame (£3.50), and pastina in brodo (£1.50) – short pasta snippets in a clear, slightly oily soup. There's a fair spread of diner staples to follow, including pork chop (£5.50) and fried scampi (£4.50), each partnered by an inevitable sprinkling of chips, but the main event here is the pasta. The bolognaise dishes – spaghetti, tagliatelli, rigatoni and ravioli (all £3.50) – are all dependable, adequately spicy and chewily meaty, and the lasagna al forno (£3.50) reassuringly button-popping, but the specials list holds more adventurous temptations. Stand-outs include the spaghetti vongole (£4.20) – which has a shoal of baby clams in a garlic, chilli and tomato sauce – and the rigatoni Alfredo (£4), a pungent swirl of cream, mushrooms, cheese, tomato and lots and lots of garlic. Rather than a small salad (£1.50), a side order of spinach (£2) adds a pleasantly slippery counterpoint to the solid bulk of the pasta.

The menu gives up the ghost a bit when it comes to dessert, sticking to just three old favourites: banana split (£1.50), apple pie (£1.50) and ice cream (£1.20), the last a tripartite triple-scoop of chocolate, strawberry and vanilla. Still, you're not here for puds. You're here for cheap food – and cheap wine. There's no licence so you can bring your own bottle for 50p corkage (£1 for a big bottle). You'll find a couple of excellent off licenses just around the corner in Old Compton St.

SOHO ⑩ MODERN BRITISH

Circus

4 Upper James St, W1 ☎ 0171 534 4000	⊖ Oxford Circus
Mon–Sat noon–3pm & 5.45pm–midnight (12.30am Fri & Sat),	
Sun 11.30am–4pm	All major credit cards

The little sister to big, brash Avenue in St James's, Circus can be a tad intimidating. You'll be greeted by a doorman in Armaniesque clothes, and supposing you're a bona fide diner, shown to your table in the colour-draining dining room. Chairs are dressed in neutral suede, walls in white, floor and customers in black. There's a pretty serious aura about it all. The name "Circus" apparently refers to the location of this restaurant, between Oxford and Piccadilly Circuses, and not to any frivolous entertainment. That said, the seriousness applies equally to the preparation of the food, which is impressive. The kitchen has the sense to buy decent ingredients and not muck about with them too much, which suits the punters – an unhealthy mix of record company executives, PRs and television people – perfectly.

The menu allows you to keep to your own expense account or blow your host's. You can start with a humble but well made French onion soup (£4.50), terrine of foie gras (£10.50) – or if the favours are in the Iranian beluga (£50) with sour cream and fluffy blinis. Follow with seared tuna with wakame & cucumber (£13.75), a classic 90s dish, prettily presented and full of East/West flavours. Heartier food includes braised faggot with bubble and squeak (£10.50), in its own way just as trendy. The less fashion-conscious are not ignored, and chicken breast wrapped in prosciutto with morels (£13.50) is well cooked, the chicken remarkably retaining and showing its own flavour. Puddings are deeply groovy but somehow miss the mark. Rice fritter with poached apricots (£4.75) is less than the sum of its parts but spiced pear with Thai ice cream (£4.95) doesn't pull its punches. The wine list, encompassing all the major wine making areas around the world, is sensibly divided into types rather than regions.

Annoyingly, the rather attractive Japanesey bar downstairs becomes a members only club during the evening, which means that if you are the first of your party to show up, you will have to sit at your table like a lemon. Arrive very early or very late, however, and you get a bargain: pre- and post-theatre menus (5.45–7.30pm & after 10.15pm) at two courses for £14.75, three for £16.75.

CENTRAL

French House Dining Room

49 Dean St, W1 ☎ 0171 437 2477	⊖ Leicester Square
Mon–Sat noon–3pm & 6–11.15pm	All major credit cards

The French House Dining Room is a small room above the bar of popular French House pub in Soho. It has high ceilings, wooden floors and large windows which overlook the corner of Dean Street and Old Compton Street. Despite its cosy size (around thirteen tables), the restaurant has a light, airy feel and the enormous mirror at one end of the room creates a nice sense of space. Part of the fun of eating here is to be in the heart of Soho, yet feel worlds away from the strip shows and noisy cafes. The French House is a sister restaurant of St John (see Clerkenwell, p.226) and shares its fondness for traditional British dishes and ingredients.

Choosing is made easy by a short, sharp menu, which changes daily. The dishes all look simple and restrained, but don't be fooled; the restaurant's pig motif is a correct indication of how much it is possible to eat here. There are usually four or five starters to pick from. Fennel and wild garlic soup (£4.20) is flavoursome and creamy; wild rabbit terrine and pickled prunes (£4.80) is a great combination of tastes. Or you might kick off with grilled quail, spinach and lentil salad (£4.80). Main dishes are hearty and presented with a lot of care. Wild salmon and cucumber (£14) comes in a generous portion, while sweetbreads, shallots and red chard (£10.50) is a fine choice for carnivores. There's usually a dish for veggie customers; aubergine and goats cheese tart (£9) is moist and delicious, and served with crispy leaves of rocket. Greens are basic and wholesome; new potatoes (£2), broccoli (£2) and green salad (£3.80) all taste very fresh. And there's a choice of four or five puddings; you might go for lemon polenta cake and stewed fruits (£4.20), which is squidgy and succulent, or the unusual and tasty rhubarb ice cream (£4.20).

During World War II, the pub downstairs was the unofficial headquarters for the Free French Army, and it is said that General de Gaulle was a regular. Being French, it has a particular quirk: it only serves beer in half pint glasses.

£18–£40

The Gay Hussar

2 Greek St, W1 ☎ 0171 437 0973	⊖ Tottenham Court Road
Mon–Sat 12.30–2.30pm & 5.30–10.45pm.	Amex, Diners, Mastercard

The Gay Hussar is part of old Soho. With its dark wooden panelling, plush red seats and tables crammed together under bookshelves and framed political cartoons, it would be worth visiting for the ambience alone. Fortunately, the food – Hungarian – is also sound enough. Traditionally, the Hussar was a meeting-point for left-wingers who came here to conspire away the evening over plates piled high with goulash and dumplings. In these days of New Labour, it seems to be losing its political class but it remains an intimate sort of place, and the staff, who have been here for years, are hospitable to a fault. The comfortable seating also ensures that you won't be leaving in a hurry.

The never-changing menu offers a wide choice of Hungarian dishes. Come here hungry; portions are hefty and the ingredients pretty girth-enhancing. Only the brave would go for a full three courses, but you should certainly attempt two as there's a tempting selection of starters. Chilled wild cherry soup (£3.85) is delicious, or you could try házi pásétom (£3.75), a smooth and tasty goose and pork paté. Fried mushrooms with tartare sauce (£3.60) is also very good. For mains, there are four fish dishes and a multitude of chicken, pork and veal concoctions. Poached pink trout, cucumber salad, boiled potatoes and mayonnaise (£11.80) is prepared with care and very satisfying; Szegedi halászlé (£14) is a robust Hungarian take on Bouillabaisse, worth trying for its rich texture. Chicken dishes include cairke pejacsevica (£12.50), which is chicken in paprika sauce. Borju porkolt (£14.25) is veal goulash in "a thick sauce" served with thimble egg dumplings. Or there's brassol ermék (£15.50), a plate groaning beneath tender beef fillets accompanied by peppers, onions, tomatoes and potatoes. Side dishes to go for include paraj pozelék (£3.80), a very tasty creamed spinach puree and párolt voros kaposzta (£3.80) – well cooked red cabbage. For pudding, try the turós palacsinta, (£4), sweet cheese pancakes, or if you have room, eszterházy málnás (£4), a great slice of old-fashioned raspberry and chocolate gateau.

The Hussar does a very good-value set lunch for £17.50, or £12.50 for a main course and coffee.

Kettners

29 Romilly Street, W1 ☎ 0171 734 6112	⊖ Leicester Square
Daily noon–midnight	All major credit cards

Owned by Soho restaurateur Peter Boizot, the man who introduced pizza to Britain in the 1960s, Kettners is modelled on a Pizza Express restaurant, but with a champagne bar attached. Over the years it's built up a loyal following that starts out an evening in the bar for some excellent champagne, then moves on to a pizza in the restaurant across the hall – although going to the bar beforehand (or indeed the restaurant after) isn't obligatory. But do at least one or the other. Kettners is a gorgeous old restaurant and part of the fabric of Soho.

The pizzas are amongst the best in London, their crusts biscuit thin and crispy, their topping thick, rich and tasty. What more do you want from a pizza? If you don't want one at all, however, there are additional choices like Kettners special hamburger (£6.65), Chilli con carne (£6.25) and eggs, bacon and chips (£6.25). Given that you'll probably spend a tenner or more on champagne (you could pay up to £865 for a 20-bottle Nebuchadnezzar of Pol Roger) in the bar, this makes for a delightful paradox of cheap staple food and expensive luxury drink. The pizza list includes the usuals like American hot (£7.35), Margherita (£6.50) and Napoletana (£7.10), plus unusual ideas like the King Edward (£6.25) which has a potato base. As in Pizza Express, the Veneziana (£7.10) comes with onions, capers, olives, pine kernels, sultanas, mozzarella and tomato, and every time you buy one the Venice Fund receives 40p. Diners have already contributed over £650,000.

A trip to Kettners isn't just for the pizzas – though they're good, you're here as much for the venue. Decorated in belle époque baroque, the building was founded as a grand hotel in 1867 by Auguste Kettner, chef to Napoleon III. Stories also have it that the hotel was used by the then King Edward VII to woo and bed his mistress. Upstairs rooms sport numbers to remind you of the racy past and some can be booked for private parties of between 8 and 80. The main restaurants, however, don't accept bookings and you are advised to get there early as Kettners is a lively place that gets very busy indeed.

Kulu Kulu

76 Brewer Street, W1 ☎ 0171 734 7316	⊖ Piccadilly Circus
Mon–Sat noon–2.30pm (Sat 3.45pm) & 5–10pm	Mastercard, Visa

Kulu Kulu is a conveyor belt sushi restaurant which pulls off the unlikely trick of serving really good sushi without being impersonal or intimidating. It is light and airy and there are enough coathooks for a small army of diners. The only thing you could quibble about is the stools which are fixed to the floor and rather low – anyone over six feet tall will find themselves dining in the tuck position favoured by divers and trampolinists. The atmosphere is one of Japanese utilitarianism. In front of you is a small box containing disposable wooden chopsticks, there's a plastic tub of gari (the rather delicious pickled ginger), and a bottle of soy. After that as they say at Bingo it's "eyes down, look in, and on with the game".

The plates come round on the kaiten or conveyor and are coded by design rather than colour which could prove deceptive: A plates are £1.20, B plates are £1.80, and C plates are £2.40. All the usual sushi favourites are here, and the fish is particularly fresh and well presented. Maguri – tuna – is a B; Amaebi – sweet shrimp – is a C; Hotategai – scallops – is a C, and very sweet indeed. Futomaki – a Californian, cone-shaped roll with tuna – is a B. The wasabi/eye-watering factor, however, is a bit hit-or-miss. As soon as you wish for a bit more wasabi, you bite into something that makes you long for a bit less. As well as the sushi the conveyor parades some little bowls of hot dishes – one worth looking out for combines strips of fried fish skin with a savoury vegetable puree (it counts as an A). The bowl of miso soup is also an A. To drink there is everything from Oolong tea (£1.50) to Kirin beer (£2.60) through to Urku shochu – a particularly dangerous Japanese white spirit (£1.80).

Kulu Kulu also offers a range of set options which represent excellent value and take the strain off watching the conveyor belt. They include mixed sashimi (£10) and mixed tempura (£8.60). Look behind the bar and you may see a stack of cardboard cases which contain sake supplies. It is strange but true that one of the premium sakes is made in the Rocky Mountains – in America!

Leith's Soho

41 Beak St, W1 ☎ 0171 287 2057   ⊖ Oxford Circus

Mon–Sat noon–2.30pm & 6–11.30pm   All major credit cards

Printed at the top of the Leith's Soho menu there's a bold announcement: "If you'd like something simple please ask. If we have the ingredients in our kitchens, we'll only be too pleased to prepare it for you." What a strange suggestion – a restaurant which is prepared to consider what you the customer might like. Of course, when you come to eat here it would be very surprising indeed if you found nothing on the menu that tempted you – but you already feel good about it as you start to look down the card. This is a modern menu, which doffs its cap to the seasons, and to a neatly restrained extent at fashion: there may be spring rolls and couscous but the combinations of cuisine and ingredients never get too freaky. The decor is steady too, mushroom walls, and there's an attractive plain feel to everything. The cooking is accomplished.

You get off to a good start as the bread is very nice. On the starters menu is Leith's prawn cocktail (£9.75) – a nod to retro chic. If you like prawn cocktails you will like this dish. If not, then you won't be won over by larger prawns and better cocktail sauce. Better to try one of the soups. These tend to be serious – like a cream of cauliflower soup with girolle mushrooms and white truffle oil (£5.95). Or there may be a risotto – one rather successful one was duck confit and sage with bitter leaves (£8.50). Or a pasta, like fettucine with artichoke, wild mushrooms and parsley pesto (£6.50). Main courses are well presented and range from salmon and crab cake with a good tomato and caper butter sauce (£10.50), with plenty of perceptible crab running through a solid ball-type fishcake, through to a slow-roast shank of lamb with crushed new potatoes and olive oil jus (£13.50), or pan-roast brill with leeks, green beans and cod cream sauce (£17.50). Puddings are sound.

As befits an area with so many restaurants vying for your business, Leith's does a competitive set lunch priced at £16.50 for two courses, and £19.50 for three.

CENTRAL

Melati

21 Great Windmill St, W1 ☎ 0171 437 2745   ⊖ Piccadilly Circus

Mon–Sat noon–11.30pm   All major credit cards

Melati is a survivor: its walls carry certificates relating to awards won in the 1980s, and the window has a sticker proudly proclaiming that it is the 1990 Perrier "Restaurant of the Year". Thereafter the accolades seem to peter out – which is not altogether fair as the restaurant continues to serve up sound "Indonesian, Malaysian and Singaporean" food at prices which, if not cheap, are a good deal lower than many of the surrounding Thai establishments. It is not to be confused with the smaller – and unrelated – Melati around the corner in Peter Street.

When you've overcome the challenge set by the maze of doorways in the complex frontage, apply yourself to the starters. Satay here (three skewers each of chicken and beef – £6) are only so so, and can err on the side of overdone and dry – the peanut sauce is good but sweet. So go for something less familiar like pergedel daging (£2.95) – a large and filling "hamburger" with the meat on the inside and an overcoat of potato which comes with a sweet chilli sauce. Or there are lumpia (£2.95) a kind of senior spring roll, and some splendid soups – eight of them, all at £2.95. Some of the rice and noodle dishes are intended as plated meals and do not work well if you intend to share – but if you're after a quick bite, nasi goreng itimewa (£6.75) – fried rice with two skewers of satay, chicken, pickle and fried egg slices – is an imposing dish. Or there's char kway teow (£5.65) which is a plateful of broad noodles, garnished with salad ingredients and enlivened with chicken, fish cakes and shrimps. As part of a spread the simple beef curry kari daging (£5.75) is tender and served up with a tasty gravy. Sambal goreng terong (£4.25) is aubergines stewed in oil with chilli – a kind of red hot Iman Bayldi. The "plain" rice dishes designed as accompaniments are anything but. Coconut rice (£1.90) is worth a detour.

Great Windmill Street, although much cleaned up, is still a pretty sleazy corner of Soho, with doorways leading down to peepshows. Not a place to take your mum if you're easily embarrassed.

Mezzo

100 Wardour St, W1 ☎ 0171 314 4000	⊖ Piccadilly Circus
Mon–Thurs 12.30–3pm & 6pm–1am, Fri 12.30–3pm & 6pm–3am*,	
Sat 6pm–3am*, Sun noon–4pm & 6-11pm	All major credit cards
*Last food orders 1am except crustacea bar (open to 3am).	

When Sir Terence Conran unveiled Mezzo in 1995 people came to look at it just because it was there, and just because it was so . . . big. Nobody had opened a restaurant in London with space for 700 diners in decades and this was on a grand scale, encompassing a bar, an "informal" ground floor restaurant (Mezzonine), and a full-on restaurant (Mezzo) at the bottom of a sweeping staircase with a stage for performers. All of these areas have been busy ever since. This is not a place for a quiet night out. The restaurant tables are packed close and there's a fashionable mayhem of noise. But if you like a buzz with your food, Mezzo has few rivals – and the food, considering the huge numbers of covers, is pretty good.

The Mezzo menus send out different signals for each session. Thus you can have three courses of a short pre-theatre menu for £14; a set Sunday brunch menu of three courses for £15.50; a weekday two-course set lunch for £12.50 or three courses for £15.50. Or you can spend a good deal more ordeing à la carte. Whichever you go for, expect a mix of trad favourites and novel twists – so you may see lunch dishes like roast salmon with panzanella (£10.50) vying for attention with deep fried fish and chips with tartare sauce (£10.50). At dinner things get more elaborate and grandstand dishes make an appearance – pan-fried foie gras mango and ginger butter (£12); saddle of rabbit, black pudding and pancetta with sage jus (£15.00); or lobster Newburg with basil risotto (for two – £18.50 per person). Beware the cost of veg: a side order of "green vegetables" really shouldn't wight in at £3.25. And leave space for the puds, which are rich and greed provoking – chocolate Amaretto mousse with pistachio sauce (£5.50), or gingerbread pudding with brandy sauce and Jersey cream (£6.25).

Mezzo has live music on Weds–Sat evenings, mostly jazz, often great. You pay a £5 surcharge for a seat to watch the shows (from 10pm) – not bad value if that's what you're here for.

Pollo

20 Old Compton St, W1 ☎ 0171 734 5917   ⊖ Leicester Square

Daily noon–midnight   Cash or cheque

You won't find much haute cuisine at Pollo, but you do get great value for money. As at its neighbouring rival, Centrale, this is comfort food, Latin style – long on carbohydrate and short on frills. Sophistication is in short supply, too – the interior design begins and ends with the lino floors and tatty pictures – but no matter: devotees return time and again for the cheap platefuls of food and the friendly, prompt service. Diners are shoehorned into booths presided over by a formidable Italian mama who tips you the wink as to what you should order. Downstairs there's more space, but you still might end up sharing a table.

The spotlight of Pollo's lengthy menu falls on cheap, filling pasta in all its permutations. Tagliatelle, rigatoni, ravioli, pappardelle, tortelloni and fusilli are all available. Your choice is basically down to the pasta type, as most of them are offered with the same slection of sauces. The tortelloni salvia (£3.60), which comes with a wonderfully sagey butter sauce, is very good, as is the tagliatelle melanzana (£3.40), whose rich tomato sauce is boosted by melt-in-the-mouth aubergine. Meat courses are less successful; anchovies, for instance, are few and far between in the bistecca alla pizzaiola, steak in capers and anchovy sauce (£5.80). But vegetarians are very well catered for here. Meat free highlights include spaghetti aglio, olio e peperoncino (£3.30), a rich mix of garlic, olive oil and chilli. Meanwhile, a hearty plateful of gnocchi (£3.60) would curb even the most flamboyant appetite. Then there are pizzas, perhaps not the elegant wood-fired-oven type that are all the rage, but solid and substantial like the Regina (£3.90), a hammy, cheesy, mushroomy kind of experience. There is even a selection of risottos to choose from (all priced at £3.50). A carafe of house wine is a bargain at £5.95; and so are the puddings at £1.60. After a substantial hit of pasta, the imposing portion of tiramisu is a challenge for even the committed diner.

If Pollo isn't cheap enough as it is, it offers the same menu as take-away and then all the pasta dishes cost only £3.

Quo Vadis

26-29 Dean St, W1 ☎ 0171 437 9585	⊖ Leicester Square
Mon–Fri noon–2.30pm & 6–11.15pm, Sat 6–11.15pm,	
Sun 6-10.15pm	All major credit cards except Diners

Quo Vadis opened a couple of years ago amid a blaze of publicity. The presence of London's most fashionable chef-enfant terrible, Marco Pierre White, and backing from a Svengali of the restaurant world, Jimmy Lahoud was enough to guarantee that. Added to this top PR man Matthew Freud was a partner, and artist of the moment Damian Hirst lent not only his name but a good deal of his work by way of decoration. Smack in the buzzing heart of Soho, just when London was being described as the hippest town in the world . . . how could it not succeed?

Surprisingly, you soon cast away instinctive wariness about somewhere so tooth-grindingly trendy. The hipness of the restaurant does not take away from the excellence of its food and service. Walk in the door and you will be greeted by polite and friendly staff who will show you to your table in the surprisingly comfortable room. Peruse the menu which changes regularly and prepare to be wowed by the kitchen. A terrine of foie gras (£18.95) may seem expensive as a starter but it is faultlessly prepared, unctuously rich, and offset with a delicate sauternes jelly. By contrast carpaccio of salmon with oriental dressing (£8.50) is sweet, sharp and clean. A main course of John Dory (£14.95) served with a morel sabayon and broad beans is a daring preparation with ingredients which in other hands would have detracted from each other. A chicken pot au feu (£12.95) with brioche dumpling and vegetable broth is a hearty and surprisingly country-style dish for such a city based restaurant. Puddings (all £5.95), range from the classic lemon tart to a tarte Tatin of bananas.

Quo Vadis is not cheap but when you consider the quality of the food it does represent good value. And if your budget is tight, there is a pretty attractive set menu (choice of three starters, mains and sweets) offered at lunchtime and pre-theatre (6–6.45pm) at £14.95 for two courses, £17.95 for three.

Randall and Aubin

16 Brewer St, W1 ☎ 0171 287 4447   ⊖ Piccadilly Circus

Mon–Sat 12.30–11pm, Sun 4–10pm   All major credit cards

Formerly a butcher's, Randall & Aubin is now a self-proclaimed champagne-oyster bar, as its seafood counter and champagne buckets groaning with flowers suggest – but it's also a rotisserie, sandwich shop and charcouterie to boot. It's the oysters that draw you in, along with the 1900s shop decor, with its original white tiles, cleverly adapted with French and American diner touches – cool marble table tops and high stools that look characterful, if not exactly lending themselves to relaxed dining. But that's part of the plan: Randall's serves good food, speedily, for folk without a lot of time. In the summer months, the huge sash windows are opened up, making this a wonderfully airy place to eat – especially if you grab a seat by the window.

There's an extensive menu: an eclectic choice of starters roaming the globe from grilled haloumi and aubergine (£5.50) to warm, if rather oily, Thai fish cakes with chilli (£5.95), and Irish smoked salmon, blini, creme fraîche and caviar (£7.50). Main courses range from Caesar salad (£5.70) to duck confit with fennel relish, stewed plums and Chinese leaves (£12.50), Cumberland sausage with seed mustard (£6.50) to sirloin steak with sauce Béarnaise and pommes frites (£9.50). There are also some interesting accompaniments such as pommes Dauphinoise or couscous. If you don't mind crowds, drop in for a hot filled baguette (£5.50-£6.50) at lunch time: the salt beef, sauerkraut and gherkin (£6.50) is good. Still available in the evening, they provide an inexpensive yet satisfying meal. The fruits de mer section offers well-priced seafood, ranging from dressed crab at £7.50 to delicious, roasted scallops with caramelised fennel and chips (£12.50), and whole roast lobster, garlic butter and pommes frites (£22.50). Puddings are all at £3.95 and range from tarts and brulées to the more adventurous pear and caramel galette or chocolate truffle cake. Many of these dishes are on the inexpensive take-away menu which makes for exciting picnicking.

Look out for the ever-changing afternoon specials on offer between 3 and 6pm . . . for example a glass of champagne and six oysters for £10; or half a lobster and a glass of champagne for £12.

The Red Fort

77 Dean St, W1 ☎ 0171 437 2115   ⊖ Leicester Square/Tottenham Court Road

Daily noon–3pm & 5.30–11.30   All major credit cards

For a long while The Red Fort was the only Indian establishment in Soho serving authentic Indian food. It forged a reputation for regional dishes, accurate spicing and comfortable – even luxurious – setting, while the rest of Soho's curry houses proffered simple dishes to the crowd that stumbled in at closing time. Since then, many others have followed in the path of aspirational and regional Indian cuisine and getting a table at The Red Fort is no longer difficult – nor costly if you take up the buffet lunch offer at £10 per person (available until 2.30pm). But the buffet is really a pale shadow of the Red Fort's freshly cooked dishes and it's best to splash out, going with enough friends to have a good tour of the menu.

Start with the adraki chop (£5.95) which is based on a traditional dish using a ginger marinade. Or tamatar ka shorba (£4.95) which is a creamy soup of tomatoes, with other vegetables and curry leaves. Or lahsuni tikka (£4.95) – a chicken tikka, by any other name. Then move on to some specials. Guinea fowl Madeira (£15.95) is an original dish, braised in a stock made with cloves, cardamom and chillies. Sula salmon (£13.95) is based on a Rajasthani dish where salmon is cooked as a kebab. Then there is gosht kohlapuri (£8.95), a regional dish of lamb braised in gravy with whole chillies. Or murga rara (£8.95) which is a Punjabi dish of chicken cooked with black cardamom. Or Kerala konju curry (£8.95) which is a traditional hot prawn curry with coconut. Just occasionally, however, the highly commendable search for new dishes over-reaches itself – and methi kangaroo (£14.95) is perhaps one such occasion.

If you look up from your table it's likely that you will recognise various exalted diners from the House of Commons or the Lords – don't rub your eyes and blame it on the spicy food. The proprietor here has had the good sense to found a Parliamentary Privilege Club which gives special terms to over 1,000 MPs and Peers. It seems that the honourable members are just as keen as everyone else both on going for a curry and on claiming a discount.

Richard Corrigan at The Lindsay House

21 Romilly St, W1 ☎ 0171 439 0450 ⊖ Leicester Square

Mon–Fri 12.30–2pm & 6–11pm, Sat 6–11pm | All major credit cards

Even amongst chefs – who are not usually regarded as overly calm and level-headed people – Richard Corrigan is regarded as something of a wild man. He has arrived at this eponymous restaurant in Soho after a lengthy voyage of discovery which has taken him from Michelin stardom in Fulham to a restaurant in the City, via a spell bringing haute cuisine to a dog track in the East End! At the Lindsay House he seems to have found his niche. The restaurant is split up into a series of small rooms, the service is attentive, and the food is very good indeed. The menus are uncomplicated and change regularly to keep in step with what is available at the market. Dinner means a choice of six starters, six main courses and six puddings and costs £34, while at lunch the line up is five, five and five – priced at £21 for three courses. As a way to see for yourself why all that fuss is made about fine dining, lunch at Richard Corrigan's is a genuine bargain.

Only a fool would predict what dishes Richard Corrigan will have on his menu tomorrow, but you can be sure that they will combine unusual flavour combinations with verve and style. Starters surprise – like beetroot bavarois with cured sea bass and caviar – or are reassuringly delicious like a veloute of langoustine and roasted artichoke. Or there are combinations that seem familiar but come with a twist, like home-cured herrings with potato and bacon salad. Main courses follow the same ground rules, so you might be offered a confit of duck leg, cabbage and pork sausage, or a lasagne of home-salted cod and lobster pistou. The puddings soar towards dessert lover's heaven with such as chocolate fondant with clementine sorbet, or roast banana with rum raisin and caramel jus. The wine list is extensive and expensive.

If there is one thing that marks out the cuisine at the Lindsay House, it is Corrigan's love affair with offal. Sweetbreads, kidneys, and tongue all find their way onto the menu, in dishes which perfectly illustrate his deft touch with hearty flavours.

Soho Soho

11–13 Frith St, W1 ☎ 0171 494 3491   ⊖ Leicester Square/Tottenham Court Rd

Mon–Fri noon–2.30pm & 6–11.30pm, Sat 6–11.30pm   All major credit cards

Upstairs at Soho Soho all is cool and calm, the softly bleached tones acting as a palliative for those whose nerves have been battered by the storm of Frith Street below. And then there's the silence: there's not a squeak of background music, and the only tinkling you'll hear is the sound of chinking glasses. The tables are spaced out so that it's virtually impossible to eavesdrop, and the waiters glide around like guardian angels. Even the wines are caged, as if to inhibit any potential outbreaks of rowdiness. This seductive, soporific ambience lulls you into a sense of tranquil bonhomie and steadies your nerves, while outside Soho rages unabated. A full meal here doesn't come cheap, and a romantic dinner for two can easily set you back £100. But as well as the ambience to commend it, Soho Soho offers sound cooking in a vaguely Provencal style. There may be no culinary fireworks, but it is a comfortable and comforting venue.

From the starters listed the mussels cooked with white wine, tomatoes, fennel and herbs (£5.95) may seem an overly cautious choice, but it is a lovely dish, delicately flavoured. Or try the warm salad of cep mushrooms, truffles, new potatoes, roasted fennel and pancetta bacon (£6.25), a good combination of tastes. For a main course, turn to the menu's costliest item – rack of lamb with a herb and nut crust and potato gratin (£16.65). Well-cooked, and very tender. For something a bit earthier and more rustic in tone, there's wild boar stewed in red wine sauce with sautéed chestnuts and Swiss chard (£13.95). A selection of vegetables costs a further (£1.35).

Of the nine ice creams, Soho Soho en Ete (£4.80), a zingy glass of lemon sorbet, vodka, melon, pineapple and kiwi – with cherries on top – is among the lightest. The other desserts are even more indulgent, like the lemon tart with a raspberry coulis and creme fraiche (£4). Best of all, though, is the assiette de dégustation (£6.50), a selection of all the house sweets.

Soho Spice

124–126 Wardour St, W1 ☎ 0171 434 0808   ⊖ Leicester Square

Mon–Thurs 11.30am–12.30am, Fri & Sat 11.30am–3am,

Sun 12.30pm–10.30pm   All major credit cards

Soho Spice is the new face of Indian restaurants. It's large – seating 100 in the restaurant and 40 in the bar – and takes bookings only for parties of six or more. It's busy, with loud music and late opening at the weekends. The decor is based around a riot of colour. And it is very, very successful. Which must be mainly down to the food, which is an equally large step from curry house fare – the main menu featuring contemporary Indian cuisine and a regularly changing special menu showcasing dishes from particular regions. What's more when you order a main course it comes on a thali – with pulao rice, naan, dal and seasonal vegetables of the day – which makes ordering simple and paying less painful.

On the main menu there are starters like spiced prawns (£5.25) – prawns rolled in vermicelli and then deep fried so that each is presented within its own little haystack. Or try barwaan baigan (£3.75) – aubergine slices stuffed with cheese and deep fried. Or there's chicken chaat (£3.75) in a suitably peppery sauce, or khumb kabab (£3.75) – chilli-hot pan-fried wild mushrooms and root vegetables. Main courses represent good value, given their accompaniments. Good choices are the tandoori lamb chops (£9.95), trout (£10.95), or select'n veg (£12.50) or the Kandhari pasanda (£9.95) – lamb with onions and almonds in a saffron gravy. Desserts (all £2.95) offer a nice range of Kulfi (Indian ice cream) and that sweet comfort food, gulab jamun – a steamed dumpling in syrup.

The regional menu makes more exciting reading but it does change – so on one visit it may be the foods of Rajasthan and the next dishes from Bengal. As an example, when the chosen region was the North West Frontier there were starters like gilafi kebab – lamb dumplings with pearl onions and button mushrooms; and makai palak – fritters made with chick peas and spinach. Mains were the celebrated murg malai Peshwari – a kebab made with chicken breast and cheese; and Kandhari pasanda – lamb with onions tomatoes almonds and saffron. The regional menu is a three course meal for £15.95. This is a bargain.

Spiga

84–86 Wardour St, W1 ☎ 0171 734 3444	⊖ Tottenham Court Rd
Mon & Tues noon–3pm & 6–11pm, Wed–Sat noon–3pm & 6pm–midnight,	
Sun noon–11pm	Amex, Mastercard, Visa

Spiga has an impeccable pedigree. It comes from the same stable as
Aubergine, L'Oranger and Zafferano and has that piece of kit that identi-
fies an Italian restaurant as serious – a wood-fired oven. However,
despite such low-tech modernity, you don't need to pay a king's ransom
to eat here, nor do you have to dress up. This is a pleasantly casual affair,
the atmosphere is lively – sometimes the music is too lively – and the
look is cool. Spiga may have cut the prices but they haven't cut corners:
the tableware is the latest in Italian chic.

Menus change monthly, with occasional daily specials, but there's a definite pattern. Starters will get you in the mood. The buffalo mozzarella
with baked aubergine and oregano (£6.00) is deliciously creamy. Or try
something like the thinly sliced raw beef with rocket and parmesan
(£6.00), or the pan-fried prawns with saffron vinaigrette and potatoes
(£5.50); both are good. But the home-made pasta course is where it's at
and what's good is that, like the starters, most pasta dishes come in large
or small portions. Think Italian and enjoy an extra course, such as the
ravioli stuffed with potato and mint (£7.00) – surprisingly light. Then
consider a Spiga pizza – thin crust, crispy and the size of a dustbin lid,
lovingly smothered with the likes of stracchino cheese and cured
smoked ham (£6.50) or bresaola, rocket and parmesan (£7.50); they are
very filling. Or for something a bit more unusual try the bruschetta
with carrots and tuna roe (£9.50). Alternatively, main courses offer up
char-grilled and pan-fried dishes, like spring leg of lamb with peppers
and aubergine (£12.50) or salmon with spinach and balsamic vinegar
(£12.50), both excellent. And if you aren't already full, the pudding
section is well worth a look, too. They are all £4.50 and highlights
include a wickedly indulgent lemon and mascarpone tart and an excellent tiramisu.

Full marks will be awarded to the person who can work out what the
large loofah-like objects are hanging on the walls. Wafer-thin slices of
giant ciabatta, perhaps?

£25–£50

The Sugar Club

21 Warwick Street, W1 ☎ 0171 437 7776   ⊖ Piccadilly Circus

Daily noon–3pm & 6–11pm   All major credit cards

After a triumphant spell just off the Portobello Road, the Sugar Club moved to these elegant premises in Soho. Much larger. Much more stylish. Much more blonde wood. But still the same passionate, eclectic, and well-executed food. The food here typifies all that is best about the irreverent attitudes of Antipodean chefs – ingredients from all over the world are brought together with panache. A starter may be composed from careful selection of top quality Spanish foods, and then a main course may have Japanese ingredients as its mainspring. Done well (and it is done well at the Sugar Club), this approach is terrifically exciting, and the menu here changes regularly to reflect seasons and markets.

Some of the finest starters at the Sugar Club are assemblies, rather as if you had helped yourself to a plateful of goodies from a fabulously well-stocked fridge. Leon Iberico chorizo with piquillo peppers, guindilla chillies, Garroxta, Marcona almonds and caper berries on toasted sourdough (£8.20): what a thoughtful selection – rich cheese, soft peppers, crunchy almonds, chewy bread. Or there are simpler arrays like grilled scallops with sweet chilli sauce and creme fraiche (£8.60), or sashimi of Iki Jimi red snapper with black bean and ginger salsa (£8.60). Exotic fish from the other side of the world will certainly feature amongst the main courses, perhaps pan-fried Pink Sea Bream, marinated in shiso leaves, on new potatoes with baby spinach, red cabbage, galangal and truffle salad (£17) – a stunning piece of fish, teamed with a splendid array of tastes and textures. Or try roast lamb chump on herbed couscous with grilled leeks and harissa (£14.40). Vegetarians are well served by a lemon grass, ginger and Parmesan risotto cake with spinach and sweet potato coconut curry, flat bread and coconut chutney (£11.50). And the desserts make even the most ardent puddingist roll over in ecstasy – terrine of coffee–chocolate chip and Bailey's ice creams, and mango sorbet (£5). Aaaah!

For recreation watch elegant and fashionably-thin diners as they taste a forkful of the mustard mash which they ordered as a side dish, and then another, and . . .

Teatro

93–107 Shaftesbury Ave, W1 ☎ 0171 494 3040	⊖ Leicester Square.
Mon–Fri noon–3pm & 6–11.45pm, Sat 6–11.45pm	All major credit cards

Appropriately, eating at Teatro is something of a theatrical experience. You pass by a rather intimidating, and industrial, street-level entrance and up metal stairs to the reception, where the atmosphere starts to feel a touch friendlier, then it's along the curved corridor, past the members' bar, into the open and elegant dining room. This restaurant has celebrity owners (Lee Chapman and Leslie Ash), the input of a celebrity chef (Gordon Ramsey), and celebrity customers (not only hiding in the members' bar but plying the knife and fork in the main arena). Given all these potential complications, the food is remarkably good and not too extravagantly priced. Indeed there's a two-course prix fixe lunch for £15 (plus an iniquitous £1.50 cover charge), or you can have three courses for £18 (£19.50 when marked up).

The menu changes seasonally and offers a mix of old favourites and updated classics, thus you might find starters like chilled green gazpacho (£4.25), or Teatro salad Nicoise (£7.25), or mushroom and Swiss chard risotto (£7.50). There is even a pleasing extravagance which takes the plat du jour approach to new heights – foie gras du jour (£11.25). Main courses are more or less equally divided between fish and meat, so seared John Dory fillets may be teamed with grilled leeks, Parmesan and balsamic vinegar (£14.50); or a grilled fillet of sea trout may come with langoustine cous cous and shellfish dressing (£15.25). The meat orientated dishes also have novel accompanimentss: the confit of Barbary duck, is served with frisée, sauté ratte potatoes and shallots (£14.50); and the grilled calves' liver, spring onion mash and pepper jus (£15.25). The standard of cooking is high and the standard of presentation higher still. The wine list runs from an eminently reasonable French Chardonnay at £11 to a rather more pocket challenging 1969 Petrus at £325.

Desserts (all £5.50) bring off the difficult trick of being both elegant and satisfying at the same time. The espresso sorbet with chocolate granita and biscotti is unreservedly good: one taste makes you feel like a celebrity.

£6–£12

The Toucan

19 Carlisle St, W1 ☎ 0171 437 4123   ⊖ Leicester Square /Tottenham Court Road

Mon–Sat 11am–11pm   Mastercard, Visa (over £10)

When they opened the Toucan the proprietors' first priority was to approach Guinness and ask if they could become a stockist. They explained that they wanted to open a small bar aimed single-mindedly at the drinking public, just like the ones they had enjoyed so much in Dublin. Guinness replied that, providing they could shift two barrels a week, they'd be happy to put them on the list. Neither party imagined that within a couple of years the weekly order would be more like thirty barrels a week! It's an impressive intake but then the Toucan is a terrific place, serving home-made, very cheap, very wholesome, and very filling food, along with all that Guinness. Its success has meant expansion from the original hot, dark, cellar premises to include the ground floor – and a Toucan Two at 94 Wimpole Street, W1.

Start with 6 Galway Bay oysters (£5), or the vegetable soup with bread (£1.50). Go on to Guinness pie and champ (£4.50) – champ is a kind of super-charged Irish mashed potato, with best butter playing a leading role alongside the spring onions, or try the large bowl of Irish stew with bread (£3.50). Then there are some novelty items – you can have chilli and champ (£3.95) or ratatouille and champ (£3). Although these two dishes are also available with rice for the less adventurous diner. The JPs (jacket potatoes) come with various fillings and there's an array of sandwiches. The food service is subject to one important proviso – there are times when the Toucan becomes so packed with people that you can scarcely lift a pint for the press – then all attempts at serving are abandoned. At quieter times – 11.30am, perhaps – the gastronaut will also enjoy the smoked salmon plate (£5), great value.

Of course, if things have got out of hand, you could spend a happy evening at Toucan without actually eating. As some Irish sage once remarked, "There's eating and drinking in a pint of Guinness." And if it's a chaser you're after, then be aware that the Toucan also makes a feature of Irish whiskies – including the exotic and stratospherically expensive Middleton Rare. If you have to ask how much it costs you cannot afford it.

Vasco and Piero's Pavilion

15 Poland St, W1 ☎ 0171 437 8774	⊖ Oxford Circus
Mon–Fri noon–3pm & 2–11pm	All major credit cards

Very much a family-run restaurant, the Pavilion has been a Soho fixture for the past twenty years. But there's nothing old or institutional about the cooking or decor. Vasco himself cooks for his regulars and Paul his son supervises front of house. The establishment has long been a favourite with diners who appreciate the best family cooking, fairly simple, and with top class ingredients. Customers include the famous and the Pavilion's modern yet comfortable atmosphere guarantees anonymity. Dishes are biased towards Umbrian cuisine.

There's an à la carte menu at lunchtime only but the basic deal at the Pavilion is that you choose either two courses for £14.50 or three for £17.50. With its quality, freshness of ingredients and detail this makes Vasco and Piero's exceptional value. A starter of carpaccio of roast pink lamb, rucola and parmesan is a moreish and clever variation on traditional carpaccio. Duck salad, mixed leaves, mostarda di Cremona is plate-wipingly good with the duck shreds crispy yet moist. Pastas (all home-made) are excellent, too, particularly the spaghettini with fresh tomato and basil – perfectly cooked and with a sauce that is prepared from fresh ingredients and tastes like it. For carnivores, however, there is nothing to beat the calves' liver with fresh sage – paper thin liver that literally melts in the mouth with just a hint of sage, and crisp vegetables that have been cooked at the moment rather than re-heated. Puddings continue the quality story. A panna cotta that is gelatinously creamy, a praline semi-freddo that is rich and soft as well as being crunchy, and a torta della Nonna that reveals buttery sponge pastry, custard and flavours that remind you of a cross between bread and butter pudding and ambrosia. There is a good selection of the less usual Italian wines and good Italian pudding wines too.

Whilst Vasco and Piero's Pavilion is closed at weekends, a select mailing list is informed of special Italian gastronomy evenings on selected Saturdays. If you like exceptionally good Italian home cooking then a quick phone call gets you on the list. Ask for Paul Matteucci.

£8–£25

Yo!Sushi

52/53 Poland St, W1 ☎ 0171 287 0443   ⊖ Oxford Circus/Piccadilly Circus

Daily noon–midnight   All major credit cards

When Yo!Sushi burst upon the scene it was to the accompaniment of fanfares and a tidal wave of publicity. This was an event beyond just another kaiten (or conveyor belt) sushi bar. Robot sushi makers, robot drinks trolleys, video screens – not many restaurants credit "sponsors" like ANA, Sony and Honda. In amongst all this there is some food, and though purists may shudder, it's more consistent than the hype would have you suspect.

Plates are marked in lime (£1.50), blue (£2), purple (£2.50), orange (£3), and pink (£3.50): when satiated you call for a plate count, and your bill is prepared. You sit at the counter with a little waiters' station in front of you – there's gari (pickled ginger), and there's soy, and wasabi, little dishes and a forest of wooden chopsticks. Sapporo beer costs £2.80, a small warm sake £2.80. Unlimited Japanese tea is £1. You're ready to begin. YoSushi! claim to serve more than 100 sushis so be leisurely and watch the belt – and if in doubt ask. The nigiri sushi range from fruit and crabstick (both £1.50) to salmon, French bean and mackerel (at £2); on to tuna, prawn and squid (at £2.50) and so on up to yellow tail and fatty tuna which carry the warning that they are "as available" and a pink price tag of £3.50. There are about 20 different maki rolls (with vegetarians well catered for) and at all prices. There are seven different sashimi and seven different gunkan all of which command orange and pink prices. As do the handrolls – which are nori funnels, Californian style. Yo!Sushi does call for some restraint and mental arithmetic as the tower of brightly badged empty plates building up in front of you can end up costing more than you expected.

Yo!Sushi are at the forefront of restaurant merchandising and no age group is safe. There are Yo!Sushi t-shirts, fleeces, coats, and even baby-grows. You can even buy badged mousemats and as you'd expect Yo!Sushi are on the Web – www.yosushi.co.uk You'll find other branches of Yo!Sushi within the Fifth Floor Food Market at Harvey Nichols (Knightsbridge) and in Selfridges on Oxford Street.

Zilli Fish

36–40 Brewer St, W1 ☎ 0171 734 8649	⊖ Piccadilly Circus
Mon– Sat noon–11.30pm	All major credit cards

Bright, brittle and brash, Zilli Fish is a companion to Aldo Zilli's other Soho venues, Signor Zilli and Zilli Bar (in Dean Street). In a hectic, young atmosphere it serves a modern Italianate fish menu to London's media workers and the rest of the Soho crowd. Tables are close and everything is conducted at a racy pace. Not ideal for a secret conversation or for plighting your troth unless you want the whole place to cheer you on.

Seared king scallops on rosemary sticks with baby spinach salad and vintage balsamic dressing (£8.50) are huge, tender and sweet, each scallop speared on the rosemary giving just enough of the herb flavour. Wild rucola with Parmesan and sun dried tomatoes (£7.50) is sharp, simple, and fruity with the tomato oil. Escalope of salmon on spinach with tarragon sauce (£14.50) is excellent, the salmon crisp on the outside, the spinach not over cooked, the tarragon sauce refreshingly astringent. Chargrilled swordfish served on Caesar salad (£15.50) proves an excellent flavour alliance. Hot fish and cool salad is a difficult combination, but one Zilli Fish does well. Dishes like breadcrumbed cod and chips (£10.50) and whole lobster with garlic butter and herbs with chips (£17.50) demonstrate restraint too. Whilst the list is predominately fish, there are daily specials with some modern Italian vegetarian and meat items, from risotto with wild and field mushroom with white truffle oil (£9.90) to roast suckling pig with apple sauce (£16.00) Puddings include an espresso creme brulée (£6). Coffee lovers take note, with its soft creamy interior it's like eating double cream cappuccino. Very moreish. Strawberries with limoncello liqueur and pistachio ice cream (£6) is a refreshing way to enhance the fruit.

Aldo Zilli has built up a popularity in Soho which guarantees that his bar and restaurants are almost always packed. Zilli Fish is good food, but also good fun. In keeping with so many restaurants nowadays, Signor Zilli is quite happy to give away his secrets. Signed copies of Aldo's latest book are always available in the restaurant.

South Kensington

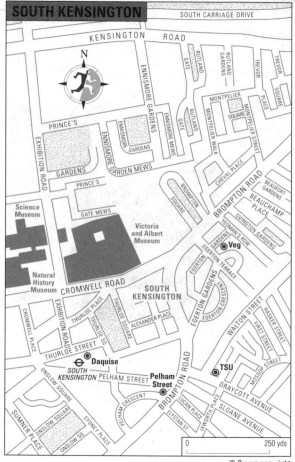

SOUTH KENSINGTON

SOUTH CARRIAGE DRIVE

KENSINGTON ROAD

N

PRINCE'S

EXHIBITION ROAD

ENNISMORE GARDENS

ENNISMORE MEWS

ENNISMORE GARDENS

ENNISMORE GARDEN MEWS

PRINCE'S

GARDENS

GATE MEWS

RUTLAND GATE

RUTLAND GARDENS

RUTLAND GATE

MONTPELIER WALK

MONTPELIER SQUARE

MONTPELIER STREET

TREVOR PLACE

TREVOR SQUARE

CHEVAL PLACE

BEAUFORT GARDENS

BROMPTON SQUARE

BROMPTON ROAD

BEAUCHAMP PLACE

OVINGTON GARDENS

Science Museum

Victoria and Albert Museum

YEOMAN'S ROW

EGERTON GARDENS

EGERTON TERRACE

● Veg

Natural History Museum

CROMWELL ROAD

SOUTH KENSINGTON

EGERTON GARDENS

EGERTON CRESCENT

WALTON STREET

HASKER STREET

CROMWELL PLACE

EXHIBITION ROAD

THURLOE PLACE

THURLOE PLACE

THURLOE SQUARE

ALEXANDER PLACE

FIRST STREET

THURLOE STREET

MOSSOP STREET

⊖ Daquise

SOUTH KENSINGTON

PELHAM STREET

Pelham Street

BROMPTON ROAD

TSU

ONSLOW SQUARE

PELHAM CRESCENT

DRAYCOTT AVENUE

SUMNER PLACE

ONSLOW SQUARE

SYDNEY PLACE

LUCAN PLACE

WORTH PLACE

SLOANE AVENUE

ONSLOW SQ.

ELYSTAN ST.

0   250 yds

© Crown copyright

174

CENTRAL

Daquise

20 Thurloe St, SW7 ☎ 0171 589 6117	⊖ South Kensington
Mon–Fri 11.30am–11pm, Sat & Sun 10am–11pm	Mastercard, Visa

Daquise is more old-fashioned than you could possibly imagine. High ceilings, murky lighting, oilcloth table covers, charming service, elderly customers: the full monty. During the day it serves coffee, tea and cakes to all-comers, breaking off at lunch time and in the evening to dispense Polish home cooking, Tatra Zwiecka beer, and shot glasses of various vodkas. Several novels have been completed here by penniless writers seeking somewhere warm to scribble – buying a cup of coffee here gets you a full ration of patience from the management. The food is genuine. Portions are serious, and prices are very reasonable.

Start with Ukrainian barszcz (£2.50), rich and red. Or there's a starter prosaically called herring and potato (£5.80): this brings a plate with a small Alp of thinly sliced red onion, some warm, plain boiled potatoes, a large dollop of sour cream and two amazing herring fillets. Thick cut, pleasantly salty, and with a luxurious smooth texture. Memorable. Go on to the kasanka (£6.00) a large buckwheat sausage (a cousin to black pudding) made using natural skins. Or for the fearless there is giant golonka (£8.80), a marinated pork knuckle which has been boiled and is served with horseradish sauce. Also welcome back an old friend, Vienna Schnitzel with a fried egg on top (£9.50). Particularly appealing, but only available in season, is the dish of forest mushrooms stewed and served with boiled potatoes (£6.50). And it is hard not to be tempted into ordering an extra dish of potato pancakes (£5.50), which are large, flat and crispy and come with sour cream or apple sauce. The other side dish options are a strange sauerkraut (£1.50), served cold and very mild; cucumbers in brine (£1); and kasza (£1.60) the omnipresent buckwheat. For purists there's also that classic Central European dish, boiled trout (£8.50).

Every now and then a speculator proposes to knock down the entire block of Thurloe Street, behind South Ken station, and redevelop it. On such occasions the locals and regulars band together to defend the Daquise. Thankfully, so far they have always won.

Pelham Street

93 Pelham St, SW7 ☎ 0171 584 4788   ⊖ South Kensington

Mon–Sat noon–3pm & 7–11pm, Sun noon–3pm   All major credit cards

This elegant restaurant sits opposite the Michelin Building at the heart of what estate agents call Brompton Cross. And like the American car rental company whose slogan was "We're number two, we try harder", it seems to shout defiance at the bigger gastro-guns all around. The cooking at Pelham Street is accomplished and presentation of the dishes original. Prices are not cheap but represent pretty good value, while the service is "keen". The dining room is modern and well set up, although tending towards the dark side of atmospheric. The menu changes regularly and features some good-value set meals – a dinner menu at £12.95 for three courses, and a three-course Sunday brunch for £14.95.

More than most candidates, the food here is "modern British", pulling in the usual suspects: Thai spicing, Italian ingredients, French techniques. The eight different starters may range from the classic – Swiss cheese soufflé with garlic cream sauce (£5.50) – through warm salad of seared scallops, dill and mussel jus (£7), thickly sliced, large scallops, precisely cooked and very sweet – to terrine of confit pork and foie gras with a warm boudin noir tart (£7), a grand combination of textures and flavours with a delicate little black pudding tart complementing the cold terrine. Main courses also range widely: from salmon, to sturgeon, to red mullet, to lobster and then chicken, lamb and beef. The salmon may come in a nage with saffron and tomato chives (£13.50). The steamed corn-fed chicken with leeks bacon and white wine cream sauce (£13.50) is a very good dish indeed, the chicken providing a perfect foil for the creamy leeks. And for the unreconstructed carnivore how about fillet of beef with girolles and fondant potatoes (£17.50)?

The presentation of each dish is most important here and the desserts are particularly good in this respect. Look out for pistachio creme brulée, with dark chocolate sorbet (£5.50) – the brulée fills the bottom of a soup plate to a depth of about 1cm and the chocolate sorbet sits proudly in a biscuit cup on top. It tastes very good, too, well bruléed and with an intense flavour of pistachios.

Tsu

118 Draycott Avenue, SW3 ☎ 0171 584 5522	⊖ South Kensington
Mon–Sat noon–11pm, Sun noon–10pm	All major credit cards

At first glance you would think that Tsu is an ultra-fashionable, conveyor-belt sushi bar, very like the Yo!Sushi chain (see p.170) – and you'd nearly be right. Where Tsu differs is on the plate. To appropriate a little of television's finest dialogue – "It's sushi, Jim . . . but not as we know it". And not really as the Japanese would know it, either. Traditionalists would certainly recognise some of the little plates whizzing round here, but others would invoke shudders of horror or delight depending on the shudderer's open-mindedness. It could, in fact, be reported as a sighting of "Nouvelle sushi": no bad thing in its way, so long as you're not looking for classic sushi qualities. Mind you, if you are moderate with the sake and you don't order too many of the day's most special sushi you shouldn't get a classically high bill either.

Those people who eat with their eyes will get on famously at Tsu. Spinach goma-ae (£2.25) is a fat wheel of spinach in a sea of tahini with a jaunty vegetable-crisp hat. Salmon sushi (£2.25) comes with its edges dressed with black sesame seeds. Then there's prawn sushi (£2.50); vegetarian maki (£2.25); tuna sushi (£2.95); and cured salmon sashimi (£3.25). There are a handful of daily specials, too, which could range all the way from sweet omelette to soup. Some of the plates are fairy portions of more complex dishes – chicken soba noodles (£3.25) is a miniature meal, as is King prawn wakame (£3.25). As with all conveyor belt missions, where they count the plates to devise your bill, you would do well to keep track of numbers – otherwise a momentary fad, for a couple of extra smoked salmon and avocado maki rolls (£2.25), say, can carry quite an escalation of the bill.

There's a great sake list here, though servings are not overgenerous. The "small" sized flask is small and the "standard" sized flask is pretty small as well. Try Jouzen (£7.95 and £14.25) served ice cold and pleasantly dry. Or Tsukasa – ice cold (£8.85 and £15.25). Or Sawandi from the mountains of Okutama – ice cold (£6.45 and £11.75).

SOUTH KENSINGTON Ⓥ CHINESE/VEGETARIAN

Veg

8 Egerton Gardens Mews, SW3 ☎ 0171 584 7007	⊖ South Kensington

Mon–Sat noon–2.30pm & 6–11.15pm, Sun noon–2.30pm & 6–11pm	Cash only

Veg is a no-smoking, vegetarian Chinese restaurant tucked away in a quiet little mews in South Kensington. Down some fairly unprepossessing steps and you find yourself in a dark and homely sort of place. The walls are rag-rolled yellow, the table cloths are red and some of the furnishings are a little scuffed around the edges. For a tête-à-tête, book one of the two cubby holes at the back. During the week the place is fairly quiet, and the staff are helpful and charming.

If you're the sort of person who has found themselves longing for vegetarian crispy duck, you need look no further: here it is on the menu. But even the most confirmed flesh-eater is likely to be pleasantly surprised by the taste sensations on offer here. The cook serves up imaginative 'assimilations' of chicken, fish and meat-based dishes, and everything tastes light and fresh. Good starters include a veggie dim sum (£3.50) – five fat soya dumplings filled with cabbage, Chinese leaf, Chinese mushroom, fresh ginger and water chestnut. You could also kick off with sesame 'prawns' (£4.50) or the spring rolls (£3.50), which are crispy and golden, or the yin yang seaweeds (£3), marinated in ginger, onions and sesame. The sunsing aromatic crispy veg duck (£7.50) makes for a good mid-course. The 'duck' is strips of tofu and looks a bit like an omelette: roll it up in a pancake and it works wonderfully – very light and succulent. For mains, go for the meatier-sounding dishes. Crispy chilli veg beef (£6.50) is spicy and delicious (the 'beef' here is strips of soya). Also good is squid in black bean sauce (£5.90) – very squid-like creations in fact made of rice. Then there's veg chicken and cashew nuts (£5.90), with the soya 'chicken' marinated in soya sauce and mixed with golden cashew nuts. For pudding, try the mango sorbet (£3.50) – refreshing and quite luxurious.

Don't ask for the wine list – there isn't one. But you can have a glass of sound house white or red for £3. And there's Chinese beer on offer – Tsing-tao at £3 a bottle.

CENTRAL

Victoria & Westminster

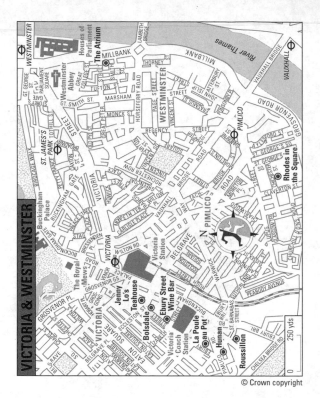

VICTORIA & WESTMINSTER

© Crown copyright

The Atrium

4 Millbank, SW1 ☎ 0171 233 0032	⊖ Westminster
Mon–Fri noon–3pm & 6–10pm	All major credit cards

4 Millbank is a large and forbidding office block and there is little sign, apart from a tatty notice board on one side of the huge doors, that there is a restaurant hidden within. Once you have entered the building, signage is still minimal but those in the know – and we're talking a lot of MPs, Lords and politicos here in Westminster-land – walk behind the giant sized reception desk and down a rather dramatic staircase into the light-well. There, surrounded by giant plants and with daylight streaming down from a rooftop skylight high above, is The Atrium, a potentially fabulous space that somehow contrives to look a little like the set of an old soap opera – El Dorado, to be precise. If this appeals, and you like Antony Worrall Thompson style cooking – the chef designed the menu a few years back but has since moved on – The Atrium is a pretty good choice for this rather barren neighbourhood.

The Antony Worrall Thompson menu remains largely intact, both in format and in content. Among the starters, pan-fried field mushrooms in filo with melted brie (£6.75) uses the filo as a tart base and the melted brie as a crust, with a generous filling of herby mushrooms and is an excellent dish. The Thai chicken and soba noodle soup (£3.95) manages to be at once raw with chilli and on the thin side. The strong point of the "deep fried cod fillets, chunky chips, dill pickle and caper relish" (£11.25) – fish and chips with tartare sauce, in other words – is the precisely cooked fish, while a millefeuille of herb crusted salmon (£12.95) comes with good pastry and a nice saffron butter sauce. Puddings (all at £4.50) are sweet and simple. Try Baileys Irish Cream cheesecake or a mango Pavlova.

The Atrium is just two minutes' walk from Parliament Square and well within the Division Bell radius, so it comes as no surprise to find MPs and Lords in abundance. There's a huge range of wines by the glass which means lobbyists and the parliamentary press can occupy their afternoons, as well as a decent full bottle list so that The Lords can while away theirs.

£15–£50

Boisdale

15 Ecclestone St, SW1 ☎ 0171 730 6922   ⊖ Victoria

Mon–Fri noon–2.30pm & 7–10.30pm. Sat 7–10.30pm   All major credit cards

Boisdale is owned by Ranald Macdonald, who is next in line to be the Chief of Claranald, and if that information gives you a premonition of what the restaurant is like you are probably thinking along the right lines. This is a very Scottish place, strong on hospitality, and with a befuddlingly large range of rare malt whiskies. Fresh produce – correction, fresh Scottish produce – rules wherever possible, and it is no wonder that the clubby atmosphere and reliable cooking makes this a haven of choice for local businessmen – who are also likely to be found in the ultra-Scottish back bar, home to a formidable malt whisky collection.

There are three Boisdale menus, one of which is admirably simple – for £12.90 diners choosing the "haggis menu" can enjoy leek and potato soup with truffle oil, followed by roast MacSween's haggis with mash and neeps. By way of glossary: MacSween is a famous haggis maker and haggis devotees spend hours arguing whether MacSween of Edinburgh or Lindsay Grieve of Hawick makes the ultimate haggis. Either way, it is still sheeps' innards and oatmeal, a sound peasant dish. Neeps is the Scottish term for what everyone else calls swede. If that sounds a bit hardcore for your tastes, the "Boisdale" set menu offers a choice of six starters and seven mains for £16.90. Starters range from salad of smoked Highland venison and pistachio, to the slightly less Scottish tagliatelle with fines herbes pesto. Main courses veer from Scotch salmon, through smoked haddock and cod fishcakes, to Scotch sirloin steak Béarnaise with pommes frites.

The à la carte includes a good many luxury ingredients; as well as foie gras, and oysters, there's spiced potted lobster, rocket and warm toasted brioche (£7.90). Commendably, the mains feature "fresh fish of the day" and "fresh offal of the day". Plus roast fillet of Highland venison with bitter chocolate sauce (£19.90); or fillet of Aberdeen Angus beef roast with a stilton sauce (£19.90). Sensibly enough, you can mix and match the carte with any of these menus. And there is an impressive and extensive wine list, paving the way for an after dinner malt.

Ebury Street Wine Bar

139 Ebury St, SW1 ☎ 0171 730 5447   ⊖ Victoria

Daily noon–3pm & 6–10.30pm (Sun 10pm)   All major credit cards

Ebury Street may call itself a wine bar, but the food is not the kind of stuff that springs to mind when wine bars are mentioned. The regulars – from those swingeingly expensive houses in Belgravia and the offices around Victoria – come for a bottle of decent claret in the front area or to eat at the restaurant out the back. They overlook the rather chintzy decor and the closely packed tables, they will even overlook the somewhat uncomfortable chairs. They pitch up for the food, and to enjoy the rather old-fashioned but undeniably friendly service.

The food is well-cooked, adventurous, and always interesting in an almost radical counterpoint to the decor. The menu changes regularly, but starters might include wild greens and herb fritter, yoghurt dressing (£4.50); or a black pudding ham and bread terrine with tomato relish (£4.50); or, at the top of the price range, marinated venison fillet, artichoke and Parmesan salad (£9). Rare meats like kangaroo, ostrich and emu all make the occasional guest appearance, and there is a magnificent "plate of savouries" (£6.75) offering a complete tour round such tastes and textures. Then there's a menu section devoted to salads – in tune with the local customers – offering the likes of pear, peas and blue cheese with toasted walnuts (£4.50); or the laconically named parsley salad (£4). The main courses are also inventive: grilled rare tuna ginger and sesame rice (£13.50); goat's cheese stuffed artichoke with rice raisins and lemon (£9.50); or "Perigord" sausages with mash and braised onions (£9.75). These are very good dishes indeed, made with well-chosen ingredients and well-presented.

Desserts are equally moody – such as figs poached in "Shiraz" (£5). And a dish that has a generation of chefs arguing over who invented it first – the Mars bar spring roll (£4) aka the deep fried Mars bar, which was probably (it's worth stressing the probably as there's a good deal of debate amongst chefs, claim and counter claim) first devised some years ago by Josh Hampton, who's in charge of the kitchens here.

Hunan

51 Pimlico Rd, SW1 ☎ 0171 730 5712   ⊖ Sloane Square

Mon–Sat noon–2.30pm & 6–11.30pm   All major credit cards

The Hunan is the domain of Mr Peng. As you venture into his restaurant you put yourself into his hands, to do with what he will. It is rather like being trapped in a 1930s B movie. You order the boiled dumplings ... and the griddle fried-lettuce wrapped dumplings turn up, "because you will like them more". And most likely you will. Probably at least ninety percent of Mr Peng's regular customers have given up the unequal struggle, submitting themselves to the "feast" – a multi-course extravaganza varied according to the maestro's whims and the vagaries of the market that might include pigeon soup, or a dish of cold marinated octopus, or goose . . . This fine food and attentive service is matched by the Hunan's elegant surroundings – but be warned the prices are Pimlico rather than Chinatown.

If you want to defy Mr Peng and act knowledgeable, you could actually try asking for the griddle-fried lettuce-wrapped dumplings (£4.80), which are exceedingly delicious; or the platter of assorted hot appetisers (£12 for two) – a triumph, with crispy bits of chicken, stuffed mushrooms, deep fried green beans in peppery chilli, spare ribs, crispy seaweed and other goodies, all piping hot and strewn higgeldy piggeldy across the plate in a delicious lucky dip. Alternatively, try the camphorwood-and-tea-smoked duck (£17.50 for a half, £32 for a whole): once again this dish is as interpreted by Mr P, so as well as a south-western Chinese version of crispy duck (with pancakes etcetera) there's a sweet and sourish sauce (apparently his regulars felt that it was "too dry" without). Other standouts include spicey-rich beef in Hunan sauce (£5.50), and stir fried squid "any style" (£6.50), which is accurately cooked.

However, for all but the strongest wills, resistance is useless and you'll probably end up with what is described on the menu as "Hunan's special leave-it-to-us feast – minimum two persons, from £23 a head. We recommend those not familiar with Hunan cuisine to leave it to the chef Mr Peng to prepare for you his favourite and unusual dishes". Quite so.

Jenny Lo's Teahouse

14 Eccleston St, SW1 ☎ 0171 259 0399 ⊖ Victoria

Mon–Fri 11.30am–3pm & 6–10pm,

Sat noon–3pm & 6–10pm   Cash or cheque only

Jenny Lo's Teahouse in Victoria is the complete opposite of the typically stuffy, over-designed Chinese restaurants: it is bright, bare and utilitarian – and somehow stylish and fashionable, too. From the blocks of bright colours and refectory tables to the artifice of framing the emergency exit sign like a picture over the door, this is a comfortable – if somewhat smart – place to eat. And that just about sums up the food too. Service makes you think that you're in the politest cafeteria in the world and the prices don't spoil the illusion. The food is freshly cooked and generally delicious, although portion sizes and seasoning can vary.

The menu is divided into three main sections: soup noodles; wok noodles and rice dishes. Take your pick and then add some "side dishes". The chilli beef soup hofun (£6.95) is a good choice. A large bowl full of delicate, clear, chilli-spiked broth which is then bulked out with yards of slippery hofun – ribbon noodles like thin tagliatelle – plus slivers of beef and fresh coriander. The black bean seafood noodles (£6.95) is an altogether richer and more solid affair, made from egg noodles with prawn, mussels, squid and peppers. Rice dishes range from long cooked pork and chestnuts (£5.95) to gong bao chicken with pine nuts (£6.95), and the simpler Sichuan aubergine (£5.50). The side dishes are great fun. There are good spare ribs (£2.75); onion cakes (£2) – Beijing street food, a flat, griddled bread laced with spring onions and served with a dipping sauce; or guo tie (£3.95) which are pan-cooked dumplings and can be filled with either vegetables or pork.

Try the tea here, too. As well as offering different Chinese and herbal teas, Jenny Lo has enlisted the help of herbalist Dr Xu who has blended two special therapeutic teas. Long life tea (£1.65) – described as "a warming tonic to boost your energy" – and cleansing tea (£1.65) – "a light tea for strengthening the liver and kidneys," which tastes . . . light, refreshing and faintly gingery, and is doubtless cleansing, too.

La Poule au Pot

231 Ebury St, SW1 ☎ 0171 730 7763	⊖ Sloane Square
Daily 12.30–2.30pm & 7–11.15pm (Sun until 10.30pm)	All major credit cards

You are in trouble at the Poule au Pot if you don't understand some French. It is unreservedly a bastion of France in England and has been for over three decades. What's more several of the staff have worked here for most of that time, and the restaurant itself has hardly changed at all, with huge dried flower baskets and a comfortable rustic atmosphere. The character of the place, however, is very different at lunch and dinner. The wide windows make it light at lunch, but by night candle light ensures La Poule is a favourite for romantic assignations.

A small dish of crudites in herb vinaigrette is set down as a bonne bouche. Different fresh breads come in huge chunks. The menu is deceptive as there are usually more additional fresh daily specials than on the menu itself. The patient waiters struggle to remember them all and answer your questions about the dishes. As a starter, les escargots (£6.75) delivers classic French authenticity with plenty of garlic and herbs. La soupe de poisson (£6.50) is not the commonly-served thick soup but a refined clear broth with chunks of sole, scallop, prawns and mussels. A main course of le bifteck frites (£13.75) brings a perfectly cooked, French cut, steak with red hot chips. Ask for mustard and you get Dijon. Le gigot aux flageolets (£13.00) is pink and tender with beans that are well flavoured and not over cooked. The pudding menu features standards like crême brulée (£4.50), huge, served in a rustic dish, and classically good, and banane à sa façon (£4.50), lightly cooked with a caramel rum sauce and a scoop of ice cream, very rich. There is also a selection of good pudding wines and a·glass of Monbazillac (£2.95) makes an excellent companion to the richness of the desserts.

If you are a francophile, you'll find all your favourites, from French onion soup to boeuf bourguignon, from quiche to cassoulet. And such is the atmosphere of the place that, for a few hours at least, you forget that you are in England.

Rhodes in the Square

Dolphin Square, Chichester St, SW1 ☎ 0171 798 6767	⊖ Pimlico
Sun–Fri noon–2.30pm, Mon–Sat 7–10pm	All major credit cards

Get him away from all that television hype, and Gary Rhodes is a very good cook. In his restaurants there is a real respect for genuine British ingredients, and the resulting dishes are always good to eat. It's hard to understand why restaurant critics tend to rank his food below that of his more French inspired peers. Rhodes in the Square is the place to make up you mind – a large, plush dining room with dark blue velvet and gleaming metalwork, how you'd imagine first class to have been on some swish 1950s ocean liner. This is not a cheap restaurant though you could maybe console yourself by thinking of all the bond dealers tucking in at Gary's City restaurant – they're paying a bit more. And, as always seems to be the case, this quality of food is most wallet friendly at lunch: two courses for £16.50 (£21.50 on Sundays) and three courses for £19.50 is not so bad.

Starters are simple and stunning. Fillet of smoked haddock glazed with Welsh rarebit on a tomato and chive salad (£9.80) is a wholly successful dish. Pigeon faggot on a potato cake with mustard cabbage (£8.20) is earthy and rich, a grand combination of tastes and textures. But the one starter every self respecting hedonist must try is the lobster omelette Thermidor (£9) – presented in its own little pan, this is a melting omelette with a rich sauce and chunks of lobster. Main courses are equally rich and reassuring, grilled calves liver with sweet seared carrots and soubise creamed potato (£19.50) will please liver lovers. The glazed duck with bitter orange (£19.80) is the most grown up duck à l'orange in town. For pudding you should pass up the famous Rhodes bread and butter pudding – though it is reliable as ever – and try the prune and Armagnac black cap rice pudding instead; or opt for the intriguing Jaffa cake pudding. All puds are £6.80.

It's an unkind blow, but the vegetables here are all priced at £3 and come as extras, which would be fair if you could legitimately ignore them. Unfortunately the mashed potatoes are very good indeed.

VICTORIA & WESTMINSTER ⑩ MODERN FRENCH

Roussillon

16 St Barnabas St, SW1 ☎ 0171 730 5550　　　　　⊖ Sloane Square

Mon–Sat noon–2pm & 7–10.15pm　　　　　All major credit cards

The people who run Roussillon are both brave and single-minded. When they opened a bar and restaurant called Marabel's on this site in 1998 they installed a very bright and very young, French chef called Alexis Gauthier. Things did not go exactly as they wished and within six months they had closed it down. It re-opened almost immediately as Roussillon, without the bar but with Alexis and most of the dishes that had won him acclaim still in place. If anything, the Roussillon menu reads even better than its predecessor with dishes combining strong flavours and making good use of fine English ingredients. Why is the use of fine local produce both a natural thing for French chefs and a strategy that is rarely adopted by their British counterparts? To see the advantages of being season- and market-driven try the terrific value set lunch at Roussillon – £13.50 for two courses and £16 for three. Or splash out on one or other of the five course showing-off menus – the all-vegetarian "Garden Menu" (£24) and the "Autumn Menu" (£35).

The menu changes four times a year but you can expect to start with good soups and risottos – perhaps the particularly good pumpkin risotto with veal jus (£7.50) – or maybe a salad of blue Bembridge lobster, with Gloucestershire purple potatoes (£12.50). Main courses are divided rather coyly into "the sea" and "the land", with four dishes to a section. Fish dishes may include braised halibut, leek, confit tomatoes and purple basil cooked together in a pot (£14), or pan fried seabass on its crunchy skin with chick pea beignets (£16). The beef is Aberdeen Angus. The veal gets a commendable subtitle – "élevé sous la mère" – and has much more flavour than factory farmed veal. Puddings are suitably extravagant. All cost £5.50, while £9 brings you a pixie portion of everything.

At the bottom of the menu is written: "Our home-made breads are all prepared with organic yeast from wild apple, grape and white wine". Now that would be the height of pretension were it not for the fact that they are very delicious breads indeed.

Waterloo &
The South Bank

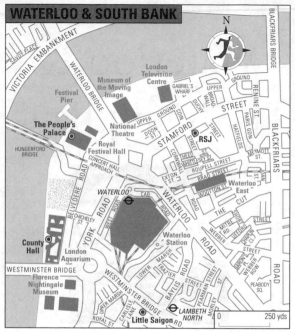

WATERLOO & SOUTH BANK

N

VICTORIA EMBANKMENT

BLACKFRIARS BRIDGE

SAVOY PLACE

WATERLOO BRIDGE

Festival Pier

Museum of the Moving Image

London Television Centre

GABRIEL'S WHARF

GROUND WALL

RENNIE ST

PARIS GDN

UPPER GROUND

STAMFORD STREET

BLACKFRIARS

The People's Palace

National Theatre

UPPER DOON ST.

GROUND

DUCHY STREET

RSJ

MEYMOTT ST.

HUNGERFORD BRIDGE

Royal Festival Hall

CONCERT HALL APPROACH

CORNWALL RD

WHITTLESEY ST.

THEED

ROUPELL STREET

HATFIELDS

BLACKFRIARS RD

BELVEDERE ROAD

EXTON ST.

BRAD STREET

Waterloo East

WATERLOO

CAB

WOOTTON ST.

WATERLOO

ROAD

THE CUT

MITRE RD.

STREET

UFFORD

WEBBER

STREET

County Hall

YORK ROAD

BECHLEY ST.

WEST SQUARE

Waterloo Station

ROAD

STREET

WEBBER ROW

BARONS PL.

WEBBER

London Aquarium

MARSH

PEABODY SQ.

WESTMINSTER BRIDGE

Florence Nightingale Museum

WESTMINSTER BRIDGE

LOWER MARSH

FRAZIER STREET

BAYLIS ROAD

PEARMAN STREET

MORLEY

ROAD

UPPER MARSH

CARLISLE LANE

ROYAL ST.

Little Saigon

LAMBETH NORTH

0   250 yds

© Crown copyright

The County Hall

Queens Walk, SE1 ☎ 0171 902 8000   ⊖ Westminster

Mon–Sat 6.30am–11pm, Sun 7am–10.30pm   All major credit cards

What a handsome room – and what a view to go with it, the river and the Houses of Parliament laid out before you. This restaurant lies behind the curved section of County Hall, London's old seat of government, now a Marriott Hotel – a Grade One building, painstakingly restored. To reach it, either walk over Westminster bridge, or get your taxi to drop you off beside the statue of the lion at the south end of the Queens Walk embankment. Down some steps and the restaurant entrance is just along the riverside walk on your right. This is another of those restaurants which is within a hotel but still asserts its own identity. The benefit for customers is that it opens at 6.30am for breakfast (the full works, £13.95); serves lunch until the pre-theatre meals take over; and then dinner until 11pm. It's a full day.

The food is ambitious, elegantly presented, and cooked with some flair. Starters range from the classic – Caesar salad (£5.50) – right through to the complex – spiced veal rump, girolles, roquette and Parmesan galette (£9.50). Midway between these poles are such dishes as jellied rabbit with prunes and hazelnuts (£8) – an elegant terrine in which the moisture from the jelly offsets any tendency for the rabbit to be dry – and a velouté of corn with crab and ginger ravioli (£6.50). Main courses range from roast cod, pommes forestière, capers and anchovies (£12.50) to a dish of sweetbreads, haricots blanc, saffron and chorizo (£13.50) – a good combination of tastes, rich and satisfying. There is also a particularly fine risotto – Gorgonzola, pea and pine nut risotto (£12.50) – well cooked, and presenting a splendid range of textures.

The set menu represents decent value at two courses for £16.50 and three courses for £19.50. Choosing from the dishes on offer you could end up with cracked wheat, mint, apricots and grilled sardines, followed by corn-fed chicken, tagliolini and roast onions, followed by banana Tatin with vanilla ice cream . . . and then perhaps, stumble back over the bridge to get on with the business of Government!

Little Saigon

139 Westminster Bridge Rd, SE1 ☎ 0171 207 9747	⊖ Waterloo
Mon–Fri noon–3pm & 5.30–11.30pm, Sat & Sun 5.30–11.30pm	Mastercard, Visa

After ten years running a restaurant in Frith Street, the Long family had had enough. Soho rents were hitting the stratosphere and the lease was up for renewal. So Mr Long and his wife opened Little Saigon, just behind Waterloo Station, a homely restaurant serving good Vietnamese food from a comprehensive menu. Stick to the Vietnamese dishes and take the opportunity to get to grips with Vietnamese spring rolls – both the crispy deep-fried kind and the "crystal" variety. The latter are round discs of rice pastry like giant, translucent communion wafers which you soak in a bowl of hot water until pliable and then roll around a filling made up of fresh saladly items, interesting sauces, and slivers of meat grilled on a portable barbecue.

Run amok with the starters. Sugarcane prawns (2 for £3.20) are large prawn "fishcakes" impaled on a strip of sugar cane and grilled. Vietnamese Imperial spring rolls (£2.60) are of the crisply fried variety, but to practice your wrapping they are served cut into chunks and with lettuce leaves to roll them up in. Also good is the strangely resilient Vietnamese grilled squid cake (£3.50). Topping the bill are crystal spring rolls (4 for £2.60); these are "pre-rolled" – delicate pancakes, thin enough to read through, filled with prawns and fresh herbs – quite delicious. It's as if each of the starters comes with its own special dipping sauce, and the table is soon littered with an array of little saucers – look out for the extra-sweet white plum sauce and the extra-hot brown chilli oil. For mains, ha noi grilled chicken with honey (£5.30); special Saigon prawn curry (£6.40); and the house special fried crispy noodles (£4.80) can all be recommended.

Do try and master the "specialities" – an intermediate course where you soak your own crystal pancakes and wrap up crunchy salads and meats barbecued at the table. Soak the pancakes too long and they stick to the plate, not long enough and they won't wrap. Grilled slices of barbecued beef (£12), and grilled slices of pork in garlic sauce (£12), are both splendid.

The People's Palace

Level Three, Royal Festival Hall, South Bank, SE1 ☎ 0171 928 9999   ⊖ Waterloo

Daily noon–3pm & 5.30–11pm   All major credit cards

When this restaurant first opened there were tales of diners who had finished their dinner late being locked into the Festival Hall and of others wandering for ages between levels. It is still not the most straightforward venue to find but it has it's own entrance now, opposite Hungerford Bridge. And it's worth persevering. The dining room looks out over the Thames and has a fabulous view. The restaurant is very large and runs with the kind of competence you would hope for considering that it is within the South Bank Centre and many of the customers are either pre- or post-concert which makes timings crucial. The food is well presented and accurately cooked, there may not be too many culinary high jinks but the menu is composed of well-balanced, satisfying dishes at reasonable prices. Add the view, some pretty sound service, a child-friendly policy (they're nice to kids, and provide high chairs and children's menus), and it makes an attractive package.

The bargains at the People's Palace are its fixed price menus. Lunch menus are available daily: £12.50 for two courses, £17.25 for three (£15.50 and £20.25 on Sundays). Pre-theatre is £15.50 and £20.25. For this, you choose from a good spread of daily selections. You might have confit of duck terrine with spiced oranges and Balsamic, followed by fillet of plaice with spinach, watercress and beurre noisette. On the à la carte you'll find starters like plum tomato tian and cream cheese (£5.50); warm buttered artichoke with truffled leeks (£7.50); ham hock and vegetable terrine (£5.75); and a particularly good char-grilled squid with spiced aubergine salad (£6.75). Mains run from roast salmon with piperade, bacon and sage (£13.50); to rump of lamb, roast tomato and grilled vegetables; and a well cooked dish of seared scallops with braised fennel and dill (£16.75) – a very good portion and accurately cooked so that they are sweet but not rubbery.

When visiting it's worth figuring the Festival Hall's concert programme into your plans. On a popular night, you'll need to book for pre- or post-concert timings. When you call to make a reservation ask the receptionist who will know just what's on and when it finishes.

WATERLOO & THE SOUTH BANK ⑪ FRENCH

RSJ

13a Coin Street, SE1 ☎ 0171 928 4554 ⊖ Waterloo

Mon–Fri noon–2.30pm & 5.30–11pm, Sat 5.30–11pm | All major credit cards

Rolled Steel Joist may seem a curious name for a restaurant, but it is appropriate as there is an RSJ holding up the first floor if you really want to see it. What's more interesting about RSJ is that it's owned and run by a man with a passion for the wines of the Loire. Nigel Wilkinson has compiled his list mainly from wines produced in this region and it features dozens of lesser known Loire reds and whites – wines which clearly deserve a wider following. Notes about recent vintages both interest and educate and each wine is well described so that you know what you're going to get.

The menu is based on classical French, but with a light touch and some very innovative combinations. Tomato sorbet with gazpacho coulis (£5.25) is densely flavoured but refreshing. Lobster and halibut sausage with asparagus and Pernod sauce (£7.25) is delicate and fine with a sauce that demands extra bread to use up. Leg of rabbit stuffed with squid, peppers and tomato confit, with pearl barley risotto and fondant potato, tarragon jus gras (£13.25), is a mixture of tastes that blends very well indeed. Halibut wrapped in potato with baby spinach, carrots and asparagus, red wine sauce and garlic velouté (13.75) is equally well judged, the dark deep sauce working well with the light and fresh fish. Puddings are adventurous, too, and the choice includes champagne mouse with a peach jelly (£4.75), assiette of liqueured creme brulées (£5.25), terrine of three fruit sorbets with fresh berries and lime syrup (£4.25), and chocoholic platter (£5.95). This last brings you five different ways to enjoy the cocoa bean from white chocolate sorbet to fresh raspberry and chocolate tart. Worth saving room for.

RSJ is situated close to the South Bank Centre's cinema, concert halls and theatres and is clearly enjoyed by arts patrons. It appears to cater for both an early and a late crowd and it's not rushed in any way. Always a good sign.

CENTRAL

CITY & EAST

Brick Lane
& Spitalfields

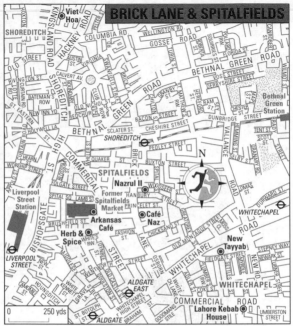

BRICK LANE & SPITALFIELDS

© Crown copyright

Arkansas Café

Unit 12, Old Spitalfields Market, E1 ☎ 0171 377 6999	⊖ Liverpool Street
Mon–Fri & Sun noon–3pm; evening meals by arrangement	Mastercard, Visa

As you approach the Arkansas Café the glow from its steel-pit barbecue invites you in. Bubba Helberg and his wife Sarah claim that they serve the best barbecue food this side of the pond, and they may just be right, for they are regularly in demand as the US Embassy's barbecue experts (they also open the Arkansas Café here for evening parties of twelve or more). Their food is fresh and simple, and Bubba only uses the highest quality ingredients, choosing his own steaks individually from Smithfield market to make sure that the meat is marbled enough for tenderness. The provenance of his lamb and sausages is listed for all to see. He marinates and smokes his own beef brisket and ribs, his recipe for the latter winning him a soul food award back home. His secret home-made barbecue sauce is on every table, but he won't sell the recipe to anyone.

The Arkansas ambience is spartan – simple scrubbed tables, canvas chairs and paper plates do not intrude on the quality food. There are no starters, so you just get stuck in. Any of the steaks – Irish rib eye (£8.00), American T Bone (£12.50) – are good bets, barbecued with Bubba's special sauce and served with potato salad and a vegetable salad. Cornfed French chicken (£6.00) is tender and full of flavour, and a side order of chilli (50p) provides a spicy sauce-like accompaniment. USA beef brisket (£9.00) is meltingly tender and smoky. Most of the other dishes on the menu come as platters or as sandwiches, the latter including choices like duck breast sandwich (£4.90), free range pork rib sandwich (£3.50), and, of course, hot dog (£2.75). Puddings (all at £2) include New York style cheesecake and New Orleans pecan pie. They are as sweet and solid as they should be. The wine list is short and simple, but the beer list is long, with a large selection of unusual beers including, in the USA section, Anchor Steam (£2.30) and Apollo craft beer (£3.00).

The diners at Arkansas usually include some expatriate Americans getting a refill of barbecue authenticity, which has to be a good sign. Eat in and take an extra order home.

BRICK LANE & SPITALFIELDS ① INDIAN

Café Naz

46 Brick Lane, E1 ☎ 0171 247 0234   ⊖ Aldgate East

Mon–Fri & Sun noon–3pm & 6–11pm, Sat 6–11pm   All major credit cards

"Contemporary Bangladeshi Cuisine" is what it says on the menu here and generally speaking that is what you get. You will find some of the Indian restaurant standards – a list of "baltis" and, of course, chicken tikka masala – but lots of less familiar and more interesting dishes as well. And the decor is certainly contemporary: bright colours, modern furniture and a gleaming open kitchen putting the chefs on display. Prices are low – having thirty curry restaurants within a stone's throw makes for serious competition – and service is attentive.

Start with the boti kebab (£2.45) – either lamb or chicken cooked in the tandoor and served with a plateful of fresh salad. Or there's adrok chop (£3.95), small pieces of lamb chop which have been marinated in ginger and garlic before getting the frazzling treatment in the clay oven. Fish cutlet (£2.95) brings pieces of a Bangladeshi fish called the Ayre, deep fried and then served with fried onions. These would be called goujons if they weren't quite so large and didn't contain a good many large bones. For main courses, the dhansak (£4.50) comes with either mutton or chicken and is very tasty – it's cooked with lentils and turns out hot, sweet and sour at once. Or how about palak gosht (£4.50), a simple dish of lamb and spinach? Then there's gosht kata masalla (£5.95), a splendid, rich lamb curry; lemon grass chicken (£4.95) made with lime and cream; or chicken sour masalla (£4.95) which is chicken in a very tomatoey tomato sauce sharpened with a little vinegar. Naan bread (£1) is freshly cooked, and wiped with butter – delicious. And there are a range of vegetable dishes (all £2.25) – niramish, mutter aloo, bindi, sag aloo, brinjal. Very sound and very good value.

There's an attractive weekday option of a buffet lunch – a chance to go through the card for £6.95, sampling curries, tandoori chicken, rice dishes and a constant flow of hot naans. If you want to do this feast some justice pick a day when all is serene – a nap after such a lunch is almost obligatory.

CITY & EAST

£6–£15

Herb & Spice

11A Whites Row, E1 ☎ 0171 247 4050	⊖ Aldgate East
Mon–Fri 11.30am–2.30pm & 5.30–11.30pm	Amex, Mastercard, Visa

Do not let the tiny, rather gloomy dining room and huge swags of plastic flowers put you off this treasure of a curry house on Whites Row, which is a small street just off Commercial Street and tucked in behind Spitalfields. A loyal clientele from the City means that to secure one of the 22 seats you'll probably have to book! The menu here includes all the curry classics, plus one or two dishes you may not have spotted before, but what sets Herb & Spice apart from the pack is that although the food is freshly-cooked and well-prepared, the prices are still reasonable. When the food arrives it will surprise you: it's on the hot side with plenty of chilli and bold fresh flavours.

It's not often that the popadoms grab your attention. They do here. Fresh, light, crisp popadoms (55p each) are accompanied by equally good home-made chutneys – fresh and perky chopped cucumber with coriander leaf, and a hot, yellowy-orange, tamarind-soured yoghurt. The kebabs make an excellent starter: murgi tikka (£2.55) is chicken, very well cooked; shami kebab (£2.25) is minced meat with fresh herbs; gosht tikka (£2.55) tender lamb cubes. For a main course you might try the unusual murgi akhani (£5.75), a dish of chicken cooked with saffron rice and served with a good, if rather hot, vegetable curry. Or there's bhuna gosht (£3.95), a model of its type – a rich, well-seasoned lamb curry with whole black peppercorns and shards of cassia bark. Murgi rezalla (£4.95) is chicken tikka in sauce: much hotter – and with more vegetables – than its cousin the chicken tikka massalla. The breads are good here, too; there is a nice nan (£1.45), or why not try the shabzi paratha (£1.55), a thin, crisp wholemeal paratha stuffed with vegetables?

For a real tongue-trampler, try the dall shamber (£2.15), a dish of lentils and mixed vegetables which is often overlooked in favour of that popular garlicky favourite tarka dall. Traditionally served hot, sweet, and sour, at Herb & Spice dall shamber comes up hot (very hot with the almost chemical bite of large amounts of chilli) and very very sweet indeed. Not for the faint-hearted

Lahore Kebab House

2 Umberstone St, E1 ☎ 0171 481 9737   ⊖ Whitechapel.

Daily noon–midnight   Cash or cheque only

The Lahore was for years a bit of cherished secret amongst curry lovers – a nondescript, indeed downbeat-looking, kebab house that served excellent and very cheap fare. Recently, however, there have been a lot of changes. Gone are the sticky carpet and the bleak Formica table tops; there are no longer sacks of gram flour stacked inside the door; even the theatre of the open kitchen has been tamed. Thankfully the food is still good and spicy, the prices are still low, and the service brusque enough to disabuse you of any thoughts that the round marquetry-topped tables and new shop front have taken the Lahore upmarket. What they do here, they do very well indeed – and if you need any further proof look at all the other similarly named places which have sprung up all over town.

There is no menu at the Lahore – merely a board on the wall listing half a dozen dishes, and during your meal rotis (50p) tend to arrive unordered, your waiter watching your eating habits and bringing bread as and when he sees fit. For starters, the kebabs are stand-outs. Seekhe kebab (50p), Mutton tikka (£2), and Chicken tikka (£2) are all very fresh, very hot, and very good, served with a yoghurt and mint dipping sauce. The biryanis are also splendid – meat or chicken (£5), well spiced and with the rice taking on all the rich flavours. The karahi meat and karahi chicken (£4.50 for a regular portion or £9 for a huge one) are simple and uncomplicated dishes with tender meat in a rich gravy. The dal tarka (£3.50) is made from whole yellow split peas, while sag aloo (£3.50) brings potatoes in a rich and oily spinach purée. Among the more esoteric offerings is paya (£4.50 only available here on Fridays), a dish made from long-stewed sheep's feet thought by some to be the hallmark of any genuine Pakistani restaurant. Much more palatable, if you want a very Lahore kind of delicacy, is the home-made kheer (£2). This is a special kind of rice pudding with cardamom.

This Lahore is unlicensed but happy for customers to bring their own beer or wine – and there's a nearby off-licence ready to oblige. You will certainly need some compliment to the generally hot food here – though note that alcohol isn't the best cooling agent. For that you need to order a lassi.

Nazrul II

49 Hanbury St, E1 ☎ 0171 247 5656   ⊖ Aldgate East/Liverpool Street

Daily noon–2.30pm & 5.30pm–midnight (12.30am Fri & Sat)   Cash or cheque only

Nazrul II is a prodigious, almost industrial curry house. Its individual curries are not over sophisticated but what's on offer is astonishing. In an attempt to cover all of the angles the establishment bills itself as both a Tandoori and Balti restaurant, and then its menu goes on to offer everything else besides. You can choose from nearly fifty different baltis, ten tandoori dishes, a dozen chef's specials, six bhuna, six kinds of rogon josh, six each of dupiaza, madras, vindaloo, kurma, dhanzak, a dozen biryanis, side dishes, sundries, appetisers. The dining room is almost as long as the menu with tables stretching away far into the interior and they are usually packed with hordes of students and large parties of local office workers, all drawn by the magnet of the amazing value. Service is brisk and battle scarred. Ignore the decor.

The Nazrul is a bargain any day of the week and startlingly so on Sunday, when they offer a five-course spread at an impressive £5.95 per person. But ordering off the regular menu, prices are little higher. Starters run the gamut from an onion bhazi (£1.20) to a rather good garlic chicken (£2.30) which is chicken tikka served in an admirably garlicky sauce and with a good deal of salad. For a main course, you might order a meat bhuna (£2.95), which brings a good-sized portion of tender meat in a no-frills sauce with plenty of onion and a welcome kick of fresh coriander. The fifty baltis are mainly priced between £3.10 and £4.40 and equally dependable. Strange touches of sophistication pierce the gloom here – a very welcome wedge of lemon in a stainless steel squeezer comes with the garlic chicken – and how odd to be offered one of those "hot towels" as you finish the last of your chicken curry and rice and call for a bill totalling perhaps as little as £3.50. The breads are fresh and excellent, from the 60p chapati to the soaring extravagance of a Peshwari nan (£1.50). And if you really want to indulge yourself, try the chef's recommended set meal for two – papadoms, onion bhaji, sheek kebab, chicken tikka masalla, meat rogon, sag aloo, pillau rice, and nan – eight items (£14.80)!

Remember to "bring-your-own" beer along – no Nazrul II regular would be seen dining without a carrier bag of lager beside the table – and a good appetite.

£3–£10

New Tayyab

83 Fieldgate St, E1 ☎ 0171 247 9543   ⊖ Whitechapel/Aldgate East

Daily 5pm–midnight   Cash or Cheque only

Since the Tayyab first opened in 1974 it has continued to spread out: after the initial cafe, there was the sweetshop, and now that the New Tayyab occupies what was once the pub there is an uninterrupted sweep of Tayyab enterprises on the north side of Fieldgate Street. Inside the New Tayyab (which is open only in the evenings) it looks as if someone has made a determined assault on the "greatest number of chairs in the smallest possible space" record. The food is straightforward Pakistani fare: good, freshly cooked, served without pretension, and at prices lower than you would believe possible – something that is much appreciated by the hordes of impoverished students who make up a large proportion of the customers. Service is rough and ready. This is not a place to umm and err over the menu.

The simpler dishes are terrific, particularly the five pieces of chicken tikka served on an iron sizzle dish, with a small plate of salady things and a medium fierce, sharp, chilli dipping sauce (£2). They do the same thing with mutton (also £2). Four lamb chops – albeit thin ones – cost £2.50. Sheekh kebab are 70p each. Shami kebab 60p each. Round fluffy nan breads 50p each. The Karahi dishes are simple and tasty: karahi chicken – chicken in a rich sauce – costs £3.50 a normal and £6 for a large portion. Karahi batera (quails) – £4 and £8. Karahi aloo gosht (£3) is lamb with potatoes in a rich sauce heavily flavoured with bay leaves. Or there's karahi mixed vegetables (£2.50). There is also a list of daily specials which range from paya on Monday (the dreaded and gluey sheep's feet stew – £3.50), to the splendidly named meat pillo (£3.20) every Wednesday – chunks of mutton slow-cooked in rice, rich, satisfying, and seeded with whole peppercorns for bite.

The Tayyab is strictly bring your own bottle if you want alcohol; indeed to judge by its own drinks offerings it is something of a shrine to Coca Cola. But whether you're going for beer or coke, make sure you try the Tayyab lassi, a yoghurt drink served in a pint beer glass; sweet or salted £1.20, mango or banana £2.

Taja

199a Whitechapel Rd, E1 ☎ 0171 247 3866	⊖ Whitechapel
Mon–Thurs & Sun 11am–11pm, Fri & Sat 11am–11.30pm	Mastercard, Visa

Taja's exterior of black and white vertical stripes certainly jolts the eye. Venture in and you find a dining area accommodating 60 covers over two floors. The counter is ultra-modern in stainless steel and the seating is made from thick slabs of honey coloured wood. From the ground floor large windows look out onto the hurly burly of passing traffic – inches away. The food tastes very fresh, and is markedly cheap. So far so good. By now those in the know will have recognised that the restaurant in question is a converted toilet in the Whitechapel Road. And as if that is not novelty enough, Taja is a genuine rarity – a thoroughly modern Bangladeshi restaurant. The menu is both enlightened and lightened, as a host of vegetarian dishes balance the traditional favourites. Prices are low and standards are high.

Start with that great test of a tandoor chef, chicken tikka (£1.95): at Taja you get half a dozen sizeable chunks of chicken, cooked perfectly (not a hint of dryness), with the obligatory salad garnish (a waste of time) and a yellowish "mint sauce". Or try chotpoti (£1.95), described on the menu as "green peas and potatoes with spices, served with a tamarind chutney – high in protein". Move on to a biryani – mixed vegetable, lamb, chicken or prawn – all at £4.49; a good-sized portion comes with a dish of really splendid vegetable curry by way of added lubrication. There are also a host of curry house favourites. Chicken bhuna (£3.49) is an outstanding choice; a really fresh sauce, hot but not too hot, and liberal with fresh herbs. Very good indeed. The nan breads – plain, Peshwari, or keema (£1.59) – are large, thick-rimmed and very fresh; everything a nan should be. By paying a small amount in corkage you can bring your own alcohol but healthier people will enjoy the fresh juices – orange and carrot (£1.95) is specially good.

Taja offers all sorts of set meals and deals. The "Fast set snack – chotpoti with a can of Coca Cola" weighs in at a quite remarkable £2.49. Or you could splash out on the "All day and every day buffet eat as much as you like non-vegetarian and vegetarian £4.95 per person" (the "day" in question being restricted to 11am–6pm).

BRICK LANE & SPITALFIELDS ⑪ VIETNAMESE

Viet Hoa Café

72 Kingsland Road, E2 ☎ 0171 729 8293   ⊖ Old Street

Tues–Sun noon–3.30pm & 5.30–11.30pm   All major credit cards except Amex

The Viet Hoa dining room is large, clean, light and airy and has an impressive golden parquet floor. The café part of the name is borne out by the bottles of red and brown sauce which take pride of place on each table. The brown glop turns out to be hoisin sauce and the red stuff a simple chilli sauce, but they have both been put into recycled plastic bottles on which the only recognisable words are, "Sriracha extra hot chilli sauce – Flying Goose Brand". Apparently this has made all but the regulars strangely wary of hoisin sauce.

As befits a café there are a good many splendid "meals in a bowl" – soups, and noodle dishes with everything from spring rolls to tofu. For diners wanting to go as a group and share dishes, an appetiser called salted prawn in garlic dressing (£4) is outstanding: large prawns are marinated and fried with chilli and garlic. From the list of 15 different soups, Pho (£3 or £3.95) is compulsory. This dish is a Vietnamese staple eaten at any and every meal – including breakfast. Ribbon noodles and either beef, chicken or tofu are added to a delicate broth. It comes with a plate of mint leaves, Thai basil, and chillis, your job being to add the fresh aromatics to the hot soup – resulting in astonishingly vivid flavours. Main courses include shaking beef (£6.50) – cubes of beef with a tangy salad – and drunken fish (£6.50) – fish cooked with wine and cloud ear mushrooms. Both live up to the promise of their exotic names. Bun bi (£3.95) is a splendid one pot dish – noodles with shredded pork and moreish spring rolls and plus a side dish of "fish sauce" – light, chilli hot, sharp, sweet, and fishy all at once.

This is a good restaurant to make a first foray into Vietnamese food. It is very much a family-run place, with the grandparents sitting at a table dextrously rolling spring rolls and the younger generations waiting the tables. They're very helpful to novices.

City

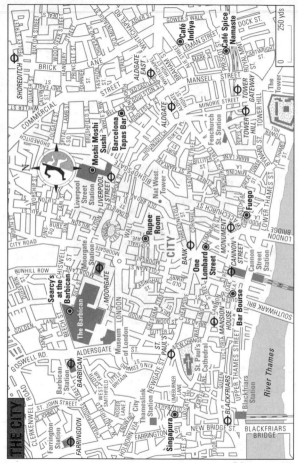

© Crown copyright

Bar Bourse

67 Queen St, EC4 ☎0171 248 2200   ⊖ Mansion House

Restaurant Mon–Fri 11.30am–3.30pm;   All credit cards except Diners

Anyone who says City people are boring hasn't been to Bar Bourse. As much bar as restaurant, it is run by Louise Mayo, herself an ex-City stockbroker. Her mission is to bring interesting food and fun to the bright-jacketed traders in the area and, as the pictures by the entrance attest, she and her staff do it well. Operating to the City beat, Bar Bourse offers a restaurant menu at lunchtime, but becomes a noisy and crowded bar after 6.00pm with a young clientele intent on testing the cocktail menu and champagne list to destruction.

The bar snacks (served Mon–Fri 11.30am–10pm) are innovative. For £5.50 you get a baked-on-the-premises focaccia stuffed with fillings like smoked chicken, basil crema and lettuce, white anchovy, rocket and roast tomato, crisp smoked pancetta, avocado and tomato. There is a huge cocktails list as well, from favourites like Margaritas to classics like whisky sour, to flavoured martinis. All are £5.00 and worth it. On the restaurant menu starters of porcini white beans and truffle soup (£6.00), foies gras, and celeriac and ham hock terrine (£8.00) are well executed. The terrine is rich with chunks of ham like a good jambon persilée. Main courses on offer may include char-grilled rib eye or fillet of beef, frites and Béarnaise sauce (£14.50–£17.50); smoked chorizo and poached egg risotto (£11.00); or organic chicken, black pudding, potato galette and tomato coulis (£15.00), which sounds a mouthful, but works well. There are some interesting salads too. Try artichoke, potato and beans, or avocado, red onion and blue cheese. You can have them for £3.50 as a side order or £5.00 as a starter. For pudding try banana tart with prune and armagnac (£5.00) or vanilla pod and redcurrant brulée (£5.00).

Wines range from thoughtfully priced "house" at £11.50 a bottle to more exotic items like Chateau Latour 1983 (£170) and Le Montrachet 1994 (£130). Champagnes run from J.Lemoine (£26) to Krug Grande Cuvée at £100, with Bollinger at £42 in between. It's not cheap, but Bar Bourse is good fun and a great place to meet and mix with the City bonus boys and girls.

£10–£25

Barcelona Tapas Bar

1a Bell Lane, E1 ☎ 0171 247 7014	⊖ Aldgate
Mon–Fri 11am–11pm	All major credit cards

At the start of the East End, not a hundred yards from the towering buildings of the City, you find yourself amongst the market stalls of Petticoat Lane and Middlesex Street. On one of the less salubrious corners you'll see a banner with the legend "tapas". Note that the arrow points down, and as you descend the stairs into this cramped basement which seats about twenty, try to still the thought that this is an inauspicious start to your lunch or evening. This is one of London's best tapas bars, producing a range of snacks that wouldn't be sniffed at in Barcelona or Madrid, and including a fair few Catalan specialities and trademarks – such as the classic tomato- and garlic-rubbed bread, a good accompaniment to any tapas session.

You'll find a number of tapas lined up in typical Spanish style along the back half of the bar – but these are only a few of the selection on offer. The Barcelona has a vast (in more ways than one) menu written in a mixture of Spanish and Catalan, with English translations. Many are simple like pa amb pernil (£6.95) – Serrano ham on the aforementioned garlic and tomato croutons, or queso Manchego (Manchego cheese, £3.95) or aceitunas (olives, £1.50–£2.50), and rely on the excellent quality of the raw ingredients. More skill is involved in creating the paellas, and the paella Valenciana (£10.95 pp) is particularly good. But for those with meetings within 24 hours, avoid anything that advertises its garlic. The Spanish seem blithely unaware of the havoc they wreak with the social lives of unsuspecting diners. And here, as well as being delicious, the gambas con all-i-olli (£6.95) is pungent enough to give you heartburn and the kind of breath that gets you space in a rush hour tube.

Unusually for such a small place with a huge choice of food, there's no need to worry about freshness. There is another bigger, smarter, newer and less charming Barcelona nearby, and the apparent lull between ordering and receiving your dish may be because the girl is running around the corner to the other kitchen and fetching a portion.

Café Indiya

30 Alie St, E1 ☎ 0171 481 8288   ⊖ Aldgate East

Mon–Fri noon–3.30pm & 6–11pm   All major credit cards

Café Indiya is a new wave Indian restaurant – bright colours, jars of spices spotlit in alcoves, wood floor, modern furniture. Then as you sit down on the surprisingly comfortable chairs, you see a really promising sign. This is a restaurant which has an additional menu offering weekly specials. Hallelujah! Batch-cooked food, evenly-balanced spicing, what a splendid idea. The menu here is tailored to the clientele, who are predominantly City types breaking out for lunch. What they want is a good, well-flavoured, not-too-outlandish curry and as a result some of the more complex dishes on the menu seem to have been reined in somewhat. Each dish on the menu comes with a coloured blob beside it to indicate its strength: yellows are mild, greens are medium and reds are hot. But only the chicken peri-peri (a tandoor dish, and so omitted from the coding system) gets anywhere near "really hot".

Start with childa (£1.95) – savoury coriander and ginger pancakes, served with yoghurt – or murgh puda, which is a more conventional pancake wrapped around chunks of chicken. Or share the mix kebab karaha (£7.95) which is a complete rainbow of grilled meats from the tandoor, going all the way from tandoori chicken to a decent, spicy chicken peri-peri, by way of sheekh kebab and suchlike. The main courses come in large portions, within attractive plain white serving bowls. Goan fish curry (£4.95) has a good concentrated sauce. Nariel gosht (£5.95) is a welcome twist on korma with a rich coconut sauce. There's chicken xacutti (£5.75) – said to be the most complex curry of all. The naan breads (£1.50) are good. The lemon rice (£1.95) is amazing – smelling intensely of lemons. And one of the side dishes – baingan (£2.50), stewed whole baby aubergines – has real star quality.

You have to approve of an Indian restaurant that offers live music on certain nights of the week. You also have to admire a sales line that links soul music and soul food. But it takes a real aficionado to stomach a pun like … "Pappa dom preach!"

£12–£30

Café Spice Namaste

16 Prescott St, E1 ☎ 0171 488 9242   ⊖ Aldgate East/Tower Hill

Mon–Fri noon–3pm & 6.15–10.30pm, Sat 6.30–10pm   All major credit cards

During the week this restaurant is packed with movers and shakers, all busily moving and shaking. They come in for lunch at 11.59 and they go out again at 12.59. Lunchtimes and even weekday evenings the pace is fast and furious, but come Saturday nights you can settle back and really enjoy Cyrus Todiwala's exceptional cooking. What's more in the City "shut for the weekend" parking is no problem. It is well worth turning out, for this is not your average curry house. Parsee delicacies rub shoulders with dishes from Goa, North India, Hyderabad and Kashmir; all are precisely spiced and well presented; and the tandoori specialities are awesome – fully flavoured by the cunning marinades but in no way dried out by the heat of the oven.

Start with a voyage around the tandoor – the Goan "galinha cafreal" (£3.85) is how every chicken tikka should taste – mint, coriander, chillies all playing their part. Or there's "venison tikka aflatoon" (£4.50) which originates in Gwalior, flavoured with star anise and cinnamon. Also notable is the "dahi kachori" (£3.85), a Gujerati pastry case filled with moong beans and fried. For a main course, fish-lovers shouldn't stray past the fish cooked "ambotik ani xit" (£10.25) – hot and sour, with the tang of palm vinegar. Choose meat and you should try the beef xacutti (£10.25 – including mushroom pulao rice), reputedly the most complex of all curries, containing more than twenty ingredients. Breads are also excellent while some of the accompaniments and vegetable dishes bely their lowly status at the back of the book-sized menu. "French beans jeera" (£3.95) are beans cooked with chopped shallots and roasted cumin seeds – simple and very good. "Choney ani oemio chey ussal" (£4.25) is a splendid Goan dish of chickpeas and mushrooms with coconut in the masala.

Watch those "diners in-the-know" and they will all be eating off the weekly speciality menu. Cyrus Todiwala is almost unique amongst Indian chefs in that he runs a specials menu which changes every week. He has recently started a South London branch at 247 Lavender Hill, Battersea, SW11 (☎0171 738 1717).

Fuego

1a Pudding Lane, EC3 ☎ 0171 929 3366	⊖ Bank/Monument
Mon–Fri 11.30am–4pm & 5.30–9.30pm (restaurant)	
Mon–Fri 11.30am–2am (tapas bar)	All major credit cards

Fuego, a subterranean tapas bar and restaurant, is sited in Pudding Lane where the first flickerings of the Great Fire of London started out on their path of destruction. A good many contemporary paths to destruction likely set out from these parts, too, as, unlike many City establishments, Fuego doesn't close mid-evening but braves it out until 2am on weekdays. As a result, and because of its good value snacks and meals, it's a popular haunt for reckless City folk who don't care what time they go home. Typically, the clientele are suit-clad and arrive in single-sex groups. However, the segregation doesn't last long, as from 8pm, from Tuesday to Friday, music is pumped out and Fuego transforms into a disco. For a more sophisticated atmosphere, you could try the lunchtime-only restaurant or come on a Monday night.

The menu is the same whichever bit of Fuego you choose to dine in: typical tapas fare with hot and cold dishes ranging in price from £2.25 for soupa de pueras (onion and leek soup) to £4.95 for the more expensive meat and seafood dishes. A couple of these and some French fries, or better still, fiery tomato patatas bravas (both £2.35) make a good foundation. The gambas gabardinas (£4.95) – crispy, battered tiger prawns in garlicky paprika sauce – are particularly good. Or try pulpo encebollado (£4.35) – a generous plateful of octopus in a pink pepper sauce. Or after a bad day at the office, the albondigas en salsa (£3.25), meatballs in tomato sauce, reassuring comfort food. More lively are the chorizo y polenta (£3.45) with red wine sauce; and the rinones al Jerez (£3.25) or kidneys in sherry, while you should look out for the weekly specials which are often interesting. For the less adventurous, homemade hamburgers (£5.50–£5.95) and sizeable toasted sandwiches (£4.75–£5.95) are available with French fries. And if you're not drinking beer or sherry, there's a decent house wine at £9.50 a bottle.

Anyone more interested in architecture than dancing, can try to puzzle out why the menu proclaims Fuego as a "Gaudí" restaurant. And the decorative iron matadors do not count!

Moshi Moshi Sushi

Unit 24, Liverpool Street Station, EC2 ☎ 0171 247 3227	⊖ Liverpool Street
Mon–Fri 11am–9pm	Mastercard, Visa

Moshi Moshi Sushi serves healthy fast food, Japanese style – its dishes circulating on a kaiten or conveyor belt. There are a dozen or so such places in London, these days, but this one claims to have been the first. Its location, inside Liverpool Street Station, meshes perfectly with the concept, and with its glass walls and ceiling, and no-smoking policy, it is a great and very wholesome place to eat before setting off on a train journey. It is, however, much more than a refuelling stop for commuters and, reassuringly, you'll find both local office workers and Japanese diners enjoying leisurely meals. You can either sit at the bar and watch your dinner circulate, or opt for table service, with some nice views of the old Liverpool Street station arches.

If you opt for a bar seat, the ordering system is child's play – you just pluck your chosen dishes from the conveyer belt as they trundle past. The billing system is slightly more complex: it's all down to the pattern of your plate. All the sushi is good and fresh and there's a decent range of authentics – from the somewhat acquired taste (or texture) of uni (sea urchin, £2.50) through to flying fish roe (£2.50) – as well as some delicious California hybrids, combining avocado and crabstick with a sweet, sticky sushi rice rolled with sesame seeds. Regular sushi choices such as negitoro temaki, a seaweed-wrapped roll of tuna and spring onion (£2.50), or shakemaki (salmon roll, £2.00), are done well, too, as is the Nigiri sushi (£1.20–2.50, depending on fish and plate pattern). Of the puddings, all at £2.50, the custard pancake, or dorayaki, is good, as are the various ice creams. Unless you're a fan, avoid adzuki dishes, no matter how dark, sticky and mysterious they look, as they consist of over-sweetened red bean paste – definitely an acquired taste.

Look out for the cartoons on the laminated cards which give you handy tips and warn newcomers to Japanese food just how to treat the fiery ground wasabi.

One Lombard Street
The Brasserie

1 Lombard Street, EC3 ☎ 0171 929 6611	⊖ Bank
Mon–Fri 11am–3pm & 5–10pm	All major credit cards except Diners

The Brasserie at One Lombard Street was formerly a banking hall and the circular bar sits under a suitably imposing glass dome. This is a brasserie in the City, of the City, by the City, and for the City. It is a restaurant which is connected to Bloomberg – a sort of elitist ceefax-cum-email which keeps City traders in touch with each other, rather like passing notes at school – and messages flash in and out. "Can you confirm your reservation at One Lombard Street?". "Yes. But we'll be ten minutes late". The Brasserie menu is a model of its kind, long but straightforward with a spread of dishes that is up to any meal occasion – Starters and Salads, Soups, Egg and Pasta, Caviar, Fish, Crustacea, Meat, Puddings. It delivers on pretty much every front, serving satisfying dishes made with good fresh ingredients, and surprisingly it manages to be both stylish and unfussy at one and the same time. The bar, meanwhile, is like any chic City watering hole – loud, brisk and crowded, with simultaneous conversations in every European language.

The Brasserie menu changes every month, to ring the changes for its band of regulars, and in addition there are daily specials. The starters can be ambitious, like a pig's trotter galette (£7.25) with truffle jus, or simple like a medley of asparagus (£7.95), while further down the menu there will be some even more comfortable options like a soft boiled free range egg (£6.75 or £9.95 main course) served with a grilled muffin, spinach and wild mushroom ragout. There's enough listed under crustacea to fuel even the wildest celebrations, but including feuillete of Burgundy snails (£7.25); and clam stew (£7.95 or £9.95 large). Then the meat section features a very well-made coq au vin Bourguignon (£12.50) plus steaks, sausages, liver and chops. During the season you may also find roast partridge with braised cabbage and Riesling jus (£15).

There is a smaller, forty seater room at the back of the bar set aside for fine dining at fancy prices. It's interesting to note, however, that caviar is a Brasserie dish – 50 grams of Beluga will set you back £78.

£25–£60

Rupee Room

10 Copthall Ave, EC2 ☎ 0171 628 1555   ⊖ Liverpool St

Mon–Fri 11.30am–3pm & 5.30–11pm   All major credit cards

The Rupee Room is a modern cellar restaurant smack in the middle of the City of London. Upstairs, suited warriors skirmish in the on-going financial world war, downstairs they pause for a curry. It won't be a cheap curry, or even a wildly original one, but that hardly matters when you've worked up a thirst while putting yet another multi-national to the sword. At the Rupee Room the decor is slick, the service is superb, and the after-dinner drinks trolley legendary.

The chutneys which arrive with the menu and poppadums are worthy of special note – five small bowls including a very fresh, tart and hot lime pickle, and an excellent tamarind sauce. Then look at the specials menu which changes regularly. Hope for hara channa bharta (£4.50), a cross between houmus and guacamole served with hot bread – the breads are good here. Or the Indian street food speciality which seems to be all the rage – sev batata puri (£4.75), diced potatoes with chutneys and crisp puris. Grilled meats from the tandoor are well-judged, and chicken nilgiri (£8.50), green and mild, makes a pleasant change from more familiar fare. Chicken daalwala (£7.95), subtitled dansak, comes as bites of chicken in a gravy boosted with lentils. Gosht banjara (£8.95) is meat in an oniony gravy with black pepper sauce. Both these sauces tend towards raw chilli heat.

It is rumoured that the Rupee Room has achieved record levels of spending per head for an Indian restaurant, particularly during the pre-Christmas scramble when large parties of revellers have been known to while away the afternoon and part of the evening, too. There's even talk of a major financial player whose inspired linking of the traditional foodfight with the humble peashooter came close to causing a riot. The catalyst for these events was the Rupee Room drinks trolley, on which you'll find (as well as brandies geriatric enough to make your wallet blanch) a range of Indian liqueurs. Branded "Pandit's", there are three ornate bottles: Kulfi – a kind of viscous, white, Indian "Bailey's"; Mango Sorbet; and Paan. Whatever will they think of next?

Searcy's at the Barbican

Level 2, Barbican, Silk St, EC2 ☎ 0171 588 3008	⊖ Barbican

Mon–Fri noon–2.30pm & 5–11pm, Sat 5pm–midnight,	

| Sun noon–2.30pm & 5–6.30pm ("pre performance") | All major credit cards |

Offering a delightful view of St Giles Cripplegate church across the fountains of the Barbican lake, Searcy's is tucked away on Level 2 of the Barbican Centre. It is a favourite with the Barbican's concert goers and if it were elsewhere (it's hard to imagine going to the Barbican just for a meal) its cooking would attract a wider audience. As you would expect from a venue catering for a pre- and post-concert audience, service is excellent, brisk and understanding of time pressures. There are special pre- and post-performance menus too.

The menu changes regularly and is seasonally based, so expect changes. Starters might include salt cod croquettes. avocado, capers and parsley (£5.50), or beef carpaccio, blue cheese souffle, rocket (£7). Both are well presented – the cod creamy and crisp with a good fresh bite from the salsa-like avocado accompaniment, the carpaccio like ultra-thin slices of slightly seared fillet steak, with its subtle flavoured souffle. Main courses might feature roast leg of lamb, spring vegetables and rosemary oil (£13), which comes pink and studded with fine slivers of garlic, the spring offering of baby carrots, leeks and turnips biting hot but still crisp. Baked dover sole with garlic and almonds (£18) is accompanied by an extra scoop of herb breadcrumbs fragrant with olive and basil. Other of the generally sophisticated offerings include skate salad, citrus fruit, lemon grass vinaigrette (£6.90), and roast rack of kid, aubergine and goat cheese cannelloni (£18.00). It's all very well done. The side dishes are good, too. A dish of mashed potatoes is swirled with butter oil, but still remains creamy smooth rather than over rich, and the chips are terrific – perfect long, uniform chips, crisp on the outside, fluffy inside and served too hot to pick up. Puddings are worth the extra course on a set menu. A sultana parfait, rum and tea (£5.50), for example, comes with its icy top fiercely bruleed to add an unexpected bite.

If you had problems finding Searcy's, or the Barbican, spare a thought for George Best, who used to have an apartment here. Winning the European Cup must have seemed a doddle.

£20–£40

Singapura

1-2 Limeburner Lane, EC4 0171 329 1133	⊖ Blackfriars/St Paul's
Mon–Fri 11.30am–3.30pm & 5.30–10pm	All major credit cards

This large, modern restaurant just off Ludgate Hill has won a succession of accolades as "London's most beautiful restaurant", and it is one of only a handful of places outside of Singapore where you can sample Nonya cuisine. Singapore boasts four great culinary traditions: Chinese, Indian, Malay and Nonya – which belongs to the people once known as the "Straits Chinese". Nonya food is a fusion of the Malayan and Chinese traditions and ingredients, it is generally (but not always) spicy, and is characterised by good deal of garlic, galangal, sweetness, and lime leaves. At Singapura it's very well done, if at some cost.

In many ways the starters are the stars here – and not just because you hit them with a fresh appetite. Siput (£5.95) is described as "mussels stir-fried with lemon grass, lime leaves, chillies and ginger in a sherry sauce" but resembles an Oriental moules matiniere: small, sweet mussels are cooked in a broth that would make a delightful (if fiery) soup. Chicken satay (£5.75), is juicy and comes with an assertive peanut sauce. Udang goreng (£12.50) is an indulgence – four large tiger prawns, butterflied, deep fried and served with chili and garlic sauce. From the main courses you might try babi tauceo (£6.50) which is made from crispy pork slices with the classic Nonya sauce based on yellow bean paste. Char kuayteow (£7.50) is Singapore street food, broad rice noodles, stir fried with fairly pungent chunks of fish cake, eggs and prawns. In the vegetable section choi sum (£4.95) is a super-charged version of the Chinese favourite "greens with oyster sauce", stronger, fishier, and with liberal garlic and ginger. By the time the puddings come around your tongue is probably only fit for the home-made ice creams which come in moody varieties like Earl Grey, marmalade parfait, and brown bread – two scoops £4.50.

In deference to Western palates, Maureen Suan-Neo, masterchef of the Singapura restaurants, has had to reduce or eliminate the blachan used in some dishes. Blachan is made from dried, salted shrimps, and smells a bit like rotten fish, Surprisingly enough, it is yummy.

Clerkenwell

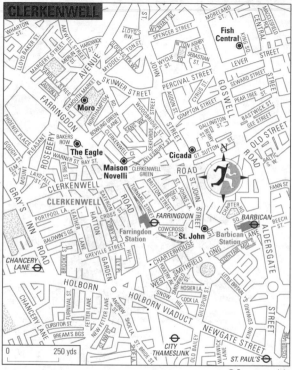

CLERKENWELL

Fish Central

Moro

The Eagle

Maison Novelli

Cicada

Farringdon Station

St. John

BARBICAN

Barbican Station

CHANCERY LANE ⊖

CITY THAMESLINK

ST. PAUL'S ⊖

0 — 250 yds

© Crown copyright

Cicada

132 St John St, EC1 ☎ 0171 608 1550   ⊖ Farringdon

Mon–Fri noon–11pm, Sat 6pm–11pm   All major credit cards

Once Clerkenwell was where you went for printing and watch repairs. But it's fast becoming London's coolest inner-town area – a fact that is highlighted in its growing choice of restaurants and bars. Cicada is one of a number catering to the new residential population. Part bar, and part restaurant, it offers an unusual Thai based menu that changes three or four times a year and allows you to mix and match from small, large and side dishes. This suits a lot of modern tastes as everyone can share dishes and different flavours.

To start, you'd be hard pressed to beat the crab rice paper rolls with nahm jim sauce (£5.00) – they're delicious – fresh tasting and at the same time crunchy, sweet and spicy. Or try the tom yum (£4.50) soup, which is full of fish, very hot and very lemony. Moving on to the large plates, duck hot pot with shitake mushrooms and thick rice noodles (£9.50) is a dish for two. Chunks of falling-off-the-bone duck arrive in a huge pot of simmering soup with fresh crispy vegetables and noodles. It's very more-ish and you could easily make a good meal off that and a single other dish. Good choices might be the sweet ginger noodles (£2.50) – a tasty bowlful; or the caramelised pork (£3.00) – sweet and crispy on the outside and tender inside, but rich with fat. Or there are fresh clams, white miso and kinome leaves (£4.50); char-grilled squid, sdjud sauce (£5.50); and inari sushi (£3.95). Puddings are tempting offerings like tapioca and young coconut (£3.50), and chocolate and lemongrass brulée (£4.25). There is a good selection of medium-priced wines and beers, including Tiger beer (£2.80) if you want to go Oriental, and a house Sauvignon (£14.50) from the part of Mexico that is almost South California – particularly good at a not too unreasonable £14.50 a bottle.

Cicada has a friendly bar atmosphere and if the weather is good it's a great place to sit outside. It's set back from the main part of the street so the pavement tables give a degree of privacy. Staff are young and easygoing and Cicada makes a good bridge between going to a bar for a drink and going to a restaurant for a meal.

CLERKENWELL ⑪ MEDITERRANEAN/PUB

The Eagle

159 Faringdon Rd, EC1 ☎ 0171 837 1353	⊖ Farringdon
Meals served Mon–Fri 12.30–2.30pm & 6.30–10.30pm,	
Sat 12.30–3.30pm & 6.30–10.30pm, Sun 12.30–4pm	Cash or cheque only

The Eagle was for years a run-down pub in an unpromising part of London, but in 1991 it was taken over by food-minded entrepreneurs who transformed it into a restaurant-pub, with an open kitchen turning out real quality dishes. It was a pioneer: there should be a blue plaque over the door marking the site as the starting place of the great gastro-pub revolution. Over the intervening years neither the food nor the decor has changed much, though activities have expanded to an enterprising and interesting gallery upstairs. The Eagle itself remains a crowded, rather shabby sort of place – and the staff still have "attitude". The kitchen is truly open: the chefs work behind the bar, and the menu is chalked up over their heads. It changes daily, or hourly, as things run out or deliveries come in. The food is broadly Mediterranean in outlook with a Portuguese bias, and you still fight your way to the bar to order and pay.

This is a pub with a signature dish. Bife Ana (£8) has been on the menu here since the place opened and they have sold tens of thousands of portions. It is a kind of steak sandwich, whose marinade has roots in the spicy food of Portugal and Mozambique and it is delicious. The rest of the menu changes like quicksilver but you may find the likes of baked brill, sautéed spinach Catalan style with pinenuts and raisins (£9); or roast marinated loin of pork, slow roast red onions, with garlic wine and Balsamico (£8). Or Caldeirada (£11), the famous Lisbon fish stew. Or conchiglie pasta with pumpkin, sage butter and Parmesan (£7.50). To finish, choose between Manchego Gold ewe's milk cheese with quince paste (£5) and those splendid Portuguese cinnamon custard tarts – Pasteis de Nata – which are £1 each.

Even with the seats outside on the pavement providing extra capacity in decent weather the Eagle is never less than crowded, the music is loud, and the staff are busy and brusque. A great place nonetheless.

CITY & EAST

Fish Central

151 King's Square, Central St, EC1 ☎ 0171 253 4970   ⊖ Barbican

Mon–Sat 11am–2.30pm & 4.45–10.30pm   All major credit cards

The Barbican may appear to be the back of beyond – a black hole in the heart of the City – but perfectly ordinary people do live and work around here. Apart from the Arts Centre and proximity to the financial district, one of the main attractions of the place is Fish Central, which can hold its own with any of the finest fish and chip shops town.

Though at first sight Fish Central appears just like any other chippie – a takeaway service on one side and an eat-in restaurant next door – one look at its menu and you'll realise this is something out of the ordinary. All the finny favourites are here – from cod (£3.45) to rock salmon (£3.45) – but there's a wholesome choice of alternatives, including grilled Dover sole (£8.65), grilled mackerel with rhubarb (£6.95), and roast cod (£6.45) with rosemary and Mediterranean vegetables. Many of these dishes would not be out of place in much grander establishments. You can eat decently here, too, even if you are not in the mood for fish. Try the Cumberland sausages (£3.45) with onions and gravy, or the spit-barbecued chicken (£4.95 per half bird – a very fair price). If you think your appetite is up to starters try the prawn cocktail (£2.45) – the normal naked pink prawns in pink sauce, but genuinely fresh – or the seafood salad (£2.95) which puts all of those run-of-the-mill Italian restaurants to shame. Chips (£1.05) come as a side order rather than as a necessary part of your dish, so those who prefer can order a jacket potato (£1.05) or creamed potatoes (£1.05). Mushy peas (£1.05) are ... mushy and Wallies (40p) – aka pickled gherkins – come sliced and prettily served in the shape of a flower.

Fish Central certainly pulls in a crowd of devoted regulars. On any given night, half the customers seem to know each other. Unusually for a chippie, it has an alcohol licence which means there's a palatable dry white Garrogny house wine (£7.50) or, at a modest splash, champagne (£19.95) – the perfect partner for mushy peas.

Moro

34-36 Exmouth Market, EC1 ☎0171 833 8336	⊖ Farringdon/Angel
Mon–Fri 12.30pm–2.30pm & 7–10.30pm	Amex, Mastercard, Visa

In its relatively short life Moro has scooped up a hatful of awards. This modern, rather Spartan restaurant typifies the new face of Clerkenwell and attracts a clientele to match. In feel it's not so very far away from the better pub restaurants, although the proprietors have given themselves the luxury of a slightly larger kitchen. This is also a place of pilgrimage for disciples of the wood-fired oven, and as the food here hails mainly from Spain, Portugal and North Africa it is both Moorish and more-ish. There is also good Spanish drink on offer: dry fino and manzanilla for an aperitif or to drink with a meal, sweet Pedro Ximenez to go with the puds. The only real problem lies in Moro's popularity. It's consistently booked out which places a bit of a strain on both kitchen and waiting staff.

Soups are among Moro's best starters. They do a perfect ajo blanco (£3.50) – chilled almond soup with grapes whose texture seems to defy such simple ingredients – and in summer an equally good gazpacho (£4). Depending on the season and the markets you may also be offered starters such as veal kidneys with garlic, paprika, fino and fried potatoes (£6) – a small earthenware dish filled with a well-seasoned and precisely cooked mixture. Or there's a classic combination of brandada – salt cod purée with olive oil and potato – with toast made from the superb sourdough bread produced in the wood-fired oven, piquillo peppers and olives (£5). Main courses are simple and often traditional combinations of taste and textures and, as with the starters, accompaniments tend to change rather than the core ingredient. Look out for wood-roasted chicken (£12) which may be served with sumac and chard or courgettes and tahini. Either way is delicious, exactly how chickens are supposed to taste. There are usually some good fish dishes, too, along the lines of charcoal-grilled sea bass with almond and caper sauce, roast beetroot and their leaves (£12.50). Or squid stuffed with egg and parsley with fino new potatoes and rocket (£12).

Do not miss the splendid Spanish cheeses (£4) served with membrillo – traditional quince paste. But that's no excuse to avoid the Malaga raisin ice-cream dowsed in Pedro Ximenez (£3.50).

Novelli EC1

30 Clerkenwell Green, EC1 ☎0171 251 6606   ⊖ Farringdon

Mon–Fri 11am–11pm, Sat 5pm–midnight   All major credit cards

Jean-Christophe Novelli must take some of the credit for the turnaround in Clerkenwell's image, as a kind of cross between Islington and Docklands. He has four restaurants in London now, and another in South Africa, but this brasserie was his first solo venture, and the neighbourhood's first real landmark restaurant. He brings a distinctive, indeed inspirational touch to the art of cooking. His menus change regularly, both to reflect the pick of the markets and to follow the seasons.

To start, you might be lucky enough to find crab bisque with cardamom and clotted cream (£5.00) – a brilliant idea and surprisingly not too rich. Main courses might include Thai fish cakes with a spicy sauce (£10.50), poached cod on a bed of spinach with aïoli sauce (£11.50), chump of lamb with cumin infused couscous and massala curry sauce (£13.50), and a simple, but perfectly cooked, sirloin steak and frites (£16.00). Whilst there's an eclectic mix of influences in all these dishes, the flavours have been assembled with a classical attention to detail and work well. The separate pudding menu offers a blueberry waffle with honey and roast almond ice cream; cold rice pudding, rhubarb compote and strawberry juice; poached peach, vanilla ice cream and raspberry coulis; and a sensational banana Tatin with calvados ice cream. They are all priced at £4.95 and all very good, the cold rice pudding with rhubarb compôte especially so – it would likely work its magic even on a child who hates the stuff.

Clerkenwell Green has a very un-London feel to it and the Brasserie, being almost on a corner, has a rather French atmosphere about it. It seems more relaxed than many restaurants of a comparable quality, with friends just dropping in for a coffee or a drink at the bar. The menu states, "Jean Christophe Novelli et son equipe vous souhaitent "Bon Appetit", and somehow you believe they mean it. Given the quality of both the cooking and the service it seems pleasantly like a bargain. The Brasserie also has private rooms and you can get the great man himself to cook for private dinner parties there.

£20–£40

St John

26 St John St, EC1 ☎ 0171 251 0848   ⊖ Farringdon

Mon–Fri noon–3pm & 6–11.30pm, Sat 6–11.30pm   All major credit cards

One of the most frequent requests, especially from foreign visitors, is "Where can we get some really English cooking?": no wonder that the promise of "olde English fare" is the bait in so many London tourist traps. The cooking at St John is genuinely English. It is sometimes old-fashioned, and it makes inspired use of all those strange and unfashionable cuts of meat – and in particular, offal – which were once commonplace in rural England. Technically the cooking is of a very high standard, while the restaurant itself is without frills or design pretensions to the point where it is almost uncomfortably bare. You'll either love it or hate it. But be forewarned: this is an uncompromising and opinionated kitchen, and no place to take anyone with remotely vegetarian inclinations.

The menu changes every session, but the tone of voice does not and there's always a dish or two to support the slogan "nose to tail eating". Charcuterie, as you'd imagine, is good here, a simple rabbit terrine (£5.70) will be dense but not dry – well-judged. Or for the committed, what about a starter of roast bone marrow and parsley salad (£5.20)? Truly delicious. Or a whole crab with mayonnaise (£8). Be generous to yourself with the bread, which is outstanding; the bakery is in the bar so you can purchase a loaf to take home. Main courses may include grilled Dexter veal kidneys and spinach (£12.40) – the tiny kidneys from these miniature cattle have an unbelievably delicate flavour. Maybe there will be grey mullet with borlotti beans (£11.20); or smoked eel, bacon and celeriac (£11) – an inspired combination of textures. Puddings are trad and well executed, along the lines of rice pudding with plums (£5), baked custard (£5), or a slice of strong Lancashire cheese with an accompanying Eccles cake.

St John has forged quite a reputation, and it's encouraging to see a party of Japanese businessmen siting down to their pot roast beef and pickled walnut toast (£10.50) rather than the usual overcooked tourist diet of "roast beef of old England". Whatever your feelings about meat and offal cookery, St John serves English food at its most genuine.

Docklands

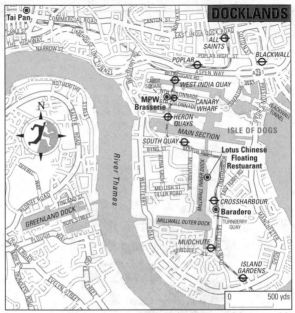

DOCKLANDS

Tai Pan
COMMERCIAL ROAD
CANTON ST.
EAST INDIA DOCK ROAD
ALL SAINTS
CABLE ST.
THE HIGHWAY
LIMEHOUSE LINK TUNNEL
BLACKWALL
NARROW ST.
POPLAR HIGH ST.
POPLAR
ASPEN WAY
A261
ROTHERHITHE
BILLINGSGATE RD.
CABOT SQUARE
WEST INDIA QUAY
NTH. COLONNADE
MPW Brasserie
STH. COLONNADE
CANARY WHARF
PRESTON'S ROAD
BLACKWALL TUNNEL
BRUNSWICK WAY
HERON QUAYS
ISLE OF DOGS
MAIN SECTION
SOUTH QUAY
BYNG ST.
River Thames
ALPHA GROVE
MARSH WALL
MILLHARBOUR
Lotus Chinese Floating Restuarant
SALTER ROAD
MELLISH ST.
TILLER ROAD
EAST FERRY RD.
MILLWALL INNER DOCK
DIEBEL WAY
WESTFERRY RD.
CROSSHARBOUR
Baradero
GREENLAND DOCK
FINLAND ST.
ROPE STREET
MILLWALL OUTER DOCK
TURNBERRY QUAY
BLORIFF ROAD
PLOUGH WAY
MUDCHUTE
SANDRIFT
ISLAND GARDENS
EVELYN STREET
RUNGERS STREET

0   500 yds

© Crown copyright

Baradero

Turberry Quay – off Pepper St, E14 ☎ 0171 537 1666	DLR Crossharbour
Mon–Fri noon–11pm, Sat 6–10.45pm	All major credit cards

Baradero is modern, light, tiled and airy. And as far as a view of Millwall dock and proximity to the London Arena will permit, you could almost think that you were in Spain. It is essentially a tapas bar but offers main courses as well as tapas – and both are of restaurant quality. Take a seat at the bar, or at one of the well-spaced tables, order up a bottle of Estrella beer or a glass of fino sherry and set about the tapas. There is even a floor show in the form of the balletic automatic orange juice machine called a Zumm which seems to wave the whole oranges about for inspection before squashing them for juice.

Start with an order of pan con aioli (95p) – good bread with a pot of fearsome but seductive garlic mayonnaise. Or pan con tomate (£1.30) – Catalan-style toast drizzled with olive oil and rubbed with garlic and tomato. Add some boquerones (£3.15) – classic white anchovies sharp with vinegar and garnished with raw garlic slices – and jamon Serrano (£4.75) – a large portion of dark, richly-flavoured, dry-cured ham. Then follow up with some hot tapas such as croquetas de pollo (£3.50) – whoever would have thought that croquettes could taste so good ? Or pulpo a la Gallega (£4.95), octopus boiled and seasoned in Galician style. Or the particularly delicious fabada Asturiana (£4.95) – an Asturian bean stew loaded with chunks of sausage, black pudding and ham hock. Also lurking on the tapas menu is paella Valenciana (£16.50). This is the real thing with chicken and shellfish and feeds two. If you can restrain your ordering, and do not end up crammed full of tapas, there is a further list of main courses which changes weekly – try chuletas de cordero al romero (£11.50), charcoal grilled lamb cutlets, which are simple and good. Or maybe lubina al horno (£12.75) – baked seabass with salted "Canary" potatoes and a Mediterranean salad.

Baradero holds notable events and food festivals when the proprietors bring in top Spanish chefs to cook serious regional food – small lambs, suckling pigs, all manner of delights and worth looking out for.

£15-£40

Lotus Chinese Floating Restaurant

38 Limeharbour, Inner Millwall Dock, E14 ☎ 0171 515 6445   DLR Crossharbour

Daily noon–11.30pm   All major credit cards except Diners

Imagine. You are on the Isle of Dogs and there, bobbing about on the Millwall Dock, is one of those floating Chinese restaurants from Hong Kong – well that's what you're supposed to think. The Lotus is certainly a boat, and it's certainly a restaurant – a very large and glitzy restaurant. And while the cooking is not quite what you'd expect of a Hong Kong boat – there are some very fine dishes but also some very bland ones toned down presumably for British tastes – it's a busy and popular place, and deservedly so. Order with care and you'll get the best Chinese food for several miles around. And the incongruity of the whole establishment, with its over-the-top decor, out in Docklands has a real charm.

To start, you could do a lot worse than the "welcome of Spring" (£3.30) – a plate of steady spring rolls, commendably crisp and dry. The jelly fish with chicken (£5.50) is a successful dish, too – rich with sesame and a good mix of textures. And the spare ribs with peppercorn salt (£5.50) are good and crispy, if needing more pepper and more salt. (Save your money on the steamed fresh scallop in shell –£1.70 each – which lack zip.) Moving on, a main course of fried squid with chilli and black bean sauce (£7) is excellent, something to challenge the tongue. The deep-fried crispy lamb with plum sauce (£7.20) is also good, crisp fatty lamb combining well with sweet plum sauce. And the steamed fillet of chicken with Chinese dates and black mushrooms wrapped in lotus leaves (£5.50) is a great dish, very tasty indeed. (Negative points here are for the steamed great prawns with crushed garlic – £7; the steamed fresh scallop in shell – £1.70 each; and the Singapore style fried noodles (£6.50); all of them are meekly seasoned and lack zip.)

You'll want to drink tea or beer here. If the latter, this is your chance to make a head-to-head comparison between two Chinese beers – Tsing Tsao (£2.50 a bottle) and Sun Lik (£3 a pint on draught).

MPW Brasserie

2nd Floor, Cabot Place East, Canary Wharf, E14 ☎ 0171 513 0513   BR Canary Wharf

Mon–Fri noon–2.30pm & 5.30–9pm   All major credit cards

Among the expensive shirt and personal accessory shops in Canary Wharf tower sits a restaurant with no name. Even its books of matches are unmarked, but to those in the know, this elliptical, Art Deco-inspired restaurant is MPW (Marco Pierre White). The Docklands restaurant world is a topsy-turvy one: here daytime is when you have to book well ahead, as the place is packed to the gunnels with power lunchers. Dinner, meanwhile, is a pretty quiet affair. Still, from 5.30pm there is a set menu (£12.95 for two or £16.95 for three courses) which, commendably, is just a paired down version of the à la carte, and as such is a bargain. But even Marco Pierre White can't install much of a night-time buzz in Canary Wharf, which from 7pm feels very much like a ghost town. And evening diners may be disappointed to find the lunchtimers have snapped up some of the choicest dishes on offer (game, especially).

Still, whenever you eat, you get the full culinary constructions of Mr W's vision – and we are talking real quality, here. The menu changes seasonally but dishes are all grandstand. You might find a started like baked sea scallop à la croque (£7.95) whose fresh vanilla sauce must be mopped up with bread – it would be a crime to waste it or carpaccio of beef (£6.95), perfectly circular and served with rocket, tapenade and generous shavings of parmesan. Main courses might include venison with braised red cabbage and honey roast parsnips (£14.50), and smoked escalop of salmon, new potatoes, asparagus sauce Hollandaise (£14.50) or a brochette of chicken with Alsace bacon and sauce bois boudran (£11.50), which is not just a bacon-wrapped chicken kebab but the most perfect, battered onion rings and waffle-cut potato crisps, fittingly stacked in towers.

The puddings, all at £6.00, are also architectural masterpieces. The lemon croustillant is served with a pyramidal forest full of red fruits and the brioche bread and butter pudding comes, mercifully, in not too big a pot, as it is so delicious you'd be forced to finish it whatever its size.

Tai Pan

665 Commercial Rd, E14 ☎ 0171 791 0118   DLR Lamb House

Mon–Thurs & Sun noon–11.15pm, Fri & Sat noon–11.45pm   All major credit cards

As anyone who has followed the adventures of Sherlock Holmes will know, Limehouse was London's first Chinatown – complete with opium dens for the "heathen Chinese". So despite the well-intentioned efforts of the Docklands Development Board to promote the area, today's Limehouse seems pretty tame in comparison. It can, however, boast about the Tai Pan. This restaurant is very much a family affair – the ebullient Winnie Man is front of house, while Mr Chen commands the kitchen. He organises a constant stream of well-cooked, mainly Cantonese dishes, and slaves over the intricately carved vegetables which lift their presentation, while she runs the light, bright dining room. He's a good cook, and as well as all the old favourites the menu hides one or two surprises.

After you've waded through the complimentary prawn cracker and seriously delicious hot-pickled-shredded-cabbage, start with "deep fried crispy squid with Szechuan peppercorn salt" (£6.80), or "fried Peking dumplings, with a vinegar dipping sauce" (£4.50), which are delicious. Or try one of the sparerib dishes (£5.60), or the soft shell crabs (£4.50 each), or the nicely done "crispy fragrant aromatic duck" with pancakes etcetera (£15.50 for a half). Or relax and order the "Imperial mixed hors d'oeuvres" which, for a minimum of two people (£8.80 a head), offers a sampler of ribs, spring rolls, seaweed and prawn and sesame toast – and has one of the carrot sculptures as centrepiece. When ordering main dishes, old favourites like "deep fried shredded beef with chilli" (£6.30), and "fried chicken in lemon sauce" (£5.50), are just what you'd expect. "Fried seasonal greens in oyster sauce" (£4.30) is made with choi sum and very delicious. "Fried vermicelli Singapore style" (£5.20) will suit anyone who likes their Singapore noodle pepped up with curry powder rather than fresh chillies.

Sometimes there are "specials" on offer which don't feature on the main menu. They're generally worth trying. "Hun tsui kau" (£2.90) – green banana or plantain encased in minced prawn and deep fried – is particularly popular. Asking Winnie to recommend something is always a good idea. Sinking your teeth into the carved vegetables is not.

Further East

Stratford, West Ham

© Crown copyright

£3–£14

Mobeen

222-224 Green Street, E7 ☎ 0181 470 2419	⊖ Upton Park
Daily 11am–10pm	Cash only

If you have never been to West Ham, the whole of Green Street is likely to come as a surprise. It has the feel of Brick Lane and Southall, but everything is much much cheaper – in the market here you can buy a whole goat for the price of a dozen lamb chops in the West End. Mobeen itself seems to operate at "factory gate" prices, offering a kind of 1950s Asian works canteen ethos – and decor. As you go in, the kitchen lies behind a glazed wooden partition to your left, while to your right are café tables and chairs. The clientele hits this place like a breaking wave – it can be impressively busy at 11.50 in the morning.

The dishes and prices are listed above the servery hatches and the food is set out in displays below. You go up to the hatch, wait your turn and then order up a trayful which will be re-animated in the microwave, then go to another hatch for fizzy soft drinks and to a further port of call to pick up cutlery and glasses. This is workmanlike food in large portions at basic prices. Most things come in two portion sizes: chicken tikka (£2.50/£3.40) is red and hot, very hot. Seekh kebabs are spicy and hot (thanks to the microwave) and are just 55p each. Meat samosas are just 55p each. Masala fish (£3.30) is rich and good. The biryani (£2.70/£3.50) is commendably un-greasy and may actually have benefited from being cooked and reheated. There's also a spinach and meat curry (£2.60/3.20); a meat curry (£2.50/£3.20); and a bhuna meat curry (£2.60/£3.50). The breads are serviceable although the bahtra (£1) which is a very thick, fried, stuffed paratha will tip you over your cholesterol allowance for about a fortnight. This establishment is just up the road from West Ham's home ground, you have to wonder what Alf Garnett would have made of it all.

Amongst the soft drinks and juices are some novelty items, for 50p you can try a fizzy mango juice in a lurid can, and if that doesn't tempt the jaded palate what about a fizzy guava juice?

£5–£20

The Piecrust

273 High Street, Stratford, E15 ☎ 0181 534 2873   ⊖ Stratford

Mon–Sat 6–11pm   Cash and cheques only

The outside of the Piecrust is rather daunting – it looks like a grubby, old-style, worker's caff. That's not very surprising, though, because from 7am to 3pm that's exactly what it is. After 6pm, however, it blossoms into a Thai restaurant that ranks with any in the capital. The food here is very fresh, very tasty, and provides the match-winning combination of large portions and small prices. It is also sophisticated. You'll find fritters made from banana flowers, and soups served in traditional charcoal-heated steamboat tureens. The service is all smiles and charm. Suchin Yoo Yai and his team have been dishing out bacon sandwiches here since 1973 but you suspect that they've been happier since 1992 when they started serving Thai food.

The first tricky choice to confront you is whether to open with starters or soup. The starters are good: poh pia (£2.50) – spring rolls; tord mun pla (£3.70) – Thai fishcakes; pek gai yut sai (£3) – stuffed chicken wings; goong sarong (£3.50) – prawns in filo; the tord mun hua plee (£3.20) – fried banana blossom with red curry paste; or there's a mixed starter (£10) which is a grand selection including all these and more. But the soups are stunning: delicate, spicy, filling, hot, sour, rich – there's something for everyone. Try tom yum gai (£4) – a hot and sour chicken soup with lemon grass, coriander and galangal - very fresh; or kadoong moo tom geamshai (£3) – a clear soup with baby spare ribs and pickled cabbage. Move on to the curries and equally tough choices are presented. Panag gai (£4.50) is chicken in thick red curry paste - spicy and good; gang kiew wan goong (£4.50) is prawns in green curry paste with coconut milk - plenty of prawns and a delicious sauce. Portions here are large. To accompany, you might try khan phud kaprouw neau (£4.20) – a meal in itself for one – comprising stir-fried rice with beef chilli and holy basil. This is one of those rare places where nothing disappoints.

In the morning The Piecrust serves egg on toast (75p). If it's half as good as the Thai food, it'll be terrific.

NORTH

Camden Town
& Primrose Hill

CAMDEN TOWN & PRIMROSE HILL

NORTH

© Crown copyright

Cheng Du

9 Parkway, NW1 ☎ 0171 485 8058   ⊖ Camden Town

Daily noon–2.30pm & 6.30–11.30pm   Mastercard, Visa

When you walk into a Chinese restaurant and see not only designer ice buckets for your wine, but also an espresso machine, your heart either sinks or soars. If you're on the side of the ice buckets, then you will enjoy Cheng Du, an elegant if slightly pricey place, improbably located in the busy heart of Camden Town. It bills itself as a Szechuan restaurant but don't expect too much in the way of raw or fierce flavours, for dishes here seem to have been "civilised", perhaps a little too much so. Yet the flavours are delicate, platefuls are pretty, and if you want a few more pyrotechnics, you can always order a saucer of chilli oil to play with and sear the tastebuds.

Steamed dumplings with Szechuan garlic dressing (£4.00 for eight dumplings) is a good starter – the dressing light and tasty. The deep-fried squid tossed with peppercorn salt (£5.00) is fresh and well-cooked, too, as are the steamed fresh scallops with garlic dressing (£4.60 for two). Main courses are all in a similar vein – peasant dishes that are heavily reliant on garlic, chilli and Szechuan pepper, "tidied-up" and made more accessible and more stylish. Try the steamed chicken with red dates, black fungi and golden lilies (£5.60), or the double-cooked pork (£5.50) in a rich sauce with capsicums, the ever-present spring onions and a red braising sauce – rich flavours predominate. The only real disappointment could be a dish of fried spring onions with black bean and green chilli (£3.90) – it carries the warning "very hot" . . . but isn't.

One section of the Cheng Du's menu is outstanding – the steamed fish, served with either ginger and spring onions, or in a black bean sauce. Various fish are priced by the pound: sea bass is £12.00 per lb.; Dover sole £15.80; turbot £12.80; and salmon £6.80. (All these prices vary seasonally). It's hard to beat a whole sea bass – firm-fleshed, delicious and perfectly cooked, arriving on a platter in all its glory, only to be meticulously filleted at the tableside by a waiter – unless, of course, your wallet will stretch to the same treatment for a Dover sole.

CAMDEN TOWN & PRIMROSE HILL ⑰ MODERN BRITISH/PUB

The Crown and Goose

100 Arlington Rd, NW1 ☎ 0171 485 2342   ⊖ Camden Town

Mon–Thurs noon–3pm & 6–10pm, Fri noon–3pm,	
Sat noon–4pm & 6–10pm, Sun noon–9pm.	Cash and cheques only.

The Crown & Goose is a lively, popular Camden pub that serves very decent food. It's a rough and ready sort of place; the wooden tables have a habit of swaying when you lean on them, and the murky green walls are hung with the odd retro sculpture and dusty nineteenth-century reproductions picked up from the markets. Staff bustle about in trendy trainers, but are friendly and attentive, and the music gets progressively louder as the evening goes on. Get here early on Saturday nights, or you'll be lucky to find a table. After eating, you're perfectly positioned to explore Camden's thriving indie music pubs, or take in some jazz at the nearby Jazz Café. Alternatively, you might prefer to lounge around; you won't be hurried on, and there's a decent choice of wines and beers.

As well as a regular menu, the Crown has a daily list of specials to choose from. Go for a dish that incorporates salad – all of which are deliciously fresh and crisp. Also good are the kitchen's home-made chips (£2), which are thick, chunky and very brown. Portions are generous; sometimes the plates seem too small to cope. Specials might include the likes of chicken supreme (£7.25) – slices of chicken breast in coriander sauce on a bed of salad – or vegetarian tomatoes (£6.50) – two beef tomatoes stuffed with rice and roast vegetables – or a Sunday Roast (£7.50 for roast meat, chips and salad). There's usually a good pasta of the day (£6.50), which might be something like fresh tagliatelle, served in a creamy dill sauce with smoked salmon. Out-and-out carnivores won't be disappointed by the 6oz Mexican burger (£6.95), a generous-sized burger topped with hot chilli sauce, melted cheese, tomato and spicy guacamole.

The choice of desserts is limited (usually two at most) but they are one of the kitchen's strengths. Home-baked almond and chocolate tart (£3.25) is warm and enticing; white and dark chocolate mousse (£3) is wonderfully creamy, and fruit salad with vanilla ice cream (£3) comes with a small pile of mint of top.

NORTH

The Engineer

65 Gloucester Ave, NW1 ☎ 0171 722 0950	⊖ Chalk Farm
Mon–Sat noon–3pm & 7–11pm, Sun noon–3.30pm & 7–10pm	Mastercard, Visa

The Engineer is one of that burgeoning rosta of gastro-pubs, whose food side has grown and grown – it now has tables in the bar, a more formal restaurant, tables in the garden (for those occasional Summer days), and a salle privée on the first floor. Wherever you end up sitting, you'll be offered the same menu (which changes every two weeks) and you'll pay the same price. The cooking is accomplished, with good strong combinations of flavours, and a cheerful, iconoclastic approach to what is fundamentally Mediterranean food.

Your hackles may rise at the charge of £1.75 for home-made bread and butter, but the bread is warm from the oven with a good crust and the butter is beurre echiré, and as they refill the basket after you've scoffed the lot you end up feeling happier about paying. Starters are simple and good. There's soup (£3.50). There may be a summery salad – such as watermelon, feta and ruby chard with roast pumpkin seeds and lime-mint dressing (£5.25), or seared tuna with white bean, flat leaf parsley and roast cherry tomato salad (£5.75). At lunchtime the mains will probably be quite light – eggs Benedict, eggs Florentine, a pan-fried organic beef burger. For dinner expect dishes like roast leg of lamb with adoba sauce (roast chilli and honey), and a prune and pistachio couscous (£11.75), or a risotto of oyster mushroom, sage and fennel with rocket and parmesan (£8.75). There's often a new twist put on an old favourite, so duck confit comes with sweet potato, watercress and bacon salad, and pickled cherries (£9.50). A very successful dish indeed. Do not miss out on a side order of baker chips (£.2.25) which are thick wedges of baked potato fried until crispy. Thanks to the Engineer's pub status, there is always a decent pint of beer to be had and the coffee is excellent, too – more reasons for why it's so busy; and more reasons for why you should book yourself a table.

At the bottom of the menu it says proudly, "Please note that all our meat is free range and organic". Hurrah! They deserve your support.

Lemonia

89 Regents Park Rd, NW1 ☎ 0171 586 7454	⊖ Chalk Farm
Mon–Fri noon–3pm & 6–11.30pm, Sat 6–11.30pm,	
Sun noon–3pm	All major credit cards

Lemons: growing outside, on tiles, in pictures, as garnishes, and in the food. They're everywhere. So it's not surprising that this popular, twenty-year-old Greek restaurant in Primrose Hill, is called 'Lemonia'. It's as good Greek food as you'll find in this swathe of London, but regulars – a mixture of greco-philes, business people and party groups – come as much for the atmosphere and friendly service. It's a big place with a main dining area that gives way to a much prettier, lower level conservatory, at the side of which is a smaller, more intimate room where the pictures are of Greek country-folk. The decor here is all trailing plants, wood, and terracotta floor tiles. Book early to ensure a table in this backwater if you wish to avoid the party crowds.

If you're indecisive, order the meze (£12.25 per person), which is an interesting combination of starters and main courses, served with a good Greek salad. Ordering off the menu, you'll want at least a couple of the starters: the spanakopitta (£3.40) – parcels of spinach, feta cheese and filo pastry – and the avocado and tarama (£3.75). The Greek salad (£2.75) is a worthwhile, too. Moving on, meat dishes are good value with generous portions of lamb in the kleftiko (£7.95) and tavvas (£7.75). The former is baked with lemon and added spices and herbs – very tender; the latter, with onions and herbs. Kalamari (£8.50) are nicely light, and fish shashlik (£8.75) is spicy. Vegetarians should go for the moussaka (£7.50). The puds range from the sweet and sticky baklava and kateifi (both £2.50) to halva (£2.70) and home-made cream caramel (£2.85). Look out for the bargain lunch special – two courses and coffee for £6.75. And there are party menus starting at £16.

The wine list includes various wines from Greece (which have greatly improved in the past few years), Cyprus and France. And they do a decent Greek coffee (£1.10) to finish the evening.

Nontas

14 Camden High St, NW1 ☎ 0171 387 4579   ⊖ Mornington Crescent

Mon–Sat noon–2.45 & 6–11.30pm   Mastercard, Visa

Nontas Vassilakas's Cypriot restaurant has been dishing up straightforward Greek food to enthusiastic Camden locals for the past quarter of a century. Endearingly tatty around the edges, it's a great-value place that doesn't need to prove itself to anyone. The Swiss-chalet-style decor – lots of dark wood and hanging lamps – is a little unusual for a Greek restaurant, but it's comfortable and relaxed, with Capitol Radio humming softly in the background, and a large cat snoozing on one of the bar chairs. At the back is a lovely garden, where in summer you can eat al fresco a world apart from busy Camden High Street. When the candles come out in the evenings, it's quite romantic – not bad for a place where you can eat well for under £10.

If there are two or more of you, go for the meze (£8.75 per person), then you'll you get a bit of everything, kicking off with some taramasalata (£1.75) and tahini (£1.55). The pourgouri (95p), which comes next, is a Cypriot speciality and very tasty – savoury ground wheat. The kalamarakia tiganita (£2.30) is also good – rings of deep-fried squid with a slice of lemon. Or start with a charcoal grilled dish – garides (£3.05), giant prawns sprinkled with chopped onions and parsley. To follow, Nontas do all the usual kebabs such as hirino – pork kebab – and kotopoulo – chicken kebab marinated in wine and served with rice (both are £5.40). Alternatively, try the pesari (£5.70) – fish kebab, or the shieftalies (£5.60) – deliciously spicy rissoles served with onions, cucumber and tomato. There's a separate vegetarian menu, where you can get a no-nonsense halloumi toasted sandwich (£2.05) or a dish such as moujendra (£1.95), lentils cooked with noodles. Desserts can be sickly sweet: avoid the pastries if you value your teeth and try the yiaourtu me meli (yogurt with honey, £1.05) instead. There's a good choice of Greek and Cypriot wines, with a bottle of retsina costing a mysterious £6.45.

Feeling sleepy? You can always check into the upstairs hotel. When it's not filled with Nontas's relatives, you can get a nice double for around £64, including breakfast.

Odette's

CAMDEN TOWN & PRIMROSE HILL ⑪ MODERN BRITISH

NORTH

130 Regent's Park Rd, NW1 ☎ 0171 586 5486 | ⊖ Chalk Farm
Mon–Fri 12.30–2.30pm & 7–11pm, Sat 7–11pm | Mastercard, Visa

Odette's is a charming, picturesque restaurant befitting equally pretty Primrose Hill. The walls are crammed with gilded mirrors and hanging plants, there's a pleasant conservatory at the back (with an open skylight in warm weather), and candles flicker throughout in the evenings. Add well-judged modern British food, the odd local celeb popping in, and staff that always try to make you feel special, and you have all the ingredients for a very successful local restaurant. In summer, try to get one of the tables that spill out onto this villagey street.

The food makes commendable use of seasonal produce so do not expect to find all the dishes listed every time you visit. However, the olive and walnut bread is a constant – warm and delicious. Starters, if you strike lucky, might include a delicate watercress soup with garlic tortellini (£3.50), or a warm salad of char-grilled Jerusalem artichokes, roasted tomatoes and rocket (£6.50). When in season, the Irish oysters (£7.50) are a good choice and well presented. Mains generally include at least one choice each of fish, meat, game and chicken. Pan-fried lemon sole comes with harissa, candied aubergines and globe artichokes (£13) – delicious. Cumin roast neck of new season lamb, soft polenta and spring greens (£12.50) is another good choice, as is sauté of black-leg chicken, fresh pasta, new season peas and broad beans (£12). Monkfish wrapped in Parma ham, served on a bed of roasted red peppers and spring onions with a warm vinaigrette (£13), is a great combination, while veggies might go for tarte tatin of caramelised onions and goat's cheese (£9). Puddings (all £4.75) are wonderfully indulgent, and include chocolate espresso tart with creme fraîche, lemon curd parfait with strawberries, and an outstanding mango and stem ginger sorbet.

Odette's has a very long wine list; so allow plenty of time to study it thoroughly, as there's something here to suit all tastes and purses. It's also nice to get such a large choice of wines by the glass and half-bottle. Try a glass of South African Chardonnay for £3.15, or a bottle of Sauvignon de Touraine for £8.25.

£12–£30

Trojka

101 Regent's Park Rd, NW1 ☎ 0171 483 3765	⊖ Chalk Farm
Daily 9am–11pm	Mastercard, Visa

Trojka is a Russian restaurant in the heart of Primrose Hill. In a spacious room decorated in bright colours, Russian, Ukrainian and Polish dishes are chalked up on the blackboard and listed on the large menu. This is a friendly, casual place, with a warm, neighbourhood atmosphere. Dishes come piled high with copious portions of well-prepared food. It is a hard worker – open for three meals a day – but it's in the evenings that Trojka really comes to life, and especially on Fridays and Saturdays when you're serenaded by a Russian musician strumming and crooning away in the centre of the room. That is, if you can get in; the place gets so packed you may have to fight for a table.

Check the blackboard for the specials before perusing the lengthy menu. Starters might include herring fillet in dill and caper sauce (£3.20), or salmon tartare (£4) – cured salmon with gherkins, capers and ginger. Otherwise, you can't go wrong with the borscht (£2.50), which is delicate and well flavoured. Trojka also does very good blinis (buckwheat pancakes, £3.70), served with a variety of fillings – smoked salmon and trout, pickled herring, aubergine caviar and taramasalata. Main dishes are generous and most come with vegetables. Good choices include pan-fried fillet of salmon marinated in ginger and dill, served on a bed of spinach with tartare sauce (£7). The Russian Pierog (£5.50) is also tasty – this is sauerkraut, sautéed vegetables and herbs in pastry served with either mushroom or tomato sauce. Pelmeni (£6) is home-made ravioli filled with a choice of vegetable or meat fillings, while galupsty (£6) are squidgy cabbage leaves stuffed with chicken and rice. Not to be missed is the latke and smetana (£1.20), crispy potato pancakes served with a dollop of sour cream. Desserts are straightforward but satisfying. There's the very good chocolate mousse torte (£3), or, for a real treat, malakoff (£3) – sponge fingers dipped in whipped cream and marsala.

Trojka (which means 'three of something') offers a small selection of flavoured, frozen vodkas to wash down all that blini and sour cream. At £1.60 a shot, you get to choose between plum, pepper, or, more intriguingly, bison grass, rowan and kosher.

Wazobia

257 Royal College St, NW1 ☎ 0171 284 1059	⊖ Camden Town
Mon–Sat 4.30pm–midnight, Sun 4.30–10.30pm	Mastercard, Visa

It says a lot for London's restaurant diversity that Camden's best-known Swedish restaurant went on to become "Wazobia", serving Nigerian and West African food. As you can discover from the menu copy, the name Wazobia is assembled from three words for "come-in" – wa in yoruba; zo in hausa; and bia in ibo – and expresses support for a united Nigeria. The restaurant is small and bright, while the service is unaffected and charming. This establishment runs on West African time. Clock watchers or busy people will probably succumb to an impatience-induced coronary while waiting for their starters. But if you can unwind enough to match velocities, you'll have a great time. The food is generally worth the wait.

Start with akara and shrimps (£2.55), a kind of small doughnut with prawns in it. Or there's puff-puff (£2.55), which is a more doughnutty doughnut. Dundun (£3.55) is very good – crisp cubes of yam served with a side dish of rich aubergine stew. But the ultimate is goat pepper soup (£3.55), a bowl of dark and incredibly rich broth that has enough chilli in it to clear the sinuses for months – seriously tasty. Choosing a main course is a more complicated business. With some sections of the menu you choose a stew and it comes with one of half a dozen kinds of staple – rice, cassava and so forth. Down the page, the procedure is reversed and you get to choose a staple dish and your choice of meat, fish or even snails. Try egusi and efo stew (£7.50), which is made from fresh spinach and ground melon seeds, with tomato and chilli sauce, then add a bit of fish, and choose rice, or semolina. More straightforward and very good is the yam and plantain pottage called asaro (£7.00), rich and tasty, especially if you choose a chicken leg from the list of optional accompaniments.

It takes a brave diner to choose amala. This is pounded cassava – an astonishingly glutinous dish, very subtly flavoured. It looks like a boxing glove made from quivering jelly and it may be an acquired taste.

Hampstead
& Golder's Green

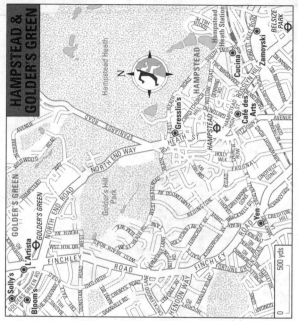

© Crown copyright

250

Bloom's

130 Golder's Green Rd, NW11 ☎ 0181 455 1338   ⊖ Golder's Green

Sun–Thurs noon–midnight, Friday 10am–2pm/3pm (winter/summer)

Sat open 1hr after sunset until 4am   All major credit cards

Bloom's goes way back. Back to 1920 when Rebecca and Morris Bloom set up the company to produce their great discovery – the original Veal Vienna. Since then the name "Bloom's of the East End" has carried the proud tag that it was "the most famous Kosher restaurant in the world". Setting aside the indignant claims of several outraged New York delis for the moment, it's a pity that the East End branch of Bloom's was forced to shut and that they have had to retrench to this, their Golder's Green stronghold, which opened in 1965. Nonetheless, it's a glorious period piece. Rows of sausages hang over the take-away counter, there are huge mirrors and chrome tables, and inimitable service from battle-hardened waiters. The food is fresh, kosher, filling and traditional.

So, the waiter looks you in the eye as you ask for a beer, "Heineken schmeineken?" he says derisively, at which point you opt for Maccabee, an Israeli beer (£1.90), and regain some ground. Start with some new green cucumbers (90p) – they are amazing, fresh, crisp, tangy, delicious – and maybe a portion of chopped liver and egg and onions (£4.50), which comes with world class rye bread. Or go for soup, which comes in bowls so full they slop over the edge: beetroot borscht (£2.90), very sweet and very red; lockshen (noodles soup – £2.90) and kreplach (dumplings soup – £3.90). Go on to main courses. The salt beef is as good as you might expect (£10.90 a plate). The stuffed breast of lamb (£9.90) is impressive, too, so long as you are a devotee of crispy bits and don't mind the sensation of fat trickling down your chin. The turkey schnitzel (£9.90) is a monster, crisp and golden. Add some side dishes, whatever you choose. Latkes (£1.90) are solid and uncompromising potato pancakes – weighty gastric depth charges. Tzimmas (£1.90) is a dish of honeyed carrots so cloyingly sweet that it could lay claim to a spot on the dessert menu. It's all filling, wholesome, comforting food. Enjoy!

Around the room are huge naive, murals representing Jewish Festivals. And who painted these complex pictures, you wonder? History doesn't relate where he's from, but he signs himself Pat O'Leary.

Café des Arts

82 Hampstead High St, NW3 ☎ 0171 435 3608   ⊖ Hampstead

Mon–Sat noon–4pm & 5.30–11.30pm, Sun noon–11pm   All major credit cards

HAMPSTEAD & GOLDER'S GREEN ⓣ FRENCH

The Café des Arts is a labyrinth of rooms, sensibly enough some are for smokers and some are not. Service is cheery and with no frills. The decor is practical with no frills. And the menu is similarly unembellished. This is a restaurant finely tuned to its surroundings: it's a fair bet that when the worthy citizens of Hampstead want fancy food they go to the West End, while closer to home they want sound bistro food at modest prices. That's what they've been getting here for the past twenty years. A chef somewhere deep in the bowels of the kitchen adds a few deft touches but the food is steady, and none the worse for that. This is the kind of good value, reliable eating out that ironically enough used to be the preserve of the French when haute cuisine ruled supreme. these days it is something of a lost art.

The menu reflects the manager's Marseilles/Provencal roots, with a few excursions around the Mediterranean. Starters range through Provencal vegetable broth with basil paste (£3.75) – on the surface a soft option, but take heart, the soup is strongly flavoured – through Elizabeth David's old inspiration – roasted peppers (£4.50), here tinkered with the addition of a ewe's milk cheese and pine nut mousse and sherry vinaigrette. Fish starters might include a swordfish carpaccio (£5.75), or saffroned cod ravioli (£5.25). As main course choices, two stand-out dishes are roast Barbary duck with artichokes stewed with garden peas (£11.25) and the lamb and broad bean fricassee with braised Cos lettuce and lemon sauce (£9.50). Both provide a welcome twist by way of the vegetable element. Fish lovers are catered for with dishes like sautéed sea bream with olive mash and peppers stewed with tomato mint and lemon (£11.25); and red mullet and monkfish stew with potatoes and saffron mussel velouté (£11.75). Desserts are simple, rich comfort dishes, such as chocolate tart, or apple and raisin butter cake (both £4.50).

The Café des Arts does an extraordinary value set lunch (Mon–Fri noon–4pm): two courses for £5, three for £7.95. It's simple fare – soup or quiche followed by steak frites or pan-fried salmon – but it's well done, and you'd be hard pushed to do it yourself for a fiver.

NORTH

Cucina

45a South End Rd, NW3 ☎ 0171 435 7814   ⊖ Belsize Park

Mon–Thurs noon–2.30pm & 7–10.30pm, Fri & Sat noon–2.30pm & 7–11pm,

Sun noon–2.30pm   All major credit cards except Diners

From the outside, this single fronted restaurant next to a bakery, just up from South End Green, looks tiny – four tables and a bar, invariably empty. But when you go in and turn right up the stairs, it opens out into a large brightly-painted, wooden-floored, roof-lit dining room. Very modern, very fashionable, very Hampstead. At the lunch service all is relatively quiet, scattered tables talking business – and there is a sensibly priced set lunch at two courses for £10, three courses for £13.50. This may feature starters like thick field mushroom soup or an anchovy salad with grilled potato celeriac, cucumber and soured cream, followed by mains such as char-grilled pork chop with barbecued beans. In the evening things are busy and the à la carte menu takes over. This menu darts about a bit from cuisine to cuisine and continent to continent, but wherever you alight each dish is well-presented, while the service is efficient (rather too speedy, sometimes) and friendly.

Dinner-time starters may include seared scallops with soba noodles, chilli, ginger and Thai basil (£6.95); or deep-fried goat's cheese and caramelised onion sandwich with walnut salad (£5.25), presented as a weighty pair of thick triangles; or perhaps buffalo and green peppercorn sausages with apple onion and thyme chutney (£5.25), solid and meaty. Amongst the main courses there is always a fish of the day, and it is often something interesting like mahi-mahi. Other fish dishes feature, too, like sweet miso marinated cod with wasabi mash, mirin and pickled ginger (£11.50). Then there may be char-grilled guinea fowl with sag aloo yoghurt and almonds (£12.95); or roast rump of lamb with moussaka Dauphinoise and red wine jus (£12.50). There may a slight suspicion that the menu reads better than the dishes turn out, but they are never short of appetising.

As an adjunct to the puddings and coffees listed on the dessert menu, there's "a selection of chocolate truffles". You get four and they are not bad at all but with a price tag of £1.95 they cost nearly 50p each, which may put a crimp in your enjoyment.

Gresslin's

13 Heath St, NW3 ☎ 0171 794 8386	⊖ Hampstead
Tues–Sun 12.30–2.45pm, Mon–Sat 7–10.45pm	All major credit cards

Gresslin's is a small, rather humble-looking restaurant on Hampstead's busy Heath Street. It has a modern glass front, wooden floors, and jolly, yellow-painted walls and modern furnishings. But don't be fooled by appearances: the minimalist, workaday decor belies a distinctive menu, which they bill as Modern European. Here you'll find a succession of dishes all given an imaginative twist – very much in the modern idiom where Mediterranean flavours meet Oriental flourishes – and presentation on the plate is taken very seriously. This combination has secured Gresslin's a considerable following.

The efficient French waiters are knowledgeable about the food, and are happy to recommend something they think you'll like, but it is hard in any case to go far wrong. The seasonal menu is short and well thought-out, underpinned by quality, fresh ingredients, and with a good balance of fish, meat and vegetarian options. Starters might include fresh steamed mussels with rice vermicelli, lemon grass and coconut milk (£4.95); grilled duck liver with teriyaki sauce (£6.50); or salad of pan-fried scallops, black pudding and potato fritters (£6.95). Everything is precisely cooked. For mains, you get a choice of eight or nine dishes, including a daily-changing special. Roast cod (£12.95) is served on a melting pile of saffron-flavoured mash, with a dollop of black olive tapenard on top, and surrounded by creamy parsley sauce – a mouth-watering combination of ingredients. The seared loin of tuna with Swiss chard, tomato and caper salsa (£13.50) produces barely cooked fish, as is the fashion, and a tangy salsa. Also good is lemon-grilled baby chicken with roasted Jerusalem artichokes and Puy lentils (£12.95). Or you might go for the very Oriental buckwheat soba with spring green, bean shoots and coriander pesto (£10.50). Desserts are good too; try the chocolate pecan brownies with hot chocolate fudge sauce and vanilla ice-cream (£4.50), or the caramelised lemon tart with raspberry coulis (£4.00).

Whilst you may not visit Hampstead just to visit Gresslin's, it's a real asset when you're there – combining well with the newly-refurbished Everyman cinema, just around the corner.

L'Artista

917 Finchley Rd, NW11 ☎ 0181 731 7501	⊖ Golder's Green
Daily noon–midnight	Mastercard, Visa

Situated opposite the entrance to Golder's Green Tube, and occupying an arch under the railway lines, L'Artista is hard to miss. It proclaims itself with its pavement terrace, abundant greenery and umbrellas: a lively, vibrant restaurant and pizzeria that exercises an almost magnetic appeal to the young and not so young of Golder's Green. At the weekend it is literally full to bursting and tables spill out onto the terrace – a perfect spot to eat al fresco, providing the traffic isn't too heavy on the Finchley Road. Inside the decor is plain but enhanced by celebrity photographs; the waiters are a bit cagey if asked just how many of them have actually eaten here, but the proximity of the tables ensures that you get to rub shoulders with whoever happens to be around you, famous or otherwise.

The menu offers a range of Italian food with a good selection of main courses such as fegato Veneziana (£6.80) – a rich dish of calf's liver with onion and white wine. The trota del pescatore (£6.80) is also good, a plain but effective trout with garlic. But L'Artista's pizzas are its forte. They are superb. As well as traditional thin crust capricciosa (£5.70) with anchovies eggs and ham, or quattro formaggi (£5.10), there are more unusual varieties such as rucola e stracchino(£5.10) – a plain tomato-less pizza topped with stracchino cheese and heaps of crisp rocket, which is actually very good. The calzone (£5.50) – a cushion-sized rolled pizza stuffed with ham, cheese and sausage and topped with Napoli sauce – is wonderful. Pasta dishes are varied and for a change the penne alla vodka (£5.10) made with vodka, prawns and cream is well worth a try. For something lighter try the excellent insalata del L'Artista (£4.80), a generous mix of tuna, olives and fennel, with an order of equally good garlic pizza bread (£2.50).

L'Artista tries hard to bring something of the atmosphere of Naples to Golder's Green and by a happy accident this ambience is enhanced by the Vesuvian tremors which occur whenever a Northen line train rumbles ominously overhead.

£16–£35

Solly's Exclusive

146-150 Golder's Green Road, NW11 ☎ 0181 455 2121   ⊖ Golder's Green

Daily except Fri 6.30–10.30pm   All major credit cards except Diners

What makes Solly's Exclusive so exclusive is that it is upstairs. Downstairs is Solly's restaurant, which is a small, packed, noisy place specialising in epic falafel – crispy balls of minced chick peas which are deep fried and served with all manner of salads. You'll find Solly's Exclusive by coming out of Solly's Restaurant, turning left, and left again around the side of the building, and then proceeding through an unmarked black door. Upstairs a huge, bustling dining room accommodates 180 customers, while a new back room provides a further 100 seats which lie in wait for functions, bar mitzvahs and so forth. The decor is . . . interesting – tented fabric on the ceiling, multi-coloured glass, and brass light fittings – while waitresses, all of them with Solly's Exclusive emblazoned across the back of their waistcoats, maintain a brisk approach to the niceties of service.

The food is tasty and workmanlike. Start with a dish that pays homage to the chick pea – hummus with falafel (£4) – three crispy depth charges and some well-made dip. Or order Solly's special aubergine dip (£3). Or the Morrocan cigars (£4.50) which are made from minced lamb wrapped in filo pastry and deep fried. Solly's pitta (95p) – a fluffy, fourteen-inch disc of freshly baked bread – has more in common with a perfect nan than Greek restaurant bread. Pittas to pine for. For a main course, the lamb shawarma (£9.50) is very good, nicely seasoned and spiced, and served with excellent chips and a good, sharp-tasting mound of shredded cabbage salad. The barbecue roast chicken with the same accompaniments (£9.50) is also good. Steer clear of the Israeli salad (£2.50), unless you enjoy a large bowl which is half full of chopped watery tomatoes and half full of chopped watery cucumber.

Solly's Exclusive is kosher and under the supervision of the London Beth Din, so rather naturally it opens and closes at different times and on different days to non-Jewish establishments. If you don't know these ground rules yourself, check before setting out.

Yen

96 West End Lane, NW6 ☎ 0171 624 8897	⊖ West Hampstead
Daily noon–2.30pm & 6pm–midnight	Diners, Mastercard, Visa

Mrs Lau and her husband used to have a smart Chinese restaurant in Manchester, over a casino. But they left all that behind to open in West Hampstead. Mrs Lau is very keen on noodles, dumplings, and dishes cooked in pots – dishes rich in coconut and chilli that come from the island of Hainan in the south of China – plus other unusual dishes that are Taiwanese in origin. The decor at Yen is modern, with light colours predominating; the chairs are good; the piped music not so good. Mrs Lau denies that she actually cooks herself but you get the impression that it would take a very brave chef to disagree with her orders – and anyone tasting the dishes would have to agree that Mrs Lau knows what she is talking about.

Start with the Sichuan-style prawns with chilli and garlic (£5.00) – large prawns on bamboo skewers, smeared with Sichuan pepper, chilli and garlic – and some crispy vegetarian spring rolls (£4.00), which are long, thin, crisp and fresh. And try at least one kind of cheow zea – pan-fried dumplings. Pork, beef, and fish are £4 for 8, £6 for 12; vegetarian £3.80 and £5.60; or try a mixture for £6. They are all freshly made (one suspects by Mrs Lau) and come with a ginger vinegar dipping sauce, the vegetarian ones are heavy with fresh coriander, pork and 'meat' are very tasty and 'fish' rather more delicate. Moving on to the main courses, Xiang woy chi (£4.50) is jasmine-flavour chicken with chilli and black bean sauce – the chilli black bean flavours vapourise any lingering jasmine but this is a good rich dish. The 'special clay pot' dishes are beautiful and delicious, especially the Sichuan sa kwoa (£6), a spicy Sichuan dish. The chia le sa kwoa (£5.50) is a chicken curry from Hainan redolent with coconut and spices. From Taiwan comes fu chein chaw (£7.20) – lettuce wraps with crab meat, prawns, egg, glass noodles, and spring onions. Altogether more serious than the more run-of-the-mill, 'meat in lettuce leaves'.

Lastly, do try the Yen 'house special' crispy noodles (£5.60). They're rather like a 1960s chow mein, but utterly delicious when – as here – freshly cooked.

£12–£30

Zamoyski

85 Fleet Rd, NW3 ☎ 0171 794 4792   ⊖ Belsize Park

Mon–Sat 5–11pm, Sun 5–10.30pm   Mastercard, Visa

Zamoyski is a small, friendly place with a long menu, supplemented by various specials written on a mobile blackboard, and a list of vodkas that is longer still. Downstairs there's room for twenty in the bar, and upstairs there's a larger dining room. The staff are cheerful and prices are low – a combination which pulls in a broad spectrum of customers from middle-aged couples taking dinner à deux, and people enjoying an early evening drink with a starter or two, to large parties (often from the nearby Royal Free Hospital) intent on laying into the vodka. The watershed here is about nine o'clock, by which point you'll need to start viewing the place through the bottom of a shot glass.

This is one of those Slavic/Polish restaurants where the starters have a distinct edge on the main courses, and as result ordering three starters per person and sharing is a very attractive strategy. The management have spotted this trend and offer a "9 course Polskie Mezze" (£6.50) – an outrageously low price (the only caveat being that it is not available after 7pm on Friday or Saturday). One daily special always worth including in your raft of starters is the soup (£2.20) which could be anything from sorrel to beetroot. Then try some herring: sledz wedzony (£4.25) is smoked herring with horseradish cream; sledz w oleju (£4.75) is the sweeter matjes fillet. You might move on to placki losos (£4.50) – little potato and walnut pancakes topped with smoked salmon; or kaszanka (£4.75) – home-made black pudding with mash; or zywiecka (£4.75) – smoked garlic sausage. And don't miss out on the pierogi rozne (£4.75) – small dumplings stuffed with potato and cheese, or mushrooms, or meat. If you get to them, main courses are made of sterner stuff, their mission is more filling than fanciful: kotlet cielecy (£8.95) is a veal escalope; kaczka z jabikami (£8.95) is a frazzled half duck; and schab ze sliwkami (£7.95) is a tenderloin of pork stuffed with prunes.

Take a look at the barrels on the bar, they are full of bisongrass vodka. You are right to feel nervous – anywhere that serves vodka by the barrel deserves respect!

Highgate
& Crouch End

HIGHGATE & CROUCH END

Highgate Wood

Queen's Wood

N

Jashan

TOPSFIELD PARADE
O's Thai Café

La Bota

BROADWAY PARADE

WESTON PARK

HARINGEY PARK

GLASSLYN RD

WOLSELEY RD

PARK ROAD

PARK ROAD

TOTTENHAM LA

WOOD VALE

QUEENS WOOD ROAD

SOUTH... WOOD LANE

CROUCH END HILL

CROUCH HILL

PRIORY GARDENS

HIGHGATE

SHEPHERD'S HILL

HURST AVENUE

CROUCH END

COLERIDGE

DRESDEN RD

HASLEMERE RD

STANHOPE GDNS

CLAREMONT ROAD

AVENUE ROAD

HOLMESDALE RD

JACKSONS LANE

ARCHWAY RD

MILTON PARK

LANE

HORNSEY LA GDN

HORNSEY RISE

HAZELVILLE RD

LANE

SUNNYSIDE ROAD

HORNSEY

HIGHGATE

The Village Bistro

WAMELEY CRES

HORNSEY LA

HORNSEY RD

HIGHGATE HILL

CHOLMELEY

HORNSEY

ROAD

DRESDEN RD

CHEVER RD

HARBERTON RD

LANE

WAY

DUNCOMBE RD

GRAND PARADE

CRABB

CROMWELL

HORNSEY ROAD

SOUTHWOOD

BISHOPS RD

HIGHGATE HILL

Waterlow Park

SWAINS LANE

DARTMOUTH PARK

MAGDALA AV

ARCHWAY

OAKESHOTT AV

| 0 | | 500 yds |

© Crown copyright

Jashan

19 Turnpike Lane, N8 ☎ 0181 340 9880	⊖ Turnpike Lane
Tues–Sun 6–11.30pm	All major credit cards

This elegant, bright and roomy Indian restaurant on Turnpike Lane has a loyal local following – all of whom seem to know The Secret. This secret – which isn't very well kept – is that the Jashan kitchens have a sideline in preparing ready meals for a number of the West End's more prestigious food halls. As to deciding which proud offerings of the foodie havens started life in N8, an intensive tasting programme is the only way you'll ever be quite sure. You're in for quite a treat for, like other leading Indian restaurants, Jashan has recently added many authentic regional dishes to its reportoire.

Take a look at the menu – and look is meant literally. The management at Jashan have taken the unprecedented step of superimposing each list of dishes on a photograph of all those dishes laid out as if for a banquet. This is a dangerous strategy . . . what if your pomfret doesn't look to be as big as the one in the picture? It also makes for an intimidatingly long and glossy menu. A good point to start would be pakora (£2.75), an array of vegetables ranging from a slice of potato to a whole chilli and a spinach leaf, all mixed in a spicy gram flour batter and fried until crisp. Or try the dehati chaas (£1.95) which is a glass of yoghurt that thinks it is a cheese, served either sweet or salty. Or share a tarah tarah ke kabab (£10.95) which presents a range of kebabs from the tandoor – the kebabs are very good here, well spiced, and precisely cooked. As a main course try murg zaibunissa (£5.95) chicken in tasty-but-mild white gravy. Or gosht kesari (£5.95), lamb in a saffron sauce. That Rajasthani classic, dal bukhara (£2.95), lentils tempered with butter, is also good. And there's a long list of breads; make sure you try phudina parantha (£1.75), a flaky fresh paratha with a sprinkling of mint.

By the time you are contemplating the dessert course the pictorial menu seems less unusual. Affable waiting staff will quite understand cries for "the pink one". This is Jashan ka falooda (£3.75), made up of malai kulfi in a sea of bilious pink, rose-flavoured, milk. Perhaps not.

La Bota

HIGHGATE & CROUCH END Ⓣ **SPANISH**

31 Broadway Parade, N8 ☎ 0181 340 3082   ⊖ Finsbury Park/Turnpike Lane

Daily noon–2.30pm (Sat/Sun until 3.30pm) & 6–11.30pm   Amex, Mastercard, Visa

This bustling tapas bar and restaurant enjoys a good evening trade – and with good reason. It's a Galician – northwest Spanish – place, and that's always a good sign, particularly for seafood. The best of its tapas fall into two categories: there are the "raw" ones like Serrano ham which simply need careful buying and some good bread as accompaniment, and there are the stews which have been made in the morning and then re-heated as necessary for the customers later on – thankfully most of the rich, unfussy dishes of Galicia lend themselves to this treatment. But your first decision is a crucial one: do you go all out for tapas (there are 21 on the menu, plus a further 15 vegetarian ones, plus another dozen or so "daily specials" chalked on a blackboard)? Or do you choose one of the main courses listed – Spanish omelette, paellas, steaks, chicken, fish and so forth? Perhaps the best option is to play to La Bota's strengths and order up a few tapas, then a few more, until you have subdued your appetite and there's no longer a decision to make.

Start with simple things. Boquerones en vinaigre (£2.95) brings forth a plate of broad white anchovies with a pleasant vinegar tang. Jamón Serrano (£4.15) is thinly sliced, ruby red and strongly flavoured, perfect with the basket of warm French bread that is on the table. Then move on to hot tapas – mejillones pescador (£3.35) is a good-sized plate of mussels in a tomato and garlic sauce; quail Tio Pepe (£2.85) is a lone quail in a sherry sauce; rinones al Jerez (£2.75) is a portion of kidneys in a different sherry sauce, rich and good. Duck a la pimenta (£3.25) is duck on the bone, cooked long and slowly in a rich gravy. Then there's egg tuna mayonnaise with potato salad (£2.70); rabbit cazuela (£2.85); chicken Riojana (£3.20); patatas bravas (£1.85) – potatoes in a mildly spicy tomato sauce. Just keep them coming until you have had enough.

If you like squid, and don't mind looking at a whole one, opt for chiprones a la plancha (£3.85) – four of squidlets grilled to tender perfection.

NORTH

O's Thai Café

10 Topsfield Parade, N8 ☎ 0181 348 6898   ⊖ Finsbury Park (then bus)

Mon 6.30–11pm, Tues–Sun noon–3pm & 6.30–11pm   Mastercard, Visa

O's Thai Café is young, happy and fresh – just like O himself. With his economics, advertising and fashion design background, and a staff who seem to be having fun, O brings a youthful zip to Thai cuisine. His café is fast and noisy with current favourite music at high volume. But that's not to say the food is anything less than excellent, and very good value too. Order from the comprehensive and well explained menu or from the blackboard list of specials which runs down an entire wall.

There are many starters and you can do no better than order the special starter (£3.75) which gives you a taster of almost everything. Satays are tasty, prawn toasts and spring rolls as crisp as they should be, and paper-wrapped thin dumplings do melt in the mouth. A tm ka chicken soup (£3.25) is hot and sharp with lime leaf and lemon grass. Main courses include Thai red and green curries – the gaeng kiew, a spicy soupy green curry of chicken and coconut cream (£4.95), is pungently mor-eish – as well as an interesting selection of specials such as yamneau, aka weeping tiger (£8.95) – sliced spiced grilled steak served on salad with a pungent Thai dressing. If you like noodles, order a pad mee si iew (£5.95), a stir fry of vermicelli with vegetables, soy sauce, peanuts and the main ingredient of your choice, either chicken, beef, pork, king prawn or bean curd. Puddings include khow tom mud – banana with sticky rice wrapped in banana leaf (£1.75), Thai ice cream (£2.25), and fruit fritters curiously served with golden syrup and ice cream (£2.25). There is a wide and varied wine list, with Budweiser Budvar, Gambrinus and Leffe beers on draught. O's does take-away too.

If you're new to Thai food, then O's is a good place to learn as the staff are happy to explain how it all works and you can specify how hot you like your food. Most main courses are around £5.50 which makes for very good value, and all of them are served with a delightfully moulded mountain of rice which is included in the price. The café also offers a discount on its prices if you eat early and vacate your table by 8.30pm.

HIGHGATE & CROUCH END · FRENCH

The Village Bistro

38 Highgate High St, N6 ☎ 0181 340 5165   ⊖ Highgate

🕐 Daily noon–3pm & 6–11pm   Mastercard, Visa

The Village Bistro is something of an institution in Highgate, serving French food of varying fashionability for decades. And you can almost forget you're in London here; all is quaint and countrified in this narrow Georgian house approached by a corridor off Highgate's main road. Inside can be a bit of a squeeze and the decor is all chintzy curtains and crooked paintings, but any sense that you're sitting in old aunt's living room is swept away by the food, which is modern French. Presumably this combination of ancient and modern is exactly what hits the spot in Highgate as this restaurant is, and has been, consistently successful. Downstairs, the windows peek out onto the hilly High street, while a spindly, winding staircase leads upstairs to the smoking floor.

Come here hungry; sauces can be rich and dishes very filling. The menu changes every few months and includes a range of old stalwarts along with a sprinkling of more contemporary creations. A really tasty starter is goat's cheese wrapped in aubergine with grilled vegetables and spicy tomato dressing (£5.95). Also good is the Parma ham with marinated leeks, baby leaves and home-dried tomatoes, with a soft boiled egg and parmesan crisp (£6.25). Traditionalists might opt for the fine French onion soup with cheese crouton (£3.95), or, when in season, asparagus with hollandaise sauce (£5.95). There's a good choice of main dishes; which always includes two specials – dishes like a panache of seafood with parmesan, lemon and olive oil (£10.95). For a well-judged mix of flavours and textures, go for the escalope of veal with parmesan mash, fried egg and capers (£11.50). Or you might try monkfish roasted with garlic, rosemary and preserved lemon on French beans and mussels (£12.95); or peppered fillet steak with gratin dauphinoise (£13.95).

Desserts (all £3.95) can be solid and formidable. Hot chocolate fondant with pistachio ice cream and white chocolate sauce is not for anyone wearing tight clothing. The classic crème brulée, and crêpe filled with vanilla ice cream and hot raspberry sauce, are wiser choices.

NORTH

Holloway
& Finsbury Park

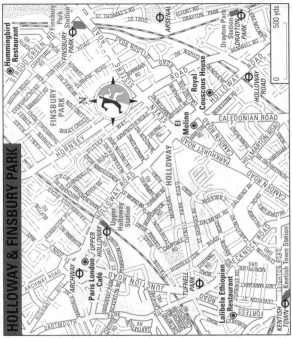

HOLLOWAY & FINSBURY PARK

Hummingbird Restaurant

Finsbury Park Station

FINSBURY PARK

HORNSEY

Royal Couscous House

HOLLOWAY ROAD

El Molino

CALEDONIAN ROAD

Drayton Park Station

Upper Holloway Station

Paris London Café

ARCHWAY

Lalibela Ethiopian Restaurant

Kentish Town Station

© Crown copyright

500 yds

El Molino

379 Holloway Rd, N7 ☎ 0171 700 4312	⊖ Holloway Road
Mon–Thurs noon–10.30pm, Fri & Sat noon–11 pm	Mastercard, Visa

El Molino is a class tapas bar and restaurant – a lot better than you might expect from its regulation bull fight posters and Spanish ceramics. Owner Tino Risquez opened in November 1992 and has built up a loyal clientele from Islington and the nearby University of North London. He offers robust Spanish food, fairly mildly spiced, and served in generous portions, belying his explanation of tapas – "The Taste of Spain in Little Dishes" – in the window. This is a place where you can dine well on the tapas alone.

Good tapas – or starters – include a fine rinones al jerez (£3.20) – well sherried and garlicky kidneys; escalivada (£2.75) – a rich dish of fried aubergine, peppers and onions; a generous round of traditional Spanish tortilla (£2.75), made fresh and served hot straight from the pan; and albondigas (£3.00) – Spanish meat balls in a thick tomato sauce. There are also the usual offerings of serrano ham (£5.00), queso Manchego – La Mancha cheese (£3.20), and patatas bravas (£2.20), as well as more spicy dishes like octopus in oil and paprika (£5.20). Main courses are reasonably priced too, with dishes like pez espada provincial – swordfish in tomato and garlic sauce (£5.00), and pollo riojana – chicken pieces in tomato, peppers, mushrooms and wine sauce (£5.45). Tin confirms that his paella is as authentic as you can get over here – ingredients permitting – and is highly flavoured rice with peppers, mussels, chicken, small and large prawns. It's properly prepared, fresh every order, so you are warned that there's a 45-minute wait. Wines are priced low and come chilled: pick between San Miguel or the slightly stronger Estrella (£2.10). Tin boasts that there's no minimum charge either and customers are welcome to come in just for one dish, except on Friday and Saturday nights, when it's advisable to book.

Although anglicised, El Molino tries to keep as authentically Spanish as possible and Tino keeps a range of drinks behind the bar to remind him of home. Try Ponche in its distinctive silver bottle. It's brandy-based, vanilla sweet, and just the thing for a nightcap.

Hummingbird Restaurant

84 Stroud Green Rd, N4 ☎ 0171 263 9690   ⊖ Finsbury Park

Mon–Sat 11am–midnight, Sun 1pm–midnight   All major credit cards

At the Hummingbird, Mark Ramgoolie combines the roles of proprietor, chef and maitre d', taking the time to guide even the most ignorant diner through the intricacies of Caribbean cuisine – what's from Guyana, what's Jamaican, which dishes come from Trinidad or Barbados, what's hot and what's not. Caribbean food is genuinely multi-cultural. There is a large Asian population in Guyana so they contribute some brilliant curries, usually with a characteristic dash of coconut milk. From Trinidad come rotis. From Jamaica callaloo soup. And from Finsbury Park, Mark's home-made ice creams, and a rum punch dangerous enough to have a fanclub all of its own.

Soups are a strong point. Consider either the crab callalloo, a thick, bright-green soup made with okra and coconut and complete with a clump of crab legs sunk in its depths (£2.50), or Humming Bird Soup, which is an altogether meatier affair with lamb and vegetables (£2.50). Or you might try the more prosaically named "fried fish" (£3.50). This turns out to be a slab of redfish perfectly cooked and accompanied by a dish of home-made green mango chutney and a home-made chili sauce with the consistency of molten lead. As a main course the Jamaican speciality ackee and salt fish (£4.50) is much nicer than it sounds and the goat curry (£4), and lamb and aubergine curry (£4.50) are both rich and tasty. The side dishes are a revelation – plantain that's nutty and tastes like chestnuts, and notably good fried green bananas (both £1.50). If you up for desserts, try corn meal pudding (£1.95), or one of the ice creams fresh from the churn – rum and raisin, pistachio, or coconut (two scoops £1.75).

Run amok with the drinks. As well as Carib lager (£1.50) and the rum-based "killer" punch (£3.50), there's Irish moss, sour sop, peanut punch, and Guinness punch (all at £2). The latter is made from Nigerian or "export" Guinness (8% abv!) with condensed milk, ordinary milk, nutmeg, cinnamon, and vanilla essence. Sounds pretty odd; looks pretty odd; is pretty odd – so why does it taste so very delicious?

Lalibela Ethiopian Restaurant

137 Fortress Rd, N5 ☎ 0171 284 0600   ⊖ Tufnell Park

Mon–Thurs 6pm–midnight, Fri–Sun 6–11pm   All major credit cards except Diners

The Lalibela is a twelfth-century Ethiopian church – carved, in the shape of a cross, from a huge outcrop of solid rock. Its namesake in Tufnell Park is remarkable for serving uncompromisingly authentic Ethiopian food and for its genuine understanding of hospitality. It has that slightly harassed, but still entirely laid-back, feel to it that is a great comfort to the diner. And however ignorant of Ethiopian cuisine and customs you may be, pure ungilded hospitality shines through. Upstairs, you will be seated on low, carved, wooden seats around traditional low tables (so that you can eat with your hands). If your knee joints won't take that kind of punishment, ask for a table downstairs and resign yourself to dripping sauce down your front.

Starters are few in number, but help banish any thought that you are merely in a strange kind of curry house. The lamb samosas (£3.25) have very dry, papery pastry and a savoury, spicy filling – delicious. The Lalibela salad (£3.25) is potatoes and beetroot fried together with a spicy sauce and served hot. Main courses are served traditionally, that is to say as pools of sauce set out on a two-foot diameter injera bread. Injera is cold, sour (as in fermented sourdough) and thin. You tear a piece off and use it to pick up something tasty. Portions are small, which makes prices seem high. But flavours are intense. If you're nervous you can have the dishes with rice or mashed potato. What goes on the injera? Wot – that's what . . . doro wot (£5.85) – a piece of chicken and a hard-boiled egg in a rich sauce, or begh wot (£5.85) – lamb with a bit more chilli. Lalibela ketfo (£7.50) is savoury mince and an amazing highly-spiced, cottage cheese – delicious. King prawn special (£6.50) is prawns in a tomato, onion and chilli sauce.

Do try the Ethiopian traditional coffee (£5), which is delicious and a spectacle. After the parading of a small wok full of smoking coffee beans through the restaurant, it is served in a round-bottomed coffee pot sitting on a plaited quoit.

Paris London Café

5 Junction Rd, N19 ☎ 0171 561 0330	⊖ Archway
Daily 9am–11pm (Sun until 10.30pm)	All major credit cards (3% surcharge)

You have to get on a train to get good, modest-priced French cooking – but not the Eurostar, the Northern line. Brothers Jerome and Frederic Boileau's Paris London Café is right opposite the exit from Archway tube station. The restaurant is small and tables are tightly packed, making for a bustling atmosphere that confirms you've made the right choice. Most of North London knows about the Paris London Café so it's often very busy. They serve breakfast, lunch and dinner – and on Sundays there's "Frunch", a mixture of brunch and lunch that includes French roasts of the day.

Starters are classic. Soupe du jour (£1.95) is freshly made and so thick you could eat it with a fork. Cassolette d'escargots au beurre d'ail (half dozen £3.25, dozen £5.25) is all you would expect of snails and garlic butter, but with a hint of Pernod, too; make sure you have plenty of French bread and be prepared for a shiny chin. Amongst the mains, boeuf miroton à la Lyonnaise (£5.95) is slowly cooked beef so tender that it cuts with the fork; confit de canard et pommes salardais au jus de cepes (£5.95) is the best confit you'll get this side of the Manche; and bavette grillée au thym frais (£5.95) is that special French cut of steak with fresh thyme. Gratin Dauphinoise (£1.95) is as creamy cheesy and garlicky as it should be, while petits pois à la Française are a must. Puddings are equally good. Tarte des demoiselles Tatin (£2.50) is sweet, tart and caramelised with solid chunks of buttery apple. Tarte aux citrons meringuée (£2.25) is creamy, rich and sharp at the same time. And profiteroles au chocolat Belge come with more than enough hot Belgian chocolate sauce. There is a very good selection of wines that includes some simple robust country choices at low prices, but finer wines as well.

The café offers a bargain prix fixe menu at £9.95 for three courses, and a Menu des Gourmands, which at £17.95 for five courses offers even better value. All in all, this is a great place to eat, and to practise your French – and, yes, les patrons do mange ici.

Royal Couscous House

316 Holloway Rd, N7 ☎ 0171 700 2188	⊖ Holloway Road
Daily 5–11pm	Mastercard, Visa

Karim Menhal is the diffident young man dressed in immaculate whites who is billed as head chef here – though he also manages to do the bills, run the bar, wait on tables, and hold the front door open. He certainly has a way about him and is described as "handsome" in one of the many admiring restaurant review clippings that adorn the front window. His restaurant is long, and the tables are topped with oil cloth. The walls show off Moroccan tourist posters, cheap carpets (you have to hope they are cheap, as they've been nailed to the decorative wood cladding), and pretend firearms. The food is very fresh, very tasty, and very good value, and Mr Menhal keeps the service well up to scratch.

Start with an array of starters and hot bread. The bread is particularly good. The aubergine dip (£1.90) is amazing, chopped aubergines have been cooked and cooked to concentrate the flavour. Smoked pepper (£1.80) is made with strips of roasted green peppers. Even the spicy olives (£1) are worthy of note – black and green olives with chunks of red chilli. Then there's the merguez salad (£3.50) – a few links of the small spicy lamb sausages with a terrific tomatoey sauce and some salad. Main courses split into couscous and tagines. The laksour couscous (£7.95) is a combination of lamb, merguez and mixed vegetables. The couscous here is light, and well-cooked. The tagines are also good. Royal tagine (£6.50) is a classic Moroccan dish of lamb with prunes, sesame seeds, and slices of boiled egg – sweet and rich. Tafraout tagine (£5.95) is made from chicken with olives and those wholly delicious brine-preserved Moroccan lemons. For pudding try the ceffae (£2.50) – a mound of couscous cooked in butter, sugar, cinnamon and almonds. Finish with mint tea (£1.20), or Moroccan coffee (£1.20) – a kind of heavily spiced cappuccino.

The Moroccan wine list features eight sound wines (all at £8.49 or £9.49) – a far cry from the days when proudly revealing a bottle of Moroccan red was enough to strike fear into the hearts of any dinner party.

Kilburn &
West Hampstead

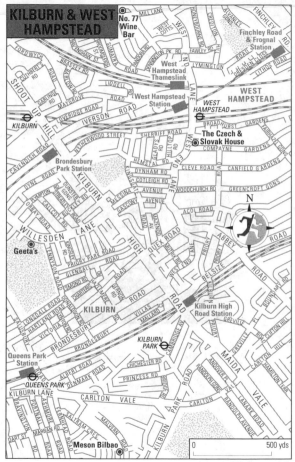

KILBURN & WEST HAMPSTEAD

No. 77 Wine Bar

Finchley Road & Frognal Station

West Hampstead Thameslink

WEST HAMPSTEAD

West Hampstead Station

WEST HAMPSTEAD

KILBURN

The Czech & Slovak House

Brondesbury Park Station

KILBURN

Geeta's

WILLESDEN LANE

Kilburn High Road Station

KILBURN

KILBURN PARK

Queens Park Station

QUEENS PARK

Meson Bilbao

| 0 | 500 yds |

© Crown copyright

The Czech & Slovak House

74 West End Lane, NW6 ☎ 0171 372 5251   ⊖ West Hampstead

Tues–Fri 6–9pm, Sat & Sun noon–3pm & 6–9pm   Cash or cheque only

A combination of low prices, an ambience to make Harry Lime feel at home, and the kind of decor that leaves design experts puzzled and wondering, fills the Czech & Slovak House with a happy mix of students and locals. It is situated in the old established Czechoslovak National House (too good an institution to be split like the nations – or even adapt its name), and its dining room is a class act. Genuine flock wallpaper gives a unique setting to some striking portraits: among them Vaclaf Havel, Winston Churchill, and a very young-looking Queen Elizabeth II with her crown and regalia picked out in glitter powder.

Menu-writers across London should be forced to study here – it is hard to improve on the concision of "meat soup (£2)". Passing that dish by, try starting with tlacenka (£2.10), which is home-made brawn with onions. Or Russian egg (£3.90), which is egg mayonnaise with salad, ham and onions. Or rather good roll mops (£2.10), again with onions. You need to like raw onions to do well at the starters. Main courses deliver serious amounts of home-made, tasty food. Beef goulash with dumplings (£7.50) is red with sweet paprika, and cooked long and slow until the meat is meltingly tender. Order smoked boiled pork knuckle, sauerkraut, and dumplings (£8.50) and you will be served a vast and tasty ham hock, good (if rather sweet) sauerkraut, dumplings, plus a small jug of wildly rich, pork gravy. If you don't fancy dumplings, the roast veal comes with creamed spinach and superb fried potatoes (£8.20). To drink, set your sights on beer – Gambrinus on draught is £1.80 a pint and there are a number of other bottled Czech beers, including one whose label is fetchingly decorated with a motorcycle and sidecar. There is a story behind this graphic which the amiable bartender will explain, not that you will be able to remember the tale after drinking the stuff.

One of the puddings must leave the cholesterol-wary clutching at their pacemakers. Apricot dumpling (£2.30) is a cricket-ball-sized lump of dough with an apricot inside. It comes under a coat of sour cream, and sits in a sea of melted butter. The only concession to modern fresh food fads is the garnish of three grapes. It is awesome.

Geeta

59 Willesden Lane, NW6 ☎ 0171 624 1713	⊖ Kilburn
Daily noon–2.30pm & 6–10.30pm (Fri/Sat 11.30pm)	All major cards (not Switch)

Some years ago, this family-run vegetarian restaurant bit on the bullet and installed a tandoor oven, and now the menu runs the gamut from South Indian vegetarian dishes to curry house favourites like beef Madras, before peaking triumphantly with "special tandoori dishes". But diversify as they might, Geeta's strengths still lie in simple, unpretentious, South Indian vegetarian food, with decor and prices to match..

Start with masala dosai (£2.00), a crisp, twelve-inch pancake folded around a savoury potato stuffing – a great combination of textures and carefully spiced. There are also all the South Indian favourites: uttapam (£1.80) – a kind of Indian pizza made from lentil dough; iddly sambar (£2.40) – steamed rice and lentil cakes; vadai (£1.20) – a deep-fried lentil doughnut. If it can be made out of rice or lentils you'll find it here. Onion bhajias (£1.30) are interesting, taking the form of onion rings crisply fried in a gram flour batter which makes them much less soggy than their cricket ball counterparts. The vegetable samosas (£1.20) are also very good. Turning to more substantial matters, the menu offers a base of "boiled rice (£1.20), fried rice (£1.50), lemon rice (£1.50), or coconut rice (£1.50)"; lemon rice is amazing – rich and lemony, speckled through with onion seeds, thoroughly delicious. Bombay aloo (£1.90) – potato, green beans with coconut (£1.90) – and black eyed beans (£1.90) are all good dishes, while in the "spicy vegetable dishes (dry)" section, there is one dish that is a favourite with local customers – green banana curry (£1.90); try it and you'll see why. If you do venture into the carnivorous section of the menu, you'll find that the sag gosht (£3.00) is an accomplished lamb curry thickened and enriched with spinach. And even the "newcomer" dishes from the tandoor – like the mixed grill (£6.90) are fresh and tasty.

It is also worth mentioning how very rare it is to see a wine list where, if you avoid the extravagance of a £10 bottle of Chablis, everything is priced at £6.50 a bottle or less.

Meson Bilbao

33 Malvern Road, NW6 ☎ 0171 328 1744   ⊖ Queen's Park/Westbourne Park

Mon–Thurs noon–2.30pm & 6–11pm, Fri noon–2.30pm & 7–11.30pm,

Sat 7–11.30pm   All major cards except Amex

Visiting this Basque restaurant-tapas bar is not so much an out-of-body experience as an out-of-country experience. The man in charge is Jose Larrucea, who has finally got his own restaurant after a career cooking for others. The pace here is gentle and to confirm your sense of displacement this is probably the only restaurant in London where three out of five of the house specials are made with hake, while one of the others features dried cod! In good weather the dining tables invade the pavement, inside there's a focal-point bar, and just when you think you've got the measure of the place you discover another large dining room in the basement.

There is an excellent value set menu at £8.90 for a soup or starter, main course, ice cream and coffee. But for the best of Meson Bilbao come in a group and run amok with the tapas. King prawns in garlic sauce (£3.90); boquerones – those wonderful, nutty tasting white anchovies (£2.75); mussels Bilbaina – both spicy and tomatoey (£3.50); chiperones en su tinta – stuffed squid in an ink sauce (£3.90). Patatas bravas (£2.50) are not over bravas but the chorizo Busturia (£3.90) is a triumph and should not be missed – this is a sandwich of two slices of aubergine cut lengthways and grilled which act as the "bread" while sliced, grilled chorizo serves as filling. Now you are at a turning point, you can either persevere with tapas, perhaps a plate of jamon serrano – strongly flavoured (£4.90), or switch to something more substantial. Like the especialidad de la casa- "merluza ala koxkera" (£18, for two people). This is a round earthenware dish of hake cooked with clams, asparagus, king prawns and peas, and is something of a favourite with the regulars, judging by the number quietly tucking in. Or you could have your hake grilled (alla plancha – £8.90), or fried (rebozada – £7.50).

Jose Larrucea's passion is for the wines of Rioja, and the list here is more diverse than you'd expect. Furthermore he has wines not on the list that are even more fascinating. Treasured bottles, wines from the vineyards of his friends – you only have to ask.

KILBURN & WEST HAMPSTEAD ⑪ BRITISH/BURGERS

NORTH

No.77 Wine Bar

77 Mill Lane, NW6 ☎ 0171 435 7787	⊖ West Hampstead
Mon–Tues noon–11pm, Wed–Fri noon–midnight,	
Sat 1pm–midnight, Sun 1pm–10.30pm	All major credit cards except Amex

"77" is the perfect neighbourhood wine bar if you like things noisy, irreverent, busy, and young. It is all that and more, and unerpinned by a thoughtful wine list and simple and tasty cooking. Don't expect haute cuisine, but the burgers here have won prizes, and there are excellent salads. This kind of place is performing the same service for today's public as neighbourhood bistros used to offer in the 1970s. What's more the proprietors are not above having a bit of fun at the expense of more gastronomical eateries – they hold an "English Noveaux" celebration when they solemnly race the first English wines to a special dinner. The menu changes quarterly to prevent boredom in the kitchen and amongst the regulars, but a core of mainstay dishes is retained to prevent riots.

Purists will be ill at ease with the menu punning here – mind you they will probably be ill at ease anyway what with the noise, informality and continual partying. Starters may include Soups you Sir! (£3.25) with the description "stirringly good stuff". Taramasalata or houmous (£3.45) is listed as "Greek dips that Aristotle was said to have described as the food of the future". Also popular are spicy merguez sausages (£3.45). Main courses run from spaghetti with mushrooms (£5.95) to Oriental style chicken with mangoes (£7.85), and chilli con carne (£6.25). The 8oz British beefburger (£6.95) comes with salad and sauté potatoes, and is very good indeed. Predictably the larger 12oz burger (£9.25) is "affectionately known as The Fat Bastard".

The wine list features wines from a dozen different countries and they are generally well-chosen if not always classical names. Like the menu, the wine list changes, but look out for delights such as Amarone Classico della Valpolicella, Allegrini 1991 (£24.95) or Three Choirs Estate Reserve, Lightly oaked, 1996 (£13.75). Anyone visiting Mill Lane for the first time should be aware that in this bit of North London the busiest night of the week is Thursday, and that is when the wine bar will be at its most lively. They certainly know how to party in these parts.

St John's Wood
& Swiss Cottage

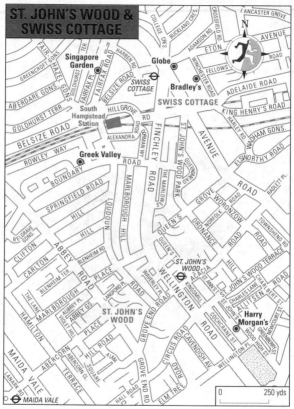

ST. JOHN'S WOOD & SWISS COTTAGE

Singapore Garden
Globe
SWISS COTTAGE
Bradley's
SWISS COTTAGE
South Hampstead Station
Greek Valley
Harry Morgan's
ST. JOHN'S WOOD

0   250 yds

© Crown copyright

Bradley's

25 Winchester Rd, NW3 ☎ 0171 722 3457	⊖ Swiss Cottage
Mon–Fri noon–3pm & 6–11pm, Sat 6–11pm,	
Sun noon–4pm & 6–11pm	All major credit cards

Hard to find, Bradley's is tucked away in a side street behind Swiss Cottage, and you get the impression that its regular clientele would prefer to keep the secret to themselves. The food here is pretty impressive – but that's not all. The atmosphere is warm and inviting, the menu covers and (metal) plates are probably the heaviest in London, and the loos are a definite must to visit. All of which forms a good backdrop for chef/proprietor Simon Bradley's cooking and presentation. Dishes revolve around a combination of fresh ingredients and are served with a view to making the most of the visual appeal. They can look terrific.

A starter of potato pancake with gravadlax, soured cream and lime chilli vodka (£7.50) is presented as a slim high tower, the frozen vodka in a tiny shot glass. Very fresh and tasty and not too much dill either. Chargrilled squid with watercress, plum and chilli sauce (£5.50) is better than good. Tagliolini with lobster, prawns, mussels and basil (£6.90) would do well as a main course. Peppered venison with artichoke mash and onion gravy (£13.50) is rich, dark and delicious – the mash subtly flavoured and a good foil for the richness of the venison. Other main courses include pan-fried veal with apple and sage Tatin and redcurrants (£12.50), herb crusted rack of lamb with mushroom, potato and tarragon gratin (£15.00), and a good selection of fish. You don't need extra vegetables but the cauliflower fritters with tomato chutney (£1.60) are delicious. And if you are still going for desserts, chocolate pudding with marmalade ice cream (£5.00) is enough for two and the ice cream is nicely tart with its caramel orange flavour.

Bradley's wine list is extensive and includes a large selection of unusual and higher priced New World wines that are often hard to find. A lively, but full-flavoured biscuity house champagne at £26.00 is good value, too, as Bradley's is a fine venue for a celebration dinner. There is also a Sunday brunch menu at £12 for two courses and £15 for three.

£15–£30

Globe

100 Avenue Rd, NW3 ☎ 0171 722 7200	⊖ Swiss Cottage
Mon–Fri noon–3pm & 6–11pm, Sat 6–11pm,	
Sun 11.30am–3pm & 7–10pm	Mastercard, Visa

Tucked away behind Swiss Cottage underground station is a bright blue and yellow seaside splash of colour. This is no accident as Neil Armishaw, owner and manager of Globe, brought back some unique hand-made blue and yellow plates from the USA and felt that the restaurant should match the plates rather than the other way round.

The food is in keeping – an accomplished mixture of modern and traditional with Pacific influences. Amongst the starters there's Malaysian vegetable and coconut laksa (£4.00); a very tasty peppered goat's cheese with warm lentils and anchovy toast (£4.50); and chicken satay and Thai fish cakes with dipping sauces (£5.00). The latter brings well salted pungent little fish cakes and very freshly curried satay sticks with a sharp chilli and sesame dip and a creamy peanut one – ideal intense tastes for starters. Main courses include fillet of Scottish beef on a mushroom, leek and potato cake with braised chicory and peas (£11.50); char-grilled snapper with wok-fried black beans and Chinese greens (£11.50). Roasted cod with spicy sweet potato, herbed butter beans and salsa verde (£11.50) was well-judged with a noteworthy salsa verde for the chunky cod. Slow roasted duck with olive oil mash and a plum and ginger chutney (£11.00) is also good value. It delivers a confit-like satisfaction and the home-made chutney is worth bottling. The mash is fruity and a demonstration of how good this is if done well. Puddings include the ubiquitous crème brulée, but with Grand Marnier and mixed berries (£4.00), and a refreshingly unusual guava and peach schnapps sorbet (£4.00). But the star item is strawberry rocky road ice cream cake (£4.00) – fresh not-too-sweet strawberry ice cream studded with marshmallow, toasted almonds and chocolate chunks that takes you straight back to childhood.

Globe is built like a conservatory with a glass roof and sliding doors that pull open and from summer 1999 there will be an open front courtyard for alfresco dining. The wines are well described on the list and there is also a popular Sunday brunch at £12.50 including a drink.

Greek Valley

130 Boundary Rd, NW8 ☎ 0171 624 3217   ⊖ St John's Wood/Swiss Cottage

Mon–Sat 6pm–midnight; lunch by arrangement   Mastercard, Visa

Heaped plates of roasted or grilled meat are the main attraction at Greek Valley: be they chicken, lamb or pork, portions are as huge as the prices are low. The sky-blue walls and Greek statues in this family-owned restaurant bring a little bit of Mediterranean sun to NW8. Considering that it doesn't benefit from passing trade (it's located a ten-minute walk from St John's Wood and Swiss Cottage) Greek Valley does well. Then again, that's hardly surprising when such warm hospitality and comforting food are on the agenda. Regulars send postcards from their Greek holiday destinations having failed to find better dishes, and at Easter there are special celebrations with all the traditional dishes cooked for those making their way back from the Orthodox midnight Mass.

Starters come hot or cold and are numerous. The garlic-rich grilled Greco pepper (£2.50) is excellent, although its feta cheese topping could be more generous. At once light and flavoursome, it's the perfect precursor to the carnivorous overload to follow. Also good is the Greek salad (£2.50) which gives you considerably more feta for your money. If pacing yourself is an alien concept, the home-made Valley sausage (£3.50), a sort of a coarse and spicy frankfurter, is worth a shot. And so to the main course. The fried kalamari (£3.50/£9.50) are perennial favourites among regulars, and the king prawns (£10.50) – grilled, garlicked and buttered – should not be overlooked. But it would be foolish not to explore the strengths of the meat dishes. For lamb-lovers there are kleftico (£6.95) and souvla (£6.75) – Friday and Saturday nights only. For both dishes slow cooking is the watchword, and the result is quite delicious. Or try the kotopoulo (£6.75), whole baby chicken grilled with oregano. With prices rising from a very reasonable £7.50 per bottle, the wine selection is affordable. It's also a little unpredictable, so safety-firsters should stick to the French section.

There are a few puddings if you insist on a sugar injection, and of these, a Greek pastry (£2) or the deliciously creamy yoghurt & honey (£2) should do the trick.

Harry Morgan's

31 St John's Wood High St, NW8 ☎ 0171 722 1869   ⊖ St John's Wood

Daily 11am–10pm   All major credit cards except Amex

ST JOHN'S WOOD & SWISS COTTAGE Ⓣ JEWISH

In 1950 Harry Morgan – a successful butcher in Park Road, St John's Wood – started to cure his own salt beef, and it proved so popular that with his wife he set up a restaurant to sell the delicacy. In 1962 the restaurant moved to its present site in St John's Wood High Street, where a couple of years ago it was taken over by a Mr Herschel. It was all change: out went the traditional little room with its handful of tables and the walls papered with pictures of famous clients . . . in came a new large airy room with acres of blonde wood on show. The salt beef, nonetheless, has weathered all these storms remarkably well; prime scotch beef is still boned-out and pickled on the premises and sandwiches can be ordered lean or fat according to taste.

Harry Morgan's sells that most famous of Jewish medicines, chicken noodle soup: with dumplings (£3.80), or with everything (£3.95). It is very good – modestly described by Herschel as the "best soup in the world" – and the customers seem to agree; they sell 250 portions a day. For more starters, try the chopped liver (£3.50) – very rich and smooth, or the egg and onion (£3.50). Then go on to a salt beef sandwich on rye bread (£4.95); ask for horseradish on it and don't be surprised when your sandwich comes as a ruby red layer – Jewish horseradish is inextricably linked with beetroot. As a side dish, you could add a latka (£1.50) – a seriously weighty, fried potato pancake. Or go your own way with any of the other specials. The menu lists everything from roast turkey (£7.50), to worsht (beef salami) and eggs (£6.50).

There is a real mystique to pickled cucumbers. What is described rather disdainfully as a "wally" in London fish and chip shops is elevated to an art form in Jewish cuisine. The subtlest is the "new green", fresh and crisp; then there's the "sweet and sour" – this one is large and nobbly; or there is the connoisseurs' choice, the "heimishe", intense and salty. And the price of all these delights? A modest £1.50 a portion.

NORTH

Singapore Garden

83a Fairfax Rd, NW6 ☎ 0171 328 5314   ⊖ Swiss Cottage/Finchley Rd

Daily noon–2.45pm & 6–10.45pm   All major credit cards

Singapore Garden is a busy restaurant – don't even think of turning up without a reservation – and performs a cunning dual function. Half the cavernous dining room is filled with well-heeled, often elderly, family groups from Swiss Cottage and St John's Wood, treating the restaurant as their local Chinese and consuming crispy duck in pancakes, money bag chicken, and butterfly prawns. The other customers are drawn from London's Singaporean and Malaysian communities, and are tucking into the squid blachan and the Teochew braised pig's trotters. So there are both cocktails with parasols and Tiger beer. But it's always busy – and the food is both interesting and good.

Start with a fresh crab fried in its shell (£12.50). This dish represents a trade off, frying (rather than baking) means that the leg and claw meat can be on the dry side, but there are sublime crispy bits encrusting the brown meat. It comes with ginger and spring onions, Singapore chilli sauce, or black pepper and butter. If you're feeling adventurous, follow with a real Singapore special – the Teochew braised pig's trotter (£10), which brings half a pig's worth of trotters slow-cooked in a luxurious, black, heart-stoppingly rich gravy. Or try the claypot prawns and scallops (£12), which delivers good, large crunchy prawns and a fair portion of scallops stewed with lemon grass and fresh ginger on glass noodles. Very good indeed. From the Malaysian list you might pick a daging curry (£6) – coconutty, rich and not especially hot. You must also try the mee goreng (£5) because this is how this noodle dish should be – a meal in itself.

At the bottom of the menu (at £31.50 per person, for a minimum of two), you'll find Steamboat listed as a "healthy alternative". This is a kind of party game. Eager participants drop tasty pieces of fresh meat and seafood into a cauldron of broth which bubbles away at the table, then experience agonies of frustration when they find that they haven't the dexterity to fish them out with chopsticks.

Stoke Newington & Hackney

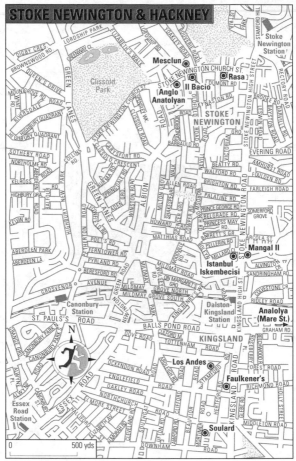

STOKE NEWINGTON & HACKNEY

Stoke Newington Station

Mesclun

Rasa

Il Bacio

Clissold Park

Anglo Anatolyan

STOKE NEWINGTON

EVERING ROAD

Mangal II

Istanbul Iskembecisi

Canonbury Station

Dalston-Kingsland Station

Analolya (Mare St.)

KINGSLAND

St. Paul's Road

Los Andes

Faulkener's

Essex Road Station

Soulard

0   500 yds

N

© Crown copyright

Anatolya

263a Mare St, E8 ☎ 0181 986 2223   ⊖ Bethnal Green

Daily 6am–11pm   Cash or cheque only

A small – five-table – functional diner, the Anatoloya has no menu other than the neon list, all in Turkish, above the counter. There are scores of such places in Hackney and on nearby Green Lanes, and there's not much, at first glance, to distinguish this from countless others. But as the regulars know, the Anatolya stands out for its unbeatable combination of consistently good and absurdly cheap, food, and extraordinarily friendly service. Waiters put everyone at their ease, patiently describing for non-Turkish speakers each dish on the mangal (grill). Anatolya takes the Turkish tradition of hospitality seriously, and, depending on the whim of the waiter, you may well find yourself plied with complimentary tea, served in delicate tulip-shaped glasses, or a sticky baklava.

Dishes change daily, but you can usually depend upon the lhamacun (£1.20), spicy minced lamb on featherlight charred flatbread enlivened with buttery juices, red peppers and herbs. For mains it's best to stick with the lamb, which comes in a variety of guises: et sote (£3), fried with chilli sauce, is a little rich, but the skewered minced lamb (£3), charred to perfection on the grill, is flawless, the red peppers and flat leaf parsley rounding off a good, robust flavour. Or try the barbecued chicken (£3), where eight crisp-skinned wings come piled onto a plate with bulghur and fresh salad. There are usually a couple of casseroles bubbling away, too; the sulu yemekler (literally 'watery meal') can take a number of forms, usually entailing chunks of meat with soft-cooked carrots, potatoes and courgettes (£3.50). Side dishes, all £1.50, include the usual humus and taramasalata, along with a punchy haydari, a kind of rough garlic paste with chopped parsley, and a creamy cacik, whose cool combination of cucumber, garlic and yoghurt makes a perfect accompaniment to the spicy grilled meats.

Even counting the three stools over the mangal, and the tiny bar at the back, Anatolya is often crowded, especially on weekend evenings, so it can be a good idea to book a table.

£8–£20

Anglo Anatolyan

123 Stoke Newington Church St, N16 ☎ 0171 923 4349	BR: Stoke Newington
Mon–Fri 6pm–2am, Sat & Sun 1pm–2am	Mastercard, Visa

The food is good at the Anglo Anatolyan, the bills are small, and tables are so crowded that you get to meet all the other diners. But the most intriguing feature of the restaurant is the large and impressive Royal crest which is engraved in the glass of the front door: under it an inscription reads, "By Appointment to Her Majesty Queen Elizabeth II, Motor Car Manufacturers". Why? Do the Windsors slip up to Stoke Newington when they feel a new Daimler coming on? Predictably, asking the waiters for provenance doesn't help much, they look at you seriously and confirm that they "got the door secondhand".

Royal warrants aside, the food at the Anglo Anatolyan is impressive. The bread in particular is amazing. Large, round flat loaves about two inches deep, cut into chunks, it is soft in the middle and crisp on the outside; it is baked at home by a local Turkish woman and is a far cry from the flat, hard, mass-produced pitta pockets of the supermarkets. To accompany it, start with ispanak tarator (£2.95), spinach in yoghurt with garlic. And a tremendous, coarse tarama (£2.45). And sigara borek (£2.95) – crisp filo pastry filled with cheese and served hot. And arnavut cigeri (£2.95) – cubes of fried lamb's liver. Dine mob-handed so that you can try more starters. The main courses are more easily summarised: sixteen ways with lamb, one with quails, two with chicken, one with prawn, and two vegetarian dishes. Kaburga tarak (£6.25) is crisp, tasty lamb "spare-ribs"; iskander kebab (£6.75) is fresh doner on a bed of cubed bread and topped with yoghurt and tomato sauce; kasarli beyti (£6.75) is minced lamb made into a patty with cheese and grilled. They are all good.

When you've eventually had your fill, you'll be presented with a hand-written bill, at the bottom of which is printed "Another cheap night out". Which for once is simply the truth.

Faulkener's

424 Kingsland Rd, E8 ☎ 0171 254 6152	⊖ Liverpool Street
Mon–Thurs noon–2pm & 5–10pm, Fri noon–2pm & 4.15–10pm,	
Sat noon–10pm, Sun noon–9pm	Cash or cheque only

Faulkener's is a clear highlight among the kebab shops and chippies that line the rather scruffy Kingsland Road: a spotless fish-and-chip restaurant, with a take-away section next door. It is reassuringly old-fashioned with its lace curtains, fish tank, uniformed waitresses, and cool yellow walls lined with sepia-tinted piscine scenes, and it holds few surprises – which is probably what makes it such a hit. Usually Faulkener's is full of local families and large parties, all ploughing through colossal fish dinners while chatting across tables. It also goes out of its way to be child friendly, with high chairs leaned against the wall, and a children's menu priced at £3.25.

House speciality among the starters is the fish cake (£1.30), a plump ball made with fluffy herby potato. Or there's smoked salmon (£3.95), which comes in two satisfying wads, or prawn cocktail (£3.25). If you fancy soup, you've got tomato (80p) or a more exotic French fish variety, peppery and dark (£1.90). For main courses, the regular menu features all the British fish favourites, served fried or poached and with chips, while daily specials are chalked up on the blackboard. Cod (£6.60) and haddock (£7.75; £7.95 on the bone) retain their fresh firm flesh beneath the dark, crunchy batter, while the subtler, classier sole – Dover (£11.50) or lemon (£9.95) – is best served delicately poached. The mushy peas (65p) are just right, lurid and lumpy like God intended, but the test of any good chippie is always its chips, and here they are humdingers – fat, firm and golden, with a wicked layer of crispy little salty bits at the bottom. Stuffed in a soft doughy roll, they make the perfect chip butty. Most people wet their whistles with a mug of strong tea (55p), but there are a couple of wines on offer, including a Merlot (£7.20) and a Chablis (£17.25).

Though always lively, Faulkener's is particularly fun at Saturday lunchtime, when traders and shoppers take time out from the local market to catch up, gossip and joke with the waitresses.

Il Bacio

61 Stoke Newington Church St, N16 ☎ 0171 249 3833 | BR: Stoke Newington

Mon-Fri 6–11pm, Sat & Sun noon–11.30pm | Mastercard, Visa

Opened in 1995 by Sardinian childhood sweethearts Luigi and Michela, Il Bacio has justly become one of the most popular fixtures on Stoke Newington's 'restaurant row'. The decor is upbeat – sunshine yellow walls are lined with splashy modern canvasses – and each (smallish) table has a vase of fresh flowers. Potted palms screen off a couple of tables for privacy, but, although Il Bacio means "a kiss", don't plan a romantic dinner here: this is a noisy place, loud with laughter and birthday parties.

If you feel you'll have room for a starter, the insalata di mare (£5.50) – packed with sea-fresh clams, calamari and prawns – or the grilled goats' cheese with poached pears (£4.95) – melt-in-the-mouth rounds of cheese perfectly set off by lightly poached fruit – work well. The garlic bread (£2.50) is good, though if you're having pizza as a main course, bear in mind that this is simply a base without the topping. Perfectly judged main course pastas include gnocchi di patate (£5.80), in a confident tomato and basil sauce, and velvety penne al salmone (£6). But it's the colossal pizzas that keep Il Bacio full every night: spilling off the plate, they never fail to produce an amazed shriek from first-timers. Bases are paper thin, cooked expertly in a wood-burning oven, so there's none of the unpleasant greasy oozing prevalent in lesser pizzas. All but the pescatora (£6.80; seafood, capers, parsley) are built on a sauce of tomato and mozzarella. The Sardegna (£6.00), with its aubergines and onion, and the Bacio (£5.80), topped with frankfurters and olives, both add a twist. Of the home-made desserts, the tiramisu (£3.50), a luscious, sozzled brick of sponge, cream and liquor, wins star prize.

In summer, French windows open out on to the street. It's a great place to survey the street life, but be warned that Il Bacio is opposite the fire station. Sudden ear-shattering sirens can shoot even the most delicious morsel of mozzarella down the wrong way.

Istanbul Iskembecisi

9 Stoke Newington Rd, N16 ☎ 0171 254 7291	BR: Dalston Kingsland
Daily 11am–5am	Mastercard, Visa

The Istanbul Iskembecisi is just over the road from Mangal II (see over-page), and at heart they are singing off the same sheet. Despite being named after its signature dish – iskembecisi, a limpid tripe soup – the Istanbul is a grill house. Admittedly its is a grill house with chandeliers, smart tables and chairs and upscale service but it is still a grill house. And because it stays open late into the morning it is much beloved by clubbers and chefs – they are just about ready to go out and eat when everyone else has had enough and set off homewards. The grilled meat may be better over at Mangal II, but the atmosphere of raffish elegance at the Istanbul has real charm.

The iskembe (£2.50) tripe soup has its following. Large parties of Turks from the snooker hall just behind the restaurant insist on it – and you'll see the odd regular downing two bowlfuls of the stuff. For most tastes, however, it's bland at best. A much better bet is to start with the mixed meze (£4.50) – good humus and tarama, superb dolma, and all the rest of the usual suspects. Then on to the grills which are presented with more panache than usual. Pirzola (£6.50) brings three lamb chops; sis kebab (£5.75) is good and fresh; karisik izgara (£8.50) is a mixed grill by any other name. For the brave, there is also a whole section of offal dishes, among them kokorec (£5) – lamb's intestines – and arvnavaut cigeri-sicak (£4.50) – liver Albanian style. And someone must be mourning two casualties of BSE which have been taken off the menu – kelle sogus – "roasted head of lamb" – and beyin salata – "boiled brain with salad".

Just when you have safely progressed to the desserts, there is still a surprise in store – kazandibi (£2.50), "Turkish type creme caramel, milk based sweet with finely dashed chicken breast". Delicious.

Los Andes

28a Stamford Rd, E8 ☎ 0171 923 3330	BR: Dalston Junction
Sun & Mon 4–10pm, Tues–Sat noon–11pm	Cash only

Los Andes is next door to one of Hackney's best pubs, the Trolley Stop, which makes it a great place to fill up before or after a night's drinking. That's not to say it's full of beer-swilling revellers who've missed the turning for the curry house – instead, there's a mixed crowd of families, homesick Hispanics and couples enjoying unfussy, good-value food and laid-back service. The chef is Chilean, and while most dishes hail from there, you can also get Argentinean churrasco (huge grilled steak), empanadas (spicy pastry pies) and other pan-American favourites. The theme is continued in the decor, the walls lined with Latin American flags, rousing political illustrations (spot the tiny Che above the bar) and bold Chilean art, along with pan pipes and a Barca FC flag for good measure.

Starters are consistently good – though the entrada Los Andes (cold beef with tuna sauce; £2.15) is best tasted for novelty value only. Sopa a la Chilena (£1.95) is a thick broth, not unlike French onion soup, packed with chunks of salmon, cod and mussels. Prawn connoisseurs will love the camarones al pil pil (£1.95) which come in a big heap, glistening, garlicky and firm. Main courses can be more hit and miss – as throughout Latin America, the protein's the thing, and the accompaniments decidedly uninspired. Thus the salmon a la parilla (£5.95), where a fresh fish steak, pepped up with Andean sauce (a garish blend of cream, cheese, garlic, wine and paprika) upstages with a vengeance the bland mashed potato and half-hearted lettuce salad. The churrasco gaucho (the most expensive thing on the menu at £9) looks impressive, a macho hunk of beef served on a plank, and though it can be fatty, will satisfy the hungriest of carnivores. Vegetarians, though acknowledged, don't have a very adventurous time, restricted to various veg and egg tartas (£4.95).

Disappointingly, the menu's promise of creme caramel, bread pudding or plantain flambéed in rum rarely materialises – there's no demand, say the waiters – so for dessert you'll likely have to make do with whatever gateau or ice cream they've got that day.

Mangal II

4 Stoke Newington Road, N16 ☎ 0171 254 7888   BR: Dalston Kingsland

Daily noon–1am   Mastercard, Visa

The first thing to hit you at Mangal II is the smell: the fragrance of spicy, sizzling char-grilled meat is unmistakably, authentically Turkish. This, combined with the relaxing pastel decor, puts you in holiday mood before you're sat down. The ambience is laid-back, too – at slack moments, the staff shoot the breeze around the ocakbasi, and service comes with an ear-to-ear grin. All you have to do is sit back, sink an Efes Pilsener (£1.50) and peruse the encyclopaedic menu.

Prices are low and portions enormous. Baskets of fresh bread are endlessly replenished, so it's wise to go easy on the appetisers. With a vast range of tempting mezeler (starters), however, resistance is nigh-on impossible. The 23 options include simple humus (£2.50) and dolma (£2.50); imam bayildi (£3), aubergines stuffed with onion, tomato and green pepper; thinlahmacun (£1.50), meaty Turkish pizza; and karisik meze (£4), a large plate of mixed dishes that's rather heavy on the yoghurt. There's a fair spread of salads (all £2.50–£3), too, though you get so much greenery with the main dishes it's a wasted choice here. The main dishes (kebablar) themselves are sumptuous, big on lamb and chicken, but with limited fish and vegetarian alternatives. The patlican kebab (£6.50) is outstanding: melt-in-the-mouth grilled minced lamb with sliced aubergines, served with a green salad of which the star turn ia an olive-stuffed tomato shaped like a basket. The kebabs are also superb, particularly the house special, ezmeli kebab (£7), which comes doused in Mangal's special sauce. Or if you don't fancy a grill, there's also a choice of three hearty daily stews (£4–£5).

After swallowing that lot, dessert might not be a feasible option, but after a long wait – there's no pressure to vacate your table – you might just be tempted by a slab of tooth-achingly sweet baclava (£2). Alternatively, round off the evening with a punch-packing raki (£3) or a slap-in-the-face Turkish coffee, which is on the house. And for a final blast of Ottoman atmosphere, pay a visit to the bathroom – the no-frills facilities are a real taste of old Istanbul.

STOKE NEWINGTON & HACKNEY ⑪ MODERN EUROPEAN

Mesclun

24 Stoke Newington Church St, N16 ☎ 0171 249 5029	BR: Stoke Newington
Mon–Sat 6–11pm, Sun noon–10pm	Mastercard, Visa

Mesclun looks like a special occasion kind of place; its stark, stylish décor incongruous on Hackney's favourite parade of cheap and cheerful ethnic restaurants. Small and elegant, with abstract paintings on the creamy walls – tasteful, muted blotches that perfectly set off the pine floor and simple, dark wood furniture – it seats about 40 people. Most of them are relaxed thirty-something locals, quietly complacent that they're onto a good thing. For despite all appearances, Mesclun is a bargain, serving astonishingly good-value, assured Modern European food.

Meals start with complementary bread and a tapenade of rough-chopped olives, sundried tomatoes and capers. Irresistibly moreish, but take it easy: the portions coming are enormous. This is especially true of the starters, most of which could pass as main courses – witness the mountainous chicken teriyaki, spring onion and noodle salad (£3.95). Though there are fancier choices, the oeuf en cocotte (£3.95) is a winner, the poached egg swirled with a savoury mixture of garlic, spinach, mushroom and bacon. The crevettes with sauce béarnaise (£5.95), are good, too. For a main course, consider the superb daily fish specials: choices may include roast cod with basil dressing or char-grilled tuna, depending on what's good at the market. Otherwise there's a judicious balance between meat (free-range/organic) and vegetarian options: stewed green lentils with couscous (£5.95) come in an unceremonious pile, the featherlight couscous jazzed up with sweet peppers, while the pan-fried calves' liver with caramelised onions, smoked bacon and mash (£10.95) is meltingly good. All come with side veg: a satisfying trio of celeriac Dauphinoise, herby ratatouille and buttery beans. Desserts (all £2.95, except for the farmhouse cheeses, at £3.95) are upper-crust comfort food: clafoutis is sweet and eggy; the raspberry crème brulée just-right with its jammy base; or for big appetites, there's a double-portion-sized chocolate tart – hot, dark and sludgy, with a slab of vanilla ice cream.

Service at Mesclun is special – patient, attentive and humorous – and though there can be long pauses between courses, no one minds much. That's especially true during the Sunday lunch, when the pace and atmosphere become, if anything, even more good-natured.

NORTH

Rasa

55 Stoke Newington Church St, N16 ☎ 0171 249 0344	BR: Stoke Newington
Mon–Fri 6–11pm, Sat & Sun noon–2.30pm & 6pm–midnight	All major credit cards

Rasa has built up a formidable reputation for outstanding South Indian vegetarian cooking. In fact when diners stop arguing as to whether Rasa is the best Indian vegetarian restaurant in London they usually go on to discuss whether it is the best vegetarian restaurant full stop. As well as great food, the staff are friendly and helpful and the atmosphere is uplifting. Inside, everything is pink (the napkins, the tablecloths and walls), gold ornaments dangle from the ceiling, and a colourful statue of Krishna playing the flute greets you at the entrance. Rasa's proprietor and the majority of the kitchen staff come from Cochin in South India. As you'd expect, booking is essential.

This is one occasion when the set meal (£15) may be the best as well as the easiest option. The staff take charge and select what seems like an endless succession of dishes for you. But however you approach a Rasa meal, everything is a taste sensation. Even the pappadoms are a surprise, served with six home-made chutneys; try the pappadavadao (75p), which is dipped in a spicy batter. If you're going your own way, there are lots of starters to choose from. Mysore bonda (£2.25) is delicious – shaped like a meatball but made of potato spiced with ginger, coriander and mustard seeds. Kathrikka (£2.25) is slices of aubergine served with a fresh tomato chutney. Main dishes are just as imaginative. Beet pachadi (£3.50) is a colourful beetroot curry cooked with yoghurt and coconut; moru kachiathu (£3.50) combines mangoes and green bananas with chilli and ginger. Or go for one of the dosas; these are paper-thin crisp pancakes folded in half and filled with a variety of goodies – masala dosa (£4.25) is filled with potatoes and comes with lentil sauce and coconut chutney. Puddings sound hefty but arrive in mercifully small portions; the payasam (£2.25) is a 'temple feast', and blends dal with jagerry (raw sugar) and coconut milk – a fine end to a meal.

The word rasa has many meanings in Sanskrit; flavour, desire, beauty, elegance and affection – something the whole of north-east London seems to feel for this restaurant.

£15–£31

Soulard

113 Mortimer Road, N1 ☎ 0171 254 1314	BR: Dalston
Tues–Sat 7–10.30pm	Mastercard, Visa

Squeezed improbably into the front room of a converted house on a residential street, Soulard pays homage to all those wonderful meals remembered from holidays in provincial France, and whisks you out of this Hackney/Islington no-man's-land – the oddly-named enclave of De Beauvoir Town – to Provence or the Dordogne. Looking for all the world like some regional French country hotel restaurant, and with the dining room centred on a large brick chimney, Soulard is a great find, serving sound food at practical prices. Everyone's in a good mood here, from the solicitous patron, who will greet you and ask after your welfare throughout the night, to the well-dressed, special occasion clientele.

The proprietors at Soulard are eager to keep things as simple as possible. Meals are prix-fixe: three courses will cost you £17.95 (ex-wine); two are £14.95 (with dessert thrown in for free if you arrive between 7pm and 8.30pm from Tuesday to Thursday). Gluttons can choose four courses for £20.95. The small, fine-tuned menu is supplemented by blackboard specials; all are written in French, but there's always someone hovering to translate. As you would hope, there's a considered wine list, including a classy selection of dessert wines. Of the starters, escargots come in a whimsical puff pastry snail, which trails a creamy, garlicky sauce and is packed with well cooked molluscs. Specials may include grilled calamari salad, all primary colours, fragrant oil dressing and the tenderest charred squid. Main courses are rich: meat-lovers will favour the traditional duck confit while the guinea fowl comes in bite-size, off-the-bone chunks, smothered in a dark sauce and cooked with mushrooms and wholegrain mustard. Various fresh fish dishes are listed on the blackboard, and precisely cooked – be it in a creamy mushroom sauce or in a sea-salty broth.

Although soulard is French for drunkard, you should try and stay sober for the desserts, which are all Gallic to the hilt. From the bavarois aux framboises, light and delicate, to an inspired black and white chocolate mousse, the bitter chocolate top layer contrasting beautifully with the sweet-as-spun-sugar white base. The creamy mint sauce isn't absolutely necessary, perhaps, but certainly doesn't hurt.

Wembley

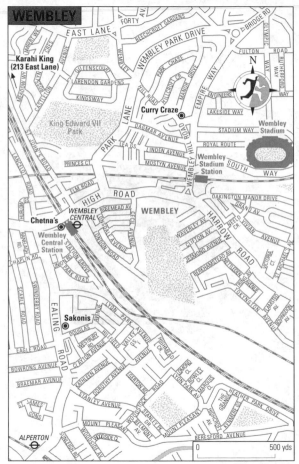

© Crown copyright

Chetna's

420 High Rd, Wembley ☎ 0181 900 1466	⊖ Wembley Central
Tues–Fri noon–3pm & 6–10.30pm, Sat & Sun 1pm–10.30pm	Cash or cheque only

Chetna's is a remarkable Indian restaurant – busy enough to need a queuing system. You register your interest at the counter and get given a cloakroom ticket, and when your table is ready your number is called. The restaurant has smart wood tables and chairs, ceiling fans and some seriously ornate brass chandeliers, but despite all these trappings it is still awesomely cheap. The food is very good indeed and the menu is a bit of a surprise, opening with a section headed "seaside savouries" – an odd claim in a vegetarian establishment – and moving through to Chetna's Pizza Corner, confirming once again that when Asians go out to dinner they often want a change from usual fare. The concept of a large "special vegetable hot pizza" (£5.10) cooked by an Indian chef and made with pure vegetarian cheese, onions, special Chetna sauce, green pepper, corn, and hot green chillies has undeniable charm.

Start with a truly amazing mouthful – Chetna's masala golgapa (£1.80); these are small, crisp golgapas filled with potatoes, onions, moong, chana, green chutney, sweet and sour chutney and topped with sev. You load them into your mouth and as you chew different tastes and textures take over. It's an astonishing sensation. Order more portions than you think you'll need. Also try the kachori (£1.80) – a crisp coat encases a well-spiced ball of green peas. Then there are the karela, bhindi, and tindora curries (£2.50). The karela dish, made from bitter melons, is genuinely bitter – very interesting. Or there's Chetna's crispy bhajia (£1.80) – slices of potatoes crisp on the outside with a batter containing bits of chilli and perfectly cooked. The most striking dish visually must be the paper dosa (£2.90), a giant cone of nutty-tasting pancake – chewy and with a vegetable sambhar and coconut chutney for dipping.

The award for most comprehensive dish must go to the Delhi Darbar thali (£5.90) which is served with one sweet, one farsan, three vegetables, chutney, vegetable biriani, dal, raita, papadum and paratha. There's a minimum charge of £3.50 per person at Chetna's – presumably to stop a large family sharing one Delhi Darbar thali for dinner.

£8–£15

Curry Craze

8–9 The Triangle, Wembley Hill Rd, Wembley ☎ 0181 902 9720   ⊖ Wembley Central

Mon 6–10.30pm, Weds–Fri 12.30–2.30pm   All major credit cards except Diners

& 6–10.30pm, Sat 6–10.30pm

On Wembley match days you'll need to book in order to get into Curry Craze, as in-the-know football regulars fill the place to take advantage of the special pre- and post-match buffets, and the weekends can be pretty busy, too. Which is no surprise, for, belying its name, this is a very good Indian restaurant indeed – a genuine and very friendly family-run place providing predominantly Punjabi food with a smattering of East African Asian dishes. And if some items on the menu have a familiar ring to them, that is because the Malhotras who run Curry Craze are related to the Anands – the dynasty responsible for the famed Brilliant and Madhu's Brilliant in Southall (see p.445 and p.447).

As at the Brilliants, you could do well starting with a share of butter chicken, or its variants, jeera, methi or chilli chicken (£6.50 for a half chicken). Or the sheekh kebab (4 for £4.75) served as a sizzler on an iron dish and very tasty. Or chilli corn (£2.95) – corn on the cob given the hot sauce treatment. Main courses range from karahai dishes to old favourites like chicken tikka masala (£6.25), birianis and pure vegetarian dishes. Karahi prawns (£7.95) come in a good rich sauce. Tinda lamb (£5.95) is a delightful dry curry of lamb and tinda – a Punjabi vegetable which is a member of the squash family, rather like you'd expect a tomato to be if it merged with a potato. Punjabi bhartha oro (£4.25) is a prince amongst side dishes, a roasted aubergine mashed and cooked with onions and peas. Pakorian raita (£2.45) is very odd indeed, but provides a perfect change of texture – pea-sized balls of gram flour are cooked and then served cold in a tangy yoghurt sauce. To dip into all these dishes, there are bhaturas (£1.00) – deep fried breads, like puffy savoury doughnuts, and not for dieters – and very delicious naan breads – peshwari (£2.25), plain (£1.20).

One house speciality well worth trying is Mrs Malhotra's dall makhani (£3.75), a rich black lentil and kidney bean dall. It is made by combining the dall with a tarka containing onions, ginger and tomatoes cooked in ghee.

Karahi King

213 East Lane, North Wembley ☎ 0181 904 2760   ⊖ North Wembley

Daily noon–midnight   Diners, Visa

Karahi King has an open kitchen and arranged around it are plastic tables and chairs for about 25 customers. Such is the fierce pace of dining here that, by the end of the evening, the immaculate kitchen is a good deal cleaner and tidier than the dining area. Service is calm and good-natured and the predominantly Asian clientele obviously rate the karahi dishes very highly. The food is all cooked freshly and curries are all finished with a handful of fresh herbs, which means they look good. They taste good as well. There's no tandoor in evidence but the kebabs (which are cooked on an open charcoal grill called a sigri which is much the same as a Turkish ocakbasi) are good and fresh.

A few words about chilli. Dishes here are aimed at local tastebuds – which seems to mean hot. When asked, "How hot you would like your meal?" you should only reply "hot" if you really mean it. Otherwise you will shortly be finding out that large amounts of fresh green chillies, combined with a top up of dried powdered chillies, can actually hurt. The chaps in the open kitchen try very hard, but cannot resist a soft smile at your discomfort. So if you want it really very hot . . . ask for medium and be prepared to quench the fire with a jug of water or a sweet lassi. Start with seekh kebabs (£1.40 for two pieces), which are good, fresh, and fierce, or chicken tikka (£2.50), or shammi kebabs (£2.50), lamb and ground lentil rissoles. On to the karahi dishes, chicken keema (£5.50) is very good, the minced chicken lending itself to the quick cooking technique. Or there's karahi aloo methi (£3.50). Or karahi gosht (£4.90), a rich lamb dish. The rotis (65p) are good, and the "fried bread" bhaturas (60p) very good. But remember, with portions this large, and dishes this hot, it is easy to end up looking just a little foolish with half your order left uneaten on the table.

You can bring your own alcohol to this establishment, and it is instructive to see a suited party of businessmen breaking the seal on a new bottle of Johnny Walker Black Label as they sit down to kebabs and karahi. Everyone appreciates a bargain.

WEMBLEY ⓥ INDIAN/VEGETARIAN

Sakonis

129 Ealing Rd, Alperton, Wembley ☎ 0181 903 9601	⊖ Alperton/Wembley Central
Sun–Thurs 11am–11pm, Fri & Sat 11am–midnight	Mastercard, Visa

Sakonis is a top notch vegetarian food factory. Crowded with Asian families, it is overseen by waiters and staff in baseball caps, and there's even a holding pen where you can wait for your turn and check out the latest videos and sounds. From a decor point of view the dining area is somewhat clinical – a huge square yardage of white tiling, easy to hose down. Nobody minds. The predominantly Asian clientele is too busy eating. The Indian vegetarian food here is terrific, but it's old hat to many of the Asian customers who dive straight into what is for them, the most exciting section of the Sakonis menu – the Chinese dishes! These tend to be old favourites like Chow Mein and Chop Suey cooked by Indian chefs and with a distinctly Indian spicing. Unless curiosity overwhelms you, stick to the splendid South Indian dishes.

Sakonis is renowned for dosas. These are pancakes, so crisp that they are almost chewy, and delightfully nutty. They come with two small bowls of sauce and a filling of rich, fried potato spiced with curry leaves; choose from plain dosa (£3.50); masala dosa (£4.35); and chutney dosa (£4.40) which has some spices and chilli swirled into the dosa batter. Try the farari cutlets (£3), not cutlets at all, in fact, but very nice, well-flavoured dollops of sweet potato mash, deep fried so that they have a crisp exterior. At Sakonis there is a very able man or men on the fryer, all the deep-fried items are perfectly cooked, very dry, with a very crisp shell, but still cooked through. A difficult feat to achieve. Also worth trying are the bhel puri (£3), the pani puri (£2.50) and the sev puri (£3) – amazingly crisp little taste bombs, pop them in whole and they go off in your mouth.

Some say that the juices at Sakonis are the best in London, and while that may be hyperbole they are certainly very good indeed. Try madaf (£2.25) - fresh coconut; melon juice (£2.25) which is only available in season; passion juice (£2.75); or orange and carrot mix (£2.50) which is subtitled "health drink" – it probably is.

NORTH

Further North

Finchley, Hendon, Kingsbury

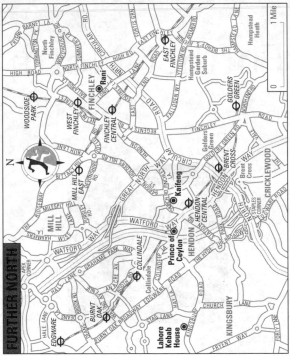

© Crown copyright

Kaifeng Kosher Oriental

51 Church Road, Hendon, NW4 ☎ 0181 203 7888   ⊖ Hendon Central

Mon–Thurs & Sun 12.30pm–2.30pm & 6–11pm, Sat 6–11pm (Sept–April only)

Sun noon–2.30pm & 6–11pm   All major credit cards

The Kaifeng Kosher Oriental Restaurant is a one-off: an opulent Chinese restaurant that claims to be (and doubtless is) the only Kosher Oriental establishment in Britain. According to the family tree displayed upon the wall the most important family of Kaifeng's former Jewish community is named Chao Luang-Ching. The inscription adds, rather enigmatically, that "Ezekiel is probably Chao Lunang-Ching Gwlyn Gym". So now you know. The long, narrow dining room fills up fast with affluent locals, happy to pay smart North London prices which have more in common with the West End than the suburbs. But you get a decent deal, friendly and excellent service that almost justifies the 15% surcharge, and fresh, well-cooked, if a trifle underseasoned dishes. If you're Orthodox Jewish, Kaifeng must make a welcome change; if you're not, then seeing how favourite dishes like sweet and sour pork, prawns kung po, and so forth turn out in their kosher variants is a lot of fun.

Start with Capital spare ribs (£6.95), which is absolutely delicious, made from lamb instead of pork and arguably even better for it. Hunan chicken with lettuce wrap (£11.50) is also fresh and good, while the usual prawn and sesame seed toast becomes sesame chicken (£6.95). On to main courses, the sweet and sour lamb (£11.95) is slightly less successful – a good sharp, sauce still makes no impression on fairly tough chunks of lamb. But there are some interesting and unfamiliar dishes like beef strips with pine seeds (£11.95), sliced mango chicken (£11.50), and mixed vegetables in coconut cream (£5.95). Shellfish dishes, meantime, turn into fish, and most often sole which is served in a variety of familiar styles including steamed with ginger and spring onion (£15.95), and drunken fish (£15.95), which is sliced sole in kosher rice wine.

Given its unique status, the Kaifeng is a pretty popular place and even early in the week it tends to fill up quickly. So take the precaution of making a booking if you're travelling out here specially.

£6–£12

The Lahore Kebab House

248 Kingsbury Rd, NW9 ☎ 0181 905 0930   ⊖ Kingsbury

Daily 1pm–midnight   Cash or cheque only

This grill house was once a branch of the famous Lahore Kebab House in East London, then in 1994 Mr Hameed bought the business and with it the right to use the name "Lahore Kebab House of East London" anywhere in Kingsbury, and a five-mile radius around. Although completely independent of the Umberstone Street establishment, this bare and basic restaurant remains faithful to the spirit of the original. Kebabs are cheap, freshly cooked and spicy, while the karahi dishes are also worth delving into. While the premises are unlicensed, there is a splendid and practical arrangement between the Lahore Kebab House and the whimsically named Sun and Sand Club next door – there's a hatch in the party wall through which curries move one way while pints of lager move the other.

There's not that much point in coming to the Lahore unless you're after some kind of kebab. If you just want a starter bite, there's seekh kebab (75p each). Or for more serious eating, there's a list of kebabs all with five pieces to a skewer – mutton tikka £2.20; chicken tikka £3; jeera chicken £4.20; chicken wings £4.20; lamb chops £5. Everyone is very helpful here, and they are happy to make you up a platter for a particular number of diners (three pieces of each kebab for example) and charge pro-rata. Strangely, for such a stronghold of the carnivore, there's a long list of vegetarian dishes all served in the karahi – include a couple with your order – perhaps karrai dal (£3.50), or karrai sag aloo (£3.50), the latter being particularly rich and tasty. Back with the meat eaters, karrai ghost (£4.70) is a rich lamb curry, while the "chef's special" (£6), a hand-chopped keema made with both chicken and lamb, is a revelation – very tasty, and with recognisable finely chopped meat, a far cry from the anonymous mince that's the backbone of keema dishes in so many curry houses. It is thoroughly recommended. As are the breads, tandoori nann (90p) and tandoori roti (60p) – fresh and good.

The Lahore's weekend special all appeal greatly, karrai nehari (slow cooked lamb shanks) (£7); karrai bindi (okra) (£4); and karrai karela (bitter melons) (£4).

The Prince of Ceylon

39 Watford Way, Hendon, NW4 ☎ 0181 203 8002	⊖ Hendon Central
Mon–Fri noon–3pm & 6–11.30pm, Sat & Sun noon–11.30pm	All major credit cards

The Prince of Ceylon has been a mainstay of London's Sri Lankan community for the past twenty years, its quality and rarity (even now there are only half a dozen Sri Lankan places in London) transcending its location. Watford Way is reminiscent of a grand prix pit lane (though you can park on it). Once inside, it's very welcoming – especially during the popular Sunday all-afternoon buffet – and there's the novelty of Sri Lankan food, which is quite distinct from most Indian dining. Whereas in an Indian curry house there's a tendency to choose a dish, and then some bread or rice to go with it, Sri Lanka turns this principle on its head. Breads, rices, and staples are strange and delightful, forcing the curries, sambals, and devilled meats and seafood into a supporting role.

Starters are deceptively named. Mutton rolls (£1.75) are delicious crispy spring rolls filled with spicy lamb and potatoes, served with a chilli-tangy tomato ketchup. The same sauce appears with fish cutlets (£1.75) – spherical, lemony fishcakes. Or there's rasam (£1.50), a spicy soup, thin, almost gritty with aromatic spices, and with a wicked chilli kick. Moving on to the main courses, start by picking your staple. Hoppers (75p) are a must: thin, crispy, bowl-shaped breads, which come either plain or with an egg to lace their base. Or there are string hoppers (£2.50), cakes of vermicelli that come into their own dowsed with a bowl of kiri hodi (coconut milk curry). The kiri hodi also accompanies pittu (£3), a plain white cylinder that looks like a roll of fax paper; it is made in a special steamer by packing the funnel with a mix of grated coconut and rice flour. Highlight among the breads is coconut roti (£1.75), a crisper, thinner kind of paratha. To mop up these delights, pick from a range of curries and devilled dishes. The mutton curry (£4) is a good meat-and-gravy dish – while the unassumingly named "Fried mutton onion" (£4.50) is even better. Good devilled dishes include crabs (£4.50) and chicken liver (£4), both of them chilli hot and piquant.

Whatever you order, be sure to get a side dish of seeni sambal (£2.25) – a spicy onion jam that adds flavour and texture. And leave room for a pud: either wattalappan (£3), Sri Lanka's second cousin to creme caramel, made with palm syrup, or (buffalo) curd and syrup (£3).

Rani

7 Long Lane, Finchley, N3 ☎ 0181 349 4386   ⊖ Finchley Central

Daily noon–3pm & 6–10.30pm   All major credit cards

Rani is something of an enigma. Simply reading the menu you would imagine that you were in one of the bustling Indian vegetarian restaurants in Wembley. You'll find all the Gujarati dishes, the breads and the street foods, all reasonably priced. But Rani is in Finchley, an altogether more upmarket and respectable neck of the woods. This is a middle class restaurant, the red and green table covers and unfussy decor put you in mind of an Italian restaurant, and just by the front door in an open kitchen they are making . . . pizzas, from bowlfuls of fresh-looking ingredients. The waiting staff are helpful and, unexpectedly, most are non-Asian. Rani has made a definite attempt to integrate with the local community and judging by the stream of respectable-looking customers they clearly seem to have succeeded.

The food is good and authentic, if a little more refined than you get in most Wembley Gujarati eateries. To start, try the vall papri chat (£2.60), a wonderful array of textures, beans, onions, crisp poori and sev. Or go for one of the bhajias – vegetable; potato; onion (all at £2.40). These come with a good coriander chutney but consider ordering a side dish of date chutney (£1.10) which is very rich, sweet and hot. The main courses go under the heading Gujarati Sak, and include some interesting curries. Banana methi (£3.90) is made with bananas rather than the more usual plantains – the sweetness of the fruit is a perfect foil for the fresh tomato and methi sauce. Undhia (£4.40) is a "kitchen sink" sort of dish: aubergines, peas, guvar, beans, and potato are cooked with fried fenugreek balls – a kind of vegetarian meatball made from lentils and methi. Breads are good here – the thin paratha stuffed with potato (£2.20) is very delicious and the deep-fried methi bhatoora (two for £1.70) are wickedly self-indulgent.

The second – pizza – menu is also worth your consideration. It's not everywhere that you have the option of a banana methi pizza (£5.35), featuring "fenugreek sauce, tomatoes, ripe banana, and mozzarella".

SOUTH

Battersea

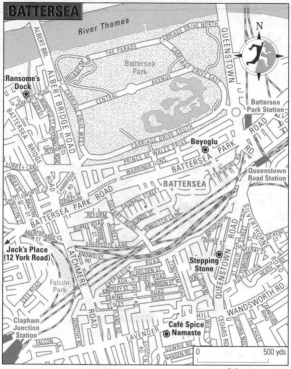

BATTERSEA

River Thames

CARRIAGE DRIVE NORTH
THE PARADE
Battersea Park
CARRIAGE DRIVE EAST

Ransome's Dock

ALBERT BRIDGE
ALBERT BRIDGE ROAD
CARRIAGE DRIVE WEST
CENTRAL
AVENUE
CARRIAGE DRIVE SOUTH

PARKGATE ROAD
WESTBRIDGE RD
BATTERSEA BRIDGE
BATTERSEA BRIDGE ROAD
SURREY LANE
PETWORTH ST

QUEENSTOWN ROAD

Battersea Park Station

Queenstown Road Station

Beyoglu

PRINCE OF WALES DRIVE
WARRINER GDNS
BATTERSEA PARK

BATTERSEA

STRASBURG RD

CAMBRIDGE RD
KERSLEY ST
BATTERSEA PARK ROAD
BAGNALL STREET
REFORM
BURNS RD
ROSENAU RD
SHEEPCOTE LANE
ABERCROMBIE ST
KNOWSLEY RD

SILVERTHORNE ROAD
BROUGHTON
PRAIRIE ST
DICKENS
HACKERAY ST
THACKERAY ST
ST PHILIP
ROBERTSON ST

Jack's Place (12 York Road)

LATCHMERE ROAD
Falcon Park

ESTE ROAD

Clapham Junction Station

EVERSLEIGH RD
HOLDEN ST
ASH
BUSY ROAD
AYSHFORD
MORRISON ST
KINGSLEY ST
SABINE
ELSLEY
ROAD
CLELAND ROAD
DOROTHY RD

Stepping Stone

QUEENSTOWN ROAD
GLYCENA

WANDSWORTH RD
CEDARS RD
THE CHASE
VICTORIA RISE

HILL
LAVENDER
SUGDEN
Café Spice Namaste
SOWRIE RD
NANSEN RD

FALCON

0   500 yds

© Crown copyright

SOUTH

314

Beyoglu

50 Battersea Park Rd, SW11 ☎ 0171 627 2052	BR: Battersea Park
Daily 6pm–midnight	Mastercard, Visa

Beyoglu has moved half way across London – from Stoke Newington to Battersea – and on the way some of the more radical specialities of the Turkish grill house have been left behind. You won't find those Turkish delicacies of brains, sweetbreads and so forth, and the grill has been tidied away out of sight in the depths of the kitchen. But the menu does proclaim "all grilled dishes cooked on real wood charcoal" and the results are here for all to see: simple but tasty fresh food at reasonable prices. This is a formula that'll guarantee a full house in Stoke Newington, Battersea or anywhere between and it's best to book before setting out. This is not a big place.

Dips and pitta always make good sense. At Beyoglu the fava (£2.50) is something of a star – broad beans are pureed with oil, onion, dill and a touch of garlic. Tarama (£2.00) is pink and perky. Muska borek (£2.90) are triangular – like tiny samosas – very light, very hot, light pastry filled with melting feta and parsley. Venture on to the grilled meats, which all come with competent rice or chips and rather good fresh-cut "assembly" salads of sliced onions, tomatoes and grilled mild chilli peppers. Special mixed grill (£7.95) comprises a quail, a slice of lamb (rolled best end of neck), a piece of lamb steak, and a lamb chop. The other combination platter is the karisik izgara (£7), which provides grilled chunks of lamb and chicken, the adana kebab (made from mince), a kidney, and seemingly whatever else is to hand! If you pine for the more obscure and traditional grilled bits the bobrek izgara (£5) delivers a portion of well-grilled and delicious lamb kidneys, while vegetarians will be pleased to find a good pilaki (white beans and potato with onions in a tomatoey sauce – £2.50) amongst the starters.

The sucuk, (£2.90), is described in the hot starters section of the menu as "char-grilled spicy Turkish sausages". They are imported from Cyprus and are very good indeed. Pleasantly spicy, they have an excellent texture – not the usual gnarled and gristly items in a pool of oil.

£12–£25

Café Spice Namaste

247 Lavender Hill, SW11 ☎ 0171 738 1717　　　　　⊖ Clapham Common

Mon–Wed 6–11.30pm, Thurs–Sat noon–3pm & 6–11.30pm,

Sun 6–10.30pm　　　　　　　　　　　　　　All major credit cards

Fans of chef Cyrus Todiwala's other restaurant – Café Spice Namaste in The City (see p.212) – will be relieved to hear that the food at this, the newer Lavender Hill outpost, is just as good. Both of them break all the curry house rules: there's no meat Madras or chicken tikka masala in sight . . . instead a long menu featuring well-spiced, fresh-tasting dishes from all over India. You will find dishes from Goa, Chettiyar, Rajasthan; then there are Parsee specialities from Madhya Pradesh, and Nepal. It's an eye-opener. And a stomach pleaser.

Start with pappads (40p) and the amazing aubergine and peanut chutney (50p for pickles). Then go on to chole aur kaju chaat (£3.50), a cold mixture of chick peas, cashew nuts, potatoes, green chillies, onions chopped together. Delicious tastes and textures. From the tandoor have the poleku masu (£3.75) – chunks of lamb in green chilli garlic mint and fenugreek paste. And the hot one – frango no espeto piri piri (£3.25) from Goa, a chicken tikka made with red chillies and palm vinegar. Equally memorable is the Goan seafood pulao with saurac (£9.25) – black tiger prawns, green lip mussels, squid, and crab meat made into a rich pulao – like a luxurious Indian paella. Then there's the kozhi vartha kari (£8.50) served with amazing lemon rice – originating in Tamil Nadu, this is the rich chicken dish from which we get the word curry. Try a vegetable dish or two, as well, like choley pindi (£3.50) – a stunning, rich dish of chick peas with ginger, green chillies and garlic cooked until almost dry. As well as the lemon rice – full of curry leaves, lemon, mustard seed, and very delicious – you must try the breads, and in particular the outstanding garlic and chilli naan (£2.25) fresh from the tandoor.

The Namaste restaurants are among the few places in London where you can try an authentic vindalho de porco (£8.50) – a hot Goan curry made with palm vinegar, garlic and pickled onions. This is a very far cry from its Friday night, post-lager, raw chilli namesake, the vindaloo.

Jack's Place

12 York Road, SW11 ☎ 0171 228 8519	BR: Clapham Junction
Mon–Sat 6pm–midnight, Sun noon–3pm	Mastercard, Visa

Jack's Place is a Battersea institution – it dates back to the days when SW11 was not the kind of postcode estate agents describe as desirable. The restaurant occupies a long, dark room decorated with pictures of Positano (the restaurant's butcher, an old family friend, is from Positano); the Royal Family; various high ranking military officers; and American presidents. There's also a dusting of Chelsea F.C. memorabilia – and it is rumoured that if you have the indecency to admit to following Arsenal, standards of both service and cuisine fall off markedly. Jack, his wife, his daughter Angela, and now her daughter Cindy, all work in the family business, and the family business is serving up steaks. The customers come from far afield, and from all walks of life. They like the lack of airs and graces, they like the simple table settings, and if truth were told they like the slightly old-fashioned feel to the place.

Jack's is an unrepentant and unreconstructed menu, dishes are as you remember them. Prawn cocktail (£4.75) is lettuce, prawns, and pink stuff. "Retro" food is more of a way of life here than the latest fad. There's also melon boat (£1.95) and stuffed mushrooms (£3.75) – home-made, like everything else. Steakwise, there's entrecôte (£14.85) either plain, Mexicaine, chasseur, or au poivre. Or fillet (also £14.85) either plain, mignon or chasseur. The meat is good quality, and the cooking precise – rare means rare. Everything comes with a mixture of six different vegetables plus potatoes, and the sauces are just as you would remember them from their heyday in the 1960s. Adventurous souls may want to try the gammon and pineapple (£11.50), or the large grilled Dover Sole (£17.50) – fresh and good.

Jack's is certainly a place where drinking men feel at home. The bar is a real bar, which makes it all the more difficult not to be stunned by the sophistication (and terrific value) represented by the wine list. You could treat yourself to a very good bottle of Spanish red – Berberana Riserva 1988 – for £13.50. And for those with cash in their wallets, there's a Croft 1963 vintage port (£64) or a Louis Roederer Cristal 1983 at a tantalising £99.50.

£15–£30

Ransome's Dock

35-37 Parkgate Rd SW11 ☎ 0171 223 1611	BR: Battersea Park
Mon–Sat 11.30am–11.30pm, Sun 11.30am–3.30pm	All major credit cards

Ransome's Dock is a restaurant you would like to have at the bottom of your street. It is formal enough for those little celebrations, or for occasions with friends, but it is still informal enough to pop into for a single dish at the bar. The food is good, seasonal, and made with carefully sourced ingredients. Dishes are well-cooked and satisfying, not fussy; the wine list is encyclopaedic; and service is friendly and efficient. All in all, Martin Lam and his team have got it just about right. Everything stems from the initial ingredients – they use a supplier in East Anglia for the smoked eels; they dicker with the Montgomerys over prime Cheddars; small producers stop by with their finest wines. The menu changes regularly here but the philosophy behind it does not. Look out for the bargain set lunch – two courses for £11.50.

Before rampaging off through the main menu look at the daily specials, then if nothing tempts you turn to the 7 or 8 starters listed. If it's on, make a bee-line for the Norfolk smoked eel with warm buckwheat pancakes and crème fraîche (£7.50), a large portion, very rich and very good. Or there may be air-dried ham from Cumbria with fresh figs (£7). Or Morecambe Bay potted shrimps with wholemeal toast (£5.85). Main courses are well balanced – Dutch calf's liver (£13.50) may come with parsely mash, field mushrooms. pancetta and red wine sauce – melt-in-the-mouth stuff. Sea bass might be accompanied by a girolle mushroom risotto and spinach (£16). Perhaps spinach, ricotta and pine-nut filo pastry with a tomato pepper sauce (£10.50) tempts? Or there may be a sirloin steak (£16.50) with mustard and tarragon sauce, roast tomatoes and chips – not just any old steak, but a well hung one from a Shorthorn steer. Puddings run from the complicated, like a hot prune and Armagnac soufflé with Armagnac custard (£5.50), to the simple – Greek yoghurt with honey (£4.25).

The wine list here is awesome reading. Long, complex, arcane – full of producers and regions you have never heard of – but prices are fair, and advice is both freely available and helpful.

Stepping Stone

123 Queenstown Rd, SW8 ☎ 0171 622 0555	⊖ Clapham Common
Mon–Fri noon–2.30pm & 7–11pm,	
Sat 7–11pm, Sun noon–3pm.	All major credit cards

Although very much a neighbourhood restaurant, Stepping Stone deserves a wider public. Its policy of using only the best ingredients, most of them organic and free range, sourced direct from many small and individual suppliers, ensures a quality of taste in simple dishes that is very rewarding. Fish is bought from the port, meat from the farm, game from the shoot. There's a separate, large no-smoking room, the whole place is air conditioned, and owner Gary Levy's policy is to encourage people to arrive early and stay late. In short it's enlightened . . . and the food is consistently good.

As you would expect, the menu changes daily and being market driven makes best use of what is available. For starters there might be grilled puffball mushrooms, rocket, gremolata and parmesan (£6.00) – it is rare to see mushrooms like this on a menu and very welcome. Cauliflower soup (£4.00) is rich and wintery; and pork terrine, toast and pickles (£5.00), is well flavoured – very different from the blandness often associated with terrines. For main courses dive in to calf's liver, beetroot and apple mash (£10.75) – the sweet mash is a good accompaniment for the rich liver. Or try roast grouse, Savoy cabbage, bread sauce (£16.00), a traditional English dish that is very well accomplished; the menu even warns you that it "may contain lead shot". Or there's rack of Norfolk Horn lamb, sweetcorn risotto, romesco sauce (£14.75); the Norfolk Horn is a rare breed that has been traditionally reared for flavour, rather than intensively farmed for size. Puddings are worth saving room for. There's roast plums with shortbread and cream (£4.50), home-made prune and armagnac ice cream (£4.00), sticky banana pudding, caramel sauce (£4.75), or a selection of cheeses from Neal's Yard dairy, London's premier English cheesemonger.

The wine policy is helpful as the list is divided by drinking type – "zesty", "aromatic", "light and fruity" and so on – which helps match wine with food. Lunch specials are two courses for £10.75 from the main menu, and there is a £10 discount all Monday evening or for early and late bookings on other nights. Sunday lunch is £15 for three courses.

Brixton & Camberwell

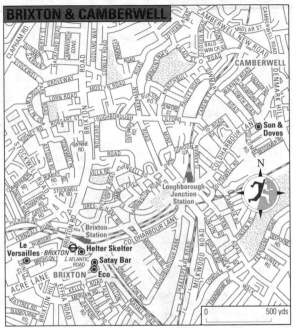

© Crown copyright

Eco (Pizzeria Franco)

4 Market Row, Brixton Market, Electric Row, SW9 ☎ 0171 738 3021	⊖ Brixton
Mon, Tues & Thurs–Sat 8.30am–5pm	Mastercard, Visa

If you're in Brixton around midday, Eco (formerly Pizzeria Franco) is a must for your lunch-break. make your way to Brixton Market – London's first market with electric light – and don't be put off by the smell from the fishmonger's shop opposite. Once inside Eco, it soon gives way to more appetising wafts of cooked cheese and coffee from your neighbour's table. Peruse the menu while you queue among the wandering shoppers, be prepared to share your table, and then sit down to perhaps the best pizza in South London. Pizzeria Franco, now technically called Eco Brixton, is the sister of Eco proper, on Clapham High Street, and has the same menu, but closes at 5pm. As it's both small and popular, things can get hectic. Still, the service is friendly, the pizzas crisp and the salads mountainous. Plus there is an identical take-away menu, at the same price.

All the famous pizzas are here: pleasingly pungent Napolitana (£5.30) with the sacred trio of anchovies, olives and capers, and quattro stagioni (£6.20) packed full of goodies. But why not try something less familiar such as coriander-topped roasted red pepper and aubergine (£5.80) or enjoy la dolce vita (£6.20) where rocket, mushrooms and dolcelatte all vie for attention; or even the amore (£5.80) with its French beans, artichoke, pepper and aubergine? Or calzone (all at £6.20). It's a difficult choice. For a lighter meal – lighter only because of the absence of carbohydrate – try a salad. Antipasto galleria (£7.20) has practically everything meaty and seafoody on top of green salad, while antipasto formaggio (£7.20) includes heaps of dolcelatte, brie, emmental and smoked mozzarella. Highly recommended side-orders are the melted cheese bread (£2.80) and mushroom bread (£3.40) – but take note, there's enough for two. For a quick sandwich, Eco also wins out, as its focaccia are stuffed with delights like Parma ham and avocado (£5.90), and salami and Emmental (£5.20).

You could also go for starters, but at lunch time they seem a little surplus to requirements. Wisely, there are only six options ranging from avocado vinaigrette (£3.30) to seafood salad (£4.90). Puddings are even fewer in number: pecan pie (£3.20), tiramisu (£3.50) and profiteroles (£3.20). As you'd expect from an Italian place, the coffee is good.

Helter Skelter

50 Atlantic Rd, SW9 ☎ 0171 274 8600	⊖ Brixton
Mon–Thurs 7–11pm, Fri & Sat 7–11.30pm	Mastercard, Visa

When John and Natasha Sverdlow got to it, the shop at 50 Atlantic Road was an Indian restaurant. It was only as they began renovating, and set about ripping away years of flock wallpaper, that they discovered beautiful original tiling depicting Dutch eel boats. Although slightly battered by time and careless builders, they decided to keep the tiling – but that is about all that can be said to be old-fashioned about Helter Skelter. The cuisine, is a disorderly mix of tastes, ingredients and styles from around the world, brought together with great care and heaps of style. It all adds up to an innovative restaurant in unusual surroundings.

The aim here is to produce good, simple, fresh food from well-chosen and carefully bought ingredients, and that is quite apparent from the menu. Starters such as char-grilled calamari with watercress and lime and chilli marinade(£4.80) and warm globe artichoke with vinaigrette and Parmesan (£5.30) are wholly successful. The Thai-inspired red chicken curry (£7.00) is a wonderfully spicy dish served on a bed of shredded vegetables; or there's the char-grilled swordfish salad Nicoise(£12.25); or for veggies, the mixed bean tagine, with roasted pumpkin, cheese and onion polenta, and rocket (£8.80). The specials board changes daily and is influenced mainly, if we are to believe the chef, by the weather. An aubergine houmous with wild rocket and parsnip ribbons (£4.80) was superb with the crisp, warm parsnip making the perfect "spoon". The puddings (all priced at £4.00) go straight for your greed bump. One – the nougat glacé with fresh fruit – is just too good to be true. The wine list offers a wide selection from both Old and New World producers and the house selection (£9.50/£12.00) is a good bet for the undecided.

Atlantic Road has had a colourful past and with this in mind the restaurant's frontage has been carefully designed: a laser cut stainless steel helter skelter mounted on bars covers the entire window. It has the double effect of not only being strikingly original but also a highly effective security grill.

Le Versailles

20 Trinity Gardens, SW9 ☎ 0171 326 0521	⊖ Brixton
Daily 6–11pm	Visa

It's hard to imagine anywhere less like Versailles than Trinity Gardens in Brixton, and in that respect the previous restaurant name (Twenty Trinity Gardens) was rather more apt. But this is now a resolute outpost of France. The staff are French. The menu is French. Even the background music is French – uncannily replicating the kind of soundtrack you'd hear in any bistro in a small, provincial, French town. Thankfully the food here is French in the best manner: the straightforward bourgeois food that used to be standard all over France. Good, fresh ingredients are simply treated and well presented. There's a bargain three-course set dinner – just £10 Monday to Thursday, rising to £13.95 on Friday and Saturday – for which Brixtonians can sit down to, say, salade Niçoise, followed by red bream with herb and basil sauce, and tart Tatin.

On the carte, the entrees list contains one or two very good dishes that may tempt you away from the set deal: salade paysanne, petit salé, oeuf poché et Parmesan (£3.95) is a well-balanced salad made with little gem lettuce and a well poached egg with a thick cut rasher of salty bacon. Crevettes Royales sautées au persil et à l'ail (£4.95) are large prawns under a haystack of crisp fried leek. On to Les Plats Principaux. Chartreuse d'agneau "pommes fondant" (£10.50) is a very tender lamb steak – simple and succulent. Then there's poulet Niçoise (£10); aiglefin fumé avec oeuf poché et pommes de terre nouvelles (£9.95) – smoked haddock and poached egg, a terrific combination; or loup de mer grillé avec tapenade, confit de fenouil and sauce Vierge (£11.95). The menu is littered with the names of classic sauces – Gribiche, Bercy, Albucera – and they are all well-made. Desserts include old favourites like "tarte au citron", "tarte au chocolat", and creme brulée; they are generally priced at under £4.

The wine list is short and to the point. Six or seven reds and the same number of whites running up to about £17 a bottle. It's a real pleasure to drink an excellent bottle of Bergerac and pay under £12.

BRIXTON & CAMBERWELL ⑪ INDONESIAN

Satay Bar

450 Coldharbour Lane, SW9 ☎ 0171 326 5001   ⊖ Brixton

Mon–Fri noon–3pm & 6–11.30pm, Sat & Sun 1pm–midnight   All major credit cards

The Satay Bar is part of the regeneration of the heart of Brixton, and is tucked away just behind the Ritzy Cinema. The first impression of this lively restaurant and bar is one of fun – pure and simple. The term laid-back was invented for here; the interior is dark and warm and there's a persistent party atmosphere, bolstered by the thumping beat of the background music. Settle in, relax and take a look at the art. If you happen to like one of the many paintings adorning the walls, ask to buy it; the management will soon replace it – the restaurant doubles as a gallery for local talent, with exhibitions changing fortnightly.

The menu is a testing one, at least when it comes to pronouncing the names of the dishes, but the food is well-cooked, service is friendly and efficient and the prices are reasonable. Your waiter will smile benignly at your attempt to enunciate udang goreng tepung (£5.95) – a delicious starter of lightly-battered, deep-fried king prawns served with a sweet chilli sauce. Obvious choices, such as the chicken or prawn satay (£5.25), are rated by some as the best in London; or try the chicken wings (£4.45) with garlic and green chilli – no less satisfying. Dishes are traditional Indonesian with the chilli factor toned down (for the most part) to accommodate European tastebuds. However, there are hot dishes to be found in the curry section. The medium kari ikan (£5.25), a salmon-based, Javanese fish curry packs a punch even in its "medium" incarnation, while the rendang ayam (£5.25), a spicy chicken dish, is only cooled somewhat by the addition of a coconut sauce. For something lighter, the mee goreng (£4.45) is a satisfying dish of spicy egg noodles fried with seafood and vegetables; or there's gado-gado (£4.25), a side dish of bean curd and vegetables with spicy peanut sauce, which is almost a meal in itself.

If terminal indecision sets in and you find yourself pinned by the menu like a rabbit in the headlights try the rijsttafel (£11.95 per person, minimum order for two), a combination of seven specially selected dishes. This has a vegetarian option.

SOUTH

Sun & Doves

61–63 Coldharbour Lane, Camberwell, SE5 ☎ 0171 733 1525	BR: Denmark Hill
Mon–Sat 11am–11pm, Sun noon–10.30pm	Mastercard, Visa (over £10)

The Sun & Doves styles itself as "Gallery, Restaurant and Bar", which may be true, but seems an overly posh title for a pub that does rather good food, has an above average wine list, and an ever-changing array of pictures on the wall. This is one of those cavernous London pubs which date back to the days before television when all manner of age groups went out of an evening. The "refurb" has been carried out sensitively, and without resorting to luxurious furnishings, it is still quite a Spartan establishment, although any Rip van Winkle awakening from a nap in the 1950's would certainly be surprised by the fresh flower arrangements. The food has also come a long way, too, as the loyal following from nearby King's Hospital will vouch.

The cooking is honest and straightforward but can be adventurous in its combinations of flavours and ingredients. The starters list will usually include a soup of the day (£3.25), and there is often a pasta dish which will do dual duty as a starter or main course – perhaps pumpkin ravioli with sage cream (£3.75/£5.50). The choice of accompaniments is generally first rate so a starter of haloumi will come with roast peppers, and lime dressing (£4.25), while escabeche of red mullet is dressed with sherry vinegar, dill and caperberries (£4.25). Another dual role dish is the vegetarian Niçoise salad (£3.95/£5.50) – green beans, cherry tomatoes, quail eggs, sugar snaps, Jersey royals, shallots, black olives and aïoli. Main courses vary with the season but run from black bean and ochra enchillada (£7.95), which comes with an avocado and tomatillo salsa, through chump of lamb with a spiced crust (£10.50) served with pea purée, sugar snaps and roast shallots, to baked ham (£8.95) with sauté sweet potatoes and pickled peaches.

The wine list is intelligently written and the selections are good value and interesting – Chenin Blanc Paarl Heights (£10.50), from South Africa; Perequita Palmela Particular (£15.50) from Portugal. And there are decent beers to be had, too, just in case you were forgetting that the Sun & Doves is, after all, still a pub.

Clapham
& Wandsworth

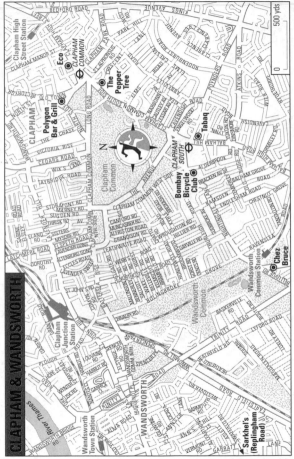

CLAPHAM & WANDSWORTH

500 yds

© Crown copyright

330

Bombay Bicycle Club

95 Nightingale Lane, Clapham, SW12 ☎ 0181 673 6217   ⊖ Clapham Common

Mon–Sat 7–11pm   All major credit cards

Local estate agents talk lovingly of the "Nightingale Triangle" – that ever-so-select group of properties just off Clapham Common – and the residents probably acknowledge the Bombay Bicycle Club as one of the assets which helps justify their premium house prices. This establishment is not a typical curry house. It is light, airy and chic, and a glimpse of the vast bowl of white lilies in the centre of the room would make any number of florists rub their hands with glee. More importantly, the food is not run of the mill either. The menu changes regularly – classics are adapted, cultures mixed, liberties taken. Generally most of it works, and stylish food tallies with a stylish setting. This is not a cheap Indian restaurant, but nobody seems to mind – after all, it is in the "Nightingale Triangle"!

The menu divides starters into two categories – "starters" and "starters from the tandoor". They range from the old-fashioned – mulligatawny soup (£3.50) – to a brochette of monkfish cooked in the tandoor (£5.50). Tellicherry squid (£4.75) is a good opening move, sliced thin and fried crisp with a good dipping sauce. Also chicken wings jeera (£4.50), and Cochin rajah prawns (£8.50) – sizzled king prawns. Onwards to main course dishes. There's a hot Madras fish curry (£8.50) and another interesting dish called gosht kalia (£7.25) – which here translates into a rich spicy sauce with yoghurt and methi (fenugreek). Or try a vegetarian dish, meerut noodles (£7.25), which comes with a rather strange and "chicken-tikka-masala-ish" pink sauce to pour over it. Rice is basmati, but pricy at "£3.25, serves two". "Daal of the day" is expensive, too, at £4, but the tarka daal made with whole pulse is certainly good. There is also a "specials menu" with dishes that are even more closely tied to seasonal availability – something that is always to be commended. Breads are hot and good.

The wine list is long, well chosen, and takes a fearful hammering – empty wine bottles must mount up by the skip load. But then Bombay Bicycle Club isn't your usual Indian.

Chez Bruce

2 Bellevue Rd, SW17 ☎ 0181 672 0114	BR: Wandsworth Common
Mon–Sat noon–2pm & 7–10.15pm, Sun 12.30–3pm	All major credit cards

In a TV poll conducted amongst London's leading chefs, Chez Bruce came out as the place they most enjoyed eating out. This was quite a coup for Bruce Poole – for his eponymous restaurant is some way from the West End, has a fairly small dining room, and lacks Michelin stars. But the chefs know cooking when they see it – and Chez Bruce delivers honest, unfussy, earthy, richly-flavoured food. It is old-fashioned food, rather than the latest gastro-tend, often featuring the likes of pig's trotters, and rabbit, and mackerel, and sometimes rather laconically described on the menu. It is also a real bargain. You'll find this restaurant described as French in other guides, but actually it represents all that is best about British cooking and British ingredients. The prix fixe three-course menus offer lunch for £18 (Sun £21.50), and dinner for £25.

The menu changes from season to season and day to day. Generally, the lunch menu is a shortened version of the dinner menu. The kind of starters you can expect to encounter are cream of onion soup with smoked bacon – rich, peasant food; or duck confit and foie gras ballotine with toasted brioche; or herb leaf salad with shallots and Parmesan. Or there might be a classic lurking, like vitello tonnato. Main course dishes are deeply satisfying. You might find roast rump of lamb with potato galette and Provençal jus; or cod fillet with horseradish crust, lentil salad and balsamico; or stuffed rabbit leg with artichokes, broad beans and tarragon. This is one of those places where everything on the menu tempts. It is also one of the last strongholds of offal (another reason for the chefs' endorsement?). Look out for sweetbreads, or perhaps calves' liver served with spinach and ricotta ravioli, sage beurre noisette and Madeira jus.

The sweets here are well executed classics – proper crème brulée; clafoutis of plums with clotted cream; tarte Tatin aux poires. No wonder this place is booked every evening well in advance. Go for lunch instead – it'll make your day.

Eco

162 Clapham High St, SW4 ☎ 0171 978 1108	⊖ Clapham Common
Mon–Fri noon–4pm & 6.30–11pm (11.30pm Fri),	
Sat noon–5pm & 6–11.30pm, Sun noon–5pm & 6–11pm.	All major credit cards

Eco is a seriously modern, seriously trendy pizzeria. It is a designer place: all sinuous curved wrought iron, simple banquettes, and a lot of plain wood. But for all that it is friendly and welcoming. There's a pizza of the day written up on a big board and they do not blanch when families turn up for lunch with a toddler in tow. In the evenings, however, things get a good deal more fashion orientated and the music quite a bit louder. On the menu you'll find a note setting out an interesting approach to the lingering problem of table turning. Each party, it says, gets the use of the table for "an hour and a half" and if you want to take more time than that you have to pre-arrange things with the manager. Quite clever that.

The whole operation, in fact, is a thoughtful one. There's a short list of starters, then pizzas, focaccia, calzone oven-baked dishes and salads. Everything that's cooked goes through the ovens, which makes a lot of sense – so there isn't any spaghetti but there are baked garlic prawns (£4.20) or melanzane al forno (£4.20) – baked aubergines, while on the starters list there's roasted pepper and mozzarella (£4.70) – served cold with anchovies and a side salad. The pizzas come both classic – Margherita (£4.80); quattro formaggi (£6.90); American hot with pepperami (£5.30); quattro stagione with artichoke, ham, mushrooms, olives and anchovies (£6.50) – and not so classic: amore – roast red pepper and green beans (£6.50); smoked salmon and baby spinach (£7.50); La dolce vita – rocket, and mushrooms (£6.50); and aubergine and sun-dried tomato (£5.90). They are all generous-sized, freshly-cooked, and well-made. Delicious, in a word. The focaccia are good, too: sandwiches made with pizza bread, including simple favourites like mozzarella and avocado (£5.50), or salami and Emmental cheese (£5.50). The calzone are folded up pizzas with tomato sauce – ricotta and spinach (£6.70) is particularly tasty.

The Eco coffee is good, too, and the puddings simple but satisfying – like tiramisu (£3.90) or raspberry chocolate truffle (£4.20).

The Pepper Tree

19 Clapham Common South Side, SW4 ☎ 0171 622 1758   ⊖ Clapham Common

Mon noon–3pm & 6–10.30pm, Tues–Sat noon–3pm & 6–11pm,	
Sun noon–10.30pm	Mastercard, Visa

Situated on the seemingly endless south side of the Common, just a stone's throw from the tube station, this open-fronted Thai eatery serves up no-nonsense, short-order dishes. It is jam-packed almost every night, with a clientele of predominantly 20-somethings, an amazing number of whom are equipped with mobile phones in order to conduct important conversations with friends other than the ones they're with – very 90s, as of course is spicy Thai food. It's bustling and noisy, and fun, if you're in the mood for company. Everyone shares mess hall tables and so each has a pick'n'mix pile of phones, which leads to a cheerful scramble whenever one rings, warbles or buzzes.

You can build your meal in stages, rather like you would a Greek meze. Vegetable rolls (£2.25) are made with vermicelli noodles, shaved carrots and Chinese mushrooms wrapped in filo pastry. Egg fried rice (£1.75), is just that; or there's a stir-fry of mixed seafood (£4.50) which is tossed with fresh chillies, garlic and sweet basil. Green prawn curry (£3.95) is simmered in coconut milk with Thai aubergines, lime leaves and sweet basil and comes medium hot. Big tum chicken noodles (£4.75) are thick, yellow and fried with chillies and sweet basil. Among the salads, the Pepper Tree (£3.95) combines marinated grilled slices of beef with lemon juice, coriander, spring onions and chilli. Many dishes use the same ingredients but ring the changes in terms of balance and preparation techniques. "Sweet things" include stem ginger ice cream (£1.95) and bananas in coconut milk (£2.50) sprinkled with sesame seeds. Sticky rice with mango (£2.50) is described on the menu as mango with sticky rice, which seems a model of accuracy.

The Pepper Tree churns out simple spicy food which is distributed by cheerful staff and sold at affordable prices. Even the drinks are reasonable – you can get a mug of tea for under £1, and there are bottles of house reds and whites at £7.95. There's also Argentine Norton Merlot (£11.95) which is a real bargain.

The Polygon

4 The Polygon, SW4 ☎ 0171 622 1199	⊖ Clapham Common
Mon–Thurs 6–11.30pm, Fri noon–11.30pm,	
Sat 11am–11.30pm, Sun 11am–10.30pm	All major credit cards

The Polygon is a super-cool addition to the old cobbled quartier of Clapham – a fine south-of-the-river representative of the new breed of bar-restaurant that continues to expand London's style boundaries beyond established chic locations. Not surprisingly, minimalism is the adopted design style, both outside and in, and it all works extremely well. A tall uncluttered bar runs the length of the restaurant separating drinkers from diners and from here you can view the sizzling dishes arriving from the rotisserie at the far end. The menu changes regularly but is hardly necessary as, by the time you're seated, it's a fair bet you've already seen what you want to order. However, the friendly staff are at pains to elaborate on anything that may have escaped your inspection.

The dividing line between starters and main courses is rather blurred here and ordering two starters can often be the way to go. You might try marinated Guinea fowl skewers with mixed pepper chutney (£5.75); grilled scallops wrapped in Parma ham with celeriac slaw (£8.25); or the seemingly ubiquitous Thai fishcakes with sweet red chilli dressing and grated coconut (£5.50). There's also a soup of the day (£4.50). The grill is key to many of the mains: Rib of beef (£26 for two); seabream with spiced tomato and chilli pickle (£13.50); simply cooked calf's liver with blueberry, red onion chutney and bacon (£10.50); and coeurs de canard served with sauce forestière (£12). In the next menu section, "From the larder", there are no fewer than three Caesar salads - classic (£7.50), with grilled chicken (£9.50), and with grilled salmon (£9.50). Whatever you're having, mustard mash (£1.75) is a good side order. And puddings are serious stuff, highlights including flourless chocolate cake with hot fudge sauce (£5.50), and banana pudding with caramel sauce and cinnamon and honey ice cream (£4.50).

The Polygon staff seem to have a sound knowledge of the wine list which is most encouraging. Among the house selections, priced at £9.50, the Terret Sauvignon blanc is good value and arrives accompanied by an ice bucket, which is more encouraging still.

CLAPHAM & WANDSWORTH ⑪ INDIAN

Sarkhel's

199 Replingham Road, Southfields, SW18 ☎ 0181 870 1483	⊖ Southfields
Tues–Thurs 6–10.30pm, Fri & Sat 6–11pm	
Sun noon–2.30pm & 6–10.30pm	Mastercard, Visa

Udit Sarkhel is a changed man. He will take you into an immaculate kitchen and enthuse about an elderly but highly polished Chester cooker. He has never, (he goes on to tell you) had a cooker that cooks rice so well, seemingly it never sticks. He shakes his head with wonder. What makes this eulogy so surprising is that before opening his own place in SW19, Udit Sarkhel was heading up the kitchens of the famous Bombay Brasserie in the West End, where he had all the latest kit and a large brigade of chefs as well. Moving to Sarkhel's in Southfields, must be like resigning as conductor of an orchestra and setting up a one-man band but it is certainly a huge asset to South London. The food here is well-spiced and there are adventurous dishes scattered through the menu – the Chettinad dishes are particularly fine, hot and fresh. Moreover, this is a pleasant, friendly, family-run restaurant offering good cooking at prices, which though not cheap certainly represent good value. There is also a bargain set Sunday lunch for £9.95.

Start by asking Udit or his wife if there are any "specials" on. These are dishes which change depending on what the markets have to offer and could be something like a starter of crab (£4.95) cooked Malabari style but with some added Chettiyar spicing – a hint of sour tamarind, a whiff of chilli. Quite delicious. Or you might try maachi Amritsari – a kind of Indian "goujons" of fish (£3.95). Or the chicken tikka (£5.95), which is as good as you'll find. For main course dishes check the specials again – it might something wonderful like a prawn pulao (£6.95) cooked slowly in a pot. On the main menu, try the chicken Chettinad, hot and clean tasting (£5.95), or the lamb roganjosh (£5.95) lamb in a simple, rich gravy. All are delicious and have no hint of a slick of oil on the surface.

Be sure to add some vegetable dishes. Baigan bhurta (£4.95) is char-grilled aubergines mashed with spices. Bhindi Jaipuri (£4.95) is a small haystack of slivered okra and onions deep-fried until crisp, then served dusted with mango powder. They are addictively good.

SOUTH

Tabaq

47 Balham Hill, SW12 ☎ 0181 673 7820	⊖ Clapham South
Mon–Sat noon–2.45pm & 6pm–midnight	All major credit cards

The owners of the Tabaq used to drive up from the suburbs to work in a smart West End restaurant and on the way they would travel up Balham Hill and past Clapham Common. They had set their sights on having a restaurant of their own – a restaurant serving the traditional Pakistani specialities – so when signs went up outside 47 Balham Hill they took the plunge. They named their restaurant after the tabaq – a large serving dish – and set about serving authentic Lahori fare. Plaudits soon arrived: in 1998 they won 'Best Pakistani Restaurant in the UK' and 'National Curry Chef' awards.

The menu here comes with a multitude of sections – appetisers, grills, seafood, curries, specialities, rice, breads, vegetables, plus another sheet of "cuisine specials" – chicken, lamb, side orders, charga. Best not to worry about the soups and appetisers; instead go straight for the tandoor and grill section as these are some of the best dishes on the menu. Seek kabab Lahori (£5.50) is made from well-seasoned minced lamb. Shish kabab lamb (£5.50) is delicious. The kingsize prawns cost £10 for five, and if you find yourself wondering whether any prawn could be worth £2 you should try them. As an accompaniment order some raita (£1.95) – yoghurt with cucumber herbs and spices – and maybe a naan-e-Punjabi (£2) which is heavy, butter-rich, bread from the tandoor, and some kachomer (£1.95) – a kind of coarse-cut Asian salsa. At this stage of your meal you may want to yield to the temptation of cancelling the rest and ordering more grills or some charga dishes. If you don't succumb, palak gosht (£6.50) – lamb with spinach – is good; as are gurda masala (£6.50) – a dish of lambs' kidneys – and the ultra-mild murgh moglai (£6.50).

Charga dishes are a speciality here. They are cooked using a "steam roasting" technique peculiar to Lahore in which the meat goes on a platform over a water tray and then into the oven. The meat retains more moisture – and it's a healthy option, too, producing less fat. Choose from charga kababs (£5.50); a whole chicken (takes 30 minutes, £13); or a leg of lamb (24 hours' notice, £35).

Greenwich
& Blackheath

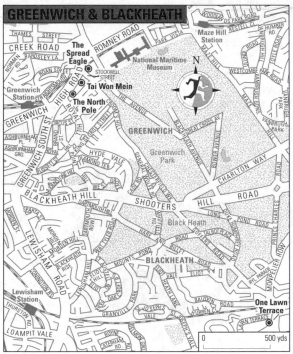

GREENWICH & BLACKHEATH

The Spread Eagle

Tai Won Mein

The North Pole

National Maritime Museum

Maze Hill Station

Greenwich Station

GREENWICH

Greenwich Park

BLACKHEATH HILL

SHOOTERS HILL ROAD

Black Heath

BLACKHEATH

Lewisham Station

One Lawn Terrace

0   500 yds

© Crown copyright

The North Pole

131 Greenwich High Road, SE10 ☎ 0181 853 3020	BR: Greenwich
Restaurant: Tues–Fri noon–2.30pm & 7–10.30pm, Sat 7–10.30pm, Sun noon–8pm	
Bar: Mon–Sat noon–11pm, Sun noon–10.30pm	All major credit cards

To say that this establishment is simply a converted pub with a nice restaurant upstairs is like saying that a Porsche is a flashy Volkswagen Beetle. The North Pole may resemble a pub from the outside but its mosaic fascia lifts it somewhat compared to the usual creaking pub sign, and once inside you find yourself in a vibrant bar area full of the local hip young things. Moving up the narrow, winding staircase, you reach the restaurant which is divided into two dining areas, the smaller of which doubles as a private dining room for a snug thirty of your best friends.

The cuisine is described as "East meets West" – and aptly so, given Greenwich's position on the Meridian. Although not vast, the menu (which changes every month) offers some fine examples of dishes which combine Pacific Rim style with European ingredients. Watercress, coriander and coconut salad (£4) is a crisp and refreshing starter – the sweet shavings of coconut complementing the peppery watercress. Hot starters such as grilled pork skewers with lime leaves (£4.50); or steamed mussels in white wine with lemon (£4.60) are well worth considering. Eastern influences are apparent in main courses such as marinated monkfish and soba noodles (£12.80); char-grilled pork and beef with corn fritter (£13); and the healthy sounding fava bean polenta, sticky rice and confit tomato. The more European saffron taglialini with shredded vegetables and pesto (£8.50), is a yellow tower with the contrasting colour of the vegetables and surrounding pesto giving the overall impression of an edible sombrero. The ubiquitous chip (£2.50) makes an appearance as a side dish; also the marvellous wok-seared greens (£3.50). Puddings, all priced at (£4.50) include lime cheesecake with roasted strawberries, and the indulgent chocolate and Brazil nut pudding. Set lunches are available at £11 for two courses and £15 for three.

As you sit back after your meal, look up and don't be alarmed if you catch sight of movement coming from the central bowl of the splendid lamps. There really are goldfish swimming about up there . . .

GREENHEATH & BLACKHEATH ⑭ MODERN EUROPEAN

SOUTH

One Lawn Terrace

1 Lawn Terrace, SE3 ☎ 0181 355 1110	BR Blackheath
Tues–Fri noon–2.30pm & 6–11pm, Sat 11.30am–2.30pm,	
Sun 11.30am–6pm	All major credit cards

One Lawn Terrace is to be found on the site of an old print works. The presses and inks have long gone but the austere brick exterior, exposed beams and pipework give clues to its past. The restaurant is located upstairs, along with a bar and greeting area, and the industrial decor is mellowed by vanilla walls and blonde wood floors. Dining is loosely divided into three zones: there's the main restaurant, and two smaller semi-private areas in an atrium and a mezzanine level. The high ceilings and vault-like feel make the main dining area seem noisy but this adds to the buzzy ambience. Opened in 1997, this is Greenwich's trendiest restaurant, and was recently sold to the Bank Group (see p.46).

The à la carte menu changes slightly every 3–6 weeks but keeps to a modern European feel. You'll find a number of salads offered as starters – leek and merguez (£5.50), hamhock and lentil (£6.95), spiced roast quail (£7.95), rocket with Parmesan and roast cherry tomatoes (£5.95) – along with the likes of crab linguine (£8.50/£11.50), or parsnip soup with curry cream (£4.50). Main courses are reassuringly solid fare such as grilled ribeye, Béarnaise and fat chips (£15.50); braised shoulder of lamb, Savoy cabbage and caper jus (£12.95); and reflecting the Bank Group's fishy heritage, fish and chips, tartare sauce (£12.95), or panfried cod, Lyonaise potatoes, red wine jus (£11.95). Puddings continue in the same kind of vein. Sticky toffee pudding comes with ginger ice cream (£4.50); chestnut meringue with ice cream and chocolate sauce (£4.50); and chocolate fondant with raspberry and red pepper coulis (£4.50). The comprehensive wine list has good descriptions by weight and taste with prices to match all pockets. A Sunday brunch menu is also available.

One Lawn Terrace has a taste for all things contemporary. Why not browse around the ground floor exhibition as you wait to collect your coat. There are some striking examples of modern art (prices start at £200 going up to thousands) so it could be a case of "been there, eaten the food, bought the paintings . . .".

The Spread Eagle

1–2 Stockwell St, SE10 ☎ 0181 853 2333	BR: Greenwich
Mon–Sat noon–2.30pm & 6.30–10.30pm,	
Sun 10am–9pm	All major credit cards

The Spread Eagle dates back to the seventeenth century, with a well documented past as tavern, coaching inn and hostelry. These days it is strictly a restaurant, not a pub, serving an imaginative range of French and traditional English dishes in a relaxed and very enjoyable atmosphere, sometimes enhanced by live Rhythm and Blues. A spiral staircase leads up to the main dining area where walls of antique theatre prints reflect the Spread Eagle's links with the nearby Greenwich theatre. Cosier banquettes are to be found downstairs. Remember this is a very old building so don't be surprised if your glasses slide towards the centre of the room – the floor has a definite slant.

The menu offers interesting seasonal dishes and changes every five to six weeks. Typical starters from the à la carte include home-smoked tuna with beetroot and napa cabbage salad (£6.25) or the chilled watercress soup, celeriac slaw, garlic and almond stuffed frogs' legs (£5.00) – good and fresh. Or you might find smoked salmon blinis and caviar (£6.75). Main dishes are well-presented and a favourite is the magret of duck with butternut squash and potato rosti (£13.50), a rich dish sweetened with a cherry and port glace du vin. The salmon grand aïoli (£13.75) is light yet satisfying. Whatever you choose, order some of the hand-cut chips (£2.25) which are wonderfully fat, square cut girders of potato cooked to perfection. And be sure to leave some room for puds, which feature such temptations as warm strawberry and green pepper Marscapone (£5.00) or brown bread ice cream with plum coulis (£5.00).

The Spread Eagle offers – in addition to the carte – a simple, three-course table d'hôte menu (£15.50) which may include starters like a serious Caesar salad with brilliant croutons and a lemon poussin for main course. On Sundays, there's a great value brunch (£5.95) available, alongside a simpler brasserie menu, with a choice of a very full English breakfast; corned beef hash with eggs and crispy skin; or that brunch staple, eggs Benedict. All good fare to round off a morning at the local markets.

Tai Won Mein

49 Greenwich Church St, SE10 ☎ 0181 858 1668   BR: Greenwich/DLR: Island Gardens

Daily 11.30am–11.30pm   Cash only

With the masts of the tea clipper Cutty Sark providing an impressive backdrop, Tai Won Mein's simple signs urge you to "eat fast food" – and the stark interior with its long, low benches reinforce the message. But while quality is often sacrificed for speed of service, that is certainly not the case here, probably because the menu is so well tailored to the demands made on it. Good quality food, together with extraordinarily reasonable prices mean that this place is always busy. It is not quite Japanese subway type busy but at the weekend, when the nearby markets are in full swing, you must expect to wait for a seat. This will give you a chance to get to know your prospective table-neighbour while you queue. Hang on in there – it is all well worth it.

Table decoration is sparse and your placemat doubles as the menu. Starters include spring rolls (£3.10) and fried spare ribs (£3.10). Make sure you ask for the chilli sauce. Main courses are divided into rice, noodles or ho fun (which are a kind of ribbon-like noodle, both flatter and softer than usual), and "noodles" are further subdivided into fried noodles and soup noodles. The house special soup noodle (£3.65) is served in an enormous bowl, a steaming vat of egg, prawn, beef, squid, crabmeat, mussels, fresh greens and finally, noodles. Less colourful but certainly no less satisfying is pork with noodles in soup (£3.10). Fried noodle dishes are equally imposing – huge plates are piled high with such delights as mixed seafood (£3.65). Then there's ho fun with king prawn in soup with vegetables (£3.65); and fried ho fun with roast pork and duck (£3.65). Rice dishes – chicken with curry sauce (£3.10) or ribs with black bean sauce (£3.10) – are equally popular.

This seems to be a "pudding-free-zone" but you can wash down the main courses with Sapporro (£2.80), a crisp Japanese beer, or for the health conscious how about the mixed fruit juice (£1.50) – a blend of apple orange and carrot. Looks odd, tastes great, but how long has the carrot been a fruit?

Kennington
& Vauxhall

KENNINGTON & VAUXHALL

The Lobster Pot

KENNINGTON

KENNINGTON

Vauxhall Station

VAUXHALL

Oval Cricket Ground

OVAL

Kennington Park

VAUXHALL

Hot Stuff

Bar Estrela

River Thames

N

0   500 yds

© Crown copyright

Bar Estrela

111–115 South Lambeth Road, SW8 ☎ 0171 793 1051   ⊖ Stockwell

Daily 8am–midnight   All major credit cards

Bar Estrela operates on various levels – literally. In the basement there's table football and a pool table, on the ground floor there's a café-bar and tapas counter, and on the mezzanine floor there's the restaurant. Visiting Estrela is very like being in Portugal – if you can overlook the weather and South London streets outside. The wines are Portuguese; the beers are Portuguese; and the TV is tuned to a Portuguese channel. The menu is long, dishes are simple and honest and . . . very Portuguese!

Start with caldo verde (£1.60) – this is the famous green cabbage soup, much enlivened by chunks of rather good sausage which help overcome a suspicion that it might be somewhat under-seasoned. Gambas Estrela (£4.50) make a brave attempt to impersonate the ones you enjoyed while sunning yourself on holiday. The buttery sauce is particularly good as it has a touch of piri piri to it and is pleasantly spicy. Then you can choose from about forty different main courses. These include most of the Portuguese favourites – indeed, more than you'll find in most restaurants in Portugal. They do a good arroz de marisco (£9) – the Portuguese version of paella – and an equally nice feijoada de marisco (£8) – bean stew with seafood – and arroz de polvo (£7.50) – octopus and rice. Bacalhau con batata, grao e ovo (£7.50) is typical of the heartier main courses: set out on the plate is a chunk of cooked salt cod, a ladleful of boiled chick peas topped with sliced raw onion, and a large boiled potato and a hard-boiled egg – you make your own dressing from the oil and vinegar supplied. Or you could try the classic carne de porco a Alentejana (£7.50) – a terracotta bowl filled with the surprisingly delicious combination of chunks of fried pork, fried potato, and tiny clams in their shells. The portions, as in Portugal, are family sized, and a couple of starters and one main should keep most couples happy.

The cooking at Estrela is resolutely unsophisticated and all the better for it, while the wine list allows you to conduct a masterclass in Vinho Verde – the perfect accompaniment to hearty Portuguese food. The four different ones on offer are all young, fresh and tart and range from a wholly reasonable £11 to a bargain £8.50 a bottle.

Hot Stuff

19 Wilcox Road, SW8 ☎ 0171 720 1480 | ⊖ Vauxhall

Mon–Sat noon–10pm | Mastercard, Visa

This tiny restaurant, run by the Dawood family in South Lambeth, is a bit of an institution. It has only 18 seats and offers simple and startlingly cheap food to an enthusiastic local following. The food is just what you would expect at home – always presuming that you live in Nairobi and are part of the Asian community.

The starters are sound rather than glorious so you'll do best to dive straight into the curries. There are eight different chicken curries and nine different meat dishes – all £3 or under – while the most expensive dish in the house is the king prawn biryani which costs £6.25 – not much more than you would pay for a curried potato in the West End. It is hard to find any fault with a curry that costs just £3! The portions aren't monster-sized and the spicing isn't subtle, but the welcome is genuine and the bill is tiny – it's a telling combination. Arrive before 9.30pm and you can sample the delights of the stuffed paratha (£1) – these are light and crispy with potato in the middle – seriously delicious. Chick pea curry (£2.20), daal (£2.20), and mixed vegetable curry (£1.80) all hit the spot with vegetarians amongst the clientele. For meat-eaters, the chicken Madras (£2.90) is hot and workmanlike, while the chicken bhuna (£2.95) is rich and very good. However, the jewel in the crown of the Hot Stuff menu is masala fish (£3.50) which is only available on Wednesday, Thursday and Friday. Thick chunks of tilapia are marinated for 24 hours in salt and lemon juice before being cooked in a rich sauce with tomatoes, coriander, cumin and ginger.

Hot Stuff closes prudently before the local pubs turn out and part of the fun here is to watch latecomers – say a party of three arriving at 9.50 – negotiating with the indomitable chef and matriarch, Bela Dawood, to secure some dinner. Promising to eat very quickly and only order simple dishes seems to do the trick. This restaurant is driven by the principles of hospitality and it puts many more pretentious establishments to shame.

£18–£45

The Lobster Pot

3 Kennington Lane, SE11 ☎ 0171 582 5556　　　　　⊖ Kennington

Tues–Sat noon–2.30pm & 7–11pm　　　　　All major credit cards

You have to feel for Nathalie Régent. What must it be like to be married to – and working alongside – a man whose love of the bizarre verges on the obsessional? Britain is famed for breeding dangerously potty chefs, but The Lobster Pot's chef-patron Hervé Régent, originally from Vannes in Brittany, is well ahead of the field. Walk down Kennington Lane towards the restaurant and it's even money whether you are struck first by the life size painted plywood cut-out of Hervé dressed in oilskins, or the speakers which relay a sound track of seagulls and melancholy Breton foghorns to the outside world. Inside, the restaurant has porthole windows behind which swim fish, while the bar upstairs is even more kitsch, with a ship's wheel to play with while you await your table.

The clues all point towards fish and doubtless Hervé will appear to greet you, moustache bristling and in nautical garb, to guide you towards his best catches of the day. The fish here is pricey but it is very fresh and very well chosen. Starters range from a good, very thick, traditional fish soup (£6.50) to a really proper plateau de fruits de mer (small £10.50, large £21). The main course specials feature strange fish that Hervé has discovered on his early morning wanderings at Billingsgate. Mahi Mahi from the Indian Ocean might arrive in a thick tranche with a "skin" of smoked sahmon, accompanied by fresh samphire (£18.50) – delicious. Simpler, and as good in its way, is la selection de la mer a l'ail (£14.50), which is a range of fishy bits – some monkfish tail, an oyster, a bit of sole, tiny squid, etcetera – all grilled and slathered in garlic butter. Or you might opt for a perfect pairing of monkfish with wild mushrooms (£16.50). The accompanying bread is notable, soft, doughy "pain rustique", and for once, le plateau de fromage "a la Francaise" (£6.50), doesn't disappoint.

The Lobster Pot's weekday set lunch for £15.50 – which could be les moules gratinees a l'ail, followed by le filet de merlan sauce creole, and la crepe sauce à la mangue – makes lots of sense. But whenever you come, do not venture here without your sense of humour.

Tower Bridge
& Bermondsey

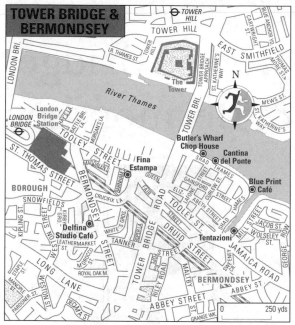

TOWER BRIDGE & BERMONDSEY

TOWER HILL

TOWER HILL

EAST SMITHFIELD

BLUE ANCHOR YD

CARTWRIGHT ST

THOMAS MORE ST

LR. THAMES ST.

TOWER HILL

The Tower

TOWER BRIDGE APPROACH

ST. KATHERINE'S WAY

MEWS ST.

ST. KATHERINE'S WAY

N

River Thames

TOWER BRI.

LONDON BRI.

LONDON BRIDGE

London Bridge Station

BATTLE BRI.

MORGAN'S LA.

TOOLEY STREET

Butler's Wharf Chop House

Cantina del Ponte

SHAD THAMES

Blue Print Café

ST. THOMAS STREET

BERMONDSEY STREET

MAGDALEN

BARNHAM

Fina Estampa

Queen

FAIR

TOOLEY STREET

GAINSFORD STREET

LAFONE STREET

ELIZABETH STREET

CURLEW STREET

SHAD THAMES

MILL STREET

JACOB ST.

WOLSELEY ST.

BOROUGH

SNOWFIELDS

KIPLING ST.

KIRBY GRO.

WHITE'S GROS.

NEWTON STREET

Delfina Studio Café

LEATHERMARKET ST.

MOROCCO ST.

ROYAL OAK M.

CRUCIFIX LA.

TANNER STREET

NEBULA ST.

TOWER BRIDGE ROAD

DRUID STREET

RILEY ROAD

MALTBY STREET

SWEENY

Tentazioni

JAMAICA ROAD

GEORGE ROW

LONG LANE

STAPLE ST.

MANCIPLE ST.

PARDONER ST.

WESTON ST.

DECIMA ST.

ABBEY STREET

BERMONDSEY

ABBEY ST.

GRANGE WK.

0   250 yds

SOUTH

Blue Print Café

Design Museum, Shad Thames, SE1 ☎ 0171 378 7031　　⊖ Tower Hill/London Bridge

Mon–Sat noon–2.45pm & 6–10.45pm, Sun noon–2.45pm　　All major credit cards

On the first floor of the Design Museum is the Blue Print Café – the oldest of Sir Terence Conran's gastrodome restaurants. It has since acquired his Pont de la Tour, Butler's Wharf Chop House and Cantina del Ponte as neighbours just along the quay, but the Blue Print has an identity that borrows from no one. It can turn out pricier than you might expect from a cursory look at the menu, and the service can occasionally be a bit uptight, but the cooking is sound, the dishes imaginative, and the setting and views are as good as London gets.

Starters are a must at the Blue Print. You might find a saffron risotto with parmesan (£6.00) – well flavoured with the rice smooth and nutty – or a baby beetroot salad with a soft-boiled egg, mustard and horseradish (£5.50), as brilliantly coloured as it is tasty, the pungent mustard and horseradish revving up the leaves and egg. Main courses can be simple, like a pizza with portobello mushrooms, persillade and Mascarpone (£10.00) – the pizza paper-thin and piled high with a huge fluff of mascarpone and mushroom slivers – or a raie au beurre noir (£13.75) – skate crisply glazed under a grill with a salty capery beurre noir, turning an under-rated fish into a highly-rated dish. Side orders include a light and airy olive oil mash (£2.00) – not to be missed with any fish dish. Puddings are pretty unmissable, too, including favourites like crème brulée (£5.00) – thinly-crusted with slightly soft crème brulée, just how it should be done – or a Marsala parfait with chocolate sauce (£5.50) – the bitterness of the chocolate working off the Marsala sweetness. The eclectic wine list has many unusual and surprising offerings as well as a particularly good house champagne (£29.95) – and the Blue Print is a fine place to celebrate.

The Blue Print Café has superb river views and as evening comes the lights of the city skyline opposite, and those of Tower Bridge, make London seem really Metropolitan. Book well in advance and ask for a table near a terrace window – or, when it's open (and they are reluctant on all but midsummer days and nights) out on the terrace itself.

£10–£50

Butler's Wharf Chop House

36e Shad Thames, SE1 ☎ 0171 403 3403	⊖ Tower Bridge

Restaurant: Mon–Fri noon–3pm & 6–11pm, Sat 6–11pm, Sun noon–3pm

Bar: Mon–Sat noon–11pm, Sun noon–3pm	All major credit cards

Butler's Wharf Chop House is a Conran creation that deserves everyone's support. For this is a restaurant that makes a genuine attempt to showcase the best of British produce. There's superb British meat, splendid fish, and epic British and Irish cheeses, and dishes are well-cooked. What's more the Chop House wisely caters for all – you could enjoy a simple dish at the bar, a well-priced set lunch, or an extravagant dinner. The dining room is large and airy and the view of Tower Bridge a delight, especially from a terrace table on a warm summer's evening.

Lunch in the restaurant is priced at £18.75 for two courses and £22.75 for three. The menu changes regularly but tends to feature starters such as roast tomato soup with cheese straw; or Loch Fyne smoked salmon; or peppered chicken livers on toast. Mains will include dishes like wild boar and apple sausages with sage and onion mash, as well as the house speciality of spit roasts and grills. They do a flawless roast rib of beef with Yorkshire pudding and gravy, here, and excellent double lamb chop, rocket, new potatoes and mint. After that you just might be able to find room and an extra four quid for a pud like Cambridge burnt cream with marinate raspberries. Dinner follows the same principles but is priced à la carte and features more complex dishes. Thus there may be starters like pork, duck and chicken terrine with apricot chutney (£7.75), or a hot smoked mackerel salad in white wine and herb sauce (£6.50). Mains may include steak kidney and oyster pudding (£15.50); pot-roast monkfish, fennel and leeks (£17); whole grilled lobster with garlic butter (£22). There's also steak and chips, priced by size – £16.50 for an 8oz sirloin to £29.50 for 16oz fillet.

The bar menu is appealing – two courses for £7.75, three for £9.50 (Mon–Fri) – plus a host of "one-offs" like pie of the day (£8.50). You might choose Loch Fyne herrings beetroot and potato salad, then spit-roast gammon mustard and honey sauce, followed by chocolate and orange mousse – a pretty good £9.50's worth. There is also a serious weekend brunch menu in the bar at £13.95 for two courses, £16.25 for three.

Cantina del Ponte

Butler's Wharf, Shad Thames, SE1 ☎ 0171 403 5403   ⊖ Tower Hill/London Bridge

Mon–Sat noon–3pm & 6–11pm, Sun noon–3pm & 6–10pm   All major credit cards

Closed Sun evenings Jan & Feb

Jostling for attention with its more renowned (and considerably pricier) Conran-neighbour, the Ponte de La Tour, the Cantina del Ponte doesn't try to keep up but instead offers a different package. Here you are greeted with the best earthy Italian fare presented in smart Conran style. The floors are warm terracotta, the food is strong on flavour and colour, the service is refined, and the views are superior London dockside. There are many Italian restaurants around town within the same price range but this is one of the better ones – if only for setting which rivals a fair few Italian cities. Book ahead and bag a table by the window or, better still in the summer, brave the elements and sit under the canopy watching the boats go by. Inside is okay but less memorable and the low ceilings a bit caustrophobic if you're seated at the back.

The seasonal menu is a meander through all things good, Italian-style, with a tempting array of primi, pasta, risotto, pizza and secondi, as well as side orders, pudding and cheese. If you can't meet the minimum order of £10 per head from this little lot then you must be exceptionally choosy. Perfect for balmy evenings is the chilled gazpacho, crab and avocado salad – a bit of a bargain at £4.75. The imaginative duck tortellini, cavalo and porcini velouté (£8.95) is a great way to line your stomach for the evening, while you'd be hard pushed to finish the risotto nero made with squid, squid ink and lemon oil (£7.95). Pizzas are equally substantial and feature imaginative toppings like marinated swordfish (£8). Il secondi – the main courses – range from £12.50 to £14.95 for serious meaty and fishy dishes. The highlights include a grilled tournedos with a spicy potato and chorizo cake and sauce Béarnaise (£14.95). It's a tall order, but if you can manage it, try a pudding of chocolate pannettone bread and butter pudding (£5.25): dark, bitter and indulgent. A lighter, but no less delicious, option is the pannacotta with raspberries and (lots of) grappa (£4.95).

If you fancy live music while you eat, book a table for Friday evening from 8.30pm. Summer nights, this is a hard act to beat.

Delfina Studio Café

TOWER BRIDGE & BERMONDSEY ⑪ MODERN BRITISH

50 Bermondsey St, SE1 ☎ 0171 357 0244   ⊖ London Bridge

Mon–Fri noon–3.30pm (lunch), 10am–5pm (snacks)   All major credit cards

Bermondsey has long been a centre for London's antique trade but in recent years it has been changing character, with art galleries moving into the old warehouses around the wharves. Delfina Studio is at the hub of this scene. It houses gallery and artists' studio space as well as a café-restaurant, and if you're out in southeast London checking out the art scene there is no better place to come for lunch. Originally a café attached to a gallery (it still functions as such outside lunchtime hours), Delfina's is now a serious restaurant – bright and modern, both in appearance and cooking, with a mix of tastes created from light fresh ingredients by head chef Maria Elia. It's moved well beyond café prices these days but the quality of ingredients and cooking justify a bit of a splurge. And it's a lot cheaper than buying a painting in these parts.

For starters you might find dishes like crispy marinated rabbit loin with salsa verde and proscuito (£5.50); or sesame battered tiger prawns, cous-cous and raita (£6.25); or carrot, lime, coriander and coconut soup (£3.95). They are all good and deliver crisp flavours that blend well. Main courses are equally satisfying. Pan-fried veal kidneys with sherried Puy lentils (£10.25) is a rare treat for offal fans; traditional flavours are well extended in a dish of smoked haddock with chive hollandaise, spinach and mash potato (£10.50); and there's a fine fish dish of roasted cod, pumpkin risotto with thyme pesto (£12.95). Puddings, all at £4.25, are deceptively simple. Depending on season, they might include roasted figs with cinnamon beignets; calvados apple tartlets with maple syrup; chocolate and banana samosas; or Picos blue cheese, plum and almond cake. The wine list offers excellent wines at reasonable prices. A good Gamay (Domaine Charmoise 97) is £14.25, and the house wines from Delfina's own vineyards in Spain cost £10.95 a bottle for very decent Iberian red, white or rose.

At its own exhibition times, Delfina extends opening hours (ring for details); normal opening hours are currently restricted to lunchtime, though if demand increases, evenings may become a feature. And yes, there is a Delfina behind it all.

Fina Estampa

150 Tooley St, SE1 ☎ 0171 403 1342   ⊖ London Bridge

Mon–Sat noon–2.30pm & 6.30–10.30pm   All major credit cards

Whilst London is awash with ethnic eateries, Fina Estampa's proud boast is that it is the capital's only Peruvian restaurant. Gastronomy may not be the first thing that springs to mind when one thinks of Peru but the husband and wife team which runs the place certainly try hard to enlighten their customers and bring a little of downtown Lima to London Bridge. With the help of a lime green interior and throbbing rhythms (live music on Friday and Saturday nights), a warm and bright ambience is achieved and the attentive, friendly staff add greatly to the upbeat feel.

The menu is traditional Peruvian and a great emphasis is placed upon seafood – this is reflected in the starters with such offerings as chupe de camarones (£6.50), a succulent shrimp-based soup; cebiche (£5.95), a dish of marinated white fish served with sweet potatoes; and jalea (£9.50), a vast plate of fried seafood. Ask for the salsa criolla – its hot oiliness is a perfect accompaniment. There is also causa rellena (£4.95), described as a "potato surprise" and exactly that – layers of cold mashed potato, avocado and tuna fish served with salsa – the surprise being how something so straightforward can taste so good. Main courses, such as the fragrant chicken seco (£10.95) – chicken cooked in a coriander sauce – or the superb lomo saltado (£12.95) – tender strips of rump steak stir-fried with red onions and tomatoes – are worthy ambassadors for this simple yet distinctive cuisine. Perhaps most distinctive of all is the carapulcra (£10.95), a spicy dish made of dried potatoes, pork, chicken and cassava, top choice for anyone seeking a new culinary adventure.

One particularly fine, and decidedly Peruvian, speciality is the unfortunately named Pisco sour (£3.50). Pisco is a white grape spirit and the Peruvian national drink, not dissimilar in taste and effect to tequila. Here they mix Pisco with lemon, lime and cinnamon, then sweeten it with honey, add egg white, and whip it into a frothy white cocktail, which is really rather good. After a couple of these you'll be perfectly in tune with the lime green walls.

SOUTH

TOWER BRIDGE & BERMONDSEY ⑪ ITALIAN

Tentazioni

2 Mill St, SE1 ☎ 0171 237 1100   ⊖ Bermondsey/Tower Hill

Mon–Fri noon–2.30pm & 7–10.30pm, Sat 7–10.30pm   All major credit cards

This small, busy, and rather good Italian restaurant has crept up behind Sir Terence Conran's Thameside flotilla of eateries and is giving them a good run for their money. The food is high quality peasant Italian, and the aim is strong rich flavours and simple quality. The pasta dishes are good here, the stews are good, and the wine list is interesting. They also offer a "Menu Degustazione" four courses at £26 or, much more interestingly £38 including a glass of wine with each course. This is a very good meal and very restful for your decision-making muscle.

The starters here are all priced at £6, unless you choose to have one of them as a main course when the price goes up to £8. The menu changes to reflect the seasons and the markets so you may find choices such as insalata di capesante allo zenzero e pep rosa – salad of scallops with ginger and pink peppercorns; or tagliolini neri con gamberoni e zucchini – black tagliolini with prawns and zucchini; or mozzarella di bufala con caponata di verdure – buffalo mozzarella with vegetable caponata. In season there is a good deal of game on the menu, and there is often a particularly good traditional dish of pasta with a richer than rich sauce made with hare or the like. Main courses offer hammer blows of flavour – fegato di vitello con cipolle fondante (£12.50) prosaically translated as calves' liver with stewed onions; or San Pietro salsa di peperoni e timballo di Melanzane (£14) – John Dory, red pepper sauce and a timbale of aubergine.

The "Degustazione" with wine included menu provides an interesting and very tempting option. How does this sound? Marinated salmon with dill and pear sauce (a glass of Riesling Drius); agnolotti with salsicca and smoked ricotta (a glass of Soave Classico); beef tagliata with port sauce (a glass of Aglianico d'Angelo); the John Dory dish mentioned above (a glass of Verdicchio di Matelica); and finally tiramisiu (a glass of Recioto di Soave). The price includes everything except bottled water and service.

SOUTH

Further South

Bromley, Dulwich, Epsom,
Forest Hill, Norbury,
Sydenham, Tooting

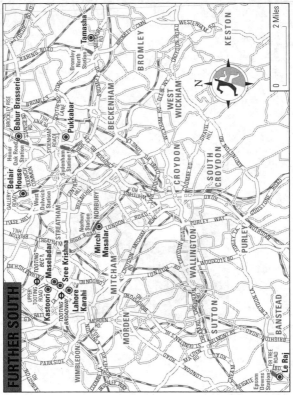

© Crown copyright

Babur Brasserie

119 Brockley Rise, Forest Hill, SE23 ☎ 0181 291 2400	BR: Honor Oak Park
Mon–Thurs & Sat–Sun noon–2.30pm & 6–11.30pm,	
Fri 6–11.30pm	All major credit cards

The Babur Brasserie is a stylish and friendly restaurant serving elaborate and interesting dishes which bear no resemblance to run-of-the-mill curry-house fare – an unexpected find in SE23. The food is both subtle and elegantly presented, and while it does cost a touch more than most suburban Indian restaurants, you are still paying a great deal less than you would in a French or Italian establishment of similar quality. And you have Chef of the Year finalist, Enam Rahman, cooking for you.

How nice to be faced with a list of appetisers and see so few familiar dishes. Patra (£2.60) is a Catherine wheel sliced off the end of a roll of avial leaves which have been glued together with chick pea paste and deep fried. The result is crispy and very tasty. Aloo choff (£2.75) is a grown-up potato croquette with vegetables and spices within an outer coat of ground cashew nuts. Chingri meerchi (£3.50) is a plate of prawns briskly cooked with green chillies, ginger, garlic, spring onions, tomatoes and coriander. Murgh tikka lasania (£3.15) is yoghurt-coated chunks of chicken cooked in a tandoor but delightfully juicy inside. And the main courses are just as good. Try shugati masala (£6.25) – chicken in a fairly mild sauce with coconut and poppyseeds. Or tuna bulchao (£7.50) – a slice of meaty fish about an inch thick served in a tomatoey-sweetish-chilli hot sauce. Sali jardaloo (£6.50) teams lamb with apricots and potatoes. Then there are ten fresh vegetable dishes for consideration – and vegetarians will applaud the option of picking four from the list with rice and a nan bread for an inclusive price of just £9.95. On the subject of bread, try the lacha paratha (£2.10) – a flaky paratha made with ghee. The dessert menu is more extensive and more elaborate than usual, too, running the gamut from Viceroy's banana pie (£2.95) to kulfi (£1.75), Indian ice cream.

Hing, or asafoetida, is a spice which not only has a distinctive flavour but also a rude name. In oonbhariu (£3.95) – a dish from the vegetables section – it is blended with lovage and cumin to accompany bananas, sweet potato, baby aubergines, and shallots. The combination is particularly good.

Belair House

Gallery Road, Dulwich Village, SE21 ☎ 0181 299 9788	BR: West Dulwich
Mon–Sat noon–2.30pm & 7–10.30pm (11pm Fri & Sat)	
Sun noon–3pm & 7–9.30pm	All major credit cards

Belair House is large, pale, and stands alone in Dulwich Park. It is a listed building which has been sensitively and painstakingly restored. In the summer the two terraces do sterling service, one filled by diners and the other by drinkers. This establishment is already justly popular with locals and Sunday lunch in particular is booked up well ahead. With the head start of tall well-proportioned rooms and a sweeping staircase, the decor is both elegant and surprisingly bright – research having shown that, when built, the interior of this Georgian Grade Two listed building would have been painted in the lurid colours fashionable at the time. Today's colour scheme is quite authentic while the food imposes Mediterranean influences onto whatever is best from the markets.

There is a good value set lunch offering starters like wild mushroom salad, and deep-fried smoked haddock fritter; mains such as shank of lamb, new potato mash, carrots and feves, or fillet of salmon, celeriac remoulade tomato and spring onion dressing; then indulgent puds like lemon soft meringue and raspberries. This is priced in an enlightened way – £12.50 for any two courses, £15.50 for three courses, Monday to Saturday; on Sundays, three courses go for £24.95. The à la carte, which is available at both lunch and dinner, offers more complex and more interesting dishes at higher prices. They might include starters like gazpacho blanc with shaved truffle (£6.50); snails in beer batter, garlic dressing (£7.50); and cured duck breast, mustard pears (£7.95). Mains may range from a wild mushroom and nettle boudin, white bean compote (£15); through new season leg of lamb, char-grilled new potatoes (£17.50); to vanilla marinated lobster, mango and tomato tian, herb salad (£21.50). Puddings are often adventurous – peach Tatin, black pepper ice cream (£6.50) – and there is always the option of British cheeses with home-made crackers (£7.50).

Look really carefully in the toilets downstairs and you will spot vestiges of a former incarnation of Belair House – for a good many years it acted as a changing room for children using the surrounding playing fields. Just imagine more rows of pegs and a lot more noise!

Kastoori

188 Upper Tooting Road, SW17 ☎ 0181 767 7027	⊖ Tooting Broadway
Daily 6–10.30pm, Wed–Sun 12.30–2.30pm	Mastercard, Visa (not Switch)

Anyone who is genuinely puzzled that people can cope on – and indeed enjoy – a diet of vegetables alone should try eating at Kastoori. Located in a rather unpromising looking bit of Balham, Kastoori is a "Pure Vegetarian Restaurant". Gujrati food is leavened with East African influences and it is so delicious that you could invite the most hardened carnivore and be pretty sure that they will be as entranced as everybody else. The large and cavernous restaurant is run by the admirably helpful Thanki family – do be sure to ask their advice and act on it.

First onto the waiter's pad (and indeed first into the mouth as they go soggy and collapse if made to wait) must be dahi puri (£2.50) – tiny crispy flying saucers filled with a sweet/sour yogurty sauce, potatoes, onions, chick peas and so forth. You pop them in whole and the marriage of taste and texture is a revelation. Samosas (3 for £1.80) are excellent but also in the revelation category are the onion bhajias (5 for £2.10) – bite size and delicious, a far-cry from the ball-of-knitting variety in most High Street curry houses. Then make sure that someone orders the vegetable curry of the day (£4.25), and others the outstanding cauliflower with cream curry (£4.25) and the special tomato curry (£4.25) – a hot and spicy classic from Katia Wahd. Leave room for the chilli banana (£4.50) – bananas stuffed with mild chillies – an East African recipe – and mop everything up with generous helpings of puris (60p) and chapatis (60p).

The smart move is to ask what's in season, as the menu is littered with oddities which come and go. For example you might find rotlo – millet loaf – (£2.50 and served only on Sunday). Or the dish called, rather enigmatically, "beans of the day" (£4.25). Another interesting and esoteric dish is drumstick curry (£4.50). Drumsticks are a thin, green, Asian vegetable about eighteen inches long and twice as thick as a pencil. You chew the flesh from the stalk. This is a place where you should always experiment.

£6–£16

Lahore Karahi

1 Tooting High St, SW17 ☎ 0181 767 2477   ⊖ Tooting Broadway

Daily noon–midnight   Cash or cheque only

Strictly speaking, the Lahore Karahi is in Upper Tooting Road but bright neon spilling onto the pavement beckons you along from Tooting High Street. It's a busy place. Behind a counter equipped with numerous bain maries stand rows of cooks, distinguishable by rather natty Lahore Karahi baseball caps, turning out a daily twelve-hour marathon of dishes. Prices are low, dishes are hot with chilli, service is speedy. Don't be intimidated, seat yourself in the Habitat chairs, don't worry if you have to share a table, and start ordering. Regulars bring their own drinks or stick to the exotic fruit juices – mango, guava, or passion . . . all are just 80p.

Unusually for what is an unreconstructed grill house there is a wide range of vegetarian dishes with the subtitle "prepared under strict precautions". Karahi karela (£2.95) is a curry of bitter gourds; karahi saag paneer (£3.95) teams spinach and cheese; and karahi methi aloo (£2.75) brings potatoes flavoured with fenugreek. Meat eaters can plunge in joyfully – chicken tikka (£2.25), seekh kabab (50p) tandoori chicken (£1.45) are all good and all spicy hot, the only fault being a good deal of artificial red colouring. There are also a dozen chicken curries and a dozen lamb curries (from £3.50 to £3.95); and a dozen specialities (from £4.50 to £7.00 for king prawn karahi). Those with a strong constitution can try the dishes of the day, like nihari (£4.50) which is lamb shank on the bone in an incendiary broth, or paya (£3.95) which is sheep's feet cooked until gluey. Breads are good here: try the jeera nan (70p) or the tandoori roti (50p).

The Lahore Karahi comes into its own as a take-away, and there's usually a queue at the counter as people collect considerable banquets – not just chicken tikka in a nan, or portions of curry, but large and elaborate biryanies as well – meat £2.95, chicken £2.95, prawn £4.75, or vegetable £2.75. For wholesome, fast-ish food, the cooking and the prices here are hard to beat.

Le Raj

211 Fir Tree Road, Epsom Downs, Surrey ☎ 01737 371371	BR: Epsom Downs
Daily noon–2.30pm & 5.30–11pm	All major credit cards

For committed Indian restaurateurs "presentation" has always been something of a Holy Grail. French chefs can plate up towering master-pieces, Thai chefs labour over ornately carved vegetables, but in curry houses everywhere stainless steel dishes are filled with . . . well, with curry. And however delicious and delicately spiced, curry tends to look like curry. Until you visit Le Raj. The food here is delicious, well cooked and quite beautifully presented. Indeed the dishes verge on the ornate.

From the starters listed why not try an old favourite, prawn puri (£3.50)? The puri is light and fluffy and the prawns have been cooked in a well-spiced tomato and coconut sauce. But instead of being pre-sented with the prawns dumped onto a puri, the prawn mixture is rolled up in the bread which is then coiled into a turban and sits proud in the middle of the plate. Elegant and delicious too. For main courses the menu lists all the standards, from vindaloo to kurma, but it's worth pick-ing out the genuine Bangladeshi dishes, which are carefully prepared as well as unusual. Good choices include the Maacher jhol (£8.95), a Ban-gledeshi fish cooked with fresh herbs, tomatoes and mustard seeds; or the ghost-e-jalali (£10.95), a spectacular dish of well-spiced lamb served under a "net" of spun egg; or murg-e-makhonee (£7.50), a superb mild dish of chicken cooked in a delicate yoghurt sauce with hard-boiled quail eggs. But equal care is taken over the more straightforward menu items. Basmati rice (£2.50) comes perfectly cooked, scented with spices and moulded into a pyramid on a side plate dressed with crisp fried onions. Puddings are original and elegant, such as spun sugar cages and fruit coulis – it's as if a talented Indian chef is cooking on Mas-terchef.

All manner of traditional delights are often available, if you ask for the day's specials, though they may not feature on the menu. Zibba ghost (£8.50) is one such dish – chopped lambs' tongues cooked with rich spices and served under a sprinkling of sev (the stringy, crunchy stuff you find in Bombay mix). Tongue is not to everyone's taste but the dish looks good, tastes good, and delivers a splendid array of textures.

£8–£20

Masaledar

121 Upper Tooting Rd, SW17 ☎ 0171 767 7676   ⊖ Tooting Bec/Tooting Broadway

Daily noon–midnight   Mastercard, Visa

What can you say about a place that has two huge standard lamps, each made from an upturned, highly ornate Victorian drainpipe, topped with a large karahi? When it comes to interior design Masaledar provides plenty of surprises – and a feeling of spaciousness that's the very opposite of most of the bustling Indian restaurants in Tooting and Balham. This establishment is run by East African Asian Muslims so no alcohol is allowed in the premises, but that doesn't deter a loyal clientele. The food is fresh, well-spiced and cheap – there are vegetable curries at under £3 and meat curries for less than £4 – plus an elegant designer dining room into the bargain. Look out Mezzo.

As starters the samosas are sound – two meat (£1.40), two vegetable (£1.25); or try the chicken wings from the tandoor (5 pieces £1.75); or the lamb chops (4 pieces £3.25), which are very tasty. You might move on to a biryani – chicken or lamb (£3.95) – both good and rich. Or perhaps try a karahi dish like karahi methi gosht (£3.95)? This is strongly flavoured and delicious although guaranteed to leave you with fenugreek seeping from your pores for days to come. Then there's chilli and lemon chicken (£4.25); or achar gosht (£4.25). The masaledar daal (£2.75) is a less successful dish unless you like your daal runny. The breads are terrific – especially the wonderful, thin rotis (60p).

Sometimes the brisk take-away trade, and the fact that all dishes are made to order, conspire to make service a bit slow, but you can always lean back and enjoy your surroundings. And, despite or because of the absence of alcohol, you can have an intresting evening's drinking. Mango shake (£1.75 a large glass, £4.50 a jug) is rich, very fruity and not too sweet; order one before your meal, however, and greed will ensure that you have finished it by the time your food comes. Both the sweet and salty lassis (£1.50 a large glass, £4.25 a jug) are also good, as is the wryly named fresh passion juice (£2.50 a large glass, £6.95 a jug), which is perhaps the best bet for accompanying your meal.

Mirch Masala

1416 London Road, Norbury, SW16 ☎ 0181 679 1828	BR: Norbury
Tues–Sun noon–midnight	All major credit cards

You'll find Mirch Masala just up London Road from Norbury Station. It may not look much from the outside but it deserves a place on any list of London's top ten Indian restaurants – something South London's Asian community appear to have cottoned on to, as they all seem prepared to make the pilgrimage. As befits such a culinary temple, the chefs take centre stage, the kitchen is on view and you can watch the whole cooking process which culminates, as likely as not, in the chef bringing the food to table. They are certainly prone to wandering out while you are enjoying the last of your starters to ask if you're ready for your main course. What's more at the end of the meal they are also happy to pack up anything you don't finish so that you can take it home. Take advantage, over order and try a lot of different dishes; this is a very friendly place serving spectacular food at low prices.

Start with a stick each of chicken tikka (£2.50) and lamb tikka (£2.50), crusted with pepper and spices on the outside, juicy with marinade on the inside. Very good indeed. Or try the butter chicken wings (£3), cooked in a light, un-greasy sauce laden with flavour from fresh spices and herbs. Then move on to some of the karahi dishes, which are presented in a kind of thick aluminium hubcap. The vegetable karahi dishes are exceptional. Try the butter beans and methi (£3.50) – an inspired and delicious combination of flavours – and karahi valpapdi baigan (£4) – aubergines cooked with small rich beans. Among the best meat dishes are the karella gosht (£5) – lamb with bitter gourd – and the deigi saag gosht (£5) – spinach, lamb and a rich sauce. Even something simple like karahi ginger chicken (£5) proves how good and fresh-tasting Indian food can be. Rice (£1.50) comes in glass butter dishes complete with lids. Breads include a good naan (70p) and an indulgent deep fried bhatura (60p).

A meal at Mirch Masala will be a memorable one. As they say on the menu "Food extraordinaire. You wish it – we cook it."

£12–£20

Pukkabar

42 Sydenham Road, SE26 ☎ 0181 778 4629	BR: Sydenham
Mon &Tues 6–11.30pm, Wed–Sat noon–2.30 & 6–11.30pm,	
Sun noon–3.30pm & 7–10.30pm	All major credit cards

The Pukkabar and Curry Hall – to give this place its full name – is like no curry house you have ever seen. It is basically a temple to beer and curry, that vice the British have been proud to make their own. It is an elegant restaurant and has the kind of smooth, sophisticated service you'd expect more in the West End than Sydenham. The long room starts as a bar, goes through a no-man's-land stage where it is a bar with dining tables, and finally ends up by the window to the kitchen as pure dining room. In the kitchen, chefs in immaculate whites work unhurriedly. The menu changes regularly but all the curries are batch-cooked. Hallelujah! None of your frying-pan-and-stock-sauce heated through stuff here. It's hard to do better than a homestyle curry and a Cobra beer.

The starters are a touch on the elaborate side – crispy deep-fried prawns with carom seeds (£4.50) is a good dish but a rather small portion. Spicy chicken pasties (£3.95) and cheese and spinach cakes (£3.50) are nice enough. But you're here, really, for the beer and the batch-cooked curries. Bengal fish curry (£6.50) is good and rich with plenty of tomatoes. Black pepper chicken (£6.25) is fierce and good. Or there's a fine Goan prawn and coconut curry (£6.25). Or a spicy aubergine curry with peanuts and sesame seeds (£5.25). For old school curry fanciers there's chicken tikka masala (£6.25). The dishes are liable to change with the seasons and the whims of the chefs but the establishment promises that everything will be cooked from scratch, homestyle – this is one of a handful of London curry restaurants that has a "spice room" where spice pastes both wet and dry are prepared freshly each day.

The breads here are terrific – the thin roomali roti; onion and green chilli bread; mint paratha; naan all priced at £1.25. The Pukkakids menu also deserves a commendation – this may be the first Indian restaurant that has put on a special menu for children including Indian fish fingers (£4)!

£10–£22

Sree Krishna

192–194 Tooting High Street, SW17 ☎ 0181 672 6903	⊖ Tooting Broadway
Daily noon–3pm & 6–11pm; Fri & Sat 6pm–midnight	All major credit cards

The Indian state of Kerala is famous for elephants, pepper and coconuts. It is also particularly famous in Tooting. Sree Krishna on Tooting High Street leads a double life as both a South Indian restaurant and unofficial Keralan embassy – the enthusiastic staff are just as happy selling you a holiday on the Malabar coast as a dinner for two. The menu here gives equal weight to both vegetarian and non-vegetarian dishes and the restaurant has built up a loyal following, something which may not be entirely unconnected with the extremely competitive pricing. And when faced with the daunting task of sorting through the unfamiliar array of iddlys, uthappams and various dosais, you could do a lot worse than be guided by the friendly staff.

Don't have pappadoms with your pre-dinner drinks, order a portion instead of cashewnut pakoda (£2.95) – a sort of savoury peanut brittle made with cashew nuts. Then try a ghee roast masala (£3.95), which is a large crisp pancake enclosing a savoury mixture of mashed potato and fried onions; large and filling, it is served with coconut chutney and a tiny portion of curry sauce with a length of drumstick vegetable floating in it. Move on to a good spread of main courses. Beetroot thoran (£1.95) is amazing – sweet, earthy and a rich ruby red. From the "Cochin specialities" chilly chicken (£6.45) gives the lie to their spelling of chilli. Ordering meen curry and kappa pulukku (£5.95) brings a duo of dishes, a rich fish curry made with fillets of pomfret is accompanied by a dish of boiled (then lightly curried) cassava with curry leaves, strangely floury and a perfect foil for the fish. From the breads list try the Malabar paratha (£1.45), which is thin, wholemeal, crisp and with an intensely sweet interior. The lemon rice (£1.95) is delicate and scented with curry leaves

On Sunday there are two "specials" – a vegetarian thali at £4.95 and a non-vegetarian thali at £6.95 – terrific value; and if you feel like an unforgettable holiday on the Malabar coast, you can start here . . .

SOUTH

£12–£25

Tamasha

131 Widmore Rd, Bromley, Kent ☎ 0181 460 3240	BR: Bromley South
Mon–Sat noon–2.30pm & 6–11pm,	
Sun noon–2.30pm & 7–10.30pm	All major credit cards

Tamasha, very roughly translated, means "a bit of a do" and this is a great place to come when you decide to push the boat out. From the moment you are greeted by the doorman, dressed in authentic costume, and shown into the mock colonial interior you know that this is no run-of-the-mill suburban curry house. Tamasha has a style all of its own, over the top and down the other side – as you can tell from its Polo bar, a cosy intimate bar perfect for aperitif or cocktail. The dining rooms – called Victorian, Raj and India Club – are light and airy, and there's a less formal room upstairs. The food lives up to these surroundings and is quite moderately priced (there's an all-in bargain Sunday buffet at £8.95). To wash it down, both ice cold Cobra beer and Dom Perignon have a strong local following.

The menu lists dishes from all over India. Starters include well known dishes such as seekh kebab (£3.95) and king prawn puri (£4.95) – both good – and extend to unusual delights such as uttapams (£3.95) – a South Indian ground rice pancake cooked with onion, green pepper and coriander, then served with creamy green coconut chutney. The chicken manchoori (£7.95) is fiery with green chilli and tomatoes although not overpoweringly so, and the Goan fish curry (£8.50) is sweetened with coconut. Vegetarian dishes such as navratan masala (£6.96), mushrooms with cream and nine dried tropical fruits, provide a sweeter, fresher alternative to the more highly spiced and richer prawn-based raja jhinga silchari (£10.95) – apparently once a very popular dish with East India Company officials. To round off your meal try the Tamasha coffee (£4.50 per person minimum four people). It sounds expensive but the theatre of the preparation alone – caramelised glasses, grapefruit peel, brandy and lots of flame – is worth the price, and the coffee isn't bad either.

If the thought of the journey home seems too daunting, why not stay in one of rooms the Tamasha has maintained from its previous incarnation as an hotel? A double costs £55 and comes with breakfast – pukka English of course.

WEST

Barnes
& Sheen

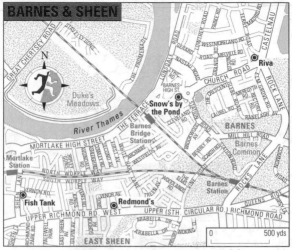

© Crown copyright

Fish Tank

45 Sheen Lane, SW14 ☎ 0181 878 3535	BR: Mortlake
Mon–Sat 7pm–11pm, Sun 1–5pm	Mastercard, Visa

Judging by the scrap for a booking, this modern fish restaurant seems to have made a favourable impression on the inhabitants of Sheen and Mortlake. So it should, the fish is well cooked, and while the portions are not likely to stop you in your tracks, the prices are neighbourhood not West End. The restaurant is designed on the premise that the customers are actually in a fish tank, thus the ceiling is the surface and if you look up there's the bottom of a boat, including the fisherman's booted feet hanging over the side and a dangling baited hook. All of which, along with some artful linen blinds, transports you into another world from the bright Texaco garage opposite.

In any case, it's the food you're here for. As a starter the crab cakes, smoked pepper aioli and mixed leaves (£5.50) is good. Small, but good. The spicy fish soup, herbes de provence and asparagus ravioli (£4) is a comfortingly rich fish soup, with a single large ravioli serving as an island. The main courses run the gamut from simple to complicated. A grilled lemon sole with flat leaf parsley and lemon (£10) perfectly cooked, neither raw nor flabby; roasted red mullet with fennel, black olive and saffron potatoes (£9.50). Prawn and shellfish green curry with basil and spring onion tempura (£9.50) is certainly a grandstand dish. For the unreconstructed meat-and-two-veggers there's chicken leg confit with roasted mushrooms, herb mashed potatoes and onion gravy (£9.50). Fish Tank chips (£2) are long and home-made; they come stacked two by two to make the sort of tower you find in a Boy Scout manual on fire-lighting – the same presentation as they use at the Savoy Grill, which seems a tad excessive in Sheen. The spinach (£2.50), however, is wonderful. Fresh green leaves, precisely cooked with a welcome splash of citrus.

Good luck when choosing a dessert as they're a bit hit-and-miss. Vanilla panna cotta with blood orange coulis and lychee (£4.25) is terrifically good, while coconut rice pudding, white chocolate and toasted ginger (£4.50) is not.

BARNES & SHEEN ⑰ MODERN BRITISH

WEST

Redmond's

170 Upper Richmond Road West, SW14 ☎ 0181 878 1922	BR: Mortlake
Mon–Fri noon–2.30pm & 7–10.30pm,	
Sat 7–10.30pm, Sun noon–2.30pm	Mastercard, Visa

Redmond Hayward is an improbably good cook to be found in a small neighbourhood restaurant. The key to this conundrum is, of course, that this is his own small neighbourhood restaurant, a pretty fifty-seater in Sheen. They tweak the menu on a daily basis, so that it reflects the best of what the season and the markets have to offer. It is not a particularly short menu – about eight starters and six mains – and it is astonishing value at £19.50 for two courses and £23.50 for three. What's even more astonishing is that the list is not splattered with supplements or cover charges; in fact a "discretionary" service charge (and then at the meagre rate of 10%) is only added to the bill when your party numbers six or more. The food here really is very good indeed; well-seasoned, precisely-cooked and immaculately presented.

If the terrine of chicken and foie gras is available when you visit, you should pounce – delicate, multi-layered, multi-textured, superlative-inducing in every way. Or there may be a crab and mussel broth with lemongrass and ginger; or razor clams marinière; or perhaps a Taleggio and Swiss chard tart with green salad. Main courses combine dominant flavours with elegant presentation: corn-fed chicken breast comes with "A" class mash, wild mushrooms and parsley oil – and it tastes how a chicken is supposed to taste. Roast rump of lamb comes with a warm salad of minted new potato, green beans and shallot, grain mustard dressing. Lemon, parsley and garlic couscous partners char-grilled scallops. The puddings are wonderful too. Praline millefeuille of crème brulée and poached peach with raspberry sauce, makes an imposing tower out of luxurious dollops of vanillary crème brulée, peach segments and craquelin. The strawberry, raspberry and elderflower jelly conceals quartered strawberries within and comes with a delicate vanilla cream.

The short wine list is littered with interesting bottles and at accessible prices – there are halves, magnums, pudding wines, and just plain bargains. Splash out on the splendid Gigondas at £22, a perfect partner for the impressive all-British cheeseboard.

Riva

169 Church Rd, SW13 ☎ 0181 748 0434	BR: Barnes
Mon–Fri noon–2.30pm & 7–11pm, Sat 7–11.30pm	
Sun noon–2.30pm & 7–9.30pm	Mastercard, Visa

When Andreas Riva opened his doors some years ago, Hammersmith Bridge allowed easy access to devotees north of the Thames who doted on his straightforward Italian cooking. Since the bridge closed his restaurant has become something of an outpost but local support keeps the kitchens busy, even without the travelling fans. It is a rather conservative looking restaurant, with a narrow dining room decorated in a sombre blend of dull greens and faded parchment, and with chairs that have clearly seen service in church. As far as the cuisine goes, Riva provides "the genuine article", so first-time customers are either delighted or disappointed.

Starters are good but not cheap: for example, the frittelle (£8.50), a tempura-like dish of deep-fried Mediterranean prawn, salt cod cakes, calamari, artichoke which is served "alla gierdea" – with a balsamic dip. If it is on the menu, a dish that must be tried is bocconcini di bufala – buffalo mozzarella with roasted peppers, red onions, cherry tomatoes and capers (£7.00), vibrant and deliciously oily. The brodetto "Mare Nostrum", a chunky saffron-flavoured fish soup (£6.75), is also superb – a delicate alternative to its robust French cousin. Serious Italian food fans, however, will find it hard to resist the sapori Mediterranei (£17 for two) – crab and fennel salad, baccala mantecato and polenta; poached pike in salsa verde; eel in tomato sauce – a combination that is unlikely to be found on many other menus outside the Po valley. Among the main courses, pesce persico alle mandorle (£12. 50) – perch fillets, almonds and lemon sauce, with courgette strips and tomatoes – seems an uncomfortable mis-match of bland and sharp tastes. But battuta di pollo – chicken breast marinated in thyme and balsamic vinegar with spinach and pumpkin gratin (£11.75) – delivers a finely balanced blend of flavours.

If there's anybody who still thinks of pizza and pasta as being Italy's staple diet, Riva's uncompromising regional menu proves otherwise. The house wines are all priced at a very accessible £9.95. Of the whites, the pale coloured Tocai is crisp, light and refreshing.

£15–£35

Snow's by the Pond

14–15 Barnes High St, SW13 ☎ 0181 876 1471   BR: Barnes

Tues–Sat noon–3pm & 6–11pm, Sun noon–3pm   All major credit cards except Diners

Provence is the inspiration behind this friendly neighbourhood restaurant on Barnes High Street – just about opposite the rather good cheese shop and a mere stone's throw from the pond or the Thames depending on your inclination. Bottle-green banquettes surround plain wood tables decorated with plants and miniature terracotta pots, adding a touch of warmth to proceedings, while the rag-rolled walls are lined with photographs depicting scenes of everyday Provencal life. The kitchen gives a nod towards Provence, too, but borders are often crossed (and sometimes totally ignored) on a refreshingly straightforward menu that bluntly dispenses with florid descriptions.

Provencal starters that might appear on the (changing) menu include a tarte fines of plum tomatoes, tapenade and pistou (£4.95), and foie gras, fried egg, and balsamic vinegar (£8.95). Still, you're as likely to find fresh and smoked salmon rillettes, pickled cucumber, country toast (£5.00), positively bursting at the seams with flavour, or Dorset air-dried ham, celeriac remoulade, bobby beans (£5.50) – as simple and tasty as the ingredients suggest. The main courses also tour European stations, encompassing dishes as diverse as char-grilled ribeye steak, parsley butter and fries (£11.00) and chicken saltimbocca, wild garlic leaves, grilled vegetables (£10.00) – the latter a mouth-watering combination alive with sunny flavours, generous in size, with a coating of garlic leaves, and attractively glazed. Chump of lamb with pea, sorrel, bacon and Jersey Royal compote (£11.75) is another hearty and filling option. Side dishes are all priced at £2 – a good way to try the aforementioned the pea and bacon compote with potatoes and sorrel. Of the desserts, sticky toffee pudding, clotted cream (£4.50) is good enough to make you feel ashamed you ordered it in public, but you can redress the balance by suggesting the cholesterol-crammed chocolate and hazelnut marquise, praline ice cream (£4.75) or rhubarb crumble and custard (£4.50) to those nearby.

Snow's by the Pond does a good value set lunch menu at £10/13, for two/three courses.

Chelsea

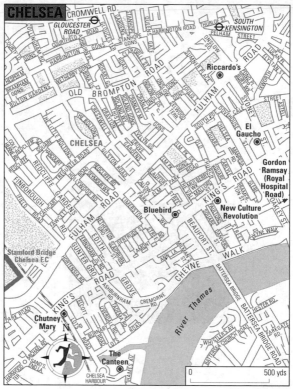

CHELSEA

CROMWELL RD.

GLOUCESTER ROAD

SOUTH KENSINGTON

Riccardo's

El Gaucho

Gordon Ramsay (Royal Hospital Road)

OLD BROMPTON

FULHAM ROAD

CHELSEA

KING'S ROAD

New Culture Revolution

Bluebird

Stamford Bridge Chelsea FC

FULHAM ROAD

CHEYNE WALK

River Thames

BATTERSEA BRIDGE ROAD

KING'S ROAD

Chutney Mary

N

CHELSEA HARBOUR

The Canteen

0   500 yds

© Crown copyright

WEST

Bluebird

350 King's Rd, SW3 ☎ 0171 559 1000	⊖ Sloane Square

Mon–Fri noon–3pm & 6–11pm, Sat 11am–3.30pm (brunch) & 6–11pm,

Sun 11am–3.30pm (brunch) & 6–10pm, All major credit cards

This is a slick place – and if you like slick places you'll like it a lot here. Conran's Bluebird complex is a large and sprawling one: there is a food-hall, a kitchenware shop, a café, a flower stall, a members-only club and the restaurant itself. The dining room is large with a central bar and manages to be both crowded as well as light and airy. The food is Modern: Modern European if that is in any way a meaningful description when the first four starters listed on the menu might be gazpacho, Chinese duck broth, Goat's ricotta, and Tataki salmon. The service is professional to a T and the prices look to be fair – although when all is finally added up you may be surprised how high the total can be. There is, however, a good-value set lunch (two courses for £12.75; three courses for £15.75) which also does service before 7pm as a pre-theatre option.

You might start with buffalo mozzarella, (£6.50), which is given some bite by tapenade and caponata, then topped with a home-made grissini. Or perhaps the Cos salad (£5.50) with proscuitto and pears. Or there's seared beef with kohlrabi and mustard (£9). The main courses are divided into fish/shellfish, pasta/eggs/vegetables, meat/offal, grill/rotisserie, woodroast, and dishes for two, which can make working through the menu a pretty concentrated operation. The line-caught seabass (£18) served with roast tomatoes and anchovies is accurately cooked and well-presented. Other sections worth browsing are the ones that are equipment led – the rotisserie turns out pretty good leg of lamb with tzatziki and tabbouleh (£13.50), while the wood-fired oven contributes tomato tart (£10.75) and peppered kangaroo with sweet potato and yoghurt (£18.50). Enlist an accomplice and you can have woodroast turbot (£33 for two). From the side dishes the mash potato (£2.50) is both generously portioned and delicious.

Strangely enough, pudding time is the perfect moment for another foray into the wood-fired oven. Woodroast peach with grappa and mascarpone (£5.25) is very delicious indeed.

£20–£45

The Canteen

Harbour Yard, Chelsea Harbour, SW10 ☎ 0171 351 7330   ⊖ Fulham Broadway

Mon 7–10.45pm, Tues–Fri noon–2pm & 7–10.45pm,

Sat 7–11.45pm   All major credit cards

Tips when eating at The Canteen: get a taxi; go in a foursome so that you can ask for a table by the window; and leave enough room for pudding. This avoids a major hike, affords stunning views across Chelsea Harbour, and provides exquisite desserts by a specialist chef-patissiere. The restaurant itself bears little resemblance to a canteen, as one might suspect of a place set up by Marco Pierre White, Claudio Pulze and Michael Caine. MPW left to create his own dynasty, while the others have wisely hung on to this special eatery. The showbiz connection is subtly apparent in the playing card and harlequin decor which, combined with the atmosphere and service, leads to a rather sophisticated evening out.

Perhaps French but fashionable is the best way to describe the seasonal menu as its foundations are classic French with Italian and Oriental overtones, hence starters such as chicken and chilli soup with coconut and spring onion won ton (£6), or risotto of smoked haddock with poached egg and curry oil – a new twist to kedgeree (£7.50). For those with bulkier wallets, the papardelle with field mushrooms and truffle oil (£8.50) or the warm salad of roasted sea scallops with apples and cashew nuts (£10.90) should set you up nicely. The main courses are all priced at £12.95 – though there is an occasional supplement such as for the delicious lobster tempura, Asian greens, Chinese leaves and ginger dressing (add £8). The main courses tend to feature some very good, sophisticated roasts – such as a saddle of rabbit with grilled polenta and mushrooms à la Grecque, or a lamb fillet with garlic mash, spinach and carrots with a marjoram jus. As for the puddings, all at £5.95: the crepe suzette soufflé is tangy and light, the tarte fine aux pommes is indeed fine, and the coffee and amaretto parfait is a work of art.

Good news for those on a budget: there are weekly changing lunch menus at £15.50 for two courses, £19.50 for three.

Chutney Mary

535 King's Rd, SW10 ☎ 0171 351 3113   ⊖ Fulham Broadway

Mon–Thurs 12.30–2.30pm & 7–11.30pm, Fri & Sat 12.30–2.30pm & 6.30–11.30pm,

Sun 12.30–3pm & 7–10.30pm   All major credit cards

For such a large, well-designed, elegant restaurant the food at Chutney Mary is remarkably close to tasting home-made – which is perhaps the greatest compliment you can pay to an Indian meal in London. Dishes here are not cheap but the food is freshly prepared and the spicing is always authentic. The menu combines regional Indian specialities with Anglo-Indian dishes from the days of the Raj – so this is an opportunity to try curiosities like Country Captain. About four dishes change each quarter but the restaurant hosts a succession of festivals which focus on the food of a particular region when you will find 15-20 of that region's specialities in pride of place on the menu. Booking ahead is advisable in the evening but lunch is a less crowded affair. On Sunday there is a very popular Jazz brunch at the wholly reasonable price of £15 for three courses.

Starters are split into vegetarian and non-vegetarian and can be conveniently ordered as a selection (£6). The former brings samosas, papri chat and veggie kebabs; the latter crab cake, papri chat and salmon samosa. Both are tempting starter options, as is the spicy calamari stir-fried with Goan spices (£6). For mains, turn to the Regional dishes which tend to be complex and interestingly spiced – green chicken curry from Goa, for instance, with fresh coriander, green chilli, mint and tamarind (£10.50), or a fiery Mangalore prawn curry cooked in an earthenware pot (£15.75), or Osmani korma – a Hyderabadi classic of lamb curry made with sandalwood, rose buds and saffron. All of these dishes come with aromatic Basmati rice. As a side dish look out for crisp fried okra and banana (£3.50) from Chettinad and Madras. Breads are also worth ordering – particularly the paratha stuffed with spicy mashed potato with lime and herbs (£2.50).

The brunch menu features one or two plain but delicious dishes – Akuri (spicy scrambled eggs served with granary toast) is one of them, and shredded lamb and potatoes fried in roasted spices is another.

El Gaucho

Chelsea Farmers' Market, 125 Sydney St, SW3   ⊖ South Kensington

☎ 0171 376 8514

Mon–Sat noon–4pm & 7–11pm   Cash or cheque only

El Gaucho is no place for the diffident – there are crowds of diners and very few frills. It is also no place for those seeking subtlety or plenty of fresh vegetables. This is a macho, bring-your-own alcohol, pitstop before embarking on the carousing and carrying-on that typifies the King's Road. At the best of times Argentinian cuisine is a fairly one tune affair and the menu here confirms that assessment. Big-boy portions of spit roast and grilled meat turn out well enough, while the side dishes and the service don't go out of their way for finesse. El Gaucho is shoehorned along the side of Chelsea Farmers' Market and there's precious little space. Having braved a (usually long) queue to bag a table, diners will either be comfortable with the brusque and brisk approach to lumps of rare meat or not!

Starters are truly Argentinian. Berenjenas asadas (£2.20) are baked aubergine – a bit ordinary; empanadas (£1.60 each) are beef pasties, given a bit of kick by the tangy chimichurri sauce that accompanies them. Bread dipped in chimichurri actually makes as good a starter as you'll find on the menu. But you're not here for starters in any case. For El Gaucho does one thing well, and that's to cook its meat – which, in the case of the steaks, is imported direct from Argentina. The striploin bife de chorizo (£9.90) and rump-steak churrasco (£9.90) both come cooked to perfection; and the pollo entero, a whole spit-roasted farm chicken (£9.90), really is finger-licking good. Problems arise when you're not feeling quite so macho and cast your eye over the vegetables and accompaniments – French fries, baked potatoes and less than inspiring salads are the extent of the offer. Again there's much to be said for a saucer of chimichurri.

Dulce de leche (which is made from much-reduced condensed milk and tastes like a toffee-flavoured custard) is the common denominator in most of the desserts. Pancakes, creme caramel and bread pudding (all £3) come laced with this syrupy, rich goo. Red meat, chips, and an unapologetic sugar overload for dessert – there are times when that's just what you need . . .

Gordon Ramsay

68 Royal Hospital Rd, SW3 ☎ 0171 352 4441	⊖ Sloane Square
Mon–Fri noon–2.45pm & 6.45–11pm	All major credit cards

The opening of Gordon Ramsay was one of the most eagerly awaited restaurant launches of 1998. Wunderkind-chef, ex-footballer Ramsay left his berth at Aubergine (two Michelin stars) and re-located to Royal Hospital Road hot on the trail of that elusive third star. And if that were not enough, the new restaurant is on the site recently vacated by La Tante Clare – long thought by many to be London's best restaurant. Foodies awaited developments with baited breath. And how did it all turn out? Well, the dining room has a more modern and spacious feel with glass screens; the service is certainly three-star service; and the food – well, there's no doubt that this is three-star cooking. At time of writing, however, it's not entirely three-star prices. There are two fixed price cartes (lunch and dinner) – £50 for three courses, £65 for seven – and a steal of a set lunch at £25 for three courses. Adding £4 for a glass of good house wine, this represents accessibly-priced great cooking.

The menu here is constantly evolving and changing as inspired by the kitchen's creativity and season's imperatives, though a good number of Ramsay favourites have made the journey from Aubergine: cappuccino of haricots blancs with sautéed girolles and grated truffle, braised shin of beef, and vanilla creme brulée with jus Granny Smith, to name just three. Look out (on the main menus) for a wonderful ravioli of lobster poached in lobster bisque served with a fine basil purée and confit tomatoes – solid, satisfying, light and fresh all at the same time. Or the pigeon from Bresse poached in a bouillon of ceps served with choux farcis. But really, you're in safe hands here: pick a dish or even an ingredient you like and see how it arrives. You won't be disappointed. This is a class act through and through, and the puddings and petits fours are just as good.

You will have to book ahead at Gordon Ramsay but sensibly enough the policy is that reservations are only taken a month in advance, avoiding a potentially huge backlog necessitating booking on your wedding day for the first anniversary. Book now, and in a month's time you could be the one with a contented smile on your face.

£7–£12

New Culture Revolution

305 King's Rd, SW3 ☎ 0171 352 9281   ⊖ Sloane Square

Daily noon–11pm   Mastercard, Visa

This is one of the latest in a series of noodle bar chains to target London, and arguably the best. New Culture Revolution brings Londoners noodles and dumplings in soup, with a North Chinese spin. There's no booking, so you may have to queue for five or ten minutes, but tables turn fast enough to make sure that your wait is a short one. Once settled in, take time to peruse the menu, which gives you a chance to catch up with the philosophy of Northern Chinese cooking, including a number of Confucius-like comments about the herbs and spices used, plus explanations about how wholesome this food is for the body. After reading the philosophy you'll find you feel better already.

The menu itself is divided into several sections – starters "specially chosen to stimulate good digestion and cleanse the palate", and various combinations of soup, dumplings noodles and rice dishes. Stimulate the juices with grilled prawns with chilli and garlic (£4.70), a "refreshing and energizing" raw juice (£2.20 – a blend of carrot and apple), or the somewhat misplaced steamed qing kou (£4.50) – New Zealand green lipped mussels. The main courses that follow are filling stuff. The vegetarian tong mein (£4.90) is thick with writhing noodles at the bottom of a huge bowl of "mellow home-made" stock, together with enough vegetables to feed a small terracotta army. A Revolution extra chow mein with sha sha spices (£5.70) is fried noodles and vegetables with a combination of beef, chicken and seafood – and a good deal better than anything the local Chinese take-away has been delivering for the last twenty years. Duck enthusiasts will find xiang su ya (£7.20) a happy solution – seasoned rice with crispy duck pan-fried with herbs and spices.

After 45 minutes you'll find yourself out on the street again, much to the relief of those waiting in the queue. It's not that you'll have been hurried or been made to feel unwelcome, rather that your tolerance of the lime green walls and uncomfortable seats will be running out. Good design feature, that.

Riccardo's

126 Fulham Rd, SW3 ☎ 0171 370 4917	⊖ South Kensington
Mon–Sat noon–3pm & 6pm–midnight,	
Sun noon–3.30pm & 6–11pm	All major credit cards

The Riccardo in question here is Riccardo Mariti, whose father was a successful restaurateur in the 1970s. Their Fulham Road site has seen a few changes in recent decades and like all good establishments has had to evolve. There is still a large area of pavement seating (suitably walled in by canvas and heated during the winter), there is still old-fashioned and courtly Italian service, and there is probably even a giant pepper mill hidden away somewhere. Thereafter things have changed. Riccardo has introduced a "spuntino" menu, which is rather like an Italian meze – you are encouraged to have several courses and this is made easier by small portions. Prices are fair but the cost of your dinner can mount as you can find yourself eating rather more than you had intended. The food is very simple, very delicious and very Italian.

This is a very relaxing, very self-indulgent way to eat. The menu lists – and for once list is the right word – some forty-five different dishes, priced between 95p (bread and butter) and £8.75 (minute steak tagliata with sautéed radicchio and chicory). In between there are soups, bruschetta, fish dishes, pastas, risotti, polenta, antipasti – a glorious array of this and that. It is essentially simple, peasant, food – very delicious and with good strong flavours. Some of the star choices are gnocchi di polenta al Gorgonzola (£4.95); insalata di spinaci (£3.95) – a spinach salad with proscuitto, avocado and Parmesan; sarde "alla Diavolo" (£4.95) – grilled sardines; ravioli de melanzane (£4.95) – ravioli with aubergine and ricotta cheese butter and sage; carpaccio (£6.95) – raw beef fillet with Parmesan; and salsiccia con lentiche (£5.95) – Italian sausages with lentils. Oh and you'll even find that old warhorse proscuito melone (£4.95) – Parma ham and melon.

On the back of the menu an imposing wine list is exclusively Italian except for half a dozen famous-name champagnes. The list repays investigation as there are a good many interesting bottles from the lesser known Italian wine regions: the offerings go all the way from house wine (£9.95) to Sassicaia (£95).

Fulham

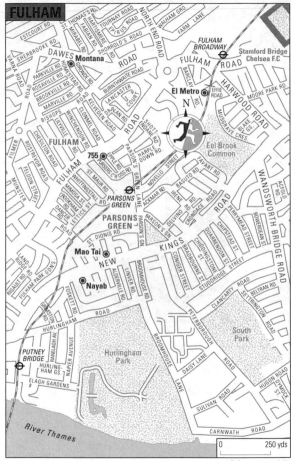

FULHAM

WEST

© Crown copyright

El Metro Tapas Bar

10–12 Effie Road, SW6 ☎ 0171 384 1264	⊖ Fulham Broadway
Daily 10.30am–11pm	All major credit cards

More taverna than tapas bar or brasserie, El Metro resurrects memories of island-hopping around the Aegean when atmosphere was the only consideration in choosing somewhere to eat. Pretentious it ain't. Asked about the origins of the pulpo a la gallega – "fresh octopus cooked in sea water" (£4.25) – the waiter replied in hushed tones, "Chelsea harbour." And as for the sea water? "It isn't." It's a popular place. Reservations are essential to secure yourself a table and even then you'll probably find yourself waiting; an amiable barman serving Mahon Spanish beer on tap (£2.60 – 33cl), and live music helps pass the time. Full blown mayhem surrounds the narrow dining area, which is presided over by a rather imposing bull's head.

The menu begins on an unintentionally authentic note with that Costa delicacy – the full English breakfast. Choose from egg, bacon, sausage, baked beans, tomato or toast (£3.95), or savour them with a nice cup of tea (£4.25). Generally accepted as the first meal of the day, breakfast here is served until 5pm. If you're ready for lunch or dinner, you might start out with sopa de ajo – spiced garlic soup with poached egg (£3.65). Or plunge straight into the calamares fritos – crispy dried flour-coated squid rings (£4.25) crisp and tender to the bite. Albóndigas (£6.45) – meatballs cooked in spicy sauce – are sound, tortilla (£3.65) is solid and filling, and they do a nice dish of gambas a la plancha – king prawns sautéed with salt and lemon (£9.95). Desserts (priced £2.75–£3.25) consist mainly of flans and ice creams . . . more fond memories of the Costas.

House red and white Rioja Vega (£8.75) is reasonably priced but most parties (for which this makes an ideal venue) prefer Sangria (£8.75 per large jug), a dangerously high-octane short-cut to merriment. You'll find more of the same at El Metro's other branch – which is usefully if a little bizarrely sited inside the Metropolitan line underground station at Hammersmith.

FULHAM ⑩ CHINESE

Mao Tai

58 New King's Road, SW6 ☎ 0171 731 2520	⊖ Parsons Green
Mon–Sat noon–2.30pm & 7–11.45pm,	
Sun 12.30–2.30pm & 7–11.45pm	All major credit cards

The Mao Tai is much more Chelsea than Chinatown, both in appearance and in the kind of food it serves. It's a pretty restaurant, cleverly lit, well-decorated, and with brisk efficient service. The food is Szechuan-sophisticated but with a satisfactory chilli burn and a nice scattering of old favourites. The clientele is just what you would expect from an area that is the very apple of any estate agents' eye. Such surroundings – and to be fair, such food – do not come cheap. Still, you'll leave well fed and well looked after: both the cooking and service are slick and chic.

Start with some steamed scallops (£6.50 for two). These are usually a pretty good indication of things to come and at Mao Tai they are well-cooked – to the point of firmness without having become rubbery. Salt and pepper prawns (£6.20 for six) are very fresh but somewhat disconcertingly fried in their shells, so the lovely crispy bits end up on the side of the plate. Firecracker dumplings (£5.80) are terrific – innocent-looking Shanghai style dumplings with a satisfactory belt of chilli lurking to surprise the unwary. For main courses, you have a choice of over fifty dishes. Two good ones to include in someone's order are Szechuan squid in a hot bean sauce (£7.20) – tender squid and a hot beany sauce, no disappointments here – and Tangerine peel chicken (£6.20), a delightful and delicate dish. Braised "Mao Tai" duck (£7.50) is a variant of duck in plum sauce, but is boneless and very tasty indeed, the ubiquitous chilli only making a small guest appearance.

In the vegetable section there's a choice of "braised lettuce or broccoli" in oyster sauce (£4.50) – opt for the lettuce. The still crisp furls of Cos are nicely wilted and make the perfect match for oyster sauce. Very good indeed.

WEST

Montana

125-129 Dawes Rd, SW6 ☎ 0171 385 9500	⊖ Fulham Broadway
Mon–Thurs 7–11pm, Fri & Sat noon–3pm & 7–11.30pm	All major credit cards

For atmosphere alone, Montana deserves the credit for livening up an otherwise dull corner of SW6. Hidden away down Dawes Road it is certainly out on its own. Its quirky Americanesque food has gained much praise despite a stream of critics pointing out that the dishes have little if anything to do with the cuisine of Montana. The decor is all ragwash and cowskin, and like that of its siblings, Dakota in Notting Hill and Canyon in Richmond, would be more at home in "Twin Peaks" than West London. Captured in two early sepia prints, Sitting Bull watches over the assembled diners – whatever would he have made of the "South Western American" food on offer here? Montana is an easy-going sort of restaurant which has very much got the measure of the youthful locals in this part of Fulham.

Your opening move is to sample the two fresh house breads, which are strongly flavoured with herbs and chilli. Then perhaps the much-lauded crab and Jerusalem artichoke chowder (£5.50) which is subject to availability – and when it has gone it has gone. Pan-fried mussels and oregano pesto (£5.25-£8.25) are juicy and pesto makes an interesting additive. The soft shell crab (£7.50-£14.95) is also pan-fried though chilli heads will be disappointed that the accompanying jalapeno sauce doesn't deliver more of a punch. The crab also comes with roast garlic polenta. Or there is pan-fried yucatan halibut (£13.25), delicious and at once both snow–white and well-cooked, although the green serrano broth may raise the hackles of a chilli lover in much the same way as the jalapeno sauce. Meat-eaters are served by chargrilled calves' liver (£11.50), served with a sweetcorn and green chilli chutney, and a warm, new potato salad as base. Desserts range from an unprepossessing mild ginger cake (£4.25) to sharp and fruity sorbets (£3.95).

There's an interesting and wide-ranging wine list with bottles starting at around £11.00. If you want a good white, splash out on the '97 Stormy Cape Chenin Blanc (£15.00) – full of soft flavour and decent value.

Nayab

309 New Kings Rd, SW6 ☎ 0171 731 6993   ⊖ Parsons Green

Daily noon–2.30pm & 6pm–midnight (Sun 11.30pm)   Amex, Mastercard, Visa

The last decade has seen enormous changes in the way Londoners think of Indian food and the Nayab has kept up with the pace. Its menu (motto: "everything you'd expect and a lot you wouldn't") features an admirable number of sophisticated and delicious specials – dishes which are probably a good deal more representative of the best cooking in Delhi than the menu section headed "old curry house favourites" – bhuna, vindaloo, rogan josh and friends. On the rest of the list good use is made of fish – it's rare to find monkfish, tiger prawns and scallops all on the same menu in an Indian restaurant. To eat well here, you should certainly ask advice and stray from the familiar.

You might start with something from the tandoor such as paneer shashlick (£3.50) – a skewer of grilled home-made cheese – or scallops shashlick (£6.95/£11.95). Or try some baingan pakoras – aubergine roundels filled with cheese (£3.50). Or murg samosas (£3.50) – filled with chicken and coriander, or even murg pakodey (£3.50) – chicken breast fillets rolled in a spiced gram flour batter and deep fried. For the main event good choices include kori gashi (£5.95) – a red chicken curry from Mangalore; monkfish ambotik (£9.95) – a Goan fish curry; king prawn haryali (£9.95) – an interesting dish of king prawns cooked in a puree of sweet basil with coconut; and the Footpath Hotel curry (£5.95) which is a Delhi style rogan josh – lamb in a rich and strongly spiced sauce without being too chilli hot. The "speciality of the house" is the nihari kohe Avadh (£7.95) which is a slow-cooked, pot-roast lamb shank. There's also a good range of vegetarian specialities. At the weekend there is a "special" special – a Hyderabadi biryani (£7.95), either lamb or chicken cooked an a sealed pot "dumm" style. Equally important, even the rice accompaniments here are special: saffron pulao (£2.50) has no splashes of food dye, just the natural flavours of saffron and a whiff of cardamom.

The Nayab is handily placed for the White Horse on Parsons Green, but being adjacent to such a trendy watering hole has its disadvantages – as the pub empties the Nayab fills up. Best try and time your visit for the early part of the evening.

755

755 Fulham Road, SW6 ☎ 0171 371 0755	⊖ Parsons Green
Mon 7–11pm, Tues–Sat 12.30–2-30pm & 7–11pm,	
Sun noon–4pm	Amex, Mastercard, Visa

Run by husband and wife team Georgina and Alan Thompson – both trained chefs – 755 is a bit of a treat. It's clearly a restaurant that the locals use for a special occasion and that means putting on the pearls, around these parts. That the treat is enjoyed often is obvious as many of the customers seem to know the couple by name and Georgina, front of house, claims that 60 percent of customers are regulars. "It's not cheap," she says, "but look what you get". Quite so: 755 prides itself on little additions, serving a canapé while you await your starter, or a tiny lemon curd brulée before dessert, turning three courses into five. And it's not as if bargain hunters are ignored, either. There's a good set menu with two courses for £18 and three for £22, and a snip of a set lunch at £12.50 a head. Whenever you come, be sure to book reasonably well ahead.

The menus change frequently but if it is offered start with griddled foie gras with Yorkshire pudding and madeira (£10.50) and you will enjoy one of the most astonishing tastes on the planet. One portion is quite enough for two. Among main courses, you might find roast sea bream with sweet chilli beignets, asparagus and crushed olive potatoes (£14.75) which comes with skin paper-crisp from the oven and the flesh at that difficult to achieve just cooked point. Or seared escalope of salmon fillet with saffron and pea risotto, basil and tomato jus (£13.75), a beautifully sandwiched tower of components, shockingly rich for fish. There are meaty offerings, too, including such robust acts as braised pig's trotter with sweetbreads and truffle jus (£14.50). For dessert, pancake of caramelised mixed fruits with cinnamon ice cream (£5.50) is a tour de force of balance – sweet, tart, hot and cold, the ice cream delicate and not too sweet. Death by chocolate (£9.50) is an orgy of a pudding that requires planning permission.

The 755 wine list is well compiled with excellent choices at pleasantly reasonable prices. There's also a decent house champagne, which at £23.50 confirms 755's party elegibility (it has a private party room).

Hammersmith & Chiswick

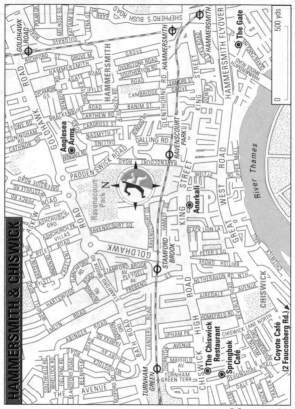

HAMMERSMITH & CHISWICK

© Crown copyright

Anarkali

303/305 King Street, W6 ☎ 0181 748 1760   ⊖ Ravenscourt Park

Daily noon–2.30pm & 6pm–midnight   All major credit cards

If you stand outside the Anarkali and glance around, you'll find that you're spoilt for choice. There are four other Indian restaurants, plus a Thai, a Middle Eastern and a Chinese all within fifty yards. The Anarkali opened over 25 years ago and is only on its second set of owners. The immediate impression is that this is a place that has been overtaken by its upstart neighbours – even the Chinese has had a dazzling facelift while the Anarkali still retains the script-based signage of a different era. Don't be put off. The Anarkali menu has some interesting dishes, and you don't survive so much competition for so long without doing something right.

There's an undeniable formality here – underpinned by pricing that's more special occasion than bargain – but everyone is attentive and friendly. The pappadams are hot and fresh and accompanying chutneys are good – a steel thali tray with half a dozen old favourites. The breads are good, too. Turning to the starters, baigun bahar (£3.50) is a slice of aubergine stuffed with panir (cheese); tandoori lamb chop (£3.95) brings a pair of small, well-marinated chops; but the star of the show is kathe kebab (£3.95) which is a savoury mixture of chopped lamb with onions served rolled up in a thin chapati. For main courses, try the shahi batak (£9.50) – strips of duck cooked with papaya, ginger and onion. Mach machli (£9.50) is a sound fish curry. And the Persian chicken pilau (£8.95) is surprisingly accomplished and quite delicious – a well flavoured dish presented under a net of spun egg, and with the unnecessary accompaniment of a side dish of vegetable curry. From the vegetables choose aloo dum haryali (£3.95), a simple but satisfying dish of potatoes cooked with coriander and fenugreek.

This is just one of Rafique Miah's five restaurants – another venture, modern and stylish, is Indian Summer, two doors down the road – and also well worth a try (☎0181 748 7345). The other three are in far-flung Wimbledon, Dunstaple and Los Angeles.

HAMMERSMITH & CHISWICK ⓦ MOD. BRITISH PUB

WEST

The Anglesea Arms

35 Wingate Rd, W6 ☎ 0181 749 1291   ⊖ Ravenscourt Park/Shepherds Bush

Food served Mon–Sat 12.30–2.45pm & 7.30–10.45pm,

Sun 1–3.45pm & 7.30–10pm   All major credit cards except Amex

The food at the Anglesea is very good indeed. Do not make the mistake of pigeon-holing this establishment as merely a pub. It is a pub, but one with a kitchen the envy of many more mainstream restaurants. The chef proprietor is Dan Evans, a seasoned campaigner who has been head chef at several of the brightest eateries of the 1990s. At the Anglesea, Dan runs the kitchen while his wife Fiona runs the bar and front of house. The menu changes at least twice a day, dishes are crossed out as they run out, and, when you've achieved "favoured local" status, you can ask for something simple that's not even on the board and if they have the ingredients you can have the dish. Pitch up early, claim a seat and not only will you dine well, but you'll leave feeling good about the bill.

Who knows what Dan will have chalked up on the blackboard when you visit? How about a starter like foie gras and pigeon terrine with brioche and onion marmalade (£4.75) – you will not often see a dish like this for under a fiver. Or there may be tomato, sweet basil and crab soup (£3.95), or home-cured gravadlax with horseradish blinis and beetroot (£4.95). Main courses may include sautéed lamb sweetbreads with fresh papardelle, peas and mint (£7.50); or a compendium dish like large warm salad of duck breast and livers, chorizo, small potatoes, flat beans and cabernet sauvignon (£7.75). Or something simple like Gloucester Old Spot ham, egg and chips (£7.50). To round things off, there is always one British cheese in perfect condition – like St Andrew's, a cow's milk cheese served with black grapes (£4.50).

As befits food such as this there's a wine list to match. A dozen wines are on offer by the glass, and the choice is thoughtful. Not very many restaurants, and very few pubs, offer a range of pudding wines by the bottle, half-bottle and glass. Among them is a Thorncroft noble harvest (£14 a bottle, £4.75 a glass), an English dessert wine, as delicious as it is unexpected.

The Chiswick Restaurant

131 Chiswick High Rd, W4 ☎ 0181 994 6887

⊖ Turnham Green

Mon–Fri & Sun 12.30–2.45pm & 7–11pm, Sat 7–11pm

All major credit cards

The menu here changes twice a day. Not completely – the puddings will probably stay the same and two or three dishes will carry over – but there's always something fresh for the large number of local regulars. And they're a lucky lot, for the Chiswick is simply one of the best neighbourhood restaurants in London. It serves delicious, well-presented dishes that major in strong flavours. Service is informal but with a steely edge of competence. Pricing is enlightened with a "one hour lunch" menu which doubles as an "early evening" menu (before 8pm). This costs £9.50 and provides two courses and coffee: you might get something along the lines of vine tomato soup and chicken confit and cash; or Greek salad and grilled mackerel and salsa verde. No wonder the place is packed.

Everything here is driven by the seasons and the markets, and with a twice-daily changing menu it's hard to make very firm suggestions. The style of cuisine is Modern British with perhaps a slight favouring of the British part of the equation. Given the chance, start with the potato pancake, wood pigeon and onion marmalade (£6.50), or the porcini and potato soup (£4); or the terrific plate of charcuterie (£6.25), each element of which is teamed with a different home-made pickle or chutney; or the warm salad of pork confit, dandelion and poached egg (£6.50). Or whatever else sounds good – since it will almost certainly be so. The inspiration for the main courses seems more widely spread. Roast halibut may be teamed with olive oil mash and red wine sauce (£12.75); calf's liver comes with melted onions and crisp sage (£11.75) and is very delicious indeed. The neck fillet of lamb with couscous, houmous and mint (£12.25) is surprisingly light and fresh-flavoured, while a fillet of seabass (£15) may come with a simple salad Nicoise. The wine list has plenty of good choices in the middle price range.

Among the puddings, keep an eye out for banana bread and chocolate malt ice cream (£4.50): for anyone old enough to remember Horlicks and Ovaltine – or Americans brought up on malted milk – this is a fine, nostalgic homage.

£12–£30

The Coyote Café

2 Fauconberg Road, W4 ☎ 0181 742 8545   ⊖ Chiswick Park

Mon–Sat 11am–11pm, Sun 11am–10.30pm   Amex, Mastercard, Visa

The proprietor here, John Wasilko, was so impressed when he visited the Coyote Café in Santa Fe that he bought the rights to use the name in Europe. Now Southwest America has a firm foothold in Chiswick, and the natives seem to be enjoying it. The bar and restaurant is packed, making booking a must, and on sunny days the crowd spills out onto pavement seating. The food is more delicate, intense and refined than your run-of-the-mill Tex-Mex; the chilli flavours may prove hot but the tastes are also sweet, sour, fruity and rich. If you are not familiar with this kind of food, you should leave your pre-conceptions behind.

As well as the regular menu there is also a sheet of specials which changes weekly. You might start with something genuinely out of the ordinary: how does South West painted bean soup (£3.55) sound? From the appetisers list try the Santa Fe Caesar salad (£6.25 or £7 with chicken) which delivers a good, fresh mound of crisp leaves, croutons and Parmesan. Or there's a nice wild mushroom quesadilla with roast corn salsa (£5.25); or Gulf coast crab cakes with creamed Creole sauce (£6.95). On the entrees list you'll see some old Tex-Mex favourites. Blackened ribeye steak with chipotle gravy, skinny fries and tobacco onions (£11.95) is worth having for the chipotle gravy, which is a kind of tomatoey, tangy, fruity chilli sauce. The "Coyote Café's" Howlin chilli burger (£7.95) is a large and delicious burger, topped with a ladleful of splendid chilli. Chilaquiles with green chilli-apple sauce (£8.95) is a layered dish of grilled vegetables between flour tortillas served with a zesty sweet sauce. Turn to the specials for even wilder and more exciting dishes – like grilled halibut with peanut chipotle sauce (£10.25), or roasted venison with green chillies and wild boar bacon (£9.75).

The Coyote Café is famed for its authentic brunch on Saturday and Sunday: biscuits and gravy (£3.95); corn beef hash (£5.55); Creole eggs Benedict (£6.25); Texas ham'n'eggs (£5.95); American pancakes with molasses (£3.35). Good enough to make you howl.

WEST

The Gate

51 Queen Caroline Street, W6 ☎ 0181 748 6932	⊖ Hammersmith
Mon–Fri noon–2.30pm & 6–11pm, Sat 6–11pm	All major credit cards

The extraordinary thing about The Gate, tucked behind the Hammersmith Apollo, is that you hardly realise it's a vegetarian restaurant. This is gourmet dining without the meat. It's not wholefood, it's not even healthy – indeed, it's as rich, colourful, calorific and naughty as anywhere in town. The clientele is a quiet and appreciative bunch of locals and pilgrims – the Gate isn't a place you stumble across. The venue is as striking as the food, a former artists' studio, with buttercup-yellow walls and huge black and white paintings of Marlon, Marilyn and Picasso, and a presiding bust of Shakespeare. It is rented from the nearby church – hence the pews – The Gate's only nod to veggie solemnities.

The short menu changes monthly, but starters are always great. There's usually a tart – like oyster mushroom and feta cheese (£4.90) – which elsewhere, with its grown-up salad, would be served as a main course. Also excellent is the noodle salad (£4.90) which transforms the humble aubergine into a crisp, nutty fritter. This is large, too, so you might want to share starters – it is certainly worth pacing yourself to sample all courses. The mains deliver more explosions of flavour. The carciofi (£8.50) is lentil-stuffed artichoke with cheesy, tomatoey polenta and asparagus, lifted with balsamic vinegar. Tortellini (£8.50) come filled with courgette and basil pesto, and a creamy leek and thyme sauce that contrasts well with a bitter olive tapenade. Puddings are splendid: the cappuccino brulée (£3.50) is good bitter chocolate and hazelnut cake (£4.50) – a thinking person's death-by-chocolate. Those without a sweet tooth should go for the cheese board (£5.00) where farmhouse varieties are accompanied by quince compote and oatcakes. The drinks list is extensive with all manner of freshly squeezed juices (£1.75), herbal teas (£1.25) and coffee (£1.25–£1.75), while the wine list has something for everyone: vegan, vegetarian, organic and carnivore alike.

This is sad place for bill-quibblers as all starters tend to be £4.90 and main courses £8.50, with a pasta of the day at £6.80, so there's not a lot of opportunity for fun with the calculator.

The Springbok Café

42 Devonshire Road, W4 ☎ 0181 742 3149	⊖ Turnham Green
Mon–Sat 6.30–11pm	Mastercard, Visa

In this quiet corner off the Chiswick High Road, Peter and Chantelle Gottgens have opened an authentic South African restaurant. The Sprinbok Café is small, informal, and centre stage is the open plan kitchen. What's more, Peter – who trained as a chef in South Africa and Italy – is passionate about both the quality and authenticity of his ingredients. He gets his fish from Mossell Bay or Port St John, and together with biltong and fresh herbs they're flown in from South Africa. Due to EC regulations he can no longer import ostrich but sources English ostrich of South African stock.

The menu changes monthly but you might start with a wild spinach, biltong, vine tomato and pecorino salad with a walnut oil lime and sunflower seed dressing (£4.50), an excellent array of tastes and textures. Or mussels peri-peri (£4), nicely spiced. For main courses turn to the specials board. You might find such exotics as Hout Bay Yellowfin Tuna chargrilled with coriander and roast plum tomatoes (£10.50), or bobotie with yellow rice and raisins (£8.50). On the regular menu dishes include wors, pap'n'sous – traditional South African sausages with maize meal (£7.50). The accompaniments are delicious, too: isijingi cakes are maize cakes; sousboontjies are butter beans in a sweet sauce, rather oddly served cold; samp'n'beans are maize kernels and beans, chewy and rich. By the time puddings come round, see if you have room to share a prickly pear with peri-peri ice cream (£4.50), or a pot of moerkoffie (£1.25) with a side order of koeksusters (£1.00) – a kind of gingery doughnut soaked in syrup.

It may be that you find the cooking here lacking slightly in salt. This is partly because South African cuisine involves a lot of fruit and meat combinations, but mainly because in the African heat salt is crucial, and every table would have a central bowl of salt so that diners could help themselves to much as they wish – indeed the blander items like isijingi cakes would be picked up and dipped in the salt bowl. Peter Gottgens approaches seasoning in much the same way as the rest of his cooking – traditionallly!

Notting Hill

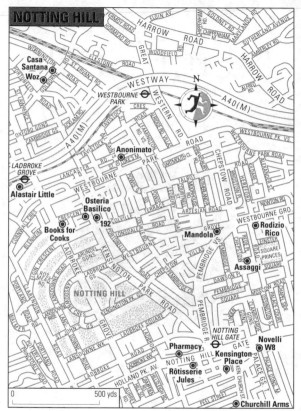

NOTTING HILL

Casa Santana
Woz
WIRLINGTON
ST STEPHEN'S
GDNS
COLVILLE

HARROW ROAD
ELGIN AV
FERMOY RD
MARYLANDS RD
CHIPPENHAM
SUTHERLAND AVENUE
SHIRLAND RD
AMBERLEY RD
HARROW ROAD
WOODFIELD
GREAT WESTERN RD
ALFRED RD

WESTWAY
A40(M)

WESTBOURNE PARK
WESTERN RD
CRES

A40(M)
LADBROKE GROVE

Alastair Little

Anonimato
LIME ST
TAVISTOCK
WESTBOURNE PARK
WESTBOURNE PK RD
WESTBOURNE PK VS
LANCASTER RD
TALBOT RD
CHEPSTOW ROAD
NEWTON RD

Osteria Basilico
192
COLVILLE
TERRACE
ARTESIAN ROAD
WESTBOURNE GRO

Books for Cooks
LONSDALE ROAD
Mandola
Rodizio Rico
LEINSTER
SQUARE
PRINCES
SQUARE

KENSINGTON
WESTBOURNE
CHEPSTOW VILLAS
Assaggi
PEMBRIDGE VS
DAWSON PL
MOSCOW RD

NOTTING HILL
LADBROKE
KENSINGTON PK RD
LADBROKE GROVE
KENSINGTON PARK ROAD
PEMBRIDGE SQUARE
PEMBRIDGE RD

LADBROKE SQUARE

NOTTING HILL GATE
Novelli W8

Pharmacy
NOTTING HILL
GATE
Kensington Place
CHURCH STREET

HOLLAND PK AV
Rôtisserie Jules
PEEL STREET
Churchill Arms

0 _____ 500 yds

© Crown copyright

Alastair Little

136a Lancaster Rd, W11 ☎ 0171 243 2220   ⊖ Ladbroke Grove

Mon–Fri 12.30–2.30pm & 7–11pm, Sat 12.30–3pm & 7–11pm   All major credit cards

Alastair Little is a name that commands respect among restaurant-going London. Back in the 80s, he was one of the main pioneers of the Anglo-Italian movement, a man without a professional catering background who wanted to serve real food – clean, fresh cooking, with home-made pastas and terrines – the sort of food that we all wish we could serve at home, but can't. Following his clean-cut eponymous site in Frith Street, he opened this much more modest-priced restaurant in 1996. Every local Notting Hill trendy rushed to try it out when it first opened but they have moved on now, returning Alastair Little back to the foodies. Forget the trends: this is a top-class place and one that feels much less like a temple than the Soho branch – indeed, the coffee-and-cream dining room has an almost careworn charm about it.

The daily changing menu is short and sweet. At lunch the price is fixed at £5 for first courses, £8.00 for pasta, £12 for main and £5.00 dessert – which is extraordinarily inexpensive for this quality of food. In the evening you'll find the same dishes but a slightly larger choice – three courses cost £27.50. Starters might be the likes of smoked mackerel, beetroot and horseradish – the whole somehow much more than the sum of its components, with unusually good mackerel, grated real horseradish and a fresh beetroot salad. Or there may be a pork and chicken liver terrine with plum chutney and toast which is good enough to put a grin on any normal, greedy person. Pastas to follow might be pumpkin and ricotta ravioli, basted with sage butter, tasting strongly of pumpkin and very rich. Or perhaps tagliatelle tordellata, with fresh spinach and a creamy cheesy sauce – true comfort food. Mains are of the order of grilled monkfish with butter beans and chermoula, or chicken breast hotchpotch. But it is really the simple pasta dishes that are Alastair Little's real strength: don't miss out on them.

Desserts are the kind of rich, indulgent things that are so good you almost feel embarrassed to be seen choosing. How about "Italian chocolate brownie"? A mixed idiom maybe, but it turns out to be completely delicious.

WEST

Anonimato

12 All Saints Road, W11 ☎ 0171 243 2808	⊖ Westbourne Park
Mon–Fri 7–11pm, Sat & Sun noon–4pm	Amex, Mastercard, Visa

All Saints Road must have changed as much as any London street in the past dozen years, from drugs'n'riots "Front Line" status to Notting Hill restaurant cool. The Sugar Club at no.33a began the media-restaurant trend here (it has since moved to Soho – leaving an offspring here in Bali Sugar). Anonimato is a rather more modest neighbour but belonging to the same school, an intimate place with Notting Hill abstract paintings adorning pastel walls and a global-trek of a menu offering some seriously weird combinations. The cooking here is original and makes a genuine effort to use the whole palate of flavours, from savoury through sweet to sharp, while balancing an equally large spread of textures.

'Pacific Fusion' is how Anonimato describe their cuisine and this can often be translated as delicious, as in the seared duck with soba noodles, mango and sweet chilli (£5.25), or the grilled asparagus with quail eggs, Parma ham and Parmesan (£5.75). Tamarind and chilli baked Devon hen (£11.75) is juicy and tender, and hoi sin roast rump of lamb with kumera mash and balsamic mint jus (£12.50) is a terrific amalgam of rich flavours. Try it with the crispy potato galette (£2.00). On the rare occasions when this otherwise inventive menu lets you down, it does so by overpowering you with different tastes. The seabass with panzanella and seven-year-old balsamic vinegar (£13.50), is such a dish. Bass is a delicate fish and cannot expect to shine when teamed with a salad that includes olives, large briny capers, onion, watercress and heavily aged vinegar. Desserts (all priced at £4.00), on the other hand, sometimes seem a tad too genteel, with rather restrained offerings of sticky toffee pudding and steamed chocolate mousse cake. Still, these are minor gripes in the context of such a pleasant restaurant which has many more hits than misses.

There are no house wines as such here but the list starts at a decent value £11.00. They include a very nice white – Norton Torrontes Argentina 1997 – at £14.50.

Assaggi

39 Chepstow Place, W2 ☎ 0171 792 5501	⊖ Notting Hill Gate
Mon–Sat 12.30–2.30pm & 7.30–11pm	All major credit cards

Assaggi is a small, ochre-painted room above The Chepstow pub. It's generally full at lunch and it is booked far in advance in the evenings. The prices are unforgiving and on the face of it paying so much for such straightforward dishes would be likely to raise the hackles of any sensible diner. But the reason Assaggi is such a gem, and also the reason it is always full, is that self-same straightforwardness. The menu may appear simple but it is littered with authentic and luxury ingredients and the cooking is very accomplished indeed. Prepare yourself for a very memorable meal.

You'll find there are a dozen starters – with the option to have the pastas as main courses as well – and half a dozen main courses. Start with some pasta – tagliolini con bottarga (£8.95), maybe – perfectly cooked fine pasta strands with the elusive and subtle flavour of smoked grey mullet roe. Or there's the Assaggi pasta loaf, (£6.95/£8.95), a pinwheel of pasta with a well flavoured filling. Or there may be a dish like fresh crab with celery, lemon and olive oil dressing (£8.95), or bresaola Punta d'Anca (£6.95). Main courses are even more pared down: calf's liver (£12.95); a plainly grilled veal chop (£18.50) with a few ceps; fish of the day (£17.95); or filletto di manzo con galletti (£18..95) – a fist-sized lump of fillet steak with a mound of chanterelle mushrooms. All are memorable, while the side salad of tomato, rucola e Basilico (£4.75) is everything you would wish for. Puddings change daily and cost a stiff £5.25. Look out for panacotta – a perfect texture – and another dish which is just ultra-fresh buffalo ricotta served with some "cooked" honey. To accompany, there is a short wine list with some splendid and unfamiliar Italian regional specialities

A hallmark of Assaggi is the bread they serve. This is the famous carta di musica, very thin, very crisp and very delicious. It's like a kind of Italian pappadom only better. The name carta di musica came about because, when well made, the bread resembles the sheets of vellum on which music was first set down.

Books for Cooks

4 Blenheim Crescent, W11 ☎ 0171 221 1992   ⊖ Ladbroke Grove/Notting Hill

Mon–Fri 12.30–1.30pm, Sat noon–1.45pm   All major credit cards

This cookery bookshop is an extraordinary little place – a Mecca for foodies throughout London and beyond. Even at 11am on a Monday morning you will find a herd of gastronomes browsing the literary undergrowth, seeking inspiration for something or other. The knowledgeable and friendly staff know all about their stock and will tell you, through experience, not only which recipes will work but where to look for further information. The reason they know what works is the test kitchen at the back of the shop, and that's where a dozen diners can enjoy a good lunch at a bargain price. At Books for Cooks the proof of each pudding is in the eating.

Though the style of cooking changes from one day to the next, depending on whether today's cookery book is by the very English Gary Rhodes or the Sugar Club's Peter Gordon, the formula is always the same. There's a soup (£3.50) followed by two or three main courses (£6.00), one of which will be vegetarian and another meat-based. Dessert (£2.50) will be a choice of two or three, depending on what they're working from. They start serving at 12.30pm and carry on until they run out of food, usually around 1.30pm. The cooking will always be competent and the food served will reflect the nature of the cookery book used rather than the temperament of the person behind the stove. Sometimes you can eat food of genius, sometimes not, but it'll never be dull. And if you are deeply impressed by your squid pie or chocolate and almond torte, not only can you discuss its preparation with the person who cooked it, you can buy the book it came from. The problem with Books for Cooks is that so many people have learnt its secret that it has become essential to book.

They do two sittings on Saturday – Portobello Market day. Book for the second sitting if you can, and drop in earlier in the morning to find out what's on the menu. The staff love it when customers bring their own wine, relax and talk about food.

Casa Santana

44 Golborne Road, W10 ☎ 0181 968 8764   ⊖ Ladbroke Grove

Daily 10am–10.30pm   Mastercard, Visa

Go up the Portobello Road from Notting Hill. Go past the fruit and veg stalls; under the motorway, past the collectors' record shops; keep going, and round the next corner you reach Portugal. The Golborne Road is (with South Lambeth Road in Vauxhall/Stockwell) London's Portuguese HQ. Just up the road from the Lisboa delicatessen is Casa Santana – a Portuguese/Madeiran restaurant. There are a dozen tall stools at the bar counter and another dozen shorter ones grouped around a handful of tables. This is a sort of super-tapas bar. Cooking is genuine and service friendly, although authentically unhurried. Non-Portuguese customers are definitely in the minority.

The Portuguese are big soup-drinkers. They're happy to start with soup, or return to it if a main course leaves a few gaps (which is unlikely given Portuguese portions). Here, you might start with caldo verde (£1.75), a a green cabbage soup enlivened with a couple of slices of sausage, or canja de galhina (£1.75) chicken soup. Or you could order a nice starter of calamares (£3.75) – deep-fried rings of squid, battered and served with lemon or a bowl of that pink sauce once the sole preserve of prawn cocktails. Moving on, consider a grilled dish – the tiny kitchen has a large charcoal grill and dishes like frango no churrasco (£5.95) – charcoal grilled chicken – are simple and good. Or there is scabbard fish – cooked in the Madeiran style – peixe espada a vilhao (£7.95). Bacalhau (reconstituted dried, salt cod) is one of those dishes which you are so sure you will dislike that you never even try them. This is the place to break your duck. Bacalhau a braz (£6.95) is a mixture of shredded salt cod fried up with scrambled egg, fried onion, and slivers of fried potato. It's a robust dish, tasty and good. Or perhaps you would prefer bacalhau an brass – which is a piece of bacalhau plainly grilled ?

Trying to sound innocuous amongst the starters lurks chourico assuado (£2.50). A pottery pig with perforated back – like an avant-garde toastrack – appears at table with a sausage laid on top of it, the "sump" is filled with aguediente – a virulent, over-proof Portuguese spirit – and a match is applied. This is a better use for aguediente than drinking it.

The Churchill Arms

119 Kensington Church St, W8 ☎ 0171 792 1246   ⊖ Notting Hill Gate

Mon–Sat 12.30–2.30pm & 6–9.30pm, Sun noon–2.30pm   Mastercard, Visa

The Churchill may look like an ordinary pub but it happens to serve some of the tastiest and most reasonably priced Thai food in London. A back room featuring acres of green foliage is the main seating area for food but don't despair if you find it full (it fills up very quickly) as meals are served throughout the pub. Service is friendly but as the food is cooked to order, be prepared to wait – it is worth it. If you really can't wait, pre-cooked dishes such as chicken with chillies (along with that other well known Thai delicacy, Stilton ploughman's) are also available.

Dishes are unpronounceable so have thoughtfully been numbered to assist everybody. The pad gai med ma muang hin-maparn (no. 15 – £5.50) is a deliciously spicy dish of chicken, cashew nuts and chilli served with a generous helping of fluffy boiled rice. Kwaitiew pad kee mao (£5.25) is a dish of pork, chicken or beef cooked with flat Thai noodles heated with red and green chillies – hot but not unbearably so. The same cannot be said for the khao rad na ga prao (£5.50) which is described as very hot. Not an understatement. This prawn dish with fresh chillies and Thai basil is an acquired taste guaranteed to bring sweat to the brow of even the most ardent chilliholic. For something milder, try the pad neau nahm man hoi (£5.25) – beef with oyster sauce with mushrooms – or the khao rad na (£5.25), a rice dish topped with prawns with vegetables and gravy. Both are good. Puddings are limited in choice and ambition but for something sweet to temper the heat try apple pie (£2.25) – a strange accompaniment to Thai food but surprisingly welcome.

Visit at lunch time and you'll get the same dishes for about 10 per cent less than in the evening when waitress service for drinks is available. Possibly the best thing about the Churchill Thai Kitchen is you get restaurant standard food with drinks at pub prices and if that wasn't enough, they even do take-aways in the traditional foil trays.

Kensington Place

2 Farmer St, W8 ☎ 0171 1 727 3184	⊖ Notting Hill Gate

Mon–Sat noon–3pm & 6.30–11.45pm.

Sun noon–3pm & 6.30–10.15pm	Amex, Mastercard, Visa

The first thing to know about Kensington Place is that it is noisy. The dining room is large, echoing, glass fronted and noisy. It's noisy because it's packed with people having a good time. Rather than music there's the busy hum of confidences, shrieks of merriment, and the clamour of parties. The service here is crisp, the food is good and the prices are fair. The menu changes from session to session to reflect whatever the market has to offer, and there is a set lunch which offers a limited choice of three good courses for £14.50. (By way of example: you might have chicken liver crostini with truffle paste and rocket; followed by wild sea trout with capers and lemon; then poached mirabelles with vanilla cream.) This is fine value for money. Regulars here claim that the set lunch menu is the key to knowing just when head Chef Rowley Leigh is cooking in person – apparently his hand-writing is very distinctive!

Rowley Leigh's food is eclectic in the best possible way. The kitchen starts with the laudable premise that there is nothing better than what is in season, and goes on combine Mediterranean inspirations with classic French and English dishes. Thus you may find (in due season) starters like fish soup with croutons and rouille (£5.50); griddled foie gras with sweetcorn pancake (£9.50); tagliarini with crayfish and baby leeks (£6); or omelette fines herbes (£4.50). These are sophisticated dishes, and well-chosen combinations of flavours. Main courses might be smoked haddock Monte Carlo (£13.50); spiced grilled quails (£14); roast guinea fowl with tajine vegetables and saffron (£13.50); or cod with parsley sauce (£12.50).

The dessert section of the menu offers what may be one of London's finest lemon tarts (£5), with well-made ice creams (£4.50) and trad favourites with a twist. Bread and butter pudding is made with pannettone (£6) while panna cotta is made with coffee and mascarpone (£5.50). For hardened pudding addicts there is the ultimate challenge – the grand selection (£10). Indulge yourself (or share) and take a glass of Tokaji Aszu 5 Puttonyos (£5) alongside.

NOTTING HILL ⑪ SUDANESE

The Mandola

139 Westbourne Grove, W11 ☎ 0171 229 4734

⊖ Notting Hill Gate

Daily noon–10.30pm

Cash or cheque only

The food at The Mandola is described as "urban Sudanese", and as that omits the doubtful pleasures of some of the more traditional Sudanese delicacies – strips of raw liver marinated in lime juice and chili and peanut butter springs to mind – it seems like a pretty good idea. This would be a small, seriously informal, neighbourhood restaurant, except for the fact that it attracts people from all over town with its sensible pricing and often strikingly delicious dishes. There's lots more to praise. The staff are so laid back as to make worriers self-destruct on the spot. The restaurant is unlicensed so everything from fine wine to exotic beer is available – if you choose to take it with you. Or you could try the deep red, citrus-sharp hibiscus tea which the proprietor describes as "sub-Saharan Ribena".

To start there is a combo of dips and salads, rather prosaically listed as "mixed salad bar" for two (£7.65). There are a few middle eastern favourites here given a twist and all strongly and interestingly flavoured. "Salata tomatim bel gibna" – tomatoes feta and parsley; "salata tahina" – a good tangy tahini; "salata aswad" – a tangy, less oily, version of the Turkish aubergine dish Iman Bayeldi; "salata daqua" – white cabbage in peanut sauce; "tamiya" – Sudanese falafel; "mish" – a spicy yogurt dip. All are accompanied by hot pitta bread. As for main courses "samak magli" (£7) is "spicy fried fish" which shows just how good simple things can be – fillets of tilapia are served crisp on the outside, fresh on the inside, with a squeeze of lime juice. "Chicken hala" is a chicken in a rich, well-reduced tomato sauce that would not disgrace a smart Italian eatery (£7). Lovers of the exotic can finish by trying the Sudanese spiced coffee – scented with cardamom, cinnamon, cloves and ginger (your own flask and coffee set – enough for nine tiny cupfuls – for £3.85).

It is lucky the bowl for the "crushed green chili with lime, onions and garlic" (£1.05) is stainless steel as the contents must be one of the hottest things in the known universe.

WEST

Novelli W8

122 Palace Gardens Terrace, W8 ☎ 0171 229 4024	⊖ Notting Hill Gate
Mon 6–11.30pm, Tues–Thurs noon–3.30pm & 6–11.30pm	
Fri & Sat noon–3.30pm & 6pm–midnight	All major credit cards

The previous restaurant on this site slumbered through the 1970s as a deeply old-fashioned French bistro. The elderly clientele must have had the shock of their lives when the ebullient Jean Christophe Novelli replaced it with a modern French restaurant which operates at a gastronomic level which is hard to classify. Novelli W8 is not so formal – and the dishes are not thought-provoking enough – as to be described as haute cuisine, but everything about it is ambitious. So we have a long, brightly painted, railway carriage of a place serving pretty good and generally pretty rich, alcohol-swathed French food. Prices are pretty steep on the carte though bargain-hunters should note the set lunches at a very reasonable £12.50 for two courses, £14.50 for three.

On the carte, there are usually ten starters to choose from. They might include tartare of salmon, mixed leaves, soft boiled quail's egg caviare top (£7.25) – a telling combination of flavours – or roast scallops on mixed leaves, with lemon couscous, tomato, and a sherry dressing (£11). Pressed cassoulet terrine served with infused lentil du Puy and haricot blanc (£6.50) is a hearty option, or try the tian of Cornish crab, red pepper gazpacho sauce (£7). Half the mains are fish and half meat. Roast mullet might come with a vanilla risotto served with a light anise broth (£14); baked cod pavé, with a tomato fondue, basil, Parmesan crackling and a mustard seed sauce (£13.50). On the meat side, you might find "pied de cochon d'aujourd'hui suivant mon humeur" – stuffed braised pig's trotter (£12.50) – which like so many dishes sounds better in the original French. Or there could be braised rabbit leg with red peppers and caramelised root vegetables (£13); or fillet of pork wrapped in pancetta and with a sage and Emmenthal glaze (£12.50); or there is roast baby chicken stuffed with aubergine caviar and served with rosemary pomme fondant and green garlic oil (£13.50).

Desserts are taken seriously here, with such treats as a hot and cold, light and dark chocolate plate (£7) and a caramelised peach Tatin with Grand Marnier ice cream (£6.25). Very indulgent. Very appealing.

£25–£40

192

192 Kensington Park Road, W11 ☎ 0171 229 0482	⊖ Notting Hill Gate
Mon–Fri 12.30pm–3pm & 7–11pm,	
Sat & Sun 12.30pm–3.30pm & 7–11pm,	All major credit cards

192 is a pretty restaurant and wine bar that attracts a young monied crowd of local Notting Hill Gate music (Virgin treat this as a house cafe), media and literary folk – most of whom seem to know each other. This makes for a friendly atmosphere with much kissing and table hopping, and you may well find yourself in conversation with singers fresh from their recording session seated at the next table. The bar section is always busy, and has a fun, clubby atmosphere.

The menu offers the kind of food that seems simple but is very hard to do well (which it is here – consistently). It is based on best quality fresh ingredients with little interference. Starters of warm foie gras with baby vegetables and wild leaves (£6.25), and crab, bacon, pousse and avocado salad (£7.50) are both very very good. The foie gras slightly pink and the crab salad with large chunks of fresh white crab meat. Main courses of ribeye steak with spinach, rösti and Béarnaise (£12.50) and roast seabass with celeriac puree and basil beurre blanc (£12.50) are exactly what you want them to be with flavours and textures all at that well-judged point. The steak comes exactly as you order it with crisp rösti and a béarnaise any classic French restaurant would be proud of. The celeriac purée complements the seabass well and the basil beurre blanc is an ideal accompanying flavour. Presentation is excellent at 192, with an eye for garnishes that enhance the anticipation of what is excellent cooking. Leave room for pudding, as there are delights like coconut and pineapple mille feuille (£4.45), which features baked pineapple in a thin biscuity mille feuille with coconut sorbet, and bitter chocolate tart with honey ice cream (£4.25) for chocoholics. Menus change daily and reflect what is in season and fresh at the market.

192 is owned by the Groucho Club and the wine list features some of the club's wines – so if you cannot get invited to the Dean Street establishment you can see how the other half drinks.

Osteria Basilico

29 Kensington Park Rd, W11 ☎ 0171 727 9372	⊖ Ladbroke Grove
Mon–Fri 12.30–3pm & 6.30–11pm, Sat 12.30–4pm & 6.30–11pm,	
Sun 12.30–3.15pm & 6.30–10.30pm	Amex, Mastercard, Visa

Long before Kensington Park Road became the borough's hottest spot for outdoor dining, there was always a restaurant on this corner. When Duveen closed, the restaurant cat stayed on to have the next establishment named in its honour – Monsieur Thompson. Then, in its turn Monsieur T became Pizza by Numbers. Then in 1992 Osteria became the latest incarnation and has flourished ever since – so they must be doing something right. Daytime stargazing is enlivened by the arguments between parking wardens, clampers and their victims, while the traffic comes to a standstill for the unloading of timber lorries and for a constant stream of mini-cabs dropping off at the street's numerous restaurants. At dusk you get more of the same with the streetlights struggling to make the heart of Portobello look like the via Veneto.

Inside, pizza and pasta is speedily delivered with typical chirpy Italian panache to cramped scrubbed tables. Go easy on the baskets of warm pizza bread as the various grilled and preserved tit-bits arranged on the antique dresser that make up the anti-pasti (£4.80) are a tempting self-service affair. Of the other starters, frito di calamari e gamberi (£4.90) and spinaci e salsiccia con aceto Balsmico (£4.90) – a rough Italian sausage served with spinach – are both delicious. Specials change daily and have no particular regional influence. Old favourites include fegato di vitello alla Veneziana (£9.50) and gamberoni alla griglia (£12.50): classic, well-prepared veal and prawn dishes. Amongst the permanent fixtures, linguine alla scroglio (£6.80) comes with mixed seafood, while fresh tomato and carré d'agnello al forno con patate e rosmarino (£9.80) is an oven-baked rack of lamb roasted with potatoes and rosemary. Pizzas vary in size depending on who is in the kitchen, perhaps staff with shorter arms throw the dough higher, resulting in a wider thinner base, but all are on the large-ish size. Pizza diavolo (£6) comes with mozzarella and a good spicy pepperoni sausage.

House wines are served by the carafe, but it is much better to opt for the Montepulciano d'Abbruzzo (£10.95), a pretty decent wine at a pretty decent price.

Pharmacy (or suchlike)

150 Notting Hill Gate, W11 ☎ 0171 221 2442	⊖ Notting Hill Gate
Daily 12.30–2.45pm & 7–10.45pm (Sun 10pm)	All major credit cards

Ferociously trendy, almost impossible to get a booking in, and with its own secret VIP reservation number, Jonathan Kennedy's Pharmacy dominates the Notting Hill scene. Its shop-like exterior, with the name arranged in some new anagram (Army Chap, etc), lights up the area. Downstairs the decor is that of a chemist's shop with shelves of pills, potions and lotions and a sign advertising prescriptions. Upstairs Damien Hirst's butterflies adorn the walls and a stunning revolving hanging mobile by Danny Chadwick transfixes as you dine. But at the end of it all Pharmacy is a restaurant. And one that's worth the trip for the grub alone. The dishes are based on simple ingredients lightly cooked, with natural reductions for sauces, fruits for sweetening, and no alcohol in the cooking.

Upstairs the main restaurant offers a full à la carte menu (which changes seasonally and often) at lunch and dinner, and a lunch special of two courses for £13.50 and three for £15.50, which is a bargain. The main carte features starters like fresh Dorset crab with avocado purée (£9.50) – very more-ish; Jabugo ham (£15) – almost black and hard with an intense flavour; or a well flavoured pumpkin soup with chives (£5.50). For the very well-heeled there's Sevruga caviar with Melba toast and crème fraîche (£40). Main courses include some excellent rôtisserie dishes. Try spit roast veal, confit of tomato, jus (£15), or spit roast Bresse pigeon, grilled ceps, roast figs and mashed potatoes (£19). Downstairs the bar and brasserie serves a simpler menu that strikes a familiar note to the quick snack bar diner and stays open later. Choose from favourites like smoked salmon and scrambled eggs (£8), Club sandwich (£6.50), chargrilled squid, rocket and fresh chilli (£8.50), or be more adventurous and sample chicken Kiev, creamed spinach and mash (£8.50), or pigeon, pancetta and quail eggs salad (£7.50). It all hits the spot after a few beers or if you're not in the mood for a full dinner. Good quality and a great if noisy atmosphere.

Pharmacy's a great people-watching place, too, as the fun and the famous have made it their own. Persevere – you'll get a table eventually.

Rodizio Rico

111 Westbourne Grove, W11 ☎ 0171 792 4035	⊖ Notting Hill Gate/Bayswater
Mon–Fri 6.30pm–midnight, Sat 12.30–4.30pm & 6.30pm–midnight,	
Sun 12.30–11pm	Maastercard, Visa

If you're a lover of smoky grilled meat, Rodizio Rico will seem a godsend. In the South of Brazil this restaurant would be pretty run-of-the-mill stuff but in W11 "churrascarias" are the exception rather than the rule. Rodizio can be a puzzling experience for first timers. There's no menu and no prices – but no problem. "Rodizio" means "rotating" and refers to the carvers who wander about the room with huge skewers of freshly grilled meat from which they lop off chunks on demand – rather like the trolleys of roast beef at Simpson's in the Strand. You start by ordering and then help yourself from both the salad bar and hot buffet to prime your plate. As the carvers circulate they dispense cheerfulness and bonhomie as they cut you chunks, slivers and slices from whichever skewer they are holding. You eat as much as you like, of whatever you like, and then you pay the absurdly reasonable price of £15.50 a head.

When you're up helping yourself to the basics, look out for the tiny bread rolls, no bigger than a button mushroom, called pao de quejo – a rich cheese bread from the south of Brazil. Also bobo, a delicious kind of bubble and squeak made from cassava and spring greens. Return to your seat and await the carvers – they come in random order, but they keep on coming. There's lamb, and ham, and pork, and spare ribs, and chicken, and silverside beef (grilled in a piece and called lagarto after a similarly shaped iguana!). Then there are grilled chicken hearts. But the star of the show is picanha – the heart of the rump skewered and grilled in huge chunks – taste it and the arguments over superiority between rump and fillet are over for ever. Brazilians seem to revere the crispy bits, but if you want your meat rare you only have to ask.

South Americans rate the impossibly sweet soft drink Antartica Guar-rana (£1.40) very highly. "Just like the guarana powder you can get in the chemist's shop", they insist. If that doesn't appeal, house wines start at a reasonable £8.90 a bottle. And, as you would expect of a Brazilian establishment, the coffee is good.

Rôtisserie Jules

133a Notting Hill Gate W11 ☎ 0171 221 3331	⊖ Notting Hill Gate
Mon–Sat noon–11.30pm; Sun noon–10.30pm	All major credit cards

This rôtisserie is one of three set up by the eponymous Jules – the others being at 6 Bute Street SW7 and 338 King's Road SW3 – and they are all admirably consistent: comfortable modern dining rooms with the kitchen open and on show, and always the rôtisserie as star. They operate a free delivery service, too, and have a constant stream of people calling in for meals to take home, but somehow they manage to avoid the atmosphere of eating in a take-away. Rôtisserie Jules make the proud claim on the menu that except for the bread and ice cream, everything is prepared on the premises from scratch and without using frozen food. It seems believable.

There is no evidence of wild flights of fancy on the starters menu: soup of the day (£2.75); corn on the cob (£2.50); Caesar salad (£2.50) – mysteriously without anchovies. All are sound enough. But you are probably here for the chicken. Careful timing is the key and the best time to visit is plumb in the middle of service when things are at their busiest. That way you'll get your chicken fresh roast and hot off the spit. There is nothing nicer. The chickens weigh about 3lb. and the pricing is complex: chicken (leg and thigh) with one side dish is £4.75, with two side dishes £6.25; chicken (breast and wing) with one side dish is £5.95, with two side dishes £7.50; chicken with one side dish £6.95, two side dishes £8.50, or chicken with two side dishes to share between two people £9.75. A whole chicken, on its own, is £9.75. Confused? Don't worry – the key factor is sound food at reasonable prices. The side dishes range from gratin Dauphinois, to ratatouille and rather good French fries. Puddings are nondescript, but a pint of Ben & Jerry's ice cream is a welcome option (£4.95).

One non-chicken menu item appeals greatly – given an hours' notice you can have a "small" (3lb – £19.50) or "large" (5lb – £27) leg of lamb cooked on the rôtisserie. Just the thing to share with friends.

Woz

46 Golborne Rd, W10 ☎ 0181 968 2200   ⊖ Ladbroke Grove/Westbourne Park

Mon 7–11pm, Tues–Sat noon–4pm & 7–11pm,

Sun noon–4pm   Amex, Mastercard, Visa

Woz – one of Anthony Worrall-Thompson's more recent ventures – is really two restaurants in one. At lunch it does an à la carte menu which changes daily, plus a set lunch for a wholly reasonable £9.95. In the evening there is a no choice, multi course, Mediterranean-style meal the price of which ranges from £23.45 for three courses to £26.45 for five. Several things about these dinners are noteworthy. The food is fresh, unfussy, and well cooked, and the atmosphere is informal – a platter is put on the table and your party help themselves. A mild bout of interrogation when you book means that allergies and most fads can be catered for and that no-one faces a meal they cannot eat. There is a glorious and welcoming informality about this. Take a large party and revel in it all.

The set lunch for £9.95 is subject to the whims of the chef and vagaries of the market. For your two courses you could choose rocket and parmesan salad, followed by cod wrapped in pancetta with slow cooked courgettes – that would certainly appeal after a hard morning on the Portobello Road. But it is the set dinners that are the most fun. Obviously you don't know beforehand just what you are going to get, but how does this sound? Start with six antipasti – fresh borlotti beans and goat's cheese salad, marinated bocconcini with balsamic and sweet onion chutney, salami and San Daniele proscuitto with fine green beans, pan-fried calves' liver with balsamic and red onion, sweetcorn fritters, carrot and pine-nut rolls with aubergine puree. Then a course of fresh egg tagliatelle with Napoli piccante. Then pan-fried guineafowl stuffed with foie gras and served with green polenta and sausages. Move on to a cheese intermission – perhaps Cashel blue with tomato and sultana marmalade and garlic and black pepper crackers. And round off with a pudding of, say, fresh apple tarte with Calvados and clotted cream.

Woz should be congratulated that the fixed price menus includes bread, olives, mineral water and coffee. Except for the wine bill, each diner knows exactly what they're in for.

Putney

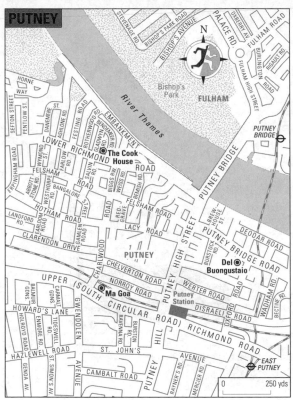

PUTNEY

PALACE RD
OXBERRY AV
FULHAM ROAD
BURLINGTON
RIGAULT RD
FULHAM HIGH STREET
FULHAM ROAD
BISHOP'S PARK ROAD
STEVENAGE RD

N

Bishop's
Park

FULHAM

HORNE
WAY

River Thames

SEFTON STREET
PENTLOW ST

HORNE
WAY

DANEMERE ST.
ASHLONE RD.
FESTING ROAD
GLADWYN RD
BENDEMEER RD
EMBANKMENT

PUTNEY
BRIDGE

LOWER   RICHMOND   ROAD

● **The Cook House**

WYMOND
FELSHAM RD.
EPPINGHAM ROAD
ABBOTT
STONE RD.
WESTHORPE RD.
BANGALORE
FARLOW
SALVIN RD.
BIGGS AV
WEISS RD
BEMISH RD.
BRIDGE
ERNE
GRAVE

PUTNEY BRIDGE

BREW-
HOUSE ST.

ROAD

FELSHAM   ROAD

PUTNEY   BRIDGE   ROAD

DEODAR ROAD

HOTHAM   ROAD
LANDFORD
RD.
EARLDOM
GAMLEN RD
CHARLWOOD
ROAD
LACY   ROAD

CLARENDON   DRIVE

PUTNEY

CHELVERTON   ROAD

BURSTOCK
RD

● **Del
Buongustaio**

RD

WADHAM RD
BECTIVE RD.

UPPER   (SOUTH

NORROY   ROAD

● **Ma Goa**

PUTNEY   HIGH   STREET

WERTER   ROAD

OXFORD   ROAD

HOWARD'S LANE
BALMUIR
GDNS
CARMALT
GDNS
ENMORE RD.
TIDESWELL
RD.
HOLROYD ROAD
RAVENNA RD.
BURSTON
RD.
Putney
Station

DISRAELI

CIRCULAR   ROAD)

RICHMOND   ROAD

GWENDOLEN

HAZLEWELL   ROAD
GENOA AV
ST. SIMON'S AV.
ST. JOHN'S

AVENUE
PUTNEY   HILL

CAMBALT   ROAD
RAYNER'S RD.
MERCIER RD.

AVENUE

EAST
PUTNEY

0   250 yds

© Crown copyright

424

Del Buongustaio

283 Putney Bridge Road, SW15 ☎ 0181 780 9361	⊖ East Putney
Mon–Fri noon–3pm & 6.30–11.30pm, Sat 6.30–11.30pm, Sun 12.30–3.30pm	
& 6.30–10.30pm (closed Sun June–Aug)	Amex, Mastercard, Visa

On the first day of each month it's "all-change" as Del Buongustaio unleashes a new menu on the appreciative residents of Putney. The menu here features well-cooked, authentic food, with a sprinkling of less familiar dishes from the Cinderella regions like Puglia and Piedmont, as well as some painstakingly-researched gems that once graced tables in Renaissance Italy. The dining room is light and airy and pleasantly informal. The cooking is good, with authentic dishes and friendly service. Take time to study the wine list which is particularly strong on classy bottles from the less-well-known Provinces.

Who knows what the next menu will bring? But you can hazard a guess that there will be interesting pasta dishes. Such as a splendid spaghetti integrale alle vongole (£5.50 starter, £7.50 main) – wholewheat spaghetti with fresh clams, chillies and spring onions. Or perhaps girello rustica con rucola, spinaci e provola affumicato (£7.50), made from pasta sheets rolled around a mixture of spinach, rocket, and cheese, and served with a chunky sauce made from chopped tomatoes and basil. Thoroughly delicious. The piatto pizzicarello (£6.50), described with disarming modesty as a "plate of savouries", is a regular starter option. And then there is the torta rinacimenttale di fave, ricotta e prosciutto (£4.95 starter, £7.50 main) – an amazing multi-layered cake of broad beans, prosciutto, ricotta and fontina cheese which comes with a rocket and egg sauce. Main course dishes may include lamb, sea bass, veal, pork, chicken, guinea fowl, cod, or a Swiss chard and ricotta pudding. Involtini di lonzo con gnocchi di polenta (£8.90) is a typical offering – medallions of pork tenderloin wrapped in pancetta and then served with polenta dumplings. Look out for the "dal campo" side dishes, particularly the puré di patate alla parmigiana (£2.20), silky mashed potato with Parmesan cheese.

There are eleven splendid pudding wines by the glass – including Vin Santo 1994 (£4.25); the befuddlingly alcoholic Aleatico di Puglia (£3.75); and a 1991 Recioto de Valpolicella (£3.75). There is also a huge selection of merciless grappas.

PUTNEY ⓥ MODERN EUROPEAN

The Cook House

56 Lower Richmond Rd, SW15 ☎ 0181 785 2300   ⊖ Putney Bridge

Tues–Sat 7–11pm   Mastercard, Visa

The Cook House is an odd sort of neighbourhood restaurant. It doesn't do lunch, doesn't open on Sundays – or Mondays – and its prices are high, for dishes and even for opening bottles (it's unlicensed – but charges a rather rapacious £2.50 per person corkage). Nonetheless, the food is very good, the service is friendly, and it delivers consistently if its popularity is anything to go by. You will certainly need to book ahead for space is at a premium. This is a small dining room and even the tables are small – side plates simply wouldn't fit – while the menu is scribbled on perspex above the tiny, open plan kitchen.

The short menu is well thought-out and changes monthly. This makes the most of seasonal ingredients and gives rein to flights of fancy emanating from the kitchen. Some of these are more successful than others but the overall result is an exotic and interesting fusion food – feta cheese and raita jostling cheek by jowl. Starters are generally priced between £5 and £7 and may include carpaccio of scallops with an Orientally influenced sauce such as sesame and ginger; or calf's liver with salty lardons on crisp mushroom bruschetta. Amongst the main courses there's usually a vegetarian option such as aubergine and feta filo parcels with raita (£9.95). Fish is accurately cooked and there's no nervousness about combining bold and strong flavours as when skate is paired with capers and garlic (£12.75). A similar deftness of touch applies to meat dishes such as the warm salad of duck which is sharpened with lime vinaigrette (£12.95). Puddings keep pace, which they should do at £4.75 each. Choice is limited but you'll find delicate and rich options such as poached nectarines with hazelnut ice-cream or a wickedly indulgent chocolate pot with raspberries and cream which would be more accurately described as a deliciously heavy truffle pot.

Be warned: due to its popularity with the local riverside set, and its meagre number of seats, the Cook House really packs them in on Saturday nights, and sometimes manages up to three sittings. This can put as much pressure on the diner as it does on the kitchen.

WEST

Ma Goa

244 Upper Richmond Rd, SW15 ☎ 0181 780 1767   BR: Putney   ⊖ East Putney

Mon–Tues 6.30–11pm, Wed–Fri 12.30–2.30pm & 6.30–11pm

Sat 6.30–11pm, Sun 12.30–3pm   All major credit cards

Despite the stylish ochre interior, complete with fans and blonde wooden floor, despite the café style chairs and tables, and the computer system to handle bills and orders, the overwhelming impression you are left with when you visit Ma Goa is of eating in somebody's home. Inspired home cooking helps. All the staff being related helps. This place is as far as you can possibly get from the chuck-it-in-a-frying-pan and heat it through school of curry cookery. And it is authentically Goan into the bargain. The food is deceptively simple, slow cooked, and awesomely tasty.

The menu is fairly compact: half a dozen starters are followed by a dozen mains, while a blackboard adds a couple of dishes of the day. Stuffed papards – papards are jolly close to pappadoms – are served as a parcel, papard wrapping spiced potatoes (£3.75). Shrimp balchao, is made from small sweet shrimps in a sauce made with achar or pickle, it's been tamed a bit for London palates but is still tasty (£4.00). The Goan sausage is, well, a sausage . . . rich with palm vinegar, cinnamon, and green chillies (£3.95). All starters come with pitta bread. Main courses are amazing. The spices properly cooked out by long-cooking which makes lifting the lids of the heavy clay serving pots a voyage of discovery. Porco vindaloo (£7.00) is sharp with palm vinegar, and enriched with lumps of pork complete with rind. Gallina achari (£7.15) is, on the face of it, a simple dish. A chicken is chopped up, marinated, and then cooked with ginger, tomatoes, garlic and chillies. What is different, is that the chicken is left on the bone, enriching the dish with its juices as it cooks slowly. Delciious. And veggies are equally well served. The vegetarian platter (£7.00) is a wonderful assortment of vegetable dishes with bread or rice and dhall. The rice here is excellent.

On the specials board you might be lucky enough to find lamb kodi (£7.25), described as "lamb with cloves, garlic, and chilli" and a long list of other ingredients; on the electronic message winging its way to the kitchen it's called Bella's lamb – dishes here really are made from family recipes.

WEST

Richmond
& Twickenham

RICHMOND & TWICKENHAM

The White Horse

Richmond Station

RICHMOND

Richmond Green
THE

Chez Lindsay

PETERSHAM ROAD

Marble Hill Park

River Thames

Cambridge Park

TWICKENHAM

ST MARGARETS ROAD

St Margarets Station

Twickenham Station

Pallavi

McClements

Twickenham R.U. Football Ground

LONDON ROAD

CHERTSEY ROAD

500 yds

Richmond Park

© Crown copyright

Chez Lindsay

11 Hill Rise Richmond Surrey ☎ 0181 948 7473 | ⊖ Richmond

Mon–Sat 11am–11pm, Sun, noon–10pm | Mastercard, Visa

At first glance Chez Lindsay looks rather like a movie of Chicago in the twenties – all around you people are drinking alcohol out of large earthenware teacups. The cups are in fact traditional Breton drinking vessels known as "bolées", the drink is cider, and Chez Lindsay lists a trio of them, ranging from Breton brut traditionnel to Norman cidre bouché. This small, bright restaurant has had a loyal local following for a good many years, attracted by the galettes and crêpes, though the menu has now expanded to include a regularly changing list of hearty provincial dishes – especially fish. It's a place for Francophiles: both the kitchen and the front of house seem to be staffed entirely by Gauls, and in this instance that means good service and tasty food.

Start with palourdes farcies (£5.95) – nine small clams are given the "snail butter" treatment, lots of garlic. Or the bavarois de saumon (£3.95) – a slice of light salmon mousse on a fine tomato coulis. There are also traditional and simple starters like artichaut a la vinaigrette (£3.95). Then you must decide between the galettes or more formal main courses. The galettes are huge buckwheat pancakes, large and lacy, thin but satisfying. They come with an array of fillings: egg, cheese and ham (£5.30); scallops and leeks (£7.95); Roquefort cheese, celery and walnuts (£5.95); and "Saisonniere" (£7.95) – egg, artichoke heart, mushrooms and lardons. The other half of the menu is very Breton, featuring a good steak frites (£12.75) and lots of fish and shellfish. The cotriade du Belon (£13.75) is an interesting dish: at the bottom of a soup plate is a pile of potato slices cooked in a saffron fish stock, while piled on top are some seriously meaty chunks of fresh halibut, cockles, queen scallops, shrimps and a large langoustine. Very good indeed. Ask the amiable staff about off-menu goodies, which depending on the market might be anything from exotic fish to roast grouse.

It takes a real pud enthusiast to opt for "chocolate and banana crepe" (£3.95) topped with a scoop of "gin and lavender ice cream" (£1.30), a bizarre combination which turns out strangely delicious.

WEST

McClements

2 Whitton Rd, Twickenham, Middlesex ☎ 0181 744 9610	BR: Twickenham
Mon–Sat noon–2pm & 7–10pm	All major credit cards

McClements is a small, comfortable restaurant whose menu runs through all sorts of luxury ingredients. It also makes something of a feature of set menus which combine a procession of dishes with matched glasses of wine. The decor and service, like the cooking, are very civilised and a strong local following seems very happy to use McClements for all those birthday and anniversary treats rather than make the voyage in to the West End. The cooking is trad French and rich, generally of a high standard, with elegant presentation and plenty of sightings of offal – up to and including the ubiquitous pig's trotter.

The menu changes periodically but starters may be seabass served with roast lobster and caviar beurre blanc (£8); or warm potato tart topped with smoked salmon, crème fraîche and caviar (£7) which takes the tried and tested "blinis" combination up a knotch. The "mixed hors d'oeuvres" (£9.50) provides a pixy portion of six starters presented on the plate with considerable élan. The main courses follow the litany of turbot-steak-lamb-duck-monkfish and just when you feel cosy . . . wham, there's cassoulet, or a pig's trotter with a lump of sweetbread, or a rather good osso bucco. All the main courses are priced between £14 and £15. to follow, the plate of six little puddings (£4.50) is obviously such a hit that it has driven everything else off the dessert menu except the hot soufflé with Calvados sauce, and the selection of mature French cheeses. All desserts cost £4.50.

The set menus operate from Monday to Friday – £23 gets you a glass of champagne with canapés, a choice of three starters with a glass of Chablis, of four mains with a glass of claret, and pudding. Or for £38 you could have a 6-course menu including a wine with each course. Both are good value. The meals start with an amuse gueule – actually four different ones – three canapés and a tablespoonful of rich lobster bisque in a coffee cup – and wind their way through to a giant plate of petit fours.

Pallavi

49 King Street Parade, Twickenham, Middlesex ☎ 0181 892 2345	BR: Twickenham
Daily noon–11pm	Cash only

This is a small outpost of an Indian restaurant empire which also includes Malabar Junction (see Bloomsbury) and Sree Krishna (see Tooting), an impressive pedigree. Pallavi is the simplest and the cheapest of the three featuring a large take-away counter and in front of it just 22 seats. The bright lighting may do wonders for the take-away trade but as you look out onto busy Twickenham it's hard to forget that this is not a gold fish bowl and that all the passers-by are not fascinated by your antics. The cooking, however, deserves the ultimate compliment – it is home style. Unpretentious dishes and unpretentious prices. True to its South Indian roots there is an impressive list of vegetarian specialities but there are enough meat and fish dishes to woo the public at large.

Start with that South Indian veggie favourite masala dosa (£2.50) – the huge, crisp, pancake is made with a mixture of ground rice and lentil flour and is a perfect match for the savoury potato mixture and chutney. There's also a meat masala dosa (£2.90), described on the menu as a "non-vegetarian pancake delicacy" – full marks for accuracy there. Or try the delightfully named iddly (£2.50) – this is a steamed rice cake made with black gram. Whatever you open with, have some cashew nut pakoda (£1.50), which is a kind of savoury peanut brittle made with cashew nuts and wholly delicious. The main dishes are simple and tasty, and are served without fuss. For unrepentant carnivores – chicken Malabar (£3.30); meat methi (£3.30); or chilli chicken (£6) all hit the spot. But it is the vegetarian dishes that are most interesting. Parippu curry (£1.85) – "split lentils with cumin, turmeric, garlic, chillies and onions"; kalan (£1.85) – "a traditional sweet and sour dish of mango, yam, coconut and spices"; cabbage thoran (£1.85) – "sliced cabbage with carrots, green chillies and curry leaves". The pilau rice, lemon rice, and coconut rice (all £1.65) are good, too. The parathas are even better. Try a green chilli or a sweet coconut paratha (both £1.55).

Pallavi is unlicensed, so you can either drink lassi (£1) or bring your own bottles of wine or beer.

£8–£12

The White Horse

Worple Way, Richmond, Surrey ☎ 0181 940 2418	⊖ Richmond
Mon–Sat noon–3pm & 6.30–10pm, Sun noon–4pm	Amex, Mastercard, Visa

All over town brave entrepreneurs are taking pubs away from the traditional breweries and transforming them into gold mines, but in this instance Fuller's brewery can be congratulated for encouraging quality themselves. The White Horse is a dark, Spartan, bar-restaurant with good large tables that are well-spread out – no sitting in your neighbour's pocket here. The food and pricing is also spot on, as is confirmed by a steady trade and a note on the menu saying "we are now taking bookings for both lunch and early evening meals".

The menu is a short one, and all the better for it – five starters and five main courses which change to accommodate whatever is best from the market. There might be a rocket salad with tomato and buffalo mozzarella crostini (£4.50) – a perky rocket salad is topped with a melted and gooey cheese and tomato on toast. Or a rich asparagus soup (£3.50) with cheesey croutons and chunks of fresh asparagus. Or salt cod fritters with rouille (£4.50). Or potato gnocchi Bolognaise (£4.50). Main courses are also simple and well executed, like an Angus rib steak with chips and béarnaise (£9.75) – great chips. Or fillet of mackerel, charred leek and potato salad horseradish cream (£7) – fresh fish, well cooked and well presented. Or a risotto (£6.75), perhaps with wild mushrooms shaved parmesan and truffle oil, or asparagus with rocket and parmesan. The wine list is wide ranging and tops out at £22 for a smart American Pinot Noir. What's more there is the intelligent option of a 250ml glassful of a dozen different wines (from £3.20 to £3.70).

The last item on the White Horse dessert section is "Vivian's cheeses with wheat wafers" (£4). The cheese in question has made the short journey from Vivian Martin's superb delicatessen a few doors down the road – call in there for all manner of goodies including top olive oils on draught. The cheeseboard here proves how much more satisfying it is to sample two or three cheeses in perfect condition than to be faced with a huge selection of the unripe and over-ripe.

Shepherd's Bush
& Olympia

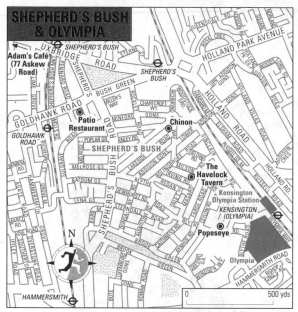

SHEPHERD'S BUSH
& OLYMPIA

Adam's Café
(77 Askew
Road)

SHEPHERD'S BUSH

SHEPHERD'S BUSH

Patio
Restaurant

Chinon

GOLDHAWK ROAD

GOLDHAWK
ROAD

SHEPHERD'S BUSH

The
Havelock
Tavern

Kensington
Olympia Station

KENSINGTON
(OLYMPIA)

Popeseye

N

HAMMERSMITH

Olympia

HAMMERSMITH ROAD

0   500 yds

© Crown copyright

Adam's Café

77 Askew Road, W12 ☎ 0181 743 0572)	⊖ Ravenscourt Park
Restaurant open daily 7–11pm	All major credit cards

Frances and Abdel Boukraa live a dual life. Each morning they run a respectable workers' cafe and every evening they transform it into a North African restaurant. Bacon and eggs in the morning; fish, grills, couscous and tagines in the evening. The kitchen here is run by a Tunisian chef with a Moroccan assistant so there are all manner of North African delicacies on offer – while the easy-going prices reflect the café heritage. You pick between three menus: rapide (£9.95 for a main course or two starters and mint tea or coffee); gourmet (£12.95 for main course and starter or dessert); or gastronomique (£14.95 for starter, main course and dessert). All exclude service, which you'll certainly want to reward. House wines start at £7.50 or you can bring your own (£1.50 corkage).

The Tunisian for ameuse-guele is kemia – complementary saucers of wonderful home-made pickles and small meatballs and harissa which arrive with the bread. As well as good home-made soups (fish or the Moroccan spicy chickpea harira), you'll find that the starters are dominated by "briks" and "ojjas". Briks are deep-fried filo parcels filled with egg and herbs, egg and tuna, or peppers, mushrooms and potatoes. Ojjas are even more delicious. They come about when a pan of scrambled egg runs headlong into a pan of ratatouille: they come with either merguez – a spicy sausage – or shrimps. There are also briwattes – filo parcels with seafood. For a main course you choose between grills (mostly brochettes – kebabs), couscous and tajine. The couscous arrives, as it should, with a tureen of vegetables in sauce and a choice of meats (or veg). If you like a little fire, mix some of the red hot chilli sludge – harissa – into a spoonful of the sauce and pour it over the couscous. Tagines hail from Morocco and are casseroles cooked and served in the eponymous pot with a conical lid: try the chicken with classic preserved Moroccan lemons. For puddings put your faith in the Moroccan lady who is assistant chef and produces brilliant almond and lemon tarts.

Beware of the Tunisian digestifs on offer. Thibarine is an aromatic liqueur made from dates which tastes of mothballs, while Boukha is an eau de vie made from figs which is faintly reminiscent of petrol.

Chinon

23 Richmond Way, W14 ☎ 0171 602 4082	⊖ Shepherd's Bush
Mon–Thurs 7–10.30pm, Fri & Sat 7–11pm	All credit cards except Diners

At first glance you might reckon this small establishment hidden behind Shepherd's Bush roundabout a good neighbourhood restaurant. But it is actually far better than that: the cooking, which has its roots in France, is very accomplished indeed. The chef is clearly meticulous, preparing superb sauces and delivering dishes that tend to include a good many little parcels. Mashed potato comes parcelled up in a cabbage leaf; chopped cabbage and bacon comes in ... a cabbage leaf; a plate with four distinct packages is the order of the day. There are few better places to dine when all is cold and damp – you'll be rewarded with rich satisfying flavours and seriously large portions. What's more there are two set menus offering three courses – at a reasonable £15 and £20.

The bread here is usually met with gasps of pleasure – wonderful, warm hunks with chewy crust and slightly sweet crumb; then there's the butter – large lumps of it. You have to be peculiarly strong-willed not to wipe out your appetite before the starters make an appearance. The menus change regularly but look out for ravioli of fresh crab with butter sauce and roast cherry tomatoes (£9) – a mound of fresh crab and crisp leeks parcelled up in delicate pasta, delicious. Or there may be smoked eel, quail eggs, and horseradish cream (£8) – simple ingredients put together well. For mains try the breast of duck with purée of Swede, and Savoy cabbage cooked with smoked bacon (£15.50) – a full complement of parcels, but stunning flavours too. Or there's a fine rack of lamb with a garlic cream sauce and ratatouille (£17).

If you are eating à la carte, forswear the desserts and opt for the plate of petits four (for two, £4). This brings half a dozen very, very good mouthfuls: a tiny lemon tart; a little raspberry barquette; a brandysnap cone filled with cream. Perfection. Great value. And about all you can fit in after that early assault on the bread.

The Havelock Tavern

57 Masbro Rd, W14 ☎ 0171 603 5374	⊖ Kensington Olympia

Food served Mon–Sat 12.30–2.30pm & 7–10pm,

Sun 12.30–3pm & 7–9.50pm | Cash or cheque only

The Havelock is one of those pubs marooned within a sea of houses, in this instance the sea of houses just behind Olympia. It's a real pub, with a sound range of beers as well as an extensive wine list. What is most attractive, though, is the attitude that lies behind the menu which is chalked up daily on the blackboard. As the chef-half of the proprietorial partnership says, "We're in the business of feeding people". And that's just what they do, serving up seasonal, unfussy food – the kind of fresh, interesting wholesome stuff you wish that you could get around to cooking for yourself. There's seating for 75 in the bar and during the summer there's a terrific garden complete with vines and a pergola. Service revolves around stepping up to the bar and ordering what you want, so there's no service charge to bump up what are very reasonable prices indeed.

The menu is different every session but at lunch there are more "one-hit" dishes as most of the customers are pressed for time. Starters might be vegetable and white bean soup with harissa (£3.50); salt cod and smoked haddock fritters, tartare sauce and lemon (£4.50); or chicken galantine, toast and chutney (£5). Main courses range from penne with spicy sausage and tomato sauce with Parmesan (£7), to monkfish saltimbocca with spinach, garlic and olive oil mash (£9). The lunch menu might feature a plate of Italian salami, Parma ham, olives and pickles (£6), or a pan-fried leek and goats' cheese risotto cake stuffed with buffalo mozzarella, rocket and baked tomatoes (£5.50). For dinner you may find a chargrilled rib-eye steak, blue cheese butter, chips and salad (£10) that has grown out of lunchtime's rib-eye steak sandwich, horseradish, mustard chips and salad (£7.50). Puddings are equally reliable – pear and apple crumble with custard (£4).

A great deal of effort goes into selecting slightly unusual, and often bargain, wines for the blackboard wine list . . . but the biggest seller is still "A glass of red".

£10–£25

Patio

5 Goldhawk Road, W12 ☎ 0181 743 5194   ⊖ Goldhawk Road / Shepherd's Bush

Mon–Fri noon–3pm & 6pm–midnight, Sat & Sun 6pm–midnight   All major credit cards

The ebullient Eva Michalik (a former opera singer) and her husband Kaz have been running this Shepherd's Bush institution for over a decade, and it's not hard to see why the show keeps on running. What you get at Patio is good, solid Polish food in a friendly, comfortable atmosphere – for a relatively small amount of money. This little restaurant is a people-pleaser; you can just as easily come here for an intimate tête-a-tête as for a raucous birthday dinner. The food is always reliable and sometimes it's really excellent. There are two floors; downstairs feels a little cosier and more secluded.

The set menu (available at lunch and dinner) is Patio's big draw card. For £9.90 you get a starter, main course, pudding, and a vodka. The menu changes daily – ask Eva to tell you what's new in the kitchen and you could get something that's not yet listed – and a dozen or so starter and main course choices are available on the set menu. The starters include blinis with smoked salmon (the blinis are plump and tasty); wild mushroom soup; Polish ham with beetroot horseradish; and herrings with soured cream. Everything is fresh and carefully prepared. For mains, there's a good selection of meat, fish and chicken dishes – the scallops in dill sauce, when available, are outstanding. Or you might try a Polish speciality such as golobki (cabbage stuffed with rice and meat); or chicken Walewska (chicken breast in fresh red pepper sauce); or sausages á la Zamoyski (grilled sausages with sautéed mushrooms and onions). Main dishes come with a hearty selection of vegetables – roast potatoes, broccoli, red cabbage. Be prepared, too, for high octane puds, such as the Polish pancakes with cheese, vanilla and rum – the fumes alone are enough to send you reeling. Also good are the walnut gateau, and the hot apple charlotka with cream. For those after more variety, including a scattering of non-Polish dishes, the à la carte offers further choice, and for not a great deal more.

Patio is a good night out. The piano crammed in near the entrance is often put to use by a regular customer, and there are frequent sightings of a roving gypsy quartet.

£12–£45

The Popeseye

108 Blythe Rd, W14 ☎ 0171 610 4578	⊖ Hammersmith.
Mon–Sat 6.45–10.30pm	Cash or cheque only

Just suppose you fancy a steak. A good steak, and perhaps a glass (or bottle) of red wine to go with it. You're interested enough to want the best steak, probably Aberdeen Angus, and you want it cooked simply. The Popeseye is for you. In Scotland rump steak is known as the Popeseye, and that is why this quirky restaurant is called what it is. Every week the proprietor buys in his meat . . . not from Smithfield or a catering butcher, but from the small butcher his family use in the North of Scotland. The meat is Aberdeen Angus and the restaurant is a member of the Aberdeen Angus Society. The dining room is small, things tend to be chaotic, and the atmosphere is occasionally pretty smoky. As to the food, there is no choice: just various kinds of steak and good chips, with home-made puddings to follow. Oh, and the menu starts with the wine list. You choose your drink and only when that's settled do you choose your steak – specifying, of course, the cut, how big it will be (and they come very big here), and how you want it cooked. The formula is now repeated at a second Popeseye, 227 Upper Richmond Rd, SW15 ☎ 0181 788 7733.

Now about these steaks. Popeseye comes in 6oz, 8oz, 12oz, and 20oz (at £7.95; £9.95; £13.95; and £17.95). Sirloin also comes in 6oz, 8oz, 12oz, and 20oz (at £9.95; £12.95; £16.50; and £20.95). Fillet also comes in 6oz, 8oz, 12oz, and 20oz (at £11.95; £15.50; £18.95; and £27.95). All prices include excellent chips and a side salad is an extra £2.95. All the puddings are priced at £3.50 and come from the "home-made" school of patisserie – such delights as apple crumble, sticky toffee pudding, and lemon tart.

The wine list is an ever-changing reflection of what can be picked up at the sales and represents good value. There are eighteen clarets, half a dozen wines from Burgundy, others picked from the Rhone, Spain and Argentina – and there are also two white wines on offer for people who have lost the plot. Ask advice. People have been seen here happily drinking Chateau Palmer 1987 for £53 a bottle, which despite being a tidy sum is also a bargain.

Southall

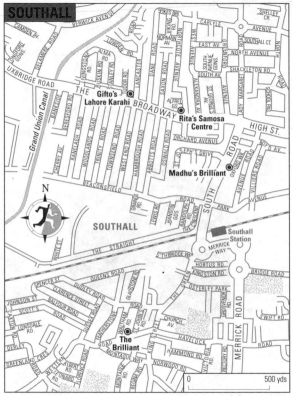

SOUTHALL

SHELLEY CR.
CAMDEN AV.
BERWICK AVENUE
SOKES BRI
VIKING RD
CARLYLE
AVENUE
SOUTHALL CT.
LONGHURST GDNS
DELAMERE ROAD
NORTHCOTE AVENUE
NORMAN AV.
EAST AV.
GRESHAM RD
NORTH AVENUE
SHACKLETON RD
TOWER RD
ALMA RD
RUSKIN RD
STANLEY RD
LANGSTONE RD
LANCASTER
DANE ROAD
SAXON ROAD
SOUTH AVENUE GDNS
SOUTH AV.
ST GEORGES AV.
LADY MARGARET RD
YORK AV.
Uxbridge Road
UXBRIDGE ROAD
THE
Gifto's
Lahore Karahi
BROADWAY
ALFRED
RD
ALEXANDRA AVENUE
HIGH ST.
Grand Union Canal
BANKSIDE
BERESFORD ROAD
RANLAGH ROAD
WOODLANDS ROAD
TRINITY ROAD
TOWNSEND ROAD
WEST END ROAD
HAMBROUGH ROAD
ABBOTS ROAD
Rita's Samosa
Centre
ORCHARD AVENUE
OSWALD ROAD
ST JOSEPH'S DRIVE
BOYD AV.
OXFORD AV.
CHERRY AV.
Madhu's Brilliant
BEACONSFIELD
ROAD
SOUTH ROAD
VILLIERS ROAD
AVENUE
N
GRANGE RD
LEWIS RD
HANSON GDNS
HARTINGTON ROAD
PARK
THE CRESCENT
AVENUE
SOUTHALL
WHITE ST.
THE STRAIGHT
Southall
Station
MERRICK
WAY
STH BRIDGE WAY
HORTUS RD.
QUEENS ROAD
KINGSTON RD.
BRIDGE ROAD
SPENCER ST.
DUDLEY ROAD
GLADSTONE RD
OSTERLEY PARK
CLARENCE STREET
THE GREEN
GROSVENOR RD.
MERRICK
ROAD
JOHNSON ST
BALFOUR ROAD
RUSSELL ROAD
JOHN'S RD
SCOTT'S
ROAD
WALTHAM ROAD
CHURCH AV.
HAVELOCK ROAD
SWIFT RD.
LONSDALE
RD.
DERLEY
RD.
LEATHERSTONE ROAD
The
Brilliant
HAMMOND RD S.
VICTORIA RD
RECTORY RD.
GREENLAND CRES.
WESTERN ALBERT RD.
LEONARD RD.
MONTAGUE WAY
MONTAGUE RD.
REGINA RD.
NORWOOD RD.

0   500 yds

© Crown copyright

WEST

444

The Brilliant

SOUTHALL ⑩ INDIAN

72–74 Western Road, Southall, Middlesex ☎ 0181 574 1928 | BR: Southall

Tues–Fri noon–2.30pm Tues–Sun 6pm–midnight | All major credit cards

The Brilliant is a Southall institution. For over 20 years the Anand family business has been a non-stop success, and for twenty five years before that the family's first restaurant – also called the Brilliant – was the toast of Kenya. The food at the Brilliant is East-African/Asian and very good indeed. D.K. Anand (known as Gulu) rules the kitchen with a rod of iron and, to quote him, "there's no frying-pan cookery here". A relatively small number of dishes are freshly cooked in bulk and if a curry needs to be simmered for three hours then that's what happens. The resulting sauces are incredibly rich and satisfying – and yet Gulu won't countenance any cream, yoghurt, nuts, or dried fruit.

To start with, you must try the butter chicken (£6 a half, £12 full). A half portion will do for two people as a starter. This dish is an enigma, somehow it manages to taste more buttery than butter itself – really delicious. There's also jeera chicken (£6 & £12), rich with cumin and black pepper. And chilli chicken (£7 & £14), which is very hot. If you're in a party, move on to the special meals section – these come in two portion sizes, suggested for three people and five people. Methi chicken, (£13.50 & £25); masaladar lamb, (£13 & £26); and palak chicken (£14 & £26) are all winners. Alternatively, choose from among the single portion curries – which include masala talapia (£6), a fish-curry of unimaginable richness with good firm chunks of boneless fish. Well-cooked basmati rice is £1.50, and as well as good rotis (50p) the breads list hides a secret weapon – the kulchay (50p). This is a fried, white-dough bread, for all the world like a very flat doughnut. Hot from the kitchen they are amazing – it's best to order a succession so that they don't go cold.

Ask to try Gulu's pickles – carrot pickle, a sharp mango pickle and a hot lime pickle. They are splendid. Also try the Kenyan beers – Tusker (with its label rather engagingly designed like a bank note) and the slightly weaker Whitecap beer. Unfortunately neither cuts much ice with the chilli chicken!

WEST

Gifto's Lahore Karahi

162–164 The Broadway, Southall, Middlesex ☎ 0181 813 8669   BR: Southall

Mon–Thurs noon–11.30pm, Fri–Sun noon–midnight   All major credit cards

In Southall they know a good thing when they taste it. Gifto's Lahore Karahi specialises in freshly-grilled, well-spiced meats and exceptionally good breads, backed up by a few curries, and one or two odd dishes from Lahore. They do these superbly well and consistently. No money has been wasted on decor and certainly none is wasted on frills. Cafe tables are lit by chandeliers mind boggling enough to give the design-aware nightmares. Plates are heavy. A row of grinning chefs seem to juggle with the three-foot skewers as meat goes into the tandoor caked in a secret marinade and comes out perfectly cooked and delicious. Despite having 85 seats downstairs and over a hundred upstairs there is a still a queue outside at the weekend.

Whatever else you order, you need some bread. Peshwari naan (£1.20) is a triumph, hot from the oven, flavoured with garlic and fresh herbs, liberally slathered with ghee and sesame seeds . . . it's hard to imagine it bettered. To accompany it, you might start with an order of chicken tikka (£2.90), which is juicy and strongly spiced. Or go straight for a portion of five lamb chops, encrusted in tandoori pastes and grilled until crisp (£4.40). Or try pomperet fish from the tandoor – a worthwhile extravagance at £6.60. Curries include saag gosht – a dark green velvety spinach base with chunks of lamb (£4.20) – and, more unusually, batera curry (quail – £5.20), magaz curry (brains – £5.20), and paya (£5.20) which the menu describes as "lamb trotters in thick gravy" – a gravy created by three hours' cooking in a pot with ginger, onions, and garlic. Specialists only, perhaps. But the side dishes should tempt all-comers, especially the tarka daal (£2.80), which is rich and buttery.

You can specify your seasonings for all the Lahore's dishes – mild, medium or hot. Hot is very hot and will have you calling for a pint of mango shake (£1.80). All drinks at the Lahore are soft, though you can bring your own beer or wine (no corkage).

Madhu's Brilliant

39 South Road, Southall, Middlesex ☎ 0181 574 1897	BR: Southall
Mon–Thurs 12.30–3pm & 6–11.30pm, Fri 12.30–3pm & 6pm–midnight,	
Sat 6pm–midnight, Sun 6–11.30pm	All major credit cards

In the beginning there was the Brilliant Restaurant and Nightclub in Nairobi; then there was the Brilliant Restaurant in Western Road Southall run by the Anand brothers (see p.445), then their nephew Sanjay set up Madhu's Brilliant which is in South Road. These are the dynastic entanglements that set up the continuing debate as to whether the original Brilliant or Madhu's serves the better food. Madhu's is a tad more sophisticated than the Brilliant, with more marble, fancier service, and slightly higher prices. But the East African/Punjabi food served at either is stunningly good and a real eye-opener to those accustomed to more standard curry house fare.

As at the Brilliant, you'll find the Anand family signature dishes here – butter chicken (£6.50 half portion, £12 whole), jeera chicken (flavoured with cumin £6.50 and £12) and chilli chicken (hot as Hades, £7 and £13). Also very good at Madhu's is the masala fried tilapia (£3) – chunks of fresh fish fried in a wonderfully exotic batter. On the chef's speciality list there are some interesting dishes such as boozi bafu (£18.00). This is a cauldron of thin lamb chops, stewed for a long while in an improbably rich curry gravy. It is cooked and served on the bone which means that not only does the sauce improve tenfold, but there are all those delicious bones to suck. Machuzi kumu (full, for up to six people, £30; half, for three people, £16) applies the same principle to chicken. From the single-portion curries list, the chicken curry with methi (£6.50) is well-spiced, and there's a very respectable chicken tikka masala (£6.50) if you're feeling unadventurous. Breads are exemplary, the keema nan (£2.50) being particularly delicious.

Choosing between the Brilliant and Madhu's Brilliant is a challenge. They both have their strengths; they are both streets ahead of your average run-of-the-mill curry house; and they can both be whole-heartedly recommended. Visit both and decide for yourself.

£3–£12

Rita's Samosa Centre

112 The Broadway, Southall, Middlesex ☎ 0181 571 2100   BR: Southall

Open Mon–Sun 11am-10.30pm   Cash and cheques (over £20)

Your first trip to Rita's will be memorable. The TV blares out Indian pro-grammes, the neon strip-lights flicker over the lurid murals, the plastic-covered tables are busy with families eating dinner, teenagers pausing for snacks. Bedlam and mayhem are all around. Both the front windows of the restaurant are fenced off and each has become a sepa-rate little shop, one selling paan leaves with their aromatic fillings for chewing after dinner and the other kebab rolls. If you are a shy, retiring type, this isn't a place for you – indeed you probably won't get served. To eat here you must go up to the counter where all the dishes are set out in giant trays, choose your meal, pay, and then seat yourself. The food will eventually arrive. There's no sign of a system but everything seems to turn up in the end.

The dishes are divided into sections – curries, bread and rice, chaats (street food), and snacks. Snacks make good starters, as do chaats. Try an onion bhaji (£1.00) – huge, and opened out flat so that it's all the crisper. Bhel puri (£2.25), alu tikki (£2) and dahi puri (£2.50) are all street food items – tasty and good value. Or how about half a pound of chicken tikka for £3.50? Or a superb fish tikka – also for £3.50 for half a pound. They both eclipse the samosas (40p each) after which this eatery is named. Main course curries are rich and simple. Try lamb (£4.50); or lamb saag (£4.50); or a deadly chilli lamb or chilli chicken (£5.50) – both of which dishes arrive scatter-bombed with halved fresh green chillies.

You can take your own beer or wine to Rita's but it is much more fun exploring the (non-alcholic) drinks section. A pint of salty lassi (£2) is wonderfully cold and pleasantly sharp with a savoury dusting of cumin seed powder. And then there's faluda. Faluda is a very thin, very soft vermicelli which comes in a glass of milk shake. The sensation of these "worms" slithering up the straw and into your mouth is most discon-certing. What's more you can have faluda with a scoop of ice cream in it (£2). What a way to end a meal.

Further West

Acton, Ealing,
Hampton, Hounslow

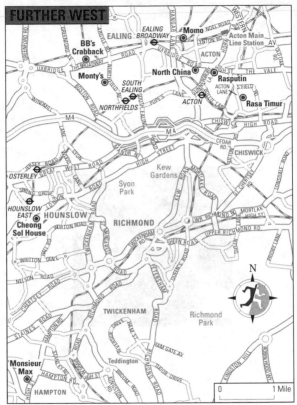

FURTHER WEST

EALING
EALING BROADWAY
Momo
NOEL ROAD
Acton Main Line Station
LYNTON RD
ACTON
BB's Crabback
THE BROADWAY
Monty's
North China
Rasputin
ACTON LANE
S'FIELD
SOUTH EALING
ACTON
Rasa Timur
NORTHFIELDS
CHISWICK HIGH ROAD
M4
CEDAR RD.
CHISWICK
M4
Kew Gardens
OSTERLEY
Syon Park
HOUNSLOW EAST
HOUNSLOW
Cheong Sol House
RICHMOND
NORTON ROAD
WHITTON
NELSON ROAD
TWICKENHAM
Richmond Park
N
Teddington
Monsieur Max
HAMPTON

0   1 Mile

© Crown copyright

WEST

450

BB's Crabback

3 Chignell Place, West Ealing, W13 ☎ 0181 840 8322	⊖ Northfields then bus
Mon–Sat 12.30–2.30pm & 6.30–11.30pm,	
Sun buffet on first Sun of month only	Mastercard, Visa

The chef at BB's Crabback is from Grenada, but his food encompasses the whole Caribbean – classic dishes from Jamaica jostling those from Trinidad, as well as Grenada itself. The restaurant, hidden away behind the Uxbridge Road, can appear a rather charming backwater, an impression enhanced by the laid-back staff. But it is not undiscovered territory. The walls are papered with awards from various "salons culinaire" – and rightly so. This restaurant has a remarkable repertoire and everything is played in tune. Visit for lunch midweek if you want to avoid the crowds – and be sure to book if you want a table on a Friday or Saturday night.

Start with salt fish souse (£3.50). This is terrific – a zesty fish salad served with molten-iron chilli salsa and "bakes", like a kind of fried dumpling. Or try the eponymous crabback (£4.50) – a crabback is nothing more complicated than a crab shell filled with crab meat and coated in a cheesy, creamy sauce. Or there's devilled salt fish balls (£3.70) – spicy, irregular fishcakes. Or callaloo soup (£3.40) served with okra. Or the Jamaican classic, ackee and salt fish (£3.75). Main courses all come with a choice of rice and peas, plain rice, or saffron rice. The rice and peas here is a revelation, dark and spicy without being chilli hot – very rich, with a waft of cloves. The saffron rice is good too, yellow and buttery. BB's special barbecued ribs (£8.90) are pork ribs marinated in ginger and fresh herbs – suitably more-ish. Parrot fish calypso (£8.20) is well-cooked, meaty fish in a lime and pepper sauce. Side dishes (all £2.20) are good fun: fried plantain; dasheen a root vegetable like a well-mannered parsnip; and roti skins – a wafer-thin, dry, delicious bread.

If you're in inflammatory mood try a dessert of banana flamed in rum and lemon (£3.80) which arrives at table quite seriously on fire. And to really indulge, finish with a cool slipper coffee (£4.50) described as "with cognac and a hint of rum. Topped with cream". It's enough to make the Irish look to their laurels.

WEST

£15–£50

Cheong Sol House

775 London Road, Hounslow, Middlesex ✆ 0181 572 3102   ⊖ Hounslow East

Mon–Fri noon–2.30pm & 6–11pm, Sat 6–11pm   Amex, Mastercard, Visa

It has to be said that the bowing can prove a little disconcerting. On the evidence of this gracious restaurant close by Hounslow bus garage, Koreans are nothing like James Bond's old adversary Oddjob – but they do bow a lot. As you come in; as the menus arrive; as each dish is presented . . . the Cheong Sol maintains a delightful courtliness. Korean food is something of a mystery to outsiders but the waiting staff here couldn't be more helpful – they'll guide you through the lengthy menu, discuss the merits of the dangerous-looking metal chopsticks, and offer you a piece of chewing gum (with the obligatory bow) as you leave. This is a fine dining adventure – though not a cheap one by any means. You will be sharing the dining room with tables of composed-looking Korean businessmen happy to pay hefty prices for good, authentic fare.

To start a meal you must try kimchee (£1.50) – salty, chilli hot, pickled cabbage – and share a sampler saucer of three other pickled vegetables (£4.50) which includes a delicious concotion of beansprouts in sesame oil. Go on to saewoo tuigim (£8.50) – large shrimp in batter, deep fried until crisp. They are described on the menu as "delicious and deeply satisfying" which isn't as hyperbolic as it at first seems. Hankuk chapche (£12) is a plateful of glass noodles with mixed vegetables and beef – sweet and rich. Then there's kimchi binatok (£6) which is flat, rather like a pizza, and made from ground-up green peas, and nakji samyein (£10) which is small octopii with mixed vegetables, noodles and hot chilli sauce. Raw food, meanwhile, gets its own section on the menu. These include yuk hwe (£9) – raw beef with pears; hanchi hwe (£25) – fresh raw squid with hot sweet sauce and mustard sauce; and hongeh hwe – raw skate (£6.50).

With such adventurous dishes to try, it is almost a shame to opt for griddled dishes, which are served in other London Korean restaurants. However, these too are done well and are quite fun. In the middle of each table there's a barbecue – to which various prepared raw meats are available to be cooked to your own taste.

£12–£40

Momo

14 Queen's Parade, West Acton, W5 ☎ 0181 997 0206	⊖ West Acton
Mon–Sat noon–2.30pm & 6–10pm	All major credit cards

The opening of a Japanese school in Acton has led to widespread Nipponification of the local shops and services – there are Japanese food shops, estate agents, and even a mysterious Aladdin's cave called the Japanese Recycling Shop which has shelf after shelf of repaired and refurbished electronic gadgetry – everything from rice cookers to typewriters. Also on Queen's Parade is a restaurant called Momo, a small establishment with 28 seats – which makes booking prudent. Service is smiling and helpful. and the long menu gives every opportunity to explore those less familiar dishes which may make you nervous in more intimidating and formal establishments.

If you don't feel up to extensive menu exploration go for the set menus – three or four dishes culminating in dessert may be had for prices ranging from £7.50 to £16 (lunch) or £15.00 to £25.00 (dinner). Assembling a meal yourself, you might start with yakitori (£3.80) – three small, very good chicken kebabs, or kanisu (£6) – a bowl of crab meat and cucumber marinated in rice vinegar, which is delicate and fresh. Soups are very intriguing, especially dobin-mushi (£3.40) which comes in a small teapot with a tiny cup on top – a rich broth with chunks of shrimp and chicken to fish out with your chopsticks. Then there's buta shogayaki (£6.50) – thin strips of belly pork grilled with ginger and soy and served with a mound of ultra-thin coleslaw. If you want to try a grand-stand dish, nigiri-zushi (£16) brings a box with a dozen pieces of assorted fish sushi, complete with gari – the amazingly delicious pickled ginger. Lovers of eel bow to the una jyu (£16.50) which is a box of rice topped with fillets of eel grilled with kabayaki sauce.

The operators at BT's directory enquiries specialise in confusing this establishment in W5 with the larger restaurant of the same name in the West End (see p.131. Fortunately the staff here have the number of the other Momo and politely ask misdirected callers whether they want Momo W1 or Momo W5; the most frequent response, of course, is that the caller doesn't know.

Monsieur Max

133 High Street, Hampton, Middlesex ☎ 0181 979 5546	BR: Fulwell
Mon–Fri 12.30–2.30pm & 6.30–11pm, Sat 6.30–11pm,	
Sun 6.30–11pm	All major credit cards

You know those tabloid stories about people being trapped in the wrong bodies? Well, Max Renzland is a Frenchman trapped inside an Englishman. Monsieur Max is the latest in a succession of restaurants from which Max and his late twin brother Mark have struggled to dispense authentic French food and Gallic culture to appreciative Londoners. It embodies all the best bits of those legendary, small French restaurants. Service is cheerful and unashamedly biased towards regulars. The wine list is short and sensibly priced (a sound Chablis for £16.50). The short menu changes every day. Dishes range from stunningly simple to French classics. And joy of joys, Monsieur Max is in London, well nearly.

Max is also a bit of a bargain. Dinner (or Sunday lunch) is £19.50 for three courses; the midweek lunch is £11 for two courses. Starters range from the simple - finest Cantabrian anchovies, cured and served with shallots, or home made rillettes of pork and duck – to the more complex – terrine of dill-marinated salmon layered with crème frâiche and cucumber salad. For a main course, if it's on the menu, you should jump at the poulet de Bresse in two services (for two, this takes 25 minutes, and has a supplement of £6 per person): first you get the breast - simply roast with a potato Dauphinoise and a vin Jaune and morel cream sauce – and then the next course is the legs with a mixed leaf salad and truffle jus. Max gets his chickens from France, and when you taste one you'll see what all the fuss is about. His fish, duck and Scotch beef offerings are equally impressive. Puddings are of the order of rum baba. Push them aside and go for the cheeseboard – twenty French farmhouse cheeses in perfect condition.

If you are a West London Francophile you're probably a regular at Max already and will be quite at home with the minor eccentricities of the menu, and service. This is the kind of restaurant London could do with a few more of – and, come to think of it, so too could post-chunnel France.

Monty's

54 Northfield Avenue, Ealing, W13 ☎ 0181 567 6281   ⊖ Northfields

Daily noon–2.30pm & 6–11.30pm   All major credit cards except Diners

The Ealing Tandoori no longer exists, but once upon a time it held west London curry lovers in thrall – it was the undisputed first choice. Then, in the late 1970s, the three main chefs left to open their own place, which they called Monty's, in South Ealing Road. As the business boomed two of the chefs moved on to set up independently – but as all three co-owned the name Monty's, they all use it, and that is why there are now three different Monty's, all fiercely independent but with the same name and logo. Unlike many small Indian restaurants these are "chef led", which is a key factor in making Monty's in Northfield Avenue an almost perfect neighbourhood curry house. You won't find banks of flowers or majestic staircases; the tables are too close together; and you may be crowded by people waiting for a take-away. But the cooking is class, the portions are good, and prices are fair.

A complimentary plate of salady crudités arrives with the chutneys and any poppadoms ordered, but starters are the exception rather than the rule here – perhaps because of well-sized main course portions. Trad tandoori dishes are good, like the tandoori chicken (£4.35 for two pieces). Or there is hasina, lamb marinated in yogurt and served as a sizzler (£5.95). The boss here remembers introducing the iron plate sizzlers at the Ealing Tandoori years ago and claims that his were the first in Britain. As you'd expect with a good tandoor chef, breads are delicious – pick between nan (£1.45) and peshwari nan (£2.25). But the kitchen really gets to shine with simple curry dishes like methi ghosth (£6.95) – tender lamb (and plenty of it) in a delicious sauce rich with fenugreek – and chicken jalfriji (£6.95), which is all the dish should be. Vegetable dishes are also made with more care than is usual – both brinjal bahji (£3.50) and sag panir.(£3.50) are delicious.

Monty's is one of very few local curry houses to serve perfectly cooked, genuine, basmati rice. So the plain boiled rice (£1.85) – nutty, almost smoky, with grains perfectly separate – is worth tasting on its own.

North China Restaurant

305 Uxbridge Road, Ealing Common, W3 ☎ 0181 992 9183   ⊖ Ealing Common

Daily noon–2.30pm & 6–11.30pm (midnight Fri & Sat)   All major credit cards

FURTHER WEST – EALING ⑩ CHINESE

The problem with "special" dishes that must be ordered 24 hours in advance, is that you tend to notice them only when you read the menu (rather than the requisite 24 hours before). The North China has such a dish. The restaurant itself has a twenty four carat local reputation: it is the kind of place people refer to as "being as good as Chinatown", which in this case is spot on, and the star turn on the menu doesn't disappoint. It is crispy Peking duck – but it is unlike all upstart crispy ducks, this Peking duck comes as three separate courses. Firstly there is the skin and breast meat served with pancakes, shreds of cucumber and spring onion plus hoisin sauce. Then there is a fresh stir-fry of the duck meat with beansprouts, and finally the meal ends with a giant tureen of rich duck soup with lumps of the carcass to pick at. It is awesome and so is the price – £38. That is, until you consider it as three courses for four people – which works out at just over £3 per person, per course.

So what goes well with duck? At the North China the familiar dishes are well-cooked and well-presented. You might start with barbecued pork spare ribs (£4.60), or the whimsically named lettuce puffs (£3.25 per person minimum two), which turn out to be our old friend "mince wrapped in lettuce leaves". For a supplementary main course, prawns in chilli sauce (£6.90), although not very chilli, is teamed with fresh water chestnuts and very good. Singapore fried noodles (£3.90) is powered by curry powder rather than fresh chilli, but fills a gap. Hidden amongst the familiar on the menu are a few more interesting dishes. One such, is grilled chicken Peking style (£4.90). This is a breaded chicken escalope that is served with quite a sharp, vinegary sauce that is redolent of pickled cabbage.

The North China also has a quality not often found in Chinese restaurants – genuinely friendly service, which in this case stems from the fact that this is a family-run establishment.

WEST

Rasa Timur

191 Acton Lane, Acton, W4 ☎ 0181 994 1049	⊖ Turnham Green/Chiswick Park
Mon–Sat noon–2.45pm & 6–10.45pm	All major credit cards

If you start at the Chiswick end of Acton Lane, Rasa Timur is about a third of the way up. Its clientele is probably more Chiswick than Acton and so is the operation. This isn't a cafe-by-day-satay-by-night operation but a "real" restaurant complete with ceiling fans and fish tank. What's more it is a restaurant that has built up a loyal following over several years. Its dishes combine the best of Malaysian and Singaporean cuisine and are both highly spiced and very tasty. Refreshingly, they tend to be authentic rather than repackaged Chinese dishes.

This is a place to start with something other than satay (though it's on offer if you want it). For example, you might try pergedel (£2.10) – a small, deep-fried, savoury potato cake served with sweet chilli sauce. Or lumpia (£2.10) – a good and crispy spring roll again served with the ubiquitous sweet chilli sauce. Chillied spare ribs (£4.80) are a treat, deep fried until very crispy and served with discs of crisply fried garlic, chillies, and onions. Udang goreng tepong (£6.95) gets you half a dozen, battered, deep-fried king prawns – delicious, even if the batter can be a touch too thick. For main courses, rendang (£5.60) comes as either beef or chicken, slow-cooked in a rich coconut sauce. Sambal ikan (£8.45) is a whole pomfret cooked in a rich and sweet chilli sauce. Char kway teow (£4.30) is a bowl of broad rice noodles fried with chicken, fish cakes and shrimps. Possibly the star of the show is to be found amongst the vegetable dishes – tumis terong (£3.80) is made from chunks of aubergine cooked in a tamarind gravy, mixed with a handful of dried anchovies that have been deep fried. Actually the "tiny fish", as they are called on the menu, look more like whitebait than anchovies and taste like Bombay duck.

Vegetarians may want to try satay sayur (£4.10), which is described on the menu as "skewers of gluten marinated with spices, charcoal grilled and served with fresh cucumber, onions, rice cakes and savoury peanut dip". Apparently when this dish was first invented it went on the menu as "skewered vegetarian".

£10–£25

Rasputin

265 High St. Acton W3 ☎ 0181 993 5802   ⊖ Acton Town

Daily 6–11.30pm   Mastercard and Visa

You'll find the "Rasputin Russian Restaurant and Wine Bar" up the Ealing end of Acton High Street. The restaurant is a cave of dark red felt, filled with English tea-room tables and chairs, and loud Russian background music which seems to alternate between Soviet covers of Boney M and Val Doonican. It's all very jolly, and the Russian specialities are homely and delicious. And all this is before you have made any inroads into the twenty different vodkas which come both as single shots and – take care here – "by the carafe".

With the menu comes a plate of cucumber, cabbage, green tomatoes, peppers, all markedly salty and with a good vinegary tang. For a starter order, try pierogi – rich little dumplings which come stuffed with a choice of potato and cheese, meat, or sauerkraut and mushrooms; they are all priced at £3.85 a portion. The blinis (small buckwheat pancakes) are also good – try them with smoked salmon and sour cream (£4.50) – and if you enjoy the special thrill of finding a bargain, with 40 grams of Russian sevruga caviar (£12.50). Sledzie is also delicious – pickled herrings with sour cream, apples, gherkins and dill (£3.45). At Rasputin they are constantly tinkering with the menu and there usually seem to be several versions extant at once. Hold out for the golubtsy (£7.50), which is permanently under threat of banishment from the menu – this is a simple but satisfying dish of cabbage leaves stuffed with meat and rice, very wholesome and very good. Or there's kotley po Kievsky (£7.95) – a chicken Kiev made with tarragon butter. Fish lovers may want to try the losos (£9.95), which is a fillet of salmon cooked with artichoke hearts, capers and a white wine sauce.

One of the desserts is an old favourite. "Charlotka" (£2.95) is none other than a classic dish, the Charlotte Russe – a mousse cake surrounded by sponge biscuits . . . welcome back. Also interesting is the Russian tea served in a glass and holder, and made with tea, lemon, and a splash of vodka (£1.95), with a small bowl of honey alongside for sweetening.

INDEX

Index of Restaurants by Cuisine

Categories below are pretty self-explanatory, though note that "Indian" includes Bangladeshi, Indian and Pakistani restaurants. The area names (in orange) are the neighbourhood sections by which this book is arranged.

INDEX

Index of Restaurants by Name

A–Z note: The Atrium appears under A not T; but Le Versailles under L, and El Molino under E. Stephen Bull is an S, Chez Gérard is a C. Well, you have to have rules.

INDEX

RESTAURANTS ⓜ A-Z INDEX

INDEX

Lotus Floating Restaurant 230

38 Limeharbour, Inner Millwall Dock, E14
☎0171 515 6445
Chinese

Ma Goa 427

244 Upper Richmond Rd, SW15
☎0181 780 1767
Indian

Madhu's Brilliant 447

39 South Road, Southall, Middlesex
☎0181 574 1897
Indian

Malabar Junction 25

107 Great Russell Street, WC1
☎0171 580 5230
Indian

The Mandalay 120

444 Edgware Rd W2
☎0171 258 3696
Burmese

Mandarin Kitchen 143

14–16 Queensway, W2
☎0171 727 9012
Chinese/Fish

The Mandeer 26

8 Bloomsbury Way, WC1
☎0171 242 6202
Indian/Vegetarian

The Mandola 414

139 Westbourne Grove, W11
☎0171 229 4734
Sudanese

Mangal II 295

4 Stoke Newington Road, N16
☎0171 254 7888
Turkish

Mao Tai 392

58 New King's Road, SW6
☎0171 731 2520
Chinese

Masaledar 366

121 Upper Tooting Rd, SW17
☎0171 767 7676
Indian

Mash London 27

19–21 Great Portland St, W1
☎0171 637 5555
Modern European

McClements 432

2 Whitton Rd, Twickenham, Middlesex
☎0181 744 9610
French

Melati 156

21 Great Windmill St, W1
☎0171 437 2745
Malaysian

Mesclun 296

24 Stoke Newington Church St, N16
☎0171 249 5029
Modern European

Meson Bilbao 277

33 Malvern Road, NW6
☎0171 328 1744
Spanish (Basque)

Mezzo 157

100 Wardour St, W1
☎0171 314 4000
Modern British

Mirabelle 111

56 Curzon Street, W1
☎0171 499 4636
French

Mirch Masala 367

1416 London Road, Norbury, SW16
☎0181 679 1828
Indian

Mobeen 235

222–224 Green Street, E7
☎0181 470 2419
Indian

INDEX

NOTES

ROUGH GUIDES: Mini Guides, Travel Specials and Phrasebooks

MINI GUIDES
Antigua
Bangkok
Barbados
Big Island of Hawaii
Boston
Brussels
Budapest
Dublin
Edinburgh
Florence
Honolulu
Lisbon
London Restaurants
Madrid
Maui
Melbourne
New Orleans
St Lucia

Seattle
Sydney
Tokyo
Toronto

TRAVEL SPECIALS
First-Time Asia
First-Time Europe
More Women Travel

PHRASEBOOKS
Czech
Dutch
Egyptian Arabic
European
French

German
Greek
Hindi & Urdu
Hungarian
Indonesian
Italian
Japanese
Mandarin Chinese
Mexican Spanish
Polish
Portuguese
Russian
Spanish
Swahili
Thai
Turkish
Vietnamese

AVAILABLE AT ALL GOOD BOOKSHOPS

ROUGH GUIDES: Reference and Music CDs

REFERENCE
Classical Music
Classical: 100
  Essential CDs
Drum'n'bass
House Music
World Music: 100
  Essential CDs
English Football
European Football
Internet
Millennium

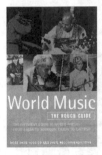

Jazz
Music USA
Opera
Opera: 100 Essential
  CDs
Reggae
Rock
Rock: 100 Essential
  CDs
Techno
World Music

ROUGH GUIDE MUSIC CDS
Music of the Andes
Australian
  Aboriginal
Brazilian Music
Cajun & Zydeco
Classic Jazz
Music of Colombia
Cuban Music
Eastern Europe
Music of Egypt
English Roots
  Music
Flamenco
India & Pakistan
Irish Music
Music of Japan
Kenya & Tanzania
Native American
North African
Music of Portugal

Reggae
Salsa
Scottish Music
South African
  Music
Music of Spain
Tango
Tex-Mex
West African Music
World Music
World Music Vol 2
Music of Zimbabwe

AVAILABLE AT ALL GOOD BOOKSHOPS

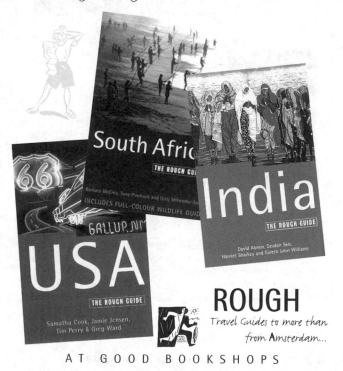

Wherever you're headed, **Rough Guides** tell you what's happening – the history, the people, the politics, the best beaches, nightlife and entertainment on your budget

ROUGH GUIDES: Travel

London
THE ROUGH GUIDE